Together
As Above, So Below

The Onereon Channels
Books One – Four

Together
As Above, So Below

The Onereon Channels
Books One - Four

Author and Channel - Jeff Michaels
Copyright © 2007 – 2022 Jeff Michaels
Printed in the United States of America
All rights reserved.

Portions of this book not exceeding 500 words may be freely quoted or reprinted without permission, provided credit is given to Jeff Michaels, *Together: As Above, So Below*.
ISBN # 978-0-9969371-6-0

An Introduction to The Onereon Channels

Onereon is a group of beings that define themselves as "together." They indicate that, during channeling, anyone that is in the room is potentially a member of the group Onereon and thus "together." This will hold equally true for any who are readers of these pages. They describe this togetherness not necessarily as an agreement, but rather as a direction of energy; together in purpose.

Onereon currently comes through to me in three main personalities, each distinct but separate and having definite points of view. I often describe them as "Human Resources," as if we are all working for a cosmic company and exist in different departments. There are others in the department as well; they just do not seem to come through as often.

There is a great deal of humor and compassion that comes through during the channeling sessions. When reading the transcriptions, be aware of the wryness and sometimes ironic tone that the communications contain. There is always underlying warmth to their comments that I find comforting and invigorating.

Above all else, the Onereon group believes in us and our ability to grow and evolve. Much of what they say is indicative of the future of humanity and the vitality of the planetary system that we are a part of, Gaia and her companion.

They point out that we are not as important as individuals but, as energetic beings that have existed essentially forever, we are, in fact, aspects of Source, the singular energy of creation. Whatever form we take is an equally important expression of creation. They also point out that we are not the pinnacle of creation.

For some this may seem disappointing. Onereon also points out that they themselves are not the pinnacle of creation. They are also quick to include themselves in the "not as important" category. The phrase we use to open the channeling sessions, "As above, so below," has an equal application to them in the realm of spirit as it does to us in the realm of physicality.

Frequent references to the idea of body, mind, and spirit punctuate the channels, helping us to understand the need to stay grounded in the physical world while we pursue our spiritual pathways and goals.

Of the word "mind" that is used in the phrase "body, mind, and spirit," Onereon is quick to indicate that it is not simply the way we think or the use of our intellectual capacities, but the balance of emotional energies of the heart with the logic energies of the brain. Thus the term "mind" takes on the meaning of heart and brain working together. Spirit, they say, cannot be comprehended by logic, but only by emotion. Still, spirit is ultimately logical.

Onereon also speaks of us as energetic beings in the same way that we can describe water. Once we change, as in birth or death, we are not the same personality. We recombine and become different than we were, in the same way as a drop of water goes into a pool and joins together its molecules with other water molecules. The chances, then, of the individual molecules all forming together into the exact same drop are extremely slim. In this same way, we do not come back to the earth repeatedly as the same personality or even the same species! We do remain life energy, however, and sometimes we are physical and sometimes we are in spirit form. The reasons for this are explained through the channels.

There is a change coming in the way that we will all communicate. Onereon indicates that this change has been going on for about two hundred years and will continue another one hundred or so. They point out that our way of communicating has already changed and continues to change dramatically in the physical realm. "So below" they say, then also "as above." In other words, look at how fast we now communicate with each other on the planet, and you will have a clue about how fast we will communicate with those in the spirit realm in the future.

Onereon reminds us that we, as a human species, have reached a level of maturity where we must now take responsibility for our lives and our future. The time for continually calling on spirit as guides or angels, to grant us some favor or blessing, is soon to pass. We are capable of doing many of these things ourselves, of creating what we choose for our life on the planet. They encourage us to see them more as companions, fellow spiritual seekers and partners in the enjoyment of all creation on all levels.

Onereon indicates that this is a returning to a way of life, one in which spirit and body are not separated but joined together with a balanced mind, acting in concert and growth towards a peaceful future, not just for life on earth but throughout the universe in all its forms.

I am happy to have been chosen as the voice of this warm, wise, and witty group and am pleased to be able to present to you this information as I am allowed to perceive it.

Entries may have been edited for better understanding in the written form, otherwise the content remains uniquely their own.

Jeff Michaels

The name Onereon is pronounced
O nair ee on

Book One - **Harmonic Coalescence**
The Future of Humanity

Book Two – **Touch the Earth**
A Path to Ascension
(starts after page 178 of Harmonic Coalescence)

Book Three – **Beings**
A Journey to Joy
(starts after page 156 of Touch the Earth)

Book Four – **Light**
The Reason for Existence
(starts after page 142 of Beings)

Always to Jill, continually my best, without whom I do not exist. My travelling companion and navigator.

To the children and women of the past, present, and future. May sorrow fade and hope return. Teach us well.

To the children I have known and to the children they will know. May the coming generations create continued joy on the planet.

To all my clients and all my students; every action must have an opposite and equal reaction.

In all ways, to the many beings of light who guide us through our days on the earth.

Book One
Harmonic Coalescence
The Future of Humanity

The future of humanity begins today!
The future of humanity begins with you.

Harmonic Coalescence offers practical guidance for thriving in these changing and challenging times.

Increase your inner strength
Gain a higher perspective on life
Connect with your spiritual companions

Regarding Channeling

We are arriving at a time of observable evolution in human communication. Over the past two centuries this has become evident in the rise of the telegraph and wired telephone systems, internet, and now, wireless communication.

Some of us are already noticing what seems to be an uncanny ability to be on the same thought as one close to us, or to have a clear thought or image drop in, seemingly out of nowhere.

Creative individuals in the arts and sciences throughout history have claimed sudden, clear inspiration to their works. The word "inspiration" shares its origins with the words "spirit" and "breath." Just as breathing is natural, so too can the action of communicating with spirit become natural. In a sense, it is communication with one's own creative spirit.

This internal communication has been with me for many, many years. I began developing it with intent in the early 1990s. Onereon is best described as a distinct group of energies, with specific personalities and specialties. They are here to assist us, offering us a different perspective, as we move through this time of rapid human development.

Channeling does not feel odd or spooky to me. In explaining it to others from many different backgrounds, I understand that it could appear very unusual. It is, in fact, one of the most natural abilities we, as humans, possess. We all hear those voices, called intuition and conscience, inside our heads and hearts, every time we choose to listen.

I would like to remind you all: there can be a fine line between true channeling, simple rambling, or even insanity. Please use your discretion in applying this and all information in your life.

Table of Contents

1. A Newer New Age 1
2. Guidance and Responsibility 9
3. Age and Passing 17
4. Do Not Waste Your Words 25
5. Be Aware 41
6. Vibrations 57
7. Perceptions 77
8. The Filter 95
9. Communication 119
    Amplification of Five Energetic Categories 151
10. Global Polarity 143
11. The Wave 147
12. Echoes 159
13. Children of the Sun 167
14. Evolution 173

1
A Newer New Age

As above, so below.

The Family Human

We are here to indicate a great change in human evolution. We are entering an age of response ability; our ability to respond is improving with experience. Not all are at the same level, in the same way as not all children in a family have the same abilities. Still, the family is a unit, and you are a member of the family of humans. Stop picking on each other.

In the spiritual realm there are many who are still immature or inexperienced in the ways of guidance. We are all of us in training and all of us learning all of the time. New experiences constantly change what we know and change how we are. Many of these new experiences are caused by you, the family of humans. It can be exasperating at times, like a child exploring their world. Still, we would not trade anything for the experiences or the challenges that our assignment has brought.

In the near future many more of you will hear us directly; more on this at a later date when we discuss the false concept of "us" and "them." For now, understand that much of what has been communicated before is adjusted. To cling to old information is to use a map of a town that you are no longer in. You have traveled far, family human, and we have sometimes been where you are while you have been here. This is difficult for some to comprehend.

The Individual Human

You are all particles of the universes, made up of smaller particles making up larger particles. This is what we mean when we say as above, so below. If it is true in small things, it will eventually prove to be true in the larger realities. If there seems to be a discrepancy in the scientific view, wait a bit. The picture continues to change. Get used to this.

To believe that the energy of the individual human is small is to believe that the solar system is small because it is not the galaxy. The family human is a system of combined energies as is the solar system, which in turn is the galaxy, which in turn is the cluster and back down to the structure of cells to the structure of molecules to the structure of atomics and as above, so below.

To believe that the energy of the individual human has a limit is to be modest and intelligent in your understanding. A container holds just so much then overflows or bursts. You are far from full. That statement will cause excitement and fear. Fear not.

We are also a part of the system of energy that is the family human, in ways that many have yet to comprehend. We will be giving you models to observe on the physical plane to instruct you on the mental, emotional, and spiritual planes. Patience as more is revealed in linear time. That is an aspect of the human limitation.

A Newer New Age

Seeds of the Future

The seeds have all been planted; it has become time to grow. The harvest is yet in your future and only a few will be alive in linear time to see the reaping. Your prophets of old foretold this time, as they also foretold a new heaven and a new earth. In fear, many felt (and rightly so for a while), that the old earth would need to be completely destroyed for this event to occur.

As above, so below. All existence is a process, not an event. The process of destroying the earth would have occurred only if heaven, the spiritual realm, had also been destroyed. Not one being believed that possible or necessary. What then do we mean by "new heaven" and "new earth?"

We now see the future in a different light. Who among us could have imagined the earth as it is today a mere two hundred years ago? Yet that is when the old energy began changing. Soon everyone will have a voice in the choices of action on the planet. Democracy, in a form you cannot conceive of now, will be the way of humanity in the linear future. Truly you already live in a "new earth" and we then live in a "new heaven."

The structures of the earth as a planet have begun to change. We are sad that some will go through these changes in pain and fear. Their lives are cut short only from another human's perspective. They return soon and are given the gift of seeing the future happen with memory of their past experiences. Will they remember every detail of their current life? No. They will, however, not have to relearn all of the spiritual skills they possessed. Their ability to respond to humanity in spiritual ways will be natural and to your way of thinking, uncanny. The lesson that they teach now is one of compassion and unity of spirit and in this way their loss of life is a time of rejoicing.

The reaping of the ripened harvest becomes a time of immense growth, a feast of spiritual information. Here is a lesson. What you sow you will reap. Yes, you have heard this all before, but now listen intently.

The Balance

The harvest will be one of balance. Balance between these three elements; the body, the mind, and the spirit. These are not separate elements; they are a system. You are that system. You are also an aspect of the larger system, as above, so below.

The earth, the planet that you walk, is the body. This body is also sentient, but more, it is the physical home of the family human.

You are the mind, the consciousness of the system. Not just you, but all life great and small. Within you dwells aspects of the energy of all life that has existed on the planet, from the first proteins and amino acids to the massive gorgons to the larger saurians and the great dragons that the ancients feared, first with purpose and respect, then with superstition and fruitless religion. All life is energy and energy cannot be destroyed, only transformed. You, and all that is alive in and on the planet today, are the mind, the mental and emotional energy of this system.

We are the spirit. Unseen, unprovable, undetectable by the logic and science of family human at this moment in linear history and yet known by all of you on levels that cannot be logiced.

As above...you must now begin to bring yourselves into a fuller balance. So many of you feel this and are at a loss for direction. The old messages no longer sound true. Many have found the newer words of spirit and feel like you have found your home. Welcome to all, there is plenty of room!

So below...there are many still who live in fear, awaiting a destiny that is no longer there. They try to create fear in an effort to achieve what will never happen. Horror and war and torture and destruction and strife have become the chosen entertainments of so much of the media.

To these ones the message that we have is perplexing and the work that we do is peculiar. The truth is that some of you are out of balance and that makes it difficult for others to approach the new earth and new heaven, to enter into the existence that you see in front of you.

Your love of spirituality is not wrong. You need to love the body and mind equally. For so many, your ability to balance your physical life has become weak. You have begun to rely so heavily on the spirit forces that you know so well that you are failing to do for yourselves.

Children learn to walk and now you must learn to stand on your own more often. We are not abandoning you. We will be as close as we have always been or closer. It is time now for you to shoulder some of tasks ahead. Do not fear. This will quickly begin to feel familiar to you; you have done this all before.

You want the spiritual gifts? Then be present fully in your own life. A hint then, touch the earth and let the earth touch you. It is not without cause that you say the phrase, "Mother Earth."

Why the rise in earth centered religions? You are all of you being drawn to the physical plane; all of you are being grounded. Not as if you are naughty children though.

You enjoy the messages from above? Then listen with equal intent to the messages from below.

Why the rise in animal communicators? Because your fellow beings have much to say to you. Soon we will be unencumbered by the old ways of communication. Soon we will return to the original forms of communication and there will be no barriers.

We have all been separate for so long after having taken on the burden of the knowledge of good and bad. Soon we will drink from waters of life that nourish us all and are free to all existence.

What now? Seek peace!

Things to remember

- The family human is in a process of gaining maturity.
- All living beings are a small part of something larger and have greater potential.
- What we are all going through on the earth has a time limit and we are each important to the outcome.
- Maintaining our personal balance is our most important work as individuals.
- The planet earth is sentient and makes choices.
- Only by being fully present in our bodies and minds can we fully gain the spiritual aspects of life.

Things to come

- Direct communication between spirit and the individual human will increase.
- A form of democracy that we have yet to conceive of will be the way of the future for all beings.
- A form of communication that was once natural to us will return.

Onereon is free with advice and information to assist us in approaching our lives in peacefully active ways. Onereon is ever mindful that we all, human and spirit alike, have free will and will do what we choose.

Onereon is not a group that is to be followed and there is no set structure or dogma that they advocate. The principles they reveal are universal.

2
Guidance and Responsibility

As above, so below.

If it is true for you on the physical plane, then it will be truth on the mental, emotional, and spiritual plane. Truth is relative to perception and experience. Expand your abilities to perceive and your truths will expand.

Guides and Angels

We will tell you about ourselves, a little at a time. We speak through a chosen voice and the process of choosing is two way. Just as on the physical plane, if you are offered a job, it does not follow that you must take the job. Remember, at some point you will all have the opportunity to speak and at some point you will all be the ones speaking through a voice.

A cooperative effort then, a system of energy consisting of several beings of energy, like the sun and the planets, like the planets and their moons, like the molecules and their atoms. What are we to you? Do you revolve around us? Do we spin about you?

You have known of us as guides and angels, in the past more as gods and goddesses. In truth, we are just like you in so many ways. We have our thoughts and, just like you, they are not always the same as each other's. We have our feelings and, just like you, they differ. We have our physical side, though not as you yet understand, and just like you we are physically different and approach the physicality differently than each other. We also have a spiritual side, and we also have our spiritual guides, just like you.

Why do we need spiritual guides? Why do you? There are and always will be times when life and consciousness enter unexplored territories. If the universe is infinite in the physical realm…as above, so below!

Our Task

Our task is to guide you when guidance is necessary. Our task is not to carry you unless you are injured or ailing. Your task is to experience the universe from the perception of the physical, mental, and emotional being that you are. Our task is to guide you to the roses; your task is to smell them. If you already know where the roses are, why ask for guidance?

Our task is not only to guide you. We have other responsibilities. If you are at a store and you ask someone where an item is, they direct you to the location of that item. They may have other work to do and may have to stop what they are doing, stocking shelves or taking inventory or repairing some part of the store, to guide you. They do not get angry. Guiding you is part of their job. There are still other parts of the job that they must get accomplished. The more they must guide you, the less they get accomplished at other levels.

You say, "Thank you" and that is often enough.

Our tasks are not always comprehensible to you, in the same way that a child does not always comprehend the activities of the parent. As the child grows, they are included more and more in the tasks of running the household and the family. Their experience and perception expands, and so does their truth.

The family human is growing up! Now you are learning new tasks in the action of running the universal house. Like the child, you are assigned a location in that structure. The child may have the task of cleaning their room. The planet earth is, in a sense, your room.

You, then, are the guides of the planet. Not the only guides, for there are others on the planet with you. You are not the owners of the planet, not even the caretakers, just the guides. The earth has things to learn still. Much work has been done on what your perception would call "cosmic scale" and that work continues. The changes in the planet require that you notice and adapt and be aware and conscious of the planet. You are growing up together and we are growing with you. We, all of us, are a system, not separate parts, but parts of a whole.

Because perception has been limited, you have seen things as separate. Because you saw things as separate, you separated things even further, dividing yourselves into parts and dividing the earth into sections, smaller and smaller.

Our task is to expand your perceptions. Why has science taken such huge leaps forward in so short a time? Why have so many things about the physical world become clearer and clearer in a mere two centuries?

Science and Spirituality

Are the scientists being guided, you ask. Yes, in as much as they are guiding humanity to a new state of physical consciousness, they are also being guided. Every action has an opposite and equal reaction, as above, so below, and here is a lesson for you. As much guidance as you receive, that much guidance you will give, not always in the same way as you received it!

The scientist is a physical being. They work with only what is provable in the realm of physicality and logic. The spiritual human, the metaphysician, works often only with what is unseen and personally experiential.

Both are observant of the universe, only in different ways. Both perceptions have equal value to the universe, for both are aspects of the universe observing itself. The universe supports diversity, not conformity.

The scientist and the spiritual human are both aspects of the whole system and necessary to each other in ways that they do not always understand. For one to deny the value of the other is for the earth to deny the value of the moon.

An element of your task is now to give your voices to the planet earth. Not just one voice, but many, and let the earth speak to its elements about the life above it from your perceptions. This is difficult for you to understand. Simple if you think of yourselves receiving guidance from your spirit guides and then creating the same energy with yourselves as the guides.

Sound and Hearing

When we speak directly to you, the individual human, you do not hear us with your ears. We do not exist in the air and cause the vibration that creates sound waves. You say that you hear us, but that is a metaphor. It is like hearing only in that you received communication that did not enter into your eyes. Some of you say you have "the sight" and we will speak of this again.

You say you hear your guides. In truth, you have received communication and now have knowledge that was not present before. Your consciousness translates at a rate that your human mind can withstand. This process is getting faster.

Some say they do not hear their guides. It may be that we have tired of being asked for help by one that should be capable of doing for themselves. It may be that we are silent.

Our voice has asked why some channels speak in an odd pattern. The energy that is around them is often more than the individual human is prepared to bear at this time. A buffering of the energy is necessary, and the human then must translate that through their own perception. The odd voice is not necessarily our voice, only the "sound" that the communication makes in the channeler's energetic form. This is why, for now, at the beginning, our voice has chosen to speak through the written word.

So be patient with the life forces of Gaia. They will "speak" slowly to you, and you must take care to hear the whole of the message. Give voice to these things only after you have removed your perceptions as much as possible.

A Change of Perception

This is all changing. The perception of the family human is expanding. Pay close attention to your science. The more you understand of your physical realm, the more you will comprehend the spiritual. When you are here, you understand this realm of spirit based on your experiences here. In the realm of spirit, your perception is one of systems and aspects. On the earth you are starting to see the completeness of the planets' systems.

You lack one part of the vision, your place in that system. Many of the family human are still trying to own the earth or at least a spot on it. This will continue to cause strife between the elements of the system. The earth will then guide you. Fear not for the planet. Its purpose is to exist and spin, experiencing the universe through forces like gravity and light. It has agreed to let you travel along.

Look to science and know that other life has traveled with planet earth and for much longer periods of linear time. You are carriers of that life energy, but like that ancient force, you are subject to change and adaptation. The family human is not the pinnacle of creation. The family human is an aspect of creation. This does not diminish you. It makes you part of something vast and eternal. Like we all are.

Our task is to guide you when needed. We have other tasks. Many of you say, "Thank you" when you receive the needed guidance. Now it is time for you to add something. Now it is time for you to start asking us, "What can I do for you? What can I, as a human, do for you, in the realm of spirit?" This will be difficult for some to understand. What could spirit possibly want of a physical individual human? Ask and you will begin to know. We have much enjoyment ahead. Together we are something so wonderful. There is your hint. For now? Seek peace.

Things to remember

- Our guides have many tasks other than us.
- The planet has tasks. Humans and animals have tasks. We are, in many ways, the same as our guides and have similar tasks.
- Our guides are really our companions.
- Science is being guided.
- Receipt of communication is not always through sound or vision.
- Saying, "Thank you" is good. Asking, "What can I do for you?" is better.
- Asking is the beginning of knowledge.

Change

We tell you these things because you sense this change coming. You have a desire for it. Many have a desire for change and yet they really strive to cling to what was and change things back. This is like the tree trying to change itself back into a seed, rather than grow more seeds.

This is the tension, this is the struggle, and this is the intensity of emotion. It is what drives many off of balance, this constant looking backwards and, were they to know the truth, it was not better. Only in the future can it be better from what it is today, and yet if they chose to live as if the future were already in existence, better would be in existence today.

3
Age and Passing

As above, so below. This is our agreed upon greeting through your channel.

It means so many more things than you can contain in your present energetic form and if we sometimes laugh or smile at you, it is with the same spirit as you finding amusement in a child's explorations.

Youth and Aging

We speak today of youth and age in the human family. Many among you have noticed a change in the way you are. Your channel likes to point out that you do not age the way your predecessors did. Look at a picture of your grandparents when they were your age now. They may look old, you do not. Have you started to age slower? Not precisely. You have started to perceive age differently and thus changed the way it affects you.

Others have pointed out the change in the children, giving them the title of Indigo. Are humans developing faster? Again, not precisely. You have started to perceive the conception process differently and thus changed the way it affects the human that grows within you. This is an expression of what is being termed the divine feminine, but is in actuality a balancing of the energies of your part of the universe.

It is more than that. We, in the spiritual realm, actually view entry into the physical plane of existence differently and thus, before we separate into smaller particles and become conceived, we have a different mindset. It is, of course, affected by the human that fertilizes and then carries the energy. We grow together.

Have you noticed, then, how many of those around you have dedicated their lives to the changing of consciousness regarding raising children? No more "spare the rod, spoil the child." That worked at one time, but no longer. Discipline is still necessary, yes. Every action has an opposite and equal reaction and thus if the child needs discipline, then the parent also receives discipline. Discipline is not punishment, this is learning, the act of becoming a disciple. You all become disciples, learning together!

Life and Death

In a short period of gravitational time, that is, linear time, the family human will begin to know through science that life and death are part of the process of all creation. The pieces of the puzzle are almost all in place. Near-death experiences will come to be understood in a wonderfully different way. You must be willing to let go of your notions of the past.

You are just starting to realize a different way of approaching the moment of death. An irrevocable change happens then, it is true, but no more saddening than the change from age seven to age eight, or thirty-one to thirty-two. It is growth, plain and simple. Fear at the moment of passing has held us all back for so long. Then, when we re-enter the spiritual realm in a frame of mind that is not conducive for growth and joy, we go into a kind of reverse hospice, where we must prepare to be alive again.

Exiting must be accomplished with more grace. Have you no faith, the assured expectation of things hoped for though not yet beheld?

Last Words

Gratitude at the end of a physical course is a key, but you cannot always wait for the end to express gratitude. You have many examples of people leaving suddenly and in surprising or shocking ways in your last seven years. The last thing on their minds in many cases were loved ones and some were even able to find ways to express gratitude at that time. You, however, would do well to not wait.

Also do waste your words! There are some situations in your lives that will not be resolved. Resign yourselves to those energies and move forward. If forward looks like dying, then understand that it is growth and enjoy the process. Hard words for many, yes, because you do not yet comprehend the bonds of energies that tie you. You do not yet comprehend the way those bonds strengthen at the moment of passing.

Words are elements of your energy. They are not physical energy, although you hear them physically. They are not mental, although you hear the thoughts you think. They are also not your emotions, although again you hear what you feel in their expression. They are not your spiritual energy either, though you often feel the need to address your spirituality through your words. What, then, are your words?

Words are the connective energy that holds you together as a species or keeps you apart. They are not your body, mind, or spirit energies that make you up individually. They bring your bodies together, your minds together, and your spirits also. Insistence on forcing meaning to old words will keep you all separate. Agreement from the heart pulls you closer.

Here is a hint, words are not as important as they once were. A better way of pulling together is occurring and those of you alive and the children you raise are the bridge that humanity crosses into a different approach to being alive together. It is being demonstrated right now and you all will have the opportunity to participate.

Not all of you will accept the opportunity and that is fine. To some this will be frightening and appear to be wrong, even evil. There is no evil. Those that sustain this point of view are followers of men who practiced this form of communication over two thousand years ago. Now they feel that no one else should exercise this ability to engage or enjoy this direct conversation. There are many ironies in our worlds.

Release Old Perceptions

Do not waste your words on ones like these. The perception that is theirs does not change the realities yet to be beheld. You, too, must be willing to release your perceptions and accept the new realities.

The old words are not wrong, only the perceptions that grew regarding them. A great destruction was foretold. That is the perception that grew regarding the energy of change. That energy, in fact, happened just as scheduled and foretold. The destruction was not one of cataclysm and fear, but one of irrevocable change. An old way has passed on and changed into a new way. The results of the change are still being felt all across the globe and will continue to be felt for seven linear years and that also is prophesied.

Release the need to wipe away the existing energy and start over. It is not necessary, for what existed was not wrong or bad. Like mother's milk to a baby, it is appropriate at the time. No one looks for mother's milk as their nourishment as they grow to adult years, and so it is now. The Source and type of energy that will sustain life on the planet has shifted and you are all part of the shifting. Leave the milk behind. There is a feast ahead!

You cannot predict how the energy will affect you. You can only increase your abilities to respond when it happens around you. One more thing you can do, you can increase your willingness to respond.

Speak and Listen with Responsibility

We speak of your words again. Your intuition is not necessarily guidance from the spiritual realm. It is guidance based on your perception from your heart and is thus limited in its scope.

Guidance from the spiritual realm is also limited in scope and there are those in both realms willing to speak without discipline. These are ones who waste their words and thus the energy of change gets weakened around them. It is natural for all of us to seek companionship, but companions are not necessarily guides and spiritual companions are not necessarily wiser than you.

This, then, will be a part of the new energy, one of individual responsibility, the personal ability to respond to the changes that are happening naturally. No more the large gathering to listen to old words which are wasted by being forced to conform to new human perception. Now the new words will flow to those who have ears that hear in the new energy. The new energy is one of releasing the old and becoming disciplined not from without, but from within. The new energy is not being a disciple of someone, but a disciplined one who acts with thought and feeling, in physical and spiritual ways all balanced together.

Thus, the family human matures and becomes adult in its evolutionary process. The change is upon you now! Embrace it and know that the journey is far from complete. Our education continues above and so below, and we are learning many things and being prepared to share these things with you at your individual levels of ability.

Say, "Thank you" to the things of the past that brought us all to this point, thank you and good-bye, for they are done and soon to be gone. It is truly a new heaven and a new earth, and it is here now, and you are alive in it as are we. One thing that has not changed, the words, "seek peace." That is our agreed upon closing at this time.

Things to Remember

- Birth is not a beginning. Death is not an ending. They are simply moments of a larger process.
- Death is growth.
- There is no need to fear your own passing. It is part of the way of the universe.
- Why wait until the end of your human life to express gratitude to everyone and everything around you?
- Release old perceptions. Look at everything with new eyes and new awareness.

Things to Come

- In a short period of time, humanity will have a scientific understanding of life that will be different than perceiving birth and death as a beginning and an ending.
- A form of communication will return to the family human, one that does not rely on words alone. There will be some who will oppose this and judge it as evil.

Questions to Stimulate Your Personal Growth

New experiences constantly change what we know and change how we are.

What new information has changed you recently?

4
Do Not Waste Your Words

As above, so below. We greet you as we enter into this session. Our voice spoke about not wasting words and that is something that we will talk about today. There are those out there who do not understand your words, so do not waste them. It is not right, and it is not wrong. They simply do not understand existence the same way that you perceive it.

Process

When you go to school, you start with ABC's. You do not start with adverbs and dangling participles. Humans have changed. You may be among those who have changed, or you may be among those who are just noticing the change, but you *will be* among those who change, perhaps not at this point in time, these linear moments that you call your life.

What we are looking at with you is the process and not the event. As humans, we sometimes believe that this process begins with the event of birth and ends with the event of death. You will understand in the future, all of the family human will, that there is a way to come into life that is not an event, and there is a way to exit life that is not an event. Some of you here already understand the exit process.

All of your life is marked because that is what humans have done in the past. You have divided time up, made things separate with things like hours, minutes, days, and years. Also by things like country, county, city and state with addresses and numbers that become important in the definition of the family human. It has served well to separate you and make you individuals. Much of that will go away.

You will all have opportunities to communicate with spirit in this way as well. The object of communicating with spirit in this way is not to glorify anyone, not to make anyone better than another. The object is to be very direct with our words and not waste our words and the energy of our words.

Words

Words are not your body, words are not your mind, and words are not your spirit. Words are things that connect you and all these linear moments that mankind, the family human, has meant to separate. Words, then, begin to connect the energy that pulls us together, but can also be the energy that pulls us apart. Wasting our words pushed us farther apart. If you cannot pull someone closer to you with your words, then do not speak. Allow your words to stay within you.

When we look at the family human, it is not, from our perspective, one of superiority. As above, so below, you begin to understand that as you look at your own children. You are not superior to your own children, although many families have thought that in the past. More and more we realize this is not true. More and more we realize that the family human is not superior to animal, and not superior to the earth. The family human is an aspect, a particle, something that occurs equally within these other systems. We in the realm of spirit do not look at you as if you are superior or inferior. We look at you as equals.

A great responsibility, a greater vision, a supervision perhaps, can help you to understand our words in a way that you comprehend your business model, but understand that your business model is changing as well. Look at the corporations around you and look at how they have changed.

As above, so below, understand that we have changed as well. Structure in the spiritual realm is different now. If you have felt lost or abandoned, that you have lost your spiritual guides, that maybe they are no longer communicating with you, well, things have changed. It is not that they are not communicating with you, they may have just changed. There may have been reassignments, there may have been switching of departments. You may feel very strongly that you were alone for a period of time, but we are all getting reacquainted, we are all entering into a different type of contract with each other, and a lot of this will be about your individual responsibility.

We are becoming much more aware. We, here in the spiritual realm, you, here on the physical plane, are becoming much more aware that it is not up to groups. It is up to individuals, undivided ones, *you*, to balance the universe. How? Start with yourself. You cannot do anything for anyone else. This is why you pull your words back in, because it is your energy, your words. Balance yourself first.

Patterns

Watch the patterns shift and watch how they have shifted. Look back two hundred years ago and notice how patterns have shifted in two hundred years of linear time, of gravitational moments. Notice how things have shifted over two hundred years. Notice how things have shifted over fifty years. Notice how things have shifted only in the last seven years. Things are going to shift similarly in the next seven.

When we say, notice how the patterns shift, look at your educational systems. Look at how people educate themselves. Look at the non-linearity of certain educational reforms. Look at your organizations. Look at your companies and the scandals that affected so many. Look at how that changed your company structure. Look at how your money organizations have changed. As above, so below, these are all patterns happening on the earth. Why? Because these changes are all happening in the spiritual realm, less the scandals, less the personal violations, less the betrayals.

When you see betrayal, take that as an opportunity for spiritual growth. Betrayal is a sign that we are trusting in something or someone to do our balancing for us. Balance yourself.

The scandals exist only because of ones trying to maintain the old energies on the physical plane. The new energy is one of personal responsibility, as above, so below.

Human Resources

Our voice would like us to talk about ourselves and our role. Consider us as human resources. We are not the CEO, we are not the supervisors, and we are not anyone that necessarily gives direct directives, although that might be so. We are information givers, we are caregivers, and we are the human resource department. Notice how your human resources departments have changed as well.

The age of humanity has changed. By that we mean maturity levels, the levels of wisdom that humanity has gained. We use the comparison of the growth of a human, an individual human, as they begin to find their voice and express who they are as an individual. This is where the family human is at. No mistake the rise of personal communication devices. No mistake separating individuals by communication devices. We begin to connect at greater and greater distances, and begin to accept the distances that we connect, while remaining separate from those standing next to us.

In the near future you will have opportunities to communicate in this way without personal communication devices. Much of what happens then in terms of spiritual growth, in terms of spiritual communication, will be a freer connectivity, but not just with each other, not just with humanity and not just with your previously called spiritual companions, but with the earth itself, with the very ground, with the very planet. Touching the planet is going to be important.

It is no mistake that you are here. What we look for with all of you is that you continue to do what you are doing but notice the changes and allow yourself to respond in a different way. We speak of responsibility, that is, your ability to respond to whatever situation comes up.

The writings of old were not wrong. They were misinterpreted. There was a preconceived notion that if a great change came, it must be cataclysmic. In fact, that change came. There are changes expected still. That energy will come true. Release the expectations that other people have imprinted upon these changes. That is the old perception, and it is not true. It is not a mistake that you are here.

Notice the animals. It is no accident that there is a rise in animal communication. Is that because humans are just now hearing it? Or is that because now is the time for them to speak? In the same way that we learn to speak with animals, the animals are training us to hear them. The earth too is training us to hear it. It would do everyone well to touch the earth.

We changed the way we approach our children. It is no mistake that schools have changed, that the way we approach our children has changed and how we communicate with them. There is no mistake that we present spirituality in a different form.

Are there questions?

I have a question about the phrase, "touching the earth." I do not get away from work often and am inside much of my time. Does working with crystals, even though they are somewhat removed from the earth, still count as touching the earth?

The earth is the earth in whatever form it is. If it is a small pot of earth, that is your earth. If you have a rock, that is your earth. If you have a plant or a piece of wood, that is your earth. Although all are removed from the earth, elements of the earth are still present. "Is it *enough*?" is your question. Being on the earth, being in the earth, being enriched by the earth in dirt…touch the earth and feel the earth as a whole living unit. That is what we mean by touching the earth. Also, it is no mistake that the earth has been covered up in this area [the Midwest of America]. From the perspective of the family human, it seems like it should be wrong. In fact, in many ways, the earth is being stored and refreshed.

This fertile soil that you live in, this Midwestern area, has drawn in many people, and that has been incomprehensible to some of you. People from areas of great beauty, from areas of great spiritual reputation are being drawn here and they do not know why. It is because there is nourishment here, there is fertility here.

Above all things, throughout the human world, spirituality now needs to become very practical and grounded. It has to become practical because there are those among you who do not sense the change and are trying to hold on to their old ways. If the old ways do not look far out to them, it is because they are used to them. If the new ways do seem far out, then we have to make the new ways seem not so far away, practical and grounded.

Part of the task here is to begin to communicate with those of the old ways so that they feel comfort, so that they understand that nothing has really changed, except that *perceptively* everything has changed, and that they may feel safe. Humans have communicated through channeling for nearly all of the family humans' existence. Now and for the last two thousand years, people have distanced themselves from and set apart this form of communication. In the future, everyone communicates through channeling once again.

Touching the earth will help ground you, it will help get you spiritually practical, and seem not so far out in other people's perception.

Again, we return to the concept of "do not waste your words." Some will not get it. Some people do not want to get it. Some want to argue. Some want *you* to change. Do not waste your words.

I find it very disturbing that so many people are flocking to this area because I think that, for me, it makes it more difficult to get in touch with nature and to experience the beauty of nature that I would like to. Now you have to go very far just to experience that. So it is hard for me to reconcile that it is the right thing that we are drawing so many people.

The nourishment that people get here, [in the Midwest] may not be directly for them, their children, or their children's children, but for *their children* and truly that is what we are looking at. It is not this generation, or the next or the next. They will take from this area energy that is different, energy that is fertile. Your concern is for yourself and that is not right, and it is not wrong. There is a greater picture, and that is what we try to communicate. It is not really that difficult to get to different and desired areas.

We have a level of freedom here in the realm of spirit. You have a level of freedom here in the realm of gravity. There are parks, there are yards, there are areas to touch the earth. It does not need to be pristine areas that are untouched by mankind. It does not need to be mountains. It does not need to be the beach. It does not need to be islands. It needs to be a yard, or a park, or a strip of land. It does not need to be ritualistic. It just needs to be your feet on the earth, your hands on the earth, not even for great periods of time.

Touch the earth, listen for a moment, and continue on with your life. There is no need to make it an event. Allow it to be a process of your daily life. Notice how you leave your house, and you avoid the ground by stepping on the sidewalk. Change your pattern to one of noticing the earth. If you do not touch the earth literally with your hands, touch it with your eyes, and allow it to touch you back though your eyes.

What we are doing to the earth, it scares me. I feel like we are destroying it and that the consciousness is changing, but I worry it is not changing fast enough.

Save the planet? Do not worry about the planet. It has taken much larger hits. The earth is an entity and is alive and has agreed to let you ride on it. When the earth no longer finds use for a form of life, when the universe no longer finds use for a life form, it goes away. The earth abides. The consciousness of this planet is very hard for you to understand because to you it is very, very slow. Touch it with your crystals, and with your minerals, and when you separate the minerals into smaller bits, the consciousness moves faster. It is easier for you to understand because you are here. The planet is just a planet, one of many, but this is your home.

The same way you have spirit guides, spirit companions, we also have guides. If we have guides, and you are being guided by us, every action must have an equal but opposite reaction and that means that you also must be guides. Guides of what? Sometimes guides for the planet. Save the planet? It is old energy. The planet is a planet, and it is hard for some people to hear these things.

Energy can not be destroyed; it can only be transformed. Everything is energy. The earth is a transformer of energy, and the sun is a transformer of energy. All of the things being done to the planet are merely things that are happening. They are happening to you as well. If you are more concerned about your own balance, do what you can for the planet in the same way that you do what you can for yourself.

The air is not pure, and the water is not pure, so you process the best you can, and you live the best you can as humans. The earth lives the best it can as earth and things change. They are changing, so "save the planet" is old energy and to be putting energy into that is pulling energy away from you. Look to yourself. Look to your form. Balance yourself first and watch the earth balance around you.

If you feel the pull to another part of the planet, allow that pull to happen. There are reasons why people get pulled in different directions. There are people present right now being pulled somewhere. By what? By the planet.

There are concerns and the concerns are true. Will the water table go down? Yes, it will. Why? Because there are more people. Is there a purpose? The planet knows. Trust your planet. It is allowing you to ride along, so enjoy the ride. Enjoy the beauty of it wherever you can, and balance yourself.

It has come to my understanding that the animals now have come to a point where they are rattling their cages. They are coming outside of their cages where they are shaking things up. They are coming forward, whether it be the whales, the elephants, the dolphins, or the coyotes coming into villages. What my understanding is, is that they are trying to make us be aware of this so that we will change. Not that it will be such a big peace movement as Save the Planet but what is going to be happening is that we as individuals are going to balance ourselves and make changes little by little. As we make changes, people are going to resonate to that energy, and they are going to make changes. People are going to come here because they feel the energy here and then maybe go and make changes elsewhere so that this is going to be happening everywhere.

Did anyone sense a question there? Your perception is very close. The animals are closer to the earth. Listen to the animals and understand them. "Rattling their cages," we like that, because all of life is rattling their cages. All life energy rattles their cages. As above, so below, we are rattling our cages as well and things change. We will talk about that later.

Intention is what we talk about, is what we discuss, and not wasting our words. Intention changes things faster than physical action. Organizing physical rallies, organizing physical activities, that is all well and good, but spirit moves instantly and your intention and your heart moves spirit. Let your heart connect with your spirit in this way and watch the changes happen more rapidly. If you become involved in the gravity of things then you must watch things happen according to gravitational time, linear time.

You have all manifested. You have all done that. It has nothing to do with acting in a physical way but acting in a spiritual way. When you manifest, you make our job so much easier because then we do not have to do it. Sometimes you feel your spirit guides cannot hear you. It is sometimes because they have stopped talking to you. They are tired of saying the same thing again and again.

And as below, so above. We changed the structure. It was not all a unanimous agreement; some of us were very attached to some of you. In the same way you attach to animals, or attach to other humans, or attach to areas of geography, we attach. Understand, the letting go will be very important, letting go of the old ideas, because if you cling to the old ideas the changes happen much more slowly.

Look, energy moves in waves. Sometimes we know that one wave will be larger than another and sometimes we know that, in the pattern of waves, we know that there may be an even larger wave amongst the large waves. We have some large waves of energy moving though right now. They are sweeping things away and it hurts us when we see living things swept away by a wave. Let the energy sweep things away that are no longer necessary to serve a purpose. Now, this is a hard statement because you wonder, did those humans serve their purpose? *[Referring to the incident of a massive tidal wave]* And in what way?

Awareness of each other, awareness of the planet, awareness of energy, awareness of power, become aware. It is not your purpose at this point to communicate awareness. Become aware within yourself. Communicate within yourself and do not waste words.

The animals are not better than you; they have a different perspective. You are not better than the animals; you are *of* the animals. The children are not better than you, and you are not better than the children. You are *of* the children. Listen to the perspectives.

Are the predictions simply indicating a bigger wave of energy?
The wave of energy is already in motion, and in ways some predicted. An "Armageddon" or an "apocalyptic"

change, a return of God, a "war in the heavens," well, there are elements of truth in all of that. The ancients and those that prophesy today, they did see a wave of energy. They were only able to interpret it from their perception. It is tempting to interpret it for this point in time, but even we do not know how it is going to affect.

In the phrases "the new heavens" and "the new earth" (and truly you are on a new heaven and earth), we say heaven because you are here in the realm of spirit sometimes. It will be a little surprising to you when you come back here, but look around at how surprising the earth is! What if someone from the earth from two hundred years ago arrived on the earth today? It would well be incomprehensible. As above, so below.

Things are changing, things have changed. Release the old ways of thinking and it will be much easier to cope with the change. Balance yourself for that energy, and then, when it comes, you will be balanced.

Many people have been thrown off when the energy has changed because they expected something horrific, with fear and terror. Some of them got it, and have it still, and you do not need to be a part of that. You do not need to oppose it. Balance yourself. Do what you can for the one in front of you at the time they are in front of you. You are the one who is in front of you all the time.

Do it for yourself, and if it sounds selfish, yes, our voice had so much trouble with this concept. Much of his life has been spent giving. It is time now to be selfish. Do not be greedy, but pull your energy back to yourself. Do not waste your words because your words are your energy, your power. Listen to how you speak and allow your speech to change.

It is hard to not make this a personal question, but as we are needed other places, will we be drawn to other places?

No one can be transferred without their will. If they do not want to go, they do not have to go. Where you are is where you are. It is no accident that you are doing what you are doing. Is it right or wrong to remain here? There are many like you who are experiencing a different point of view, a different perception in how you settle on the earth. There are bridges that we cross, and sometimes we are the bridge for others to cross. Sometimes you are the bridge for others to cross.

On an island in the Pacific, in the past, you were unable to own the land, now you can. Something changed and the earth will have something to say about that. The spirit of the earth, the consciousness of that specific place, does not want to be owned on that island. It will reclaim the ownership.

You pull and you get pulled. The action will have an equal but opposite reaction, as above, so below. If you feel the pull, cooperate with it, the same way as if you are caught in a stream of water. Do not struggle against it, swim with it or go with the flow.

Be careful not to mistake desire for pull. The shift of the earth, the shift of the energy of the earth, the shift of the energy around the earth occurred, yet it still needs to settle in. We feel the pull to different areas. We feel the change in certain areas. We must have patience to see if the pull stays strong. If the pull is constant, then it is a stream. If it is inconstant, then it is a whim.

Follow the stream. Allow yourself to be carried with it. If the flow is somewhere, you are then somewhere. If the water is still, then you float. So relax and enjoy!

There are three things: love, joy, and peace. In the past channeled writings, they were described as the fruitages of the spirit. We know that if someone is spiritual then they display these things and more.

Love what you are, who you are, where you are, love you. If you do not love you, you can not love anyone else, and no one can love you. Joy, enjoy things. Peace, seek peace. That is how we close our channel at this point in time.

Things to Remember
- If you cannot pull one closer with your words, it is better to allow your words to stay within you.
- It is up to you to balance the universe, by starting with yourself.
- Great changes in the course of life on the planet need not be cataclysmic. Think catalyst.
- Become aware; aware of each other, aware of the planet, aware of energy, aware of power.

Things to Come
- Spiritual companions may shift for you as assignments are adjusted.
- Watch for changes in the islands of Hawaii.

Question and Answer Sessions

The question-and-answer sessions are always fun and enlightening. It is at these times that Onereon's sense of humor tends to come out clearly and there is a feeling of gentle teasing in many of the responses.

The dialogue that follows after some of the channels can be equally enlightening. Though it is not directly channeled information, the energy of Onereon is still with those in attendance, and many bits of wisdom can grow from our discussion.

In my private meditation after the channels, Onereon will often comment on the discussions and build on some of these thoughts. Where appropriate, I have edited these thoughts into the transcription of the channel. Sometimes I have left the after-channel dialogue just as it is to illustrate the continuity of energy that stays with those in attendance.

Onereon describes themselves as "Together" and it is this wonderful sensation of togetherness that we wish to convey here by including the words of others in the room during the live channels.

Jeff Michaels

5
Be Aware

So we begin with the agreed upon phrase: As above, so below.

We speak about that for this reason, so that you understand that what you are going through, we also go through. There is no difference between the body, the mind, and the spirit in the human. It is all part of the system, and you are all part of the system as well. Just because we are in spirit does not mean that we experience things any differently than you do. We only experience them in a different fashion.

The events that go on in the world, around you, mirror the events that go on in spirit. What you see in the physical world is merely a reflection of what is happening in your mental world and that is a reflection of what happens in your emotional world and your spiritual world. Body follows brain, spirit follows heart.

Death and Life

There are some of you concerned about current events. You may question sometimes, "Am I losing my faith" or "Do I have a lack of faith" or "Is this stuff really real?" How can we be in a new age when there is so much violence and there is so much bloodshed and there are so many innocent lives lost? How can one person walk up to a group of innocent people enjoying their life and taking care of business and take those lives and their own away?

We say, "As above, so below." If this is happening in your world, how then does this happen in spirit? We have said before, look back at the last two centuries of human history. Look at what happened to all of those people that died young, that died by each other's hands. What happened to their spirit? What happened to their vital force? What happened as they lay in agony in deserts and frozen tundra?

Life changes. Life is change. You will begin to understand death in a different way in the near future. Birth is not an event and death is not an event. They are all still part of the process of the vital force of life and living. What happens when life is suddenly stopped by violence?

Think of the rain. Think of water. When water becomes polluted, the planet purifies this. How? With movement, and the water moves through different levels and the water sinks into the ground and the water rises into the air. The water rains back down, repeatedly over and over and over. The water becomes purified. Life force is like that; it is energy. Energy becomes purified by repeatedly going through a cleansing process, a filtering.

What caused these situations in the first place? We will speak of that at a different time. A pattern was set for many of these young people, to die young, and it has been filtering. The fear at death did not go away as they passed through. The realities of spiritual worlds cause some to be in fear at that point in time. It was not what they expected. They had an opinion. They had someone tell them, "Do this and you will be in heaven." It was not what they thought. They died in fear and, passing through the veil, they continued to live in fear. The cycle brought them back in fear. There is much fear.

We tell you these things today for this reason; do not give in to the fears. It is easy to do that, give in to fear. It is so difficult not to give in to fear in this so encompassing sphere. Trust your perceptions. Make sure they are your perceptions. Make certain that no one else has taught you your perception.

Become Self Aware

You sometimes use the word "beware," and that word instills fear. Let us bring that word back to its original meaning, "be aware." Look around. Be aware of the world around you. Are there frightful things? Yes. Are there dangerous things? Yes. Are there beautiful things? Yes. Be aware.

As above, so below; you have seen your world change. You will see it change more. Do not be afraid. Be aware. Be aware of where you are. Be aware of what goes on around you. Be aware of your thoughts. Be aware of your feelings. You have heard this so many times. Please take this to heart. Be aware of who you are, not the outside forces that have formed you. This is the problem, so many bend to the outside forces.

The growth of the family human is on time, on a course. The things that are happening around you are not an accident. They are also not necessary. Be aware of how you feel about other people. It is not your concern how they feel about you. Be aware of others and how you feel about them. They are not a danger to you. They are an opportunity for you.

Look to your history and the two hundred years past. Understand, all of those beings had to make the cycle, first into spirit and then back onto earth, back into spirit and then back onto earth. Then again, spirit to earth. Some of them made this cycle many times and experienced similar things every time. These cycles are nearing an end, slowing down. Great changes are about to happen!

The family human began at a very specific spot on the globe, on the earth, near the equator, degree 30. Look to that area now and understand how Source stays Source, the Source of life and the Source of new life. The source of maturity of the family human is beginning at the same spot as the family human began. This will be difficult for you to understand for some time.

Life energy coalesces into individuals. Individuals become personalities. When the life energy passes from that personality back into spirit, it may decide to reform with another personality, or it may decide to become more than one personality. There will come a time when the billions of personalities begin to come back together, less and less individual humans. The population will drop as we become one, one with each other. There are many changes that need to go on before that happens.

You and No Other

The qualities that we ask of you as individuals, we ask that you apply the qualities to others, yes, but we ask that you apply those qualities to yourself first. This is the new age.

You are responsible for who? Yourself. *This* is the new age. Not reaching out unnecessarily. Allowing individuals to be individuals, to stand on their own, by standing on your own yourself. There are many individuals who feel alone. We invite you to stand on your own, alone and strong, not lonely.

It is not necessary to see the images of violence. It is not necessary to see these things. You know about them. Do not review them. Allow them to exist as they are and here is the quality, forgive. Forgive them, forgive yourself.

Seek guidance, yes, but think companionship when you seek guidance and ask, "What can I do?" "What can I do for you?" This is a very important question. Begin asking now. You will be in the front, the leading edge.

It is a good world. It is one of joy. It is one of sky and air and water and fire. It is one of growth, beauty, and light and as above, so below. We enjoy this. We enjoy this energy. We enjoy this part of it. We enjoy the contact. We are spirit. We enjoy the moments that we spend together with our human companions. Please begin to enjoy the moments that you spend with your spirit companions. Ask their names. Ask what we like. Ask what we like to do and begin to understand that we are not so different. As you take a drink of water, include us, as you are asking to be included in the things we enjoy. You get to have the physical experience. When you are here on the earth, you miss the spiritual experience, and you reach for that. When you are here in spirit, you miss the physical experiences. We ask that you reach out and include us.

Touch the earth, touch the water, touch the people around you and do these all in gratitude and enjoy this. Life can be shorter, life can be longer, and the more joy you have in your life, the more gratitude, the longer life may be. There are larger forces at work than even we. Those larger forces like gratitude. They like balance. They like diversity. They like being included. Be in motion. Be grateful. Be balanced yourself. Are there questions?

Q: You say, "As above, so below." Right now we are us below, you above. Is there a place where there is an above and you are the below and so on? Does that somehow circle around together?

A: We say, "As above, so below." It really does make it sound like a hierarchy, does it not? As here, so there, but yes, there is an above for us and we assume for them as well. There is a below for you and we assume a below for those that are below you. We speak of the non-human animals; in a sense they are slightly below.

The way you could see it, the way you can sometimes glimpse it in the vast field of moments of energy, the energy spins together for awhile and then spins off to join other energies and spin together. It is really quite magnificent. It is colors that you can not see, sounds that you can not hear. It is as if you hear the colors and see the sounds. It all flows together in different directions.

The mistake is to think that you are something. You are everything. At some point, so much of the energy that is you right now has touched so many energies that you cannot see and you cannot hear now. The limits are not a mistake.

As above, so below. Yes, we have our guides too. When we reach out for guidance, we say, "Hi, what about this?" The perception is different. We have a larger perception. We look at things from a different point of view. In the same way that a child looks at things from a different point of view than you do. Are you then the child and we are the adult? In a sense, but understand that even as an adult, you have an adult that is older than you, your parent, and they have a different perspective than yours too. It is just perception.

We do not have that perspective, but we also know that as human becomes spirit and as spirit becomes higher spirit, higher spirit sometimes comes back to spirit and spirit comes back to human. Higher spirit thus sometimes goes below.

You were talking about how people who left violently by someone else's hand, what if someone takes their own life? Are they entered back into the spirit world? Do they rest for awhile and recondition themselves?

After the passing of any human being there is a short time, short in linear, short in gravity. The marvelous thing about the spiritual plane is understanding time in such a different way. A person who has died in fear is oftentimes given time, an opportunity really; think of it as hospice where someone is eased comfortably into death. They can be eased out of death as well, eased out of death into spirit. Some people react differently to earthly hospice. They still are in denial. They still die in fear. They still die in rage and anger. They still die not having said thank you. They still die without gratitude. Sometimes then, they live again in that way. The cycle of spirit for them is short because the filter is here on the earth.

There is no damnation. There is sadness when suicide happens. It is unfortunate, though sometimes it is the contract (we will refer to that as a contract) that you and the energies you are made up of create prior to your existence here. Sometimes it is illness, that inability to be at ease with your human condition.

This is why we say so often, be balanced, be practical. Remove expectation from this life. Live this life. Enjoy this life. Get dirty. Be in the dirt. Sweat. Be strong, be balanced, that will keep you on the earth for longer. If you feel the need to take your life, it is up to you. It is your perception. It is your reality. Again ask, what reality is it?

Whose reality is it? Are there things that can be changed? Take the action, change those things. Do not take up other people's action, for that is reaction. Take the action. Take your action!

I have heard that every life is supposed to be in many different realities at the same time. I know the one we are in is what we are focusing on, but while we are here, I have been told, there are many different dimensions we are living in all at the same time. How are you supposed to jump from one to the other?

Stay Here! Your light is your light. Cast it where you will. Light goes off in all directions from the sun. In multidimensionality…It is not up to you to understand that at this point. Focus on where you are now. In the same way that we understand higher spirit and higher and higher spirit, we do not reach for that. When it happens, it happens, and you allow.

As a human, and the perception that you have as humans, you are not here to understand what you see in other dimensions. There is a danger in seeking other dimensions. Not a danger to be afraid of, but a danger that this pursuit would take you off your courses and pull you away from what is in front of you and mix you up.

It is a problem that you have had in your writings. There are those that saw energies and went into other dimensions and saw the future of earth time and misunderstood and became afraid and wrote great apocalyptic pieces. Horrible blood moons, fearsome things and "be afraid" was the message they came away with. It is equally wrong to come away with the message that everything is wonderful, and everything is light. As above, so below. Look around you. Look around you and understand this is how things are, not just on the planet but throughout all planes of existence. We just deal with things differently in other areas.

We spoke earlier of the earth as a filter. Not just the earth, but to give information about where life force also exists in this universe is to give you things that are not easily comprehensible at this point. The earth is the filter, the earth by herself. Be on the earth. Do not get out of balance by reaching for things that are not of your understanding.

That is not what I meant. This is what I have been told: each person living linearly has many different dimensions they are living in at the same time, many different lives, rich, poor, here, there, each person in each different reality.

You feel those things because of the karmic experiences you carry. Focus on who is in the mirror. That is the person to care about. That is the person to love. That is the person to forgive. That is the person to be grateful to and that is the person to enjoy, the person that is in the mirror. All these other aspects, they are not in the mirror. Focus on you. Focus on that dimension. These other visions are often a mistake made by those whose perceptive abilities are not equipped to handle that information, people that have taken their training too fast or for granted or not at all, people that have reached too far.

So in effect, this is like predestination, you are where you are, no matter what. Things are brought to you where you are walking, so it has been there since the time you are born, and you are just playing it out.

There are so many variables that to begin to think of the concept of destiny…Everything has a choice and every second you make a choice that changes the destiny of everything and everyone. It is nearly impossible for the human to consciously make every choice. There are so many choices. Maintain your balance so that when choices come up you remain balanced in your choices.

There is no pre-destiny. You chose the direction you chose to go. Walk that path. It is not a different dimension. It is just a different direction. Driving in your car in Chicago, you think about a road in Denver. You do not automatically get to that road in Denver. You can get to that road in Denver by following many other roads until you arrive at that point in time. It is not the same road except that it is connected by different roads. Your path…You can change your path, but you have to follow in the dimension that you are in, earth dimension. Chose your path. There is no pre-destiny. There is choice.

I have a question on manifesting and how spirit answers our questions on manifesting. When we manifest…

Spirit rarely answers your questions on manifesting. YOU manifest. YOU do that! You are the one. You manifest. This is so interesting for us because we get the request, "Please, please help me, help me have this…" Just manifest it! You do this all the time. Family human, you do this all the time.

So what is the point of manifesting? When we go to spirit for the manifestation, but it is really us?

Exactly.

So there is really no point in manifesting?

Of course there is a point. What do you want? Define it then manifest it. You do not need to ask us, any more than you need to ask the grocer where the milk is when you have been shopping at the store for twenty years. Nobody moved the manifesting energies. If they moved the milk around, then you might need to ask one time, but you go to the grocery store and you know where things are. You know where your house is. You know where your job is. You know where the manifesting energies are. Why ask? Why not just go pick up the manifesting energy, use the manifesting energy. Understand something, sometimes there is no milk…

There has been no milk for a long time!
Then we find something else, see. Sometimes we are silent. You have known us as angels and guides. Sometimes we are silent, because the question gets asked in the wrong way or the question that is being asked has been refused. The question may be asked many times. Think again about how children ask, "Mommy can I have a cookie now?" "No, you can not have a cookie right now. You can have a cookie after you finish what is actually good for you." In a way, if you are trying to manifest a cookie and a cookie does not appear, maybe you are just being asked to eat your vegetables, what you have been given, what is good for you! Manifesting energy is an intrinsic aspect of the human family. You do not ask us to look and see things for you. You do not ask us to listen to music for you and then tell you what it sounded like. Just manifest.

I am doing it wrong then?
You just have to eat your vegetables first.
I was ignored!
You were answered.

Why have you chosen this time to come and talk with us and guide us and help us on a more outgoing, more visible basis? What would you like us to learn from you?

Think about your companies. Think about the company that has a new direction. New technologies on the earth have created opportunities for companies to work in different ways, so training needs to be done. Generally that is put in the hands of the human resources department and that is how our voice considers us, more as human resources. That makes sense to us.

We are here to keep people integrated, to keep people in motion, to keep people up to speed, to keep people learning, to keep people fresh and vibrant, to keep people on a path where they can have a career, where they can enjoy their work in a spiritual way.

Look at the ways companies have changed and understand how spirit then has changed. Look at the way your world has changed in two hundred years. The balance is this, then. With everything that went on, new things were learned, new things discovered, new technologies, new information, new aspects of understanding where the family human came from. Napoleon is not just a conqueror. Napoleon was not just one who directed weapons against others. Napoleon opened up Egypt, the Egypt of today. There is more information to come from the land of Egypt.

The technology that you enjoy, the technology around you, is also an aspect of what we have seen the last two hundred years. A wave of energy hit then and changed many, many things. Many deaths and many other things changed as well.

Your world is magic. The magic that you seek is really technology that has yet to be discovered and it will be! The more you learn about the past, the more you understand what has changed, what has not changed, and what continues to change, the more you will understand the changes in the future and the less frustrated you will have to be.

The more motion you apply to yourselves, the more natural your balance will be. Balanced motion is the key. Be balanced. Move forward in a balanced way. Stay balanced. Do not move faster than you can exist.

Stay practical. Be here. Be here now on the ground, on the earth.

Look for those moments of peace in this life, not for those moments of strife. Find the moments of peace and go towards them. You will find the moments of strife reduced, the moment of frustration reduced.

Accept the guidelines. Accept the fact that at this moment, now, you are in human form. Find the peace. Move towards peace. We say, "Seek peace."

At this point we include some of the discussion conducted after the channeling session. We feel that there is a deepening of an understanding of manifesting, revealed through the words and observations of those in attendance at this session. Attendees are designated by initials, except for Jeff, who is the channel. The words are from the humans and are not directly channeled.

A.: *Did you get your question answered N.?*

Jeff: They can seem scolding, can't they?

N.: *I always thought manifesting went through to the higher, above.*

A.: *What they said is that it is part of the human energy.*

M.: *I always thought it was supposed to be co-creation.*

Jeff: What we are really looking at is not new information but a new way to understand the information. I do not know that co-creation is so much what we are supposed to be doing. We are at a certain level of development. They use the example of little kids a lot, indicating that we are not little kids anymore. We don't have to have our hands held. We can cross the street by ourselves. The idea here is the responsibility of the individual human. At a certain point in time, the child gets on the bus by themselves, goes to school by themselves, and at a certain time the child gets their own vehicle and drives themselves.

We are at that section where we are not necessarily on our own; our parents are always willing to welcome us, for the most part, depending on what your family dysfunction is. The reliance on family has changed to a great degree. We have been accepted by family for many, many years and it is okay to come back to the family. It is better not to have to come back to the family. It is best to be self-reliant. If we have to go back to the family, we do. No judgment.

So spirit says things like, "Not guides but companions." This is something Onereon is really fond of talking about. We are companions, and at a certain point of time you can become companions with your uncles, aunts, and the other adults in your family. They are guiding you less, helping you grow up less and life becomes more like, "Why don't we all go to the museum. Let's experience this interesting thing together." That's what I get from this, that we are really supposed to be at that point.

It is all part of a greater shift involving the whole planet. Don't worry about it. It is not like *(snap)* today the shift is going to happen. We will know it, but we will know it as a wave. A wave doesn't hit like that. *(hits wall)* Even a tsunami, if you look at pictures of that, a wave came in and flowed in and flowed back out and that is the energy of how these things happen.

Armageddon happened, that's what I get, just not in a fearful way. It wasn't scary. It was scary for some as it happened because there were wars and the common things that are scary, but there were also interesting things. There were famines, but there were also interesting things. It was a wave of energy. Take a look.

W.: I thought it was supposed to be something in the future, or is that just my catholic background showing?

Jeff: Many people think it is an event that is supposed to happen, a vast destructive, cataclysmic event. If we stop thinking cataclysm and start thinking catalyst, we will gain a better perspective on the energy. A wave of something happened. Look back the last three hundred years. You can clearly see the change, the end of a long-standing way of life.

W.: When did it actually happen?

Jeff: You are asking for the date. You are still thinking event. As far as I know, it is still going on. It was a changing of sight, of vision. Apocalypse means just that, a revelatory experience. A revealing of the way things are. Onereon indicates that, as humans, we changed the way that the Armageddon energies impacted the planet. We co-created as a group. The way that spirit helped was when *we* were in spirit, between lives, we decided that destruction wasn't that much fun. I like it better this way, don't you? *The group agreed unanimously. Again!*

Things to Remember

- The earth is a filter.
- Life and death act as a filter for purifying the vital forces of Gaia.
- Be aware! This is the new age, one in which you are responsible for yourself alone.
- Stand on your own. Be balanced. Be in motion. Be here.
- Invite your spirit companions to join with you in the things that bring you pleasure on earth.
- Do not give in to fear.
- There is no damnation.
- There is no pre-destiny.
- There is choice.
- You manifest.

Things to Come

- There is more information to come from the land of Egypt.
- The family human will soon begin to understand death and dying in a different way.

6
Vibrations

As above, so below. Where Onereon speaks, we speak with a unified voice, though we are in multiple.

Sound and Vision

We speak about vibration today. You know about vibration; you know there are many vibrations. You know vibration based on sound and you know vibration based on light and as above, so below.

You know that there is visible vibration, and you know that there is non-visible vibration. You do not seek to see beyond red…infrared. You do not seek to see beyond violet…ultraviolet. As a human, as a member of the family human, you understand the limitation of physical sight. You also understand that it is a limit based on vibration. You understand the limit of sound. You understand that no matter how hard you may try, ultrasonic is not for your ears. Yet these vibrations still affect, and they still flow around you and sometimes through you.

We will speak mostly of sound and vision and yet we know that vibration also is taste. We know that vibration is also smell. We know that vibration is also touch. As above, so below. We also have our vibrations, and we have our limitations. In the acknowledgement of vibration, the closer the vibrations together, the denser the matter becomes. As humans, you have many vibrations very close together.

When we are spirit, we are many vibrations, but farther apart, harder to detect. Sometimes they are not possible for a human to detect. Sometimes the human reaches that area of spirit and their vibrations become farther apart and they become scattered. It is difficult for them to be practical, and it is not for human to be spirit.

As above, so below. There are times when spirit and those personalities, those beings on our plane, become denser. They lose track of their own light because that is, in a way, what we all are. Our voice is fond of the phrase that humans are gravitationally trapped light, and it is not entirely accurate, but poetically it works.

Notes

In a concert hall, many vibrations come together and as a family human you hear the concordance, you hear the harmonies. The notes fit together well. It is good if you think of yourselves as individual notes. It may be helpful to think of yourself as a chord. Some chords sound pleasing together; sometimes there is discord. And as above, so below. We deal with this differently. We do not try to harmonize with what is not harmonious. We allow for another song. When the vibrations become very, very dense, they can intrude.

Dark messages, deep messages and for the human that has reached too high and has allowed their vibration to separate too far, and for the spirit that has become dense and lowered their vibration, this is when miscommunication happens. Yet they seem harmonious at the point that they touch. What is a higher vibration for human is a lower vibration for spirit. So we caution those. We see much discord on your planet.

In a concert hall, prior to performance, you may hear individuals begin to warm up. The warming up is each individual playing notes for themselves and themselves only, until a conductor approaches and brings all of them together. When the performance is over, when that time has ended, when the linear lines of notes stop, each individual goes back and returns to the respective space and plays their own notes once again. The next time, they all tune up at the same time and it sounds discordant.

Harmonizing

The vibration of the planet has shifted and there is a new song. There is much discord now as the family human begins to harmonize. We have spoken in the past of the pain some have felt as they left the physical life and the inability they had to stay within spirit.

We have spoken of the earth as a filter and life on the earth as a filter. It is no accident that the population has increased. Soon the population will drop. Sometimes the population will drop in dramatic ways, and it will seem wrong.

In truth, it is just the filter, and the notes will be coming together. The vibration that was an individual human will have an opportunity to become a larger vibration, a higher vibration, part of a chord, part of a line of music, part of a measure. They will be more than a single beat. They will become unified.

It is difficult to understand from your perspective. In a sense, one human and another human and another human become one being. When you have a memory, when you have a sense that you have been somewhere before, it is a resonance, a recognition of a vibration, a similarity of vibration to what you are now. It is not a false memory; it is recognition. When you resonate, how do you feel? You feel at home.

For some, discord is all that they have known. In order for them to process and filter, it has been necessary to separate the vibrations. There are many on the planet now that feel incomplete. In a sense that is true.

Changing Vibrations

It is the tuning of the planet. The vibration of the planet has shifted and changed. It is higher. It will become easier and easier for those who feel that they are missing something to find a space within the vibration of the planet earth. As the generations of the family human move forward, there will be less and less people, fewer and fewer individuals, and more harmony.

It is a process. The capability of the human has levels that have yet to be attained. The capability has been there, but in the same way that a human from several thousand years ago does not have the capability to withstand modern life, present linear gravity, you will not have the vibration to handle one hundred years from now. It will be very different times, very different vibration, and very different gravity.

As above, so below, we see these things differently. We see the sense of change because we sense the vibrational change. We have a higher plane of existence, and by that we do not mean superior. We are partnered with you. You are partnered with us, have no fear. Be aware.

We are cautious about what we say. We have affected our voice deeply and yet we do need to speak about these things. The deaths of many, the violent deaths of many, are yet to be at an end because there were so many. If you look back, look back two centuries and you will see how this all started.

We have given you a place on the earth to look at, did you look there? This is where the vibrational change begins, for the family human has always been linked to this spot.

There is more to know about the history of humanity and much of what science knows right now is wrong and yet they know that, and they are on the right track. As they explore and as they learn to accept a vibration that can not be proven, they will begin to understand the paintings in the pictures in a different way. The illustrations in the caves, the illustrations on the rocks, the vibration of the colors and the vibration of that land will become clearer and clearer and clearer.

Our voice asks for clarification. First we were talking about Africa, we now talk about Australia. The images on the walls and on the rocks and in the caves of Australia speak of a different history of humanity. One where spirit walked the earth and human walked with spirit and there was very little difference. There is a beginning there that has yet to be uncovered.

Create the Vibration

Vibration through sound, vibration through light, vibration through touch, we asked that you touch the earth. We said, "Touch the earth." Touch the earth through the trees, touch the earth through stones, and touch the earth through flowers, through dirt, through water. You will learn through touching the earth. You will learn the vibration.

You will feel the harmony. You will sing your song in harmony and in turn what happens then is that the earth harmonizes with you. The planet itself...we say, "As above, so below," and again let us clarify this. Above is the higher vibration, not superior, but just a different perspective and you have a vibration higher than the planet and so the planet would say, "As above, so below," and look to you to be the "as above" and feel itself, "so below."

Allow the planet to have the same gift of communication "as above" as you have in communicating with us "as above," partnering with the planet in the same way that you partner with spirit. They are equal and they are important, and it is necessary for the family human's survival to partner with the planet and to harmonize.

Not just the planet, also spirit, and this is part of the discord today. Earth-centered religions have regained popularity. They have found a space and that is no accident. Ascended religions are having troubles and that also is no accident. Instead of trying to make ascended religions sing the song of earth-based religions or earth-based religions sing the song of ascended religions, allow them to harmonize where they are.

There are many types of music and not all please everyone. As above, so below, there are vibrations that we ourselves do not appreciate. It is the human way to say, "Why not stop those vibrations?" In the spirit way, we say, "Why not learn those vibrations and allow those vibrations? It is just a vibration, it is not right, it is not wrong."

Vibrations can cancel each other out. We see that with wave experiments. We see that with sound experiments, and we see that with light experiments. So we change. We change where we are at so that we do not cancel out a vibration. These are higher vibrations, and they act quickly. That is why we sometimes return to the earth quickly. That is why there may be sudden growths in population, because certain vibrations need to flow from Source and the vibrations that we are at that moment may not harmonize. So we return to a physical form where we assimilate the vibration at a slower pace.

Not just on the earth and not just as human. Some of us choose to vibrate at a much lower level: planets, asteroids, comets. The vibration of life is a very interesting vibration and one you will not understand for quite some time. There are many, many, many areas for the individual vibrations to travel to and coalesce and to solidify. There are many varied forms of life who talk about the earth. Our voice likes the idea of "life out there." We stay practical. We stay here on the earth. We sense the vibration of change now, change within this group in an elevating and of higher vibration, but not too high. As vibrations cancel each other out, some vibrations strengthen each other. Move towards those vibrations, move in trust, not fear. Are there questions?

When you speak of a conductor coming into a concert hall and harmonizing all of the individual notes, who is the conductor?

Touch the earth. It has been said life is a little bit like learning how to play the violin while the concert is going on. There has been so much training. There is a Source, you know. There are so many levels between us and the Source and between you and the Source. It is difficult to begin to describe that. There are conductors, there are many conductors, and there are guest conductors and they come in and we play together and not everyone gets to play. There are individuals that strike out on their own, who do not become part of the group and who become successful in the small venues where they play and sing. We like this idea of music.

We look at the earth, and you know of some, you know of one, who has helped to change the vibrations, the harmonics, one who has helped to make things more concordant. It is not *the* conductor, a conductor, or a group of conductors.

Your position on the earth is to learn your song, to harmonize with the earth and let the earth harmonize with you. These are your lessons and as time goes on, as things become more harmonious, the earth itself will help the harmony. This way the conductor has allowed the earth to be the tuning mechanism, so that at least many people begin to be tuned to the same vibration. In a sense it is a limiting analogy to say, concert hall. You will play in many performances. You will play in many concerts, acting in concert with others. So, not one conductor, but many, not one performance, but many. Learn your song. Learn your strength and play to your strength.

I think the reason there are many conductors is that some people may resonate with one conductor and some with other conductors. What about the conductors who say they are conductors, but they are not?

How quickly does a show close when the performance is bad? Every action will have an opposite and equal reaction. If the conductor can not bring concordancy, these things happen, no one will listen, no one will play.

Those that chose to play with a conductor of low quality do so only to excuse their own inadequacy. "It is not my fault. It is the conductor's fault. Everyone knows that the conductor is bad." Allow the show to close. Play your song. You will notice many, many, many discordant events in this world. Do not try to change them. Play your song. Your song is beautiful. Your song is important. If your song is harmonious, then people will want to play in concert with you and the conductor will want you and chose you as you have already been chosen. Play your song.

Can you give us some advice about finding our song and about becoming a clear note?

Where do you feel clear? Where do you feel like singing? What is beautiful to your eyes? What is rhythmic to you? When you find yourself not in flow, when you feel you are out of your own pattern, when you feel you do not have a pattern, when you feel that it is someone else's pattern, it is probably not your song. A skilled musician will be able to play any song, but not all songs are a musician's favorite song. What do you like to be? What do you like to see? What do you like to taste? Remember, we are talking about vibration and so it is all of these things. It is not just song. It is not just sight. We can easily apply this to visuals, to taste, to touch, to smell. Where do your senses feel activated, inspired, stimulated, all of the senses, because they are really not separate. There are no five senses. There is one human, an individual, an undivided one. The divisions are getting less and less and less as time goes on.

As the vital force of life, as the vibration of life begins to re-assimilate and coalesce, people filter through this planet. This is hard for some to understand, the necessity of the deaths, the necessity of the grief, but it is to show that we do not want this any longer, that it is not in harmony.

When the children die, when the innocent die, when the car bomb explodes, when the wave washes over people, they are moving quickly through this life. When they come back, they understand, "No more." They return to areas of what in a human sense might feel like power and they become the leaders, and they say, "No more."

It is a process, not an event, and it is in process. Nine people die, two people return. How does that happen? The vibration that is here then is a higher vibration; it is more vibrations, it is more experience, it is more lessons. They play their songs in a harmonious way. Several thousand people die, mere hundreds return, and quickly, because they want that lesson to be learned quickly. We do too.

Is the lesson being learned quickly enough?

Vibrations have changed. Look to Rwanda. You will see the beginning of the model. Look to where we all began on this planet. Look to where sentience first stood up. Watch how sentience continues to rise. The wisdom continues to rise. You will not recognize this world in one hundred years.

I'd like to ask about you. Where do you live? What do you enjoy?

We are.... we are about. In the past, as we have spoken, we had a chosen voice. In answer to this question, we want to change speakers and be softer.

Consider me as the energy of the grandmother, the one who has seen generations. I enjoy the perspective. I enjoy the nurturing. I enjoy the ruling hand of the grandmother. I enjoy the care, the tradition, and that is what I enjoy. I enjoy the nurturing and the nourishing.

Others within Onereon enjoy the organizing, the planning, and we have our strengths. Overall, why do we harmonize? I would say it is because of the fun. I would say we share the nourishing desire. We ourselves enjoy being nourished. We look for new experiences. We look for learning. We look for things that are pleasing.

We have really no specific pleasurable pastime. Sometimes we enjoy being very close to the sun. Sometimes we enjoy distance, the spaces. It is difficult to describe in human terms. One of us enjoys the spaces. It is not just the space; it is not just great distances. There is great space between cells, there is great space between molecules, between atomics, and one of us enjoys that, enjoys being small. One of us enjoys the strong forces in small places. We enjoy that. We would say that we enjoy the feeling of the force, the feeling of the movements of energy. We enjoy the flow. We like the spin of things. We are sometimes cautious not to get caught in the spin.

What, if anything, can we do for you, or would you accept from us?

Wisdom, perception. Perception. We are cautious now in our reply. Our voice has a strength about his opinion of proselytization. It is not what we ask, but the speaking of the words, the speaking of this message is important. You are beginning. We trust the flow and we trust the current, so we trust the level of frequency.

Does there not need to be an energy exchange?

If these moments are the pebbles, then you are the wave, the ripple. We would like to see more ripples. We would like to see this energy flowing outward. We would like to see these words, this information, flow out. So it is with our host, our agreed upon voice, it is with his opinions in mind that we do ask that.

Speak of these events. Speak of these moments. Be cautious with your words, it is true. Do not waste your words on those who will not hear. We are not trying to be a big splash. We want this to be a steady flow. It is a very strong partnership that we have, as Onereon, and in a very strong way you also are Onereon. Onereon is more of a purpose, not so much a personality.

How did you come to choose the term Onereon?

It is a vibration. A title was needed, and that was the chosen one.

Is there a relation between other energies with the same sounding name?

Yes. When you hear that vibration, you will recognize that vibration in other names. There is no accident; there is purpose to the vibration.

How does this correlate with Kryon?

We will switch speakers for a moment. In a business model there are those that have strong sight, oversight. Their vision is above, the supervision. That is the director. That is the one that chooses the direction of the business.

There is need to communicate the direction of the business and that one is not always the best one to choose for communication. They may be a good communicator.

Their responsibilities, their abilities, are stronger in the different directions and so, communicators are chosen.

As Onereon, we are communicators. We communicate to individuals on an individual basis. We speak of the trends, not so much policy, but the way the business is trending.

Why do we feel drawn to different physical locations on earth?
The vibration of the earth is different in all areas. Denser hard packed granites are different than hard packed sands. The temperature causes a difference in vibration. It is no accident that we seem to feel more relaxed in warmer climes.

The earth is warming back up. Part of the filtering process will be to enjoy the warmth. For a time in the linear past, the filtering process allowed humans to become denser and denser and denser because the temperature was colder and colder. For the vital force to survive in the family human they had to be a denser vibration, and less and less of a population. In the warmth, you will begin to see a lower population with a higher vibration. Go where you feel in accord, in a chord.

As the people choose to leave and not come back and the consciousness is brought up as above, so below, in the process is the earth becoming more as above per se because of the healing that is going on in the consciousness in the higher vibration?
Yes. Gaia is a living planet and in its own way has sentience, although not as you may understand sentience. In a way you are Gaia's sentience, you are not just the family human, the family feline, the family equines. You are all aspects of Gaia's sentience.

Will the planet ever become as consciously high as you in this process?

It is a potential. It is a potential in the same way that humans are just a realized potential. There was no dictate that humans would exist. Humans were not a forgone conclusion in the process of the development of life. In the same way, it was not a forgone conclusion that dinosaurs as a species would become extinct. We may yet see sentience in creatures where we just would not imagine that. It depends on the process.

Is it possible to evolve a mass consciousness separate from the planet?

Life on the planet is based on the vital force of Gaia. The diversity of life on the planet is not a separate consciousness. It may be that the planet achieves higher consciousness through the returning of vital force to the planet. It would mean less and less in terms of sentient humans, sapient humans, existing on the planet.

There is a vital force about this planet, and it expresses itself in many ways. Saurians were an expression of the vital force of this planet. The plants, the fishes, the mammals, these are all expressions of the vital force of this planet. The vital force is not going anywhere. If something were to happen to make this planet inhospitable for mammalian, saurian, fauna, flora, the vital force is not going anywhere. It will grow somewhere. It may grow into the planet at that time. The consciousness of the planet would then be raised.

Are there correlations to the legendary geographical sacred spaces of earth and higher vibrations of humans, the ability for a human to gain a higher vibration or enlightenment? Are we closer to spirit in some areas of the planet?

There is a vibration that is conducive to a Walker, one who is walking between worlds. It only makes sense that if we, in spirit, are a higher vibration than those in the physical realms, the gravitational realms, that there is gradience, a spectrum of vibration that leads to the realm of spirit. There is no real boundary, only distance between waves of energies. Be aware that not everyone can or should reach for this higher vibration.

In the linear past of the family human, some were able to access the realm of spirit through training. It is true today, but with much training required for the vibration of the family is denser. Those that reach too far become unbalanced in their physical form. Those that focus on the balance of their physical form, maintaining a level of purity, may access the higher vibration with greater ease, but training is still required. Perfect health is not required.

As the family human progressed through time, many changes occurred of which you only now are becoming aware. In a far distant past, many more were able to access spirit directly. In the near future, we will return to that wave of existence.

As linear time moved, as the vibration changed, the planet was accommodating, and areas of the globe became centers for specific vibrations. The echo of that vibration remains in some of those areas still, but the reality is that not all sacred spaces retain the energies they once did. Some that still seek those areas do so based on karmic memories, which are strong, rather than any real sense of power. Be aware of what is a true vibration and what is simply a memory, sentiment.

However, there are many areas still where the vibration has not changed. The grid, the lines of strength and energy have shifted. You should expect no less. The centers for some of the lines remain or in fact shifted only slightly. In two cases they remained the same, but the land is no longer above the water. We will address this in greater detail at a later time.

We do not discourage ones from seeking these areas out. We encourage ones to seek the sacred space within themselves first.

If you draw a straight line through the globe from where the sacred areas of the earth are believed to be you will have a clue of where other sacred areas were, are, and will be. These are centers of energy that have existed for great aeons of linear time, from before the family human stood erect. In truth, these centers of energies were what drew many species from the areas of their comfortable existence, giving them the opportunity to adapt and grow. Civilizations grew in circles around these points and centers, longer ago than is the fashion to believe.

The consciousness of the family human, the vital force that was being expressed as Homo at that time, was drawn there. There is a race in existence today that recalls the connection of earth and spirit, of human existence and the space between. They still walk between the worlds, though it is a difficult land they walk in and much has been taken from them. Draw a line from their home.

Once you could see and step into these areas without losing harmony with the physical world, without losing humanness. Once the family human, not always Homo sapien, could walk in the areas that were near to spirit and those in spirit could walk in areas that were near to Gaia.

There is still a resonance in that land, and one other. There is still peace in that land, but not in the other. There is a unity of senses, a harmony of tribal notes. The harmonic is close to what it once was, so, though the vibration of the land changes and moves in waves, the people still sense the peace, the areas between worlds. They are still able to see but not access fully the spiritual realm, what they perceive as dreamtime, until such time as their vibration changes again.

There are intervals, there are frequencies, there are no boundaries except those that you create with belief. Stay with your training. Do not exceed your grasp. Conduct yourself in the ways of your song, for there is coming a time when you will be called upon to harmonize.

In the past, sacred spaces used to need to be in harmony with the earth and people. Beings, not just human, could approach and retain balance. All could approach. As time moved forward, it became necessary for ones to ask for help in locating the sacred spaces. Individuals then trained in the arts of spirituality and rules were created. The space between spirit and human increased. Individuals then began to be perceived as the sacred area themselves. In truth, they were not wrong. In truth though, all life and all beings are potentially sacred spaces.

In the present linear time, many people have set themselves up as individual sacred spaces. This arrangement, while proper, often leaves the individuals needing strengthening. The individual as sacred space needs grounding. Otherwise, their perception is not strong and can and will be influenced by the beliefs of others around them. They can easily feel that they have lost a level of peace. Their vibration is too wide for their physical presence and the individual can and will be in danger of becoming scattered.

This is why the middle of the continent attracts so many now pursuing their spiritual path. Fertility is still strong in these areas. If you want to grow strong, you need strong soil.

During the coalescing we will be bringing light together, narrowed and focused. The denser the light, the easier it is for those in the physical realms, the gravitational realms, to see.

Today is a time of individual responsibility, a time of harmonizing energies, a time of coalescence. In this way, many are recovering their peace.

Maintain balance. Speak your peace without expectation. Seek peace.

Things to Remember

- There is a Source.
- The vibration of the planet has shifted, and all life is now harmonizing to the new song.
- Learn your song. Learn your strength. Play to your strength.
- Allow others their song.
- Perfect health is not required to access communication with spirit. A balanced physical life will lead to a balanced spiritual life.
- In the past, civilizations grew around energy centers of the earth. Those energy centers may have shifted.
- Humans no longer need to go to specific geographical areas of the planet to be in sacred places.
- Humans *are* sacred places if they so choose.

Things to Come

- The population of humans will decrease significantly in the near future.
- A different history of humanity will be revealed, possibly through the first inhabitants of Australia.

Questions to Stimulate Your Personal Growth

You are all particles of the universe. Everything is a particle of the universe.

Are you doing your part to keep the universe balanced?

Manifesting energy is a human ability. You are creative.

What are you creating?

7
Perceptions

As above, so below.

A Bit on Diversity

Our voice thinks he may have some idea of where we are going to go today because we have given information about the diversity of humans and the survival based on diversities. Very briefly, survivals of species are often due to diversity of species. There are many breeds of cat, many breeds of dog, many breeds of simian, only one breed of human. For the family human to continue to be effective, there will need to be more diversity of the family human.

This has been a potential all along. This has been a reality for much of human existence. It is encoded within you to diversify. It is not time for diversification at this point, but we are getting there. It is a long process, because it is a physical process and physical takes linear time. This is what we want to talk about.

Drawing a Line

Because humans have hands and fingers and because humans can do this action of pointing and pulling things apart, they think that this marking and separating are things that *need* to be done. The directing of energy, the pointing of something, the pointing out of something, the pulling apart of something to see what is inside, the family human is very good at this. It is strength and it is why the family human has risen to the top of the vital forces on the planet.

Unfortunately, they are making a mistake. They think that this, pointing and delineating with their hands and bodies, means that things move in a linear fashion.

Let us talk about the sun. The family human has a subconscious thought about the sun. They think it only shines on the earth, when in reality it shines outwards in all directions equally and evenly. The family human, once they grasp that, sometimes will imagine the planets orbiting the sun and the sun shining out equally in all directions on all of the planets. The light of the sun, the heat of the sun, the radiation of the sun rises outward in all directions, not simply on a planar level.

The universe itself is a curve. Information travels in a curve in the universe. Sometimes it is a curve like a sphere. Sometimes it is a curve like a straw. Your scientists are understanding this more and more. The universe is also more dimensional than the majority of humans are really able to understand at this point in time. Again, your scientists are picking up on this information nicely. They have only been able to do so by abandoning the way they used to think, by not starting at Point A and then going to Point B in a linear fashion, but by taking a wild leap.

Once that wild leap was taken, and that was not very easy for them, the humans involved, these same ones would not understand the metaphysics and yet they are supporting the metaphysical. They are not a single vibration from the past; they are many vibrations. This is why they get to think this way. This is why they get to have these moments of inspiration. They do not know where it comes from, but somehow in their heart they have a faith in what they know and then they build the proof around it. This is a new way for the family human.

You also are curved. You also are a sphere. We are going to give you this image with the understanding that you understand that you are not literally a sphere, but that in the same way as the sun, your energy, as an undivided one, radiates out in all directions. Let us talk about direction. A cell moves in any direction. Why? Why not? When mitosis happens, the cell divides, and the divided cell becomes two undivided or individual ones and they move in any direction.

Direction and Motion

As humans, you have begun to believe in the laws of the lines. The lines have benefited you by dividing the earth up, so that you know where you are. Your latitudes and your longitudes give you direction. They also separate you. It is not so much forward motion that we are looking for. You say, "I want to move forward on my path." What if your path is a plane? What if the plane is a membrane? What if you close your eyes and use your ears?

It is true that humans have developed in a physical way so that the motion, the natural motion, is in the forward direction. We do not need to always move forward. The physical energy of the human will continue to move forward, but your heart beats not only in a forward direction. Your heart also beats backwards. Your brain thinks not only in a forward direction; your brain thinks also in a backwards direction. And you radiate like the sun.

We do not want to make people nervous by taking away their path. There is security for the human in saying, "Well, this is my path," and following the path. There is also a limitation for the human.

Division

As above, so below, when a cell divides it makes two cells, which then grow up to make a greater whole. The cells that make up a human do not stop their purpose once the human is made. The human then becomes a part of a larger body, the body of family human ultimately. Because humans can do this (extend arms forward and outward), they think of ways to separate, to categorize, to limit, to rank, to put some above and some below. They begin to try to impose all of that on spirit. So as some humans transform, they enter the spiritual realm with that in mind. It is difficult...so, as above, so below.

We sometimes feel the division above. When asked what Onereon is, there are many words that we will apply to this. Together. Onereon is together. Peace. Onereon is peace. Together, not conforming. Ah, see? Peaceful, not passive. Active, not aggressive. That is Onereon. Peaceful, not passive. Active, not aggressive, and together, but moving. In what direction? In all directions. Thus, you here today are Onereon. It is not a direct path, is it? If it were a direct path, everything would all look the same. Everything would be conforming, and the efficiency of the universe would be that everything did the same thing all the time. What a boring life it would be if that were true!

Be cautious how you raise your vibration levels. In some cases, we do this because there is a great need. It will affect things around you, adversely to a certain point of view. The human being, this wonderful, wonderful miracle that holds vital life, but is also vital life, that radiates in all directions, has a limit.

The more together, the more together in peace, the more together in active peace, the higher the harmony, the higher the vibration. This is why groups pull together, because they feel the vibration raise when they are together. You know, the word "synergy" is a good word.

We have said before that there is no sixth sense. In fact, there are no five senses. There is one sense. When you begin to understand the wholeness of you, the individual, the undivided one, (stop dividing yourself!) you will begin to feel the vibration of your energy and of your power. Our voice says, "and glory," because this is the essence of what you sense when you sense God and divinity. What you sense is everything around you and how you are connected to it and that is your spiritual experience. Not separate from you, but together, all acting in concert.

We like the model of music. We spend some time with that. The more you stretch your range, the more opportunities you have to be harmonious with a variety of people. Be cautious not to stay in one range, in one vibration, in one note, for very long. It wears you down and it is annoying to those around you.

Unification

Sense now your head. Do not separate it out to skin and skull and brain, just sense your head and let your sense from the front go to the back. Without looking, know what is behind you. Let your sense go upward to the top of your head. Without looking, know what is above you.

Know what is above the ceiling. Know what is above the building. Practice and do not stay there too long.

We categorize energies in the family human. We speak of energies as being this type of energy, that type of energy. As the family human, we seek to understand the relationship of the energies one to the other. This will help. The mistake is, you cannot separate the energies and understand the unification of the energies at the same time. You begin to understand the unification of things and then the relationship of energies becomes clear. This is why science has made a great leap and they do not know it yet.

In your day-to-day life, how does this become practical? Cease being in analysis. That does not bring peace. Listen to the vibrations that are harmonious to you in your life and go to those vibrations, even if it seems like you are leaving something behind. Play to your strength, not to your weakness. Play to music that you enjoy, not limiting yourself, but growing in the direction that is harmonious to you, the vibration that feels the best, the healing vibration.

For in truth, most disease is simply that. It is a dis-ease with the vibration you are experiencing at the moment. It may be change in locale. It may be a change in partnerships. It may be a change in a cherished path, one of tradition. If your shoe does not fit, do you wear it? There are many shoes in the world.

Direction is interesting and flow can sometimes indicate direction. Go with...the flow. Radiate and sense that, sense the effect that you are having on those around you. It is not necessary to change yourself at that point in time, but you may find that you choose to.

There is an energy of coalescence approaching the planet. Our voice is correct in his understanding that people return, less and less in number, but higher and higher in the ability to vibrate at a higher rate. Not quantity, but quality will be gained for the family human.

Then the diversity begins again. You see the traits already in humans. You see some who live in the sea. Yes, they come out of the sea, but they have an affinity for the sea. You see some who live in ranges of mountains, who have an affinity for trees. There is nothing mystical about this. It is a genetic code that is within you. It has been there all along. It has been there since your knuckles were front feet.

The diversity is not going to happen in this generation or the next. Over the next century, as the population dwindles, as the concept of communication shifts, as people delight in the idea of not needing tools to communicate, we will begin to see this more and more. Homo sapien will become more. The earth will return to more, shall we say, natural ways. Not pastoral, not peaceful, the struggle for life will continue. It is part of the vital force, and yet, abundance and plenty as the earth shifts into a different vibration itself. Ah, and all along you thought it was you that was raising your vibration. It is the planet that is raising its vibration and your vibration rises with it. You are not at the top and neither are we. There are larger forces at work and there are larger forces at play. Let us play!

Are there questions?

Will humans go back to a time resembling something like the movie, "The Lord of the Rings" where there are different groups of human-type energies on the planet?

It is a natural way, is it not? It is not going back. Ergaster is gone...Erectus, Neanderthal. Rarely does the vital force go back. It may appear that it did in certain creatures. In fact, it was a new adaptation, a new development that was ripe and right for that moment.

In a business model it would be this: the engineering department is important, but more important than manufacturing? Without manufacturing, the engineering department is simply thinking. Without the engineering department, the manufacturing department has nothing to do. Without the shipping department, things get jammed up really quickly.

The diversity of human will be like this in the future. It will be a cooperative effort; it will be together. It is unfortunate that in the past there was still much of the jungle, the animalistic nature.

The rising off of the planet and the returning to the planet is a filtering. The planet itself is a filter. What we want to make clear is that the function of the planet as a filter is not to achieve an ultimate goal where all life and everyone is spirit. There will always be life and there will always be vital force involved in this planet and not this one alone. Will it always be human? Chances are no. Human is not the most successful life-form on this planet. Can they learn to be? The answer is yes, and the possibility is there, and the probability right now is very strong. Sentience does not need to have opposable thumbs.

Are we not seeing the beginning of the massive diversity of humans coming together right now as we look at the huge amount of migrations across the world where cultures are integrating with each other and people who have come from one part of the world are becoming ingrained in other cultures? For example, we see Africans in the Netherlands and we see Mexicans in Canada, etc.

Homogeneity, the bringing together of all of the strains so that the family human can be stronger again, and yes, we are beginning to see that. It is not without purpose that these issues are being raised now and the answer is really very simple, is it not? Eliminate all of the borders. Yet for how long have humans been doing this, creating lines and taking things apart? So they are very proud of their ability to indicate and separate. It is a strong energy, and it will take much time to overcome this.

The filtering process is intact. The vibrations that people feel will coalesce, if not on this planet, then here in spirit. Then as we return, understand this, we will return…you will return here, and we will return there. You will be the ones responding to "as above, so below."

I've read a lot about this concept of critical mass. Can you define for me what that means in terms of our evolution as humans and the evolution of our planet?

Critical mass. Let us criticize mass. There is that moment where there is no turning back. We reached that moment some centuries ago. There was no turning back. The course of destruction was set. When people read that, they said, "See the course of destruction. See the path that we are on? The planet will be destroyed because divinity will destroy it."

It was never the planet that was involved. It was only the society of the planet that was involved. Yet when that critical mass rolled around, we found a way to funnel that energy, to channel it, to channel it in different directions, to radiate it out. The results we still see. "Armageddon" happened. Oh, the sun did not turn blood red, the moon did not fall from the sky, but we did see earthquakes and we did see wars and we still see the remnants. We still see that. We did not all have to perish.

We chose a different way to express the energy of an apocalypse. We took the literal word, which means "a revealing," and uncovered things. Let us look out of the corner of our eye instead of directly at things. Let us be careful around the fire. There is a principal, the one that is first becomes last. The least among you, look for those who are putting themselves first and understand how they are viewed as the least.

Critical mass…you are thinking now that the population is reaching a critical mass and we are saying that we do not need to criticize this mass, we need to coalesce. Bring it back together. That is what we are seeing and what you will see shortly, before the end of your lives.

You will begin to see the population decline. There is a choice in how that happens. It does not need to be by war, by famine. It can be very natural. It can simply be the passing of people. Within the next one hundred years, the population will decline. Within that, what we indicate then is not a lack of diversity, but a lack of quantity…diversity will retain. Below it, all the races are the same. You are really starting to comprehend that in a genetic way. There is no difference genetically between one human, one Homo sapien, to the next.

We have talked about how humans are very linear, and they relate to moving forward on their path. Because that is such an integral part of what we have been taught and who we are, how do you go about changing that perspective? I understand that we all radiate energy outward, but if we are not all trying to work towards being a better person or work towards enlightenment, how do we shift that perception?

Why be a better person? Why not just be the person that you are? This is one of the things about radiating out. It is a loosening of all of those things that are around your human form. It is a releasing of the need to satisfy other people. It is a releasing of the need to do what other people expect of you. It is not a disregard for other humans. It is a living of your own life. It is a following of your own path. It is the creation of you, the human, the individual, undivided by other information coming into you.

Our voice says, "The shoulds," and he is not wrong. "You should do this." "Mother said I should live my life this way." "Father said I should handle my money this way." "The priest, the reverend, said I should believe this thing." "Scientists say we should act in this way." "Politicians say we should salute this idol."

That is a lot of shoulds! You *should* say, "I AM." That is the act of creation, and you are the creation, and you are also the creator. As above, so below. You are a creator. Following your path is simple as this: do not follow anybody else's path. Be who you are. Be the truest, purest you that you are.

Be the least divided, not focused necessarily. When we focus, we become very intense. Sunlight through a glass starts fires. Sometimes fire is good. Let your light shine in the way that the sun lets its light shine. Let your heat radiate out in the way that the sun radiates out in all directions. The sun does have a path, does it not? The sun itself is in an orbit, as are all stars, all planets, all galaxies, all molecules, all atoms, and all of the sub-atomic structures are all in an orbit. What is your orbit? What is your center? How do you spin?

Can you elaborate on the statement regarding listening to find your path rather than using your eyes. That is not a sense that we use a lot.

It is not the sense that is common, is it? We could say, smell, taste your path. Touch your path. What we want is for you to understand and comprehend that the human sense is not a divided sense. The reason we rely on eyes is because light travels quickly and we get our information so quickly and we like that. When we close our eyes, information comes slower, and we have to then do what?

Think about what we hear. Think about what we smell. What is that smell? What is that sound? What is that? With our eyes, we just look. "Oh, it is that!" We get more from our ears, do we not? We get a vibration from our ears that we can easily access. The light itself is a vibration.

We are not necessarily indicating anything specific with the indication to listen, but to increase your senses, to sense with your skin, to sense with your entire human form. As you radiate out your energies, you sense how other people radiate out their energies as well. You know their fears, their pains, and their loves. How? By sensing where they pull their energy and the way they release their energy. Listening is an avenue to increasing this ability.

A more direct avenue is to just sit quietly and reach out in back, front, top, bottom, left and right. If the vibration of sound makes sense to you, follow that path. If the vibration of light makes sense to you, then follow that path and enjoy it…play. Play along that path.

Along those same lines, would it not be more appropriate, instead of "seeking your path," to just "experience your path," to just be open to the experience, to just try to "be in the moment" all the time?

You are your path. Whatever is in your sphere at that point is an aspect of your path. Take things from all around you, rather than direct yourself towards things. Be together with those things, do not possess those things. *Be your path.* You are your path.

Dimensions are interesting. Science has got the idea of dimensionality, but they still seek to understand where the division of dimensions is and there is no division…not truly. We have talked before about spirit guide…no, *spirit companion*. We are right next to you, and if not us, others.

You are a sphere. Use your energy to sense the others around you. Allow them to get on with their work by getting on with yours. It is not too difficult this path, this physical path.

We look and we enjoy. Include your companions when you touch the earth. Include your companions when you drink water. Invite them to be with you at that moment. It is not something we get to do. In those joinings, those togethers, those peaceful moments where nothing is expected, it is just the enjoyment of existence. It is there and then you will understand peace and you will understand your connection.

And so, we say seek peace as a way to close. It is that simple. Whatever you are enjoying on the physical plane, invite your spirit companions to be with you at *that* moment, no pressure, nothing to do, simply sip the water, sip the wine. Feel the sun, feel the rain. Feel the peace.

At this point we include some of the discussion conducted after the channeling session. We feel that there is a deepening of understanding of Onereon and their purpose, revealed through the words and observations of those in attendance at this session. Attendees are designated by initials except for Jeff, who is the channel. The words are from the humans and are not directly channeled.

Jeff: The feeling of lightheartedness and play is so strong among some of the members of the Onereon group. I enjoy that and it was part of our agreement. I didn't want to just talk about gloom and doom. So what they do is bring up Armageddon every single time.

Their way of explaining it is that it was a growth cycle. Yes, there was destruction, and there was an end. Societies were completely destroyed and completely reintegrated and went back to something completely different. People from two hundred years ago would not recognize society today. They wouldn't get it; they wouldn't be able to function without extensive training. And so, in that way we unveiled things…we apocolypsed.

A: For people who haven't been here before, there is one voice, who was the main voice today, that is the voice who usually comes in.

Jeff: Yes, he's the spokesman. He's the one who makes sure that things get said exactly right. It was interesting because he was there today, but there is a much more playful individual that came in to the channel. He's quite the experimenter. I try not to categorize them and yet I end up doing it. He's really the one who loves to play; he's the curiosity guy.

I use the term "he's" and "she's" because there are yin energies and yang energies amongst the group, and he is definitely yang energy. He was very much about this today. When we talk about the way the universe moves in the great things and the way it moves in the small things, that is really where he's coming in. He really likes the pattern of the galactic spin and the pattern of the sub-atomic spin. There are ways that this gets talked about and one of the things he says is, "Small is not so small," or "Small is really pretty big," indicating that from a certain perspective, small is really pretty large.

From our perspective the universe is pretty large, but not from the perspective of a being the size of the galaxy. This is an indication that the galaxies have a level of sentience to them. They are made up of particles, in the same way as we are, so that sentience isn't necessarily something that is outside of the cells. The cells themselves help to create sentience, in the same way that the planets help to create a sentient feeling. It is just not sentience the way that we think about it.

A: They mentioned that humans are a curve or a sphere and if you think of the galaxies, they are too. So that really does seem to fit.

K: It took me awhile to get that. I was thinking very linear. Then I realized in terms of our energetic field, we aren't just our physical bodies.

Jeff: Yes, we do not stop at our skin.

T: Or DNA! Group consensus: Great thought!

Jeff: That is part of the as above, so below, to get us to think about not just our outside, but our inside as well. That is a good pickup. Genetics notices the spirals and the curves. When we draw DNA, we think in terms of the spiral, but they'll often times refer to it as a straw. The universe is not just a curve, but sometimes it is a cylindrical situation as well. But the cylinder itself is curved too. When I have that image, it is not the straight straw; it is the cylinder aspect of the straw.

A: Do you mean like an inner tube?

Jeff: I do not know that the universe goes around and connects. I think what we are talking about there is aspects of the universe, not the universe itself. There are all of these curved aspects of the universe. The feeling that I get on a lot of it is that sometimes the curve is so gentle that it seems flat. Sometimes the curve is so steep that is seems like we are wrapped up, like there is no room to evolve.

As above, so below, when we are in that situation, you might feel like there is no place to go. Those are the moments to stop looking with your eyes and stop trying to go forward and see if you can just take a step backwards and things might loosen up a lot. Because you got yourself into that situation, step back.

A: It was interesting, the idea that when you are looking for your path…close your eyes and use your other senses, which goes back to another thing they were saying about consider all of your senses together, not just sight which is what we use most often. Isn't there something in physics that says that it is the light that keeps us in this dimension? If we start using our other senses, can we cross dimensions?

Jeff: One of the things I've said since the 60s is that we are all gravitationally trapped light. I probably picked that up somewhere. They kind of tease about that because it is like it is true, but it is a poetic truth. So we are gravitationally trapped light, why try to escape gravity? Our job is not to escape gravity. They really like that you picked up on "Be the Path."

K: Maybe we should stop using the term "path." It has such linear connotations.

T: But can you really do away with that because then how do you reach your goal?

K: But to use "goal" is again indicating a linear movement. It indicates that there is an end. I do not like to think of it in those terms. What happens when you reach the end?

Jeff: They talk a lot about the undivided one. The undivided one is really everything. Because we are physical, we do act in a linear fashion, and it is not wrong to do that but understand that is not the way everything works. Be human and be linear when linear is necessary.

Understand that linear is a plane and understand that the plane is curved. We are talking about perceptions here. We have a much lower perception. It does not mean that it is an inferior perception. It is just that from our perception things are this way.

They ask a lot to be included. In one of the channels, they address that part of it. They say humans spend so much time asking their guides for help, but they have often times not said, "Thank you." If you do say, "Thank you," we like that, but the other thing is, "What can I do for you?"

When our children are little, they ask and they ask and they ask and we teach them to be polite and say, "Thank you." But isn't it nice when they say, "Mom/Dad, since you did this for me, I'm going to do this for you," without us having to ask. That is one of the things that they say to me.

Ask your guides or angels, however you visualize them, and understand that they aren't just there to guide you. They are there as companions and there is a process being worked here. You are part of the team, part of the whole, part of the unit.

It can be really, really simple and they say this a lot, "Touch the earth. Have a sip of water and invite us to be there." It is really simple because then they get to have that feeling. It is really easy then to be with each other. There is no pressure to be in deep meditation or deep prayer. It just is what it is.

Things to Remember

- The universe is not always linear.
- Energetic bodies often radiate in all directions.
- Choose to radiate your energy.
- Humans are energetic bodies.
- There are not five senses, there is one sense expressed and perceived five ways.
- Following your path is as simple as this: do not follow anyone else's path.
- You *should* say, "I am."
- You are a creator!

Things to Come

- Humanity as a species will again begin to diversify.
- Diversity may be expressed on the basis of the elements of water, air, and earth.

8
The Filter

As above, so below. We are happy to be here at this point. We welcome the interest; we hope for an increased interest.

The human individual, the undivided human, is divided, divided from the Source, the Source of all things. As are we, although we are individual, we are divided from our Source. We come together in larger vibrations. We come together as the family spirit. You come together as the family human, and you are here as the family human this evening. United in your desire to be alive. United in your desire for peace; peace, freedom, freedom from fear, freedom from uncertainty. That is not the contract the family human has.

Harmonic Coalescence

We are entering an age of harmonic coalescence, hence the feeling that many of you have of missing something. There is nothing in the human experience that is a mistake. The family human and all of the experiences of the family human have been leading us to this point and the change is upon us now.

It is not a moment of change. It is not an event of change. It is a process of change, which makes it difficult for the family human at this point in time as they believe that there is a point in time. There is nothing that is happening on the globe that is a mistake and as above, so below.

Let us now talk of wars and reports of wars. We have had much time with our voice on this. These are things that disturb him. Peace is not the absence of violence and you have heard us say this before. Peace is the cessation of againstness. Stop being against these things.

The family human, in their individual forms, makes choices. Sometimes they choose to be together and to make a choice that may not be the best choice.

We now speak of experiences. There have been many in the last two hundred years who have left this planet suddenly, fearfully, without preparation, without having completed a life by their human perception. As they become spirit, there is an abrupt transition, and it is confusing. In order to deal with this energy, that energy is separated then and returned back to the earth, not as one being, but as several, so that the energy of fear can be reduced, spread out.

We say this is a time of harmonic coalescence. We are now bringing these energies back together. It is difficult and yet this is the way the task has been assigned to us above.

It is not that important. You are not that important, but then neither are we. What is important is the energetic of all things. One hundred people, two hundred people, three hundred humans dying in violence and yet they are being returned. They are coalescing. They are coalescing, not from region to region, but from all regions together.

The Filter

Coming Together

These ancient hatreds, these ancient fears, these ancient arguments over soup and birthright, they will no longer be valid because this one and this one who argued against each other will be the same. They will be an undivided one. It will be difficult.

You see, the planet earth is a filter in the same way that the human form is a filter. We take in things in the human form, and they filter, they process. Nothing truly is waste, for everything is energy. Those that are now arguing, there will be a reduction in numbers. It is not necessary for it to be that way. It is the flow of energy. This is a process that has been going on for some time, linear time, gravitational time.

From our perception, we see farther ahead than you do. Yet what we see is not what is going to happen; what we see is probability. Each one of you can change probability by acting in a certain way, rather than reacting. When you integrate, when you coalesce in your future, remember this. Remember these ones, because you here may coalesce with some of those that died hard, that transformed in a difficult way. You, then, are the balance, you are the filter. There are some in this room now that are already in that situation. It may have been that your early life was emotionally difficult

It is now time to look at the world differently, to look at the world differently and to cease being against things, especially yourself. We say, "Touch the earth."

You have companions. You are not alone. Speak to them. Introduce yourself to them in the same way that you would do if you were moving into a new room, a new job, a new neighborhood. If you have need of a name, ask for a name, but be patient if the name does not come easily to you, because the vibration above is so much different than the vibration below. Some have heard the names right away, they have opened to it, they have been communicated with directly and it is frightening to them, and they lose their balance because they are not prepared for direct spiritual encounter.

Allow your spiritual encounters to be oblique. Invite your companions to enjoy something with you, to enjoy the light and the flower, the light of water. What do you enjoy? Invite your companions to enjoy that. What do you enjoy about that? Instead of praying for your food, invite spirit to be with you as you eat. Nothing bad will come your way.

In this way we, spirit, touch the earth. It is something that we miss. We miss it because we have been there before, and we have said this before. Now we are as above, and you are as below. In the future you will be as above, and we will be as below and let us establish a good relationship now. So that when the circumstances have shifted, we are already in concert, we are already in harmony, we are already together, Onereon.

Now as above, so below. That is an interesting question: does then a bullet make the transference from above to below? You see, a bullet is a uniquely human experience. In the same way water is a uniquely human experience. Is it then that a human dies by another human's hand and that is the law?

Let us speak of lawlessness for a moment. The law is not to waste life, not to waste energy. When the earth, when the planet, when the living planet, when Gaia strikes someone down through a rock fall, through a wave, through a lightning strike, it is not a waste of energy, it is a transference of energy. As unpleasant as that might be for the individual human, remember, the individual human does not count as much as the individual human thinks they should count.

We are all particles and aspects of the universal energy, and we cannot be destroyed. We can only be transformed. It is sometimes a natural reaction for humans to lose their lives. Why? They put themselves in areas where they are going to lose their lives. They create areas of dwelling where you should not create an area of dwelling. Then they try to force the earth to adapt.

Please. We have said this before as well. It is not the earth that needs to be saved. It is not the planet that needs saving. The planet has taken much bigger hits than a human can give. It is unfortunate when a human acts contrary to universal law.

We return to some islands. When we first referred to them, we perhaps were not clear. It will not be fire alone that reduces humanity from Hawaii, water also, and it is not long in coming.

Our voice wishes us to clarify one more thing. Yes, it is in Africa. It is the trace of the family human, it is that center, that fertile area where humans first began that we spoke of earlier. There is a solution there for you. There is the beginning of the change of all humanity growing there now and it is called forgiveness. Look to the country of Rwanda and look to the women.

Do Not Buy Perceptions

When you hear of the wars, when you hear of the rumors of war, the reports of war, step back from the report. There are things that are not truth; there are things that are only perception. Do not be sold, do not buy. Ask yourself the question, as above, so below? How then can this be? Step back from the region and look at the globe and understand the coalescing of energy that is happening today. We are in this moment coalescing energies and the earth is a filter.

We have said this before, and we will clarify. We are looking at a span of time. We are looking at two hundred years ago. We are looking at one hundred years from now. This is a significant era, but it is only an aspect of a longer era.

We will be having less human activity on the planet and yet it becomes not a burden but a blessing, because humans will begin to coalesce. Three humans become one, five humans become one. The vibration rate of life returns to a larger, higher quality being of existence. This is what you miss. You miss the rest of you, and we miss that too.

How will this end? There are two things and they both concern the past. The very first, history, and when we say do not buy the report, we mean historically as well as currently. Do not buy the prophesy either. There are many who are willing to sell the prophecy. The more fear they can put into the prophecy, the more important it is to them that you buy that prophecy. Only when you buy the prophecy and the fear do they become validated. Do not buy the past. It is not what you know, and you see that changing now, the changing of history, the repealing of "known facts." It is always an amusing phrase, "known facts."

The length of time that the family human has recorded history and the length of time that members of the family human have attempted to control and censor are not equal. In only recent memory, human memory, an attempt has been made to take reality away. In the linear past, efforts were made by the family human to build upon knowledge. In the present linear moment, much knowledge has been lost and with purpose. The humans that do these things do this for personal gain and have shortened their sight and attempt to shorten all sight. They know that time and history have gone on longer.

Be cautious now because there are some that believe it has gone on for *much* longer. Pay attention to the real evidence, the truths. The truth is very, very small. It is not to be dug up out of the ground. It is to be found within you and you are finding it. That is one, the removal of history so that we can understand what really happened. Here we need to cease being against things so that we can remove history and know what is true.

The second thing is closely linked to this. History has to stop having value. The cost to reduce the value of history is human life. This is not pleasant for us to say. When enough lives are lost over an argument that is four thousand years old and pertains to nothing, and enough lives are lost and enough blood is shed to wash away the sacredness and the holiness of a land, that is when history will no longer hold value.

As above, so below and we feel angry about this too. There is no need for this. It is a bad decision. There is a different way to do what needs to be done, longer, certainly, but more natural. Yet this has been the choice of the family human in many regions. Now, balance that. You see how I feel about that and as Onereon, we need to bring another voice in.

At this point in the channel, it was clearly perceived by all that another of the personalities stepped in, as the one that had been speaking was feeling very strongly regarding the poor choices of segments of humanity.

Still, we love those ones, those humans, and we love them deeply and despite the decisions that they make we need to continue to love them. For that is a point of spirit. Love, joy, peace, against such principles there is no law, and this is in one of your holy books.

Find a way to have joy every single day, please, and this will offset the fear that some need to feel every single day. Cease being against things every single day, little things, not big things, little things.

Tell someone every single day that you love them, beginning with yourself and watch the world balance around you. Watch love come to you and joy come to you, and peace. It is a dear thing, and it is a fine thing. It is a probable thing, and we see that for the family human in the future. Are there questions?

As we become conscious of our guides and they become our companions and friends on a very real level, are we also coalescing with them while we are here on earth and therefore affording them a greater opportunity to rise in consciousness quicker when they ascend to the earth, and we shift places?

When one voice sings, that is joyful. When several voices harmonize, it so much more, is it not? Yes, your vibration with your growth is becoming stronger and stronger and you practice, right? This is the way that we practice. We enjoy each other and it does not matter what position we take, whether it is in the physical plane, linear gravity and time, or in the spiritual plane. No matter what position we take, we sing and we vibrate together and we are more effective together. When these moments happen, we build towards the Harmonic Coalescence. So yes, your observation is correct.

You commented on the question we need to ask ourselves, "Am I willing to step up and take on more responsibility?" My question is, is that on the spiritual plane or is that on the material plane?

Yes.

Thanks for narrowing it down.

Let us address something. Let us address limitation in the human form. Far too many in the physical realm have tried to be "out of the body." That is not what the human experience is about. This is a wonderful form, no matter what shape, no matter what health. If you invite your form to be enjoyed by spirit, watch your health increase. There is no difference between the physical, the material form, and the physical spiritual form, is there? We say this, mind, body, and spirit. Those are the three elements that make up the human experience. So enjoy all of those things equally. If you are ailing in one, you will affect the others. Bring all things up equally.

As we get older on the human plane, there is loss. The more loss we see, the more it can affect us in our heart. We say farewell to the energies around us, and we maintain our spiritual connection. If we hold the loss within our heart, then our heart cannot touch or be touched by spirit. Release the pains of the heart. That is very easy to say and I, in particular, need to say that. For even from a perception of spirit as above, it is difficult to leave what we left.

So, is it when we give up the againstness, is that what makes the coalescing happen?

In science, we speak of resistance, and we create resistors to help control energy to power our communications systems. When we are resistant, then we cease the flow of energy. By lowering our resistance, energy flows freely. There is a reason for resistance. We want to caution you; it is not ceasing being against all things. It is not softness. We still need, as a human, to wear a hat in the sun.

As we test what we are against and decide and we find that we really do not need to be pushing against this thing or that person, we then realize that there is no energy except what we give to it. We can release that and then we become freer to move in a different direction and to join with others already moving in that direction.

There are many moving in a specific direction now, in spirit. There is less energy in the family human moving in that direction now than ever before. There is more opportunity for the family human to move in that direction.

Again, cease being against things. Cease giving power, cease holding things up, structures that do not need to be held up any longer. Cease being against, because when we are against something we are really holding it up, are we not? When we move away from it on the physical plane, there may be nothing to hold it up and it may just collapse and go away.

Be careful with this. It will be time of confusion when these structures that are no longer valid begin to collapse. Do not fear. Look for the love and look for the joy and it might be hard to find. The opportunities for the human to join into this wave of energy have never been greater. It is a decision.

The Filter

If I understand you correctly, instead of expressing anger about people being killed, people in wars, whatever, is it better to stay in a neutral place and send love and light to the place rather than negative energy feeding into what's going on?

You see how that is not a neutral place. It is taking action, is it not? Saying, "I will not be angry about this. I will not direct anger towards this situation. I will not direct acceptance towards this situation either. I will address this in this way."

Where is wisdom? Find wisdom. Where is coalescence? Find coalescence. Where is the structure that we need to not support? Cease being against this structure. Find harmony.

The temptation with the family human is to gather more humans around that agree with your perception. That is just validating yourself outside of yourself. Act on your own. Take your own action as an undivided one and say, "I will not accept anger and hate. I will love and enjoy and be at peace."

You do not have to get into an airplane, you do not have to get out into a boat, you do not have to fly to these areas and stand and meditate and chant and hold up a sign. You begin where you are right now. You begin with the stranger next to you in the store and in traffic and you wish them well, you wish them love, and you wish them peace. It does not have to be that you are walking up to strangers and saying, "I love you!"

It has to be your choice and it has to be from your heart and you may need to practice bringing it from your heart. In this way, much of this begins in the thought. That will be your test. If it is not your heart's desire, then you may not be of that energy. Let me tell you this, you would not be here this evening if you were not of this energy.

So many things that you speak of tonight, I understand and I am experiencing. My heart is sad for people continuing to be against things and I have just gone into silence about it because I'm not sure how to respond. I do not want to react. How can I help others to see a different view?

By being the different view, by not taking a side. It is difficult to do now, is it not? Polarity is a way of life. Creating polarity is a way of life. Do not make the mistake that your sadness is wrong. That is part of the experience of the family human. As above, so below, we too feel fears and sadness despite a perception that is different and a vibration that is different. There is more going on in this universe than you know in your present form.

Silence. When you say "silence," when you say, "not react," you are correct that action speaks louder than words, so silence is sometimes the first step to not reacting, but taking action. Sometimes we feel the need to return words for words for words. Let us not waste our words. There are those out there that love to engage in words, and they mean nothing. Do not waste your words.

When you spoke earlier about the great opportunity for individuals to move towards coalescence and to contribute towards peace and balance, I'm wondering specifically, are you referring really just to attitude, the attitude we bring in to the world or specifics. Are there specific things for an individual to do?

In the nature of questions like this, we sometimes have a sense of the individuals to whom we are about to speak. There are some things in your lives that need to go away. Some of you have done a wonderful job in eliminating so many things from life, of freeing yourself from others' behaviors. It must begin with you always. It must always begin with you.

The Filter

The coalescence has to be a voluntary situation. To be together again does not need to mean agreement. It means acceptance. We do not have to all like the same music or the same flavors. So much about that question is unanswerable at this point. Yes, there are larger, larger, larger energies, always larger energies. We feel them too and it is the wave, it is the next step of universal energies.

It is difficult for us to understand, difficult for you certainly in your current form. Let us take it down. Begin with you as the individual, follow your path…growth. Growth is the universal law, movement and growth. We have said to our voice, the universe does not support conformity. The universe does support diversity. This does not mean to be different for difference's sake. It means just be who you are.

Begin to take action, not against anything else, not to stop anything else. Take action on your part so that you grow, so that you learn, so that you continue to be more than you are currently. Not just on a spiritual level, but on an intellectual level and on an emotional level and on a physical level. Get those bodies moving, be in motion, have emotions, feel. If it is sad, then be sad. If it is happy, then be happy. Get the thoughts in motion. Read something different, something new. Learn something new and watch as those three things then become your spiritual movement. Invite us to be with you.

You mentioned that the planet earth is a filter and that everything is energy and I've observed for awhile the energy shift happening through various events, wildfires, changes in global temperatures, and in the loss of human life and I guess I'm wondering if this is part of an energy shift that is happening on our planet for the purpose of assisting us to be coalescing with these energies.

Yes. Yes. As these things happen, it is easy to blame an army, is it not? It is difficult to blame a wave. A wave is natural, a wave happens. It is hard to be angry at a wave. Easy, though, to express emotion towards those affected by a wave. A reduction of violence of human against human will also correlate towards a reduction of activities by the earth in this fashion.

There is one more question, have you chosen?

You keep asking us to invite you, is there a certain name or word that you would like us to use to draw us closer?
Not us so much, but yours, your companions, their companions. They are all around you. Introduce yourself, say hello. Allow some time for these things. Allow the vibration to sound down into you, into your physical form. Not quickly, just invite, "Those of you that are my companions, please join me in this glass of water. Please join me in touching this blade of grass. Join me in this meal. Join me as I drive a vehicle, as I go to work."

You will begin to sense through the human sense, not sight, not hearing, not taste, not touch, not smell, but through all of those and more. You may feel them at your side, at your back. You may see things in a very different way and suddenly, you say, "I have never seen that before," and it has been there all along. In these ways, you will know that your companions have joined you in that moment.

You will not be taken over. It is an invitation that you accept to allow us to be accepted. As above, so below, allow us to experience these things and you see how that comes back? Your vibration then rises, and you see things differently. This is what is happening now on the planet;

many, many opportunities to experience many, many things that we have not had the chance to do before. Do not become overwhelmed by the information. You, too, then grow in the same way that we grow.

Look to those moments where you can invite us in to assist in growth. We are all of a group, are we not? Tonight, the group is here in this room. As you leave, you each have your own group.

What can be done on the plane that we exist on often cannot be done on the plane that you exist on, and you may forget that. You may say, "Let us just do this." You may know better. So the agreement must be made and you must say, "Yes, I am willing to do that." "No, I am not willing to do this," and that agreement will be honored, perhaps after some negotiations. Do not say, "No, I am not willing to do that," simply because it is unfamiliar to you. Consider it, ask questions, allow time to go on.

In the past, men from the family human have decided that there is one that needs to be called upon and he was to be prayed to in a specific way. Spiritual is different. Spiritual experience is each one of you having your own personal experience with spirit. If you all decide that you are going to call on one being and give that one being all of your power, it is not a spiritual experience. Then it has become a religion that needs to be supported by pushing against things that do not agree with your religion. Your perception then is your reality.

Receive us in whatever way you need to. We are happy to dress up. Take responsibility for yourself. Increase your abilities. Now, begin tonight. Increase your ability to respond to situations that are around you now. Do not support fear. Support love. Support joy. Support peace.

There is still one question.

Are we in essence transformers?
The answer to the question is yes. There is another question, though. Somebody is holding back.
I think a lot of us are holding back.
Let us take these moments, please. There is one amongst you that is holding back because they feel that it might be too personal of a question. Please ask that question.

You talked briefly about Hawaii again, which you had mentioned in an earlier channel. The change that is going to affect Hawaii, will that have an affect on other parts of the Pacific Rim, or will it be more of a slow process?
What happens there will be unusual for that area, unusual in current time, not unusual in historic time. It will affect other areas, yes, but very specifically that area is due for change of energy.

More? It is alright.

Is there any way that you could assist us in knowing what areas or main areas need a change of energy?
You as an individual, again, trust your companions, but trust yourself, you know those areas. You know that area of your heart, you know that. Within the areas of the globe, once again, let us not try to affect the globe as a human being. Unless you are trying to grow something, it very rarely works for you.

More? Please ask.

I'm trying to understand what you said about coalescing and becoming one. I assume that there is no timeline, essentially it is an individual happening, so to speak. When does that come about for people like us in this room? What is that like? What is the process?

Many people may go to a store and buy the same thing or a similar item. They do not all go to the store at the same time. As they process through the line, someone may notice that two or three people have purchased the same item. It may be that five or six people have purchased the same item. The energy of the human is simply that, it is energetic. It is not something that holds together. Now, this is difficult for people to understand, because you have been taught for so long that you are the primary form of life and that your personality is thus very important. It is, but not as important as you have been taught.

After transformation, death, there are opportunities then, as above, together, to make an agreement to be together, sometimes to receive an assignment to be together and to return to the planet to continue the filtering process. The coalescing of individuals, the harmonizing of energies here, now, in physical form, takes place in the way that we do tonight, we gather as a group. Then we go off and gather as a different group for a different purpose. It is a path of diversity.

We may do this with that person. We may do something else with another person. It is our individual choice. After the transformation, and it is a transforming, the coalescence happens. It is not always three into one, it is not necessarily five into one, it may be two, it may be seven. So you see, there is no formula here…diversity. It may be that there are some that are very weak, and they come together with one that is stronger or two that are stronger and the bonding that happens creates a stronger person with weaknesses.

We together, as humans, we feel a similar vibration and we like to be around that human, oh yes! Sometimes we do not see a similar vibration. Sometimes we get a vibration that is not harmonious. Then do not be around that person. If your vibration changes, you may find that the people that you are around do not vibrate the way that you do. Thus, you may need to move on.

Be careful with this. I am giving you an illustration. I am describing things to you in terms that you can understand. Very soon, humanity is going to begin to understand the birth process in a different way, less as an event and much more a process. With understanding, the implication of death and dying will change dramatically…very soon. You are not coalescing now. You are preparing to coalesce later.

Is it a permanent state? If there are two or four or however many individuals coalescing, is that per our agreement?

It is as permanent as a human can be, and so, no. Do not look for permanency in this world. Do not look for permanency in this universe. Look for growth, look for change. Look to be the change. Look to act and create the change. Where? Within you. Is there a permanent agreement while that human is alive? Yes. The energy comes together and for energy to separate out at that level, well, it would be explosive. It would be a combustive experience. Not beneficial for the continuance of human life.

You talked about the two hundred years ago time period again briefly. As I am understanding it, that was a time that there was a lot of energy on the earth as individual humans and since that that time, especially now, as we transform, a lot of those energies are coming together, coalescing so that the next incarnation of that person or that energy might be a coalescence of many of the energies that have been separate on the earth before. Why are we at that stage now? Is it an evolutionary time period?

We need to be careful. When we speak to you, we speak in terms of limits, because there are. The process, and look to your history on this, the process really began then of separating and thus the population increased and increased and increased, because we needed to have more human bodies to hold that form of energetic life. We could easily have done this by moving everything into a different type of life form, gone back to the larger life forms that have existed on the planet.

We have chosen, we have all chosen this, to become smaller and smaller and smaller in our energy and now as part of that process, we begin to become larger energies. Not in size, you see, but in energy, in power, in ability. See, you sense this already, do you not?

There are those amongst you that sense the abilities that we do not have here as family human, the mental abilities, the emotional abilities, the abilities that the family human has created technology to replace. Look around you. Look at the technologies. Those are replacements for what you will be doing as humans within the next one hundred years. Think wireless.

There is a disconnection with the planet. There is a looking to ascend. There is a devaluing of the human experience and thus as the human experience was devalued, the wars began to become greater and greater and greater, did they not?

There was a decision that many made. It was a decision to have an experience that could have been had in a very different way, longer, longer in linear time. Some there were that wanted things to happen quickly. Well, they did and they continue. It has been said that time is speeding up and it is. There will come a time when time will slow down again and lives will become longer, happier, more joyful, more balanced and the planet itself will be more balanced. That is for the future.

For now, for you, be together in acceptance. Work to grow as an individual. Once you bring more to the table, then the agreements begin to be made. Raise your value, not by devaluing others. Above all, cease being against things by seeking peace.

Author's note...

It was clear that Onereon sensed or knew that someone in the audience had an important question and was reluctant to ask for some reason. In fact, after the channel, a woman from Northern Europe approached the subject that Onereon sensed. She had been concerned about being misunderstood due to her professed lack of ability to communicate in English. In fact, she was quite eloquent! She was also unsure of the appropriateness of the question.

She was very concerned about "ghosts" and "spirits of the dead." She was concerned about their ability to affect those still alive on the earth, and also about how we on the earth can affect them. Onereon has provided this follow up regarding "ghosts."

We will speak to this point in this way. Life is life and all life is energy. Energy cannot be destroyed, merely transformed. When life transforms, to the family human, as you perceive things now, it appears that life has stopped and is no more. Soon, you will know through science, that this is not true.

The consciousness of the individual human can be a very strong energy. If they are reluctant to go through the transformation or if they are unjustly cut off from their path of human energy or if they pass in fear, the energy of the consciousness, the emotional or mental energies, may retain a hold on a place on the earth. This results in a separation of energies that is difficult to correct.

The consciousness has separated from the body and that is correct, for the energy of the physical form then returns to the planet to be of use on the physical plane. The consciousness then should naturally return with the spiritual aspect of the individual to the spiritual realm. This is where the disconnection occurs.

For the consciousness to remain in contact with the physical plane without the physical form is uncomfortable and confusing. Behaviors that are not conducive to peace are often exhibited. Confusion and repetition of actions is observed.

As some humans are more sensitive to the spiritual realms, they may begin to "see" these points of energetic consciousness. The more that "see" an "entity," the stronger the tie to the physical realm.

There is often no harm meant by the consciousness, the entity. It is merely confused and searching for a way back to what is familiar. They are merely looking in the wrong direction, back towards the physical plane.

Directing the consciousness to the realm of spirit is the only thing that will allow this lost energy to regain peace.

The habit of erecting shrines is something that can make the passage difficult for those that pass suddenly. There is a strong pull of energy on them from those that express their love through grief on the physical plane. It is especially difficult for those that were young, those that are involved in traffic or other types of accidents, and those that cause their own human existence to come to an early conclusion, whether by choice or by misadventure.

All life is a path or a journey. When you make a decision to travel to another location, you say good-bye to those that are not making the trip with you. So it is with the end of human existence. You are traveling on. Your great faiths teach this in many forms, yet many clearly do not believe.

Expressing gratitude for having spent time together is a key to allowing the natural process of life to continue. Say, "Thank you." Say, "Farewell" and allow them to continue on their way and then you also can continue along your path.

Things to Remember

- How can a "Holy Land" be holy when it is awash in innocent blood shed by violence based on arguments that are over four thousand years old?
- How can religions be valid if they support four-thousand-year-old arguments that promote the shedding of innocent blood?
- Peace is not simply the absence of violence. Peace is the cessation of againstness.
- Cease being against things every day. Little things.
- Find a way to have joy every day. This will offset fear.
- The true fruitage of the spirit is and has always been, love, joy, and peace. There can be no dogma against these things.
- Allow your spiritual encounters to be oblique.
- Enjoy your communications with your spiritual companions.

Things to Come

- ♦ A changed perception of prophecy and history is coming soon.
- ♦ There is a beginning of a change of energy for all humanity to be found in the women of Rwanda.
- ♦ There will be changes in the land of the islands of Hawaii.
- ♦ Humanity will soon understand the birth process in a much different way. This will provide, by implication, a much different view of death and dying.
- ♦ Technologies that we possess today are indications of what humanity will be evolving towards in the future. Think of the wireless communication.

9
Communication

We say, "As above, so below." This is our agreed upon introduction. When our voice communicates for us, we are allowed to be with you this evening through someone else's voice and we appreciate that. We are grateful for it. We appreciate the presence of so many this evening. This is joy.

Communication is important and this is our topic this evening, a communiqué. There will come a time when communication between spirit and human will be very, very easy and very free. What we now do in a formal setting will become a common occurrence.

We have said before and we will say it again, it is no accident that your technology has freed you from wires. Walking anywhere, you can communicate anywhere. In the future, technology will advance to what we once had as family human, where we will communicate without wires and also without tools.

Communication comes in many forms. For the human, speaking and hearing has been the most common form of communication for recorded history. Prior to recorded history, speaking and hearing were also very common but as we began to record, the apparent need for speaking and hearing diminished.

As we began to record our thoughts, the need for directly knowing another's thoughts diminished. We began to set thoughts down as if they would never change. The thoughts then become rules, codes, laws, and religions. Here we are today, as if the thoughts never change, as if experience never affected the thought that was written down. Humanity began to be formed by thoughts rather than thoughts being formed by humanity.

Categories

Diversity of humanity has been programmed in. The undivided aspect of the human species at this point in time is undergoing change. In the future, humans will once again diversify. We will talk about 5 categories.

The Walkers - You know these humans by what they do, their actions, their activities, their explorations, and their movements.

The Watchers - You know these humans by their ability to know you without having met you, and their observational skills.

The Knowers - These are the ones who have knowledge, who keep knowledge, who disseminate knowledge, and who pass knowledge along.

The Growers - These are those beings who instigate growth, who plant, and who nurture.

Then a fifth category that we will talk about in a moment - The Harvesters.

Who is Communicating with Whom?

The experiences that the planet is undergoing now, not the humans, but the planet, are beginning to be communicated in a way unexpected to the family human who think they are the top of creation and somehow in control. In fact, it is just another expression of the vital force of the planet.

It is no accident that we see a rise in animal communicators. Is this because humans are getting better at this? That they have learned some new skill? That they now have some wisdom that allows them to access the animal's brain? No. This is because the animals are allowing the humans to have access to the animals' brains, their thoughts, and their hearts, their emotions.

We say as above, so below, you look for guides as family human, but also, as above, we look for guides. The animals, the ancients knew this, the animals communicate to us. What do they communicate? The way of the planet, the home, the mother, Gaia. The animals now have much to say about the shifting, the changing of the energies of the planet. Childlike, the humans totter into the animals' presence and say, "How are you feeling?" There is much more to be said.

Look to the larger mammals. Look to their behaviors. Look to how they change, how their behaviors change. Look to the mammals of the sea. They are holding much energy. The large mammals of the sea, they are Knowers. Ah see, the categories extend to all mammals! They are Knowers and they are not to hold knowledge forever. They are to disseminate knowledge.

The family human is unready, but getting closer, to exist for the length of time within the water, within the sea, to communicate with these creatures, to hear them, to learn from them. The large animals of the land, again, have knowledge, hold knowledge – Knowers.

The Walkers, they walk while humans ride. The Walkers have shown humans many things and humans felt they were controlling the Walker. It is a peculiar sense within the animals. They sense each other deeply. They run together, they exist together, sometimes in families, sometimes in flocks, sometimes in schools. You see, they share a mind. Sometimes the mind is very, very simple within the individual, as with the small fish, but when put together, watch how they turn, watch how they move, together, you see. Humans will never move that way.

The Point

The filter: let us clarify the filter. For the planet is, in fact, the filter. The existence on the planet is, in fact, the filter. It is a section; it is a moment within the universe, within all of existence. We will talk about the earth now. Our voice would like us to expand on the other planets. We will talk about the earth now. As above, so below.

The vital force leaves a physical being, an animal, a mammal, cat, dog, horse, human. The vital force leaves. What happens to it? It is energy. Energy transforms, and as energy, again as the ancients have known, transforms into what? Ether, ethereal things, spirit.

It is not that your personality transfers and then transfers back into the planet into a new body, one personality intact. It is that when you return to spirit, your spirit, prana, breath, returns, coalesces again, into above, where we are. All of the experiences and all of the knowledge, all of the wisdom and all of the thoughts are now added to, and they create a ripple, a ripple of energy that changes heaven, as it were.

Over the last two hundred years, so many have died in battles, in tragedies, in hard situations. They have died in fear, have died young. It is difficult to assimilate the fearful experience when they transfer to spirit. Often times, there is nothing to be done but return them to the filter, the vital force, the vital field, the energy of the planet.

In some cases, it has been so extreme that they return into smaller animals. Vital force does not necessarily mean humanity. They live their lives out and they process. You see, the human vital force is much larger than a small animal, a squirrel, a cat. Many animals then become that vital force and by spreading out that energy, the energy that was in fear, we spread the energy and it dispels in this way.

Our task now, as Onereon, is to begin coalescing these energies again.

In The Near Future

Why so many animal communicators? Because you are starting to speak in their language! They hold within their genetics deep knowledge. Not of philosophy, not of history, but of life and of living. Wisdom of the earth, wisdom of the planet, agendas certainly, but no lies. Agendas, yes, for they have their purposes. Their purposes are strongly encoded within each one, within each species, each type. But no lies. It is unique to humanity to purposefully deceive.

Humanity will coalesce, will come together. Over the next one hundred years, humanity comes together. Less humans, but of a higher quality, more integrity. Ethics not based on old thoughts. Closer kinship to the animals as the evolution of all of the species continues after some time.

The planet has shifted. The energy has shifted. Gaia has changed. You know this. Your scientists know this. Ask them. Look at your weather patterns. Look at your magnetics. Look at the behavior of people in individual countries as they struggle to maintain a purpose that no longer exists in that geography.

A Holy Land? With this much blood being shed, how can it be holy any longer? The key, the solution, you see, is forgiveness. Not from ancient arguments that are not necessary, but of current violences that are forgiven. We have given you an example in Rwanda. Look to that country. Understand the beginning of humanity is the beginning of new humans, as much energy coalesces in the center of Africa. Surprise perhaps to some, but it is the pattern. Gaia has shifted. The energy has shifted, shifted back to that area. The development of humanity and the development of animals, the development of the vital forces of life needs to be centered there and at the opposite point of the planet.

We said we would speak about the Harvesters.

The Growers nurture. The Growers heal. The Growers attempt to extend life and sometimes that becomes an imbalance.

The Harvesters process change, remove the vital forces and the energies when they are no longer useful. This is hard for some to hear. For life is sacred, and that is not wrong, but death is also sacred. The transference of energy at the end of a life, a peaceful transference, allows you to return to "heaven."

As above, so below. Peaceful transference from the family human to family spirit, how much more pleasant that is than to cling to life in pain and in suffering and in agony and a false sentimentality. The Growers are now gaining an understanding of this, and some have begun to move into the realm of Harvesters.

Harvesters do not take life. They assist in the transference. They reassure. They comfort. They allow one to relax through the transference. They create an opportunity for a change of mind, a change of thought and emotion, one that the ancients knew.

Look to those that were of the nation of the plains, nations of this continent, and understand their wisdom regarding death, their wisdom regarding the animals, their wisdom regarding themselves and their role on the planet, not owning the planet, but being owned by the planet. Know how advanced they were in their spirituality, advanced from where much of the planet is today, the family human on the planet.

The Harvesters do not take life. A Harvester out of balance, one who possesses that energy, the family human views them as evil. The Harvester in balance is a comforter, a processor, one who helps the individual, the undivided one, to make the choice and to take the comfortable path by not being against the process, the peaceful path.

There are many that claim faith. "We have faith. When we die, we go to see God." These are the ones who will fight tooth and nail to stay alive. Where is their faith? It is non-existent. It is an old idea. It is an old thought that changed, except that someone wrote it down.

Communication, based on current thinking and thought, based on living thought, how much more pure is that?

We ask that you examine your thoughts and your thinking. Why do you believe what you believe? We ask that you be willing to abandon cherished beliefs, not out of principle, but because you see things differently, clearly, currently. Not because anyone has asked you to see things differently. Not because anyone has suggested to you a different thought, but because it feels right in your heart. Spirit so rarely makes sense in the brain, and yet in the end, following your heart makes the most sense, at the end of the process of life, life as a human.

You will see more Harvesters over the next twenty years. You will see more Harvesters. Many of them will extend out from the class of Grower because, like a farmer, once you have planted a seed, the seed is only good when it is harvested and the energy transfers and is useful.

You will see a return to agriculture on this planet and a decline of manufacturing over the next one hundred years, mark this as a century (our voice reminds us that it is not an exact time period). Of necessity, industry will change. There will be less demand for so many products as the population of the family human declines in quantity but rises in quality.

You already have a number of beings on this planet that have coalesced, that are stronger in purpose, that have a better vision, that are comfortable with themselves at a very young age. They have a confidence and ability that has intuition tied in with their very actions. They do not question. They simply know, the Knowers. At a later date we will speak more about the categories.

The first responsibility in communication is this, be clear in your communication with yourself. For if you are not clear in your communication with yourself, how can you expect your spirit companions to know what you want? Are there questions?

The five categories that you mention: are they a stepping stone? Can you go from one category to another or are the majority of people just in one category?

Because of the diversity of humankind, the diversity of the energies, you will often times find strains, traits. As the family human re-integrates, coalesces, these are very strong categories. Certainly, a Watcher can be a Walker; a Walker can be a Knower. The categories are very strong. The Watchers are Watchers first. The Knowers are Knowers first. They honor their knowing by doing just that, by fulfilling the purpose of knowing. The answer is yes, at this point in time there can be many cross referencing of energies.

It is not within the energy of the majority of the family human at this point to be diverse in these categories and still function at a higher vibration. By remaining within one of these types, you will find yourselves feeling stronger and with more direction in your current life. It is best to be undivided, an individual.

Find your strength. Lean towards that strength. Allow the field, the vital energy around the planet, to help purify that.

Do animals have the same categories all at the same time?

Animals are very pure, are they not? Species of animal tend to be very strong within one category. Elephants, for example, are Knowers. They know. We have mentioned horses as Walkers. Cats of all sizes, Watchers, you see. Look at them. What do you see? They watch. Dogs…what do you think? They watch, but they also walk. So the strains again, the traits. There is diversity even within the animals. Understand that the vital force takes many shapes, not just always human. Just because you are human now does not mean that you have always been human.

The vital force, as it coalesces, as it purifies, never goes down. The amount of vital force, in the same way as water, just changes. Sometimes water is a cloud, sometimes it is a lake, sometimes it is a tear or a part of a mammal. The vital force, Gaia, it is coalescing now, becoming purer.

Planet Earth, as we know it, is defined by land masses, continents. We see more and more migration on all of the continents now. Are we starting to see a coalescence of cultures which will eventually raise our vital force?

Land mass continues under the water, does not it? The coalescence does not mean uniformity. Diversity will continue. The coalescence of populations changes the diversity of the ethnicity of the family human. Not too far in the future the land masses under the water will also be recognized as populated areas. You will understand the coalescence differently with the mammals of the sea.

We look to migrations of the past. We see that the migrations of the past slowly, slowly, slowly eliminated the diversity of the humans, Homo sapiens being the last at this point in time. The reintegration of many ethnic cultures begins to stimulate the diversity once again. This is a long process. Not so long once Gaia begins to act. Do not bore the universe. It will surely change things up!

You have spoken in many of these channels of the earth as a filter, as the family human, especially over the last two hundred years, expanding out, becoming greater in number and now it is the coalescing time. It is time for that energy to come back together again. It is becoming clear to me, because Onereon describes itself as together, that this is a purpose of yours at this time. What can others of us as members of the family human do to support this effort at this time?

Know yourself. Know yourself clearly. Create a strong identity, a pure identity, an ethical identity. Be very undivided. Be very individual. Not against anything, but for yourself. This is the purpose. These are the purification times. This is the filtering.

Make the decision to be pure. Purely you! Not to purify anyone else, to purify yourself. To accept your strength of character based on who you truly are, not on anyone else's perception of you.

Notice what is not your path. Notice what is a remembrance of other people's words. Notice what is an old thought written down and has not changed. Examine your life, fearlessly. Move forward, grow, adapt, change, evolve, you see. These are the things that keep a species fresh. These are the things that keep life alive, diverse. The universe does not support conformity. Bring yourself back into spirit as an undivided one, as a pure identity. Is that not what we are striving for? You say nirvana, the one who has purified themselves.

It is not a one-way ticket! You have the opportunity to say then, "Yes, let us be together, you and I and you and you, all of us. Let us all together return as a pure clean spirit on the planet in the shape of a human." We have some of those walking amongst you now. They do not announce themselves.

It is true our task is to assist in the coalescence. There is a concept, and our task is more the concept, to communicate the concept of being together, without having to be the same or even in agreement. Tonight you are Onereon, together.

Can you tell us more about Rwanda?

When a being is confronted with their crime, with the horrors that they have perpetrated against other lives, calmly and peacefully and they have nothing they can be against at that moment, (their energy has been strongly against an ethnicity or gender) and the one confronting them takes one more step and says, "I forgive," the structure of energy that was hatred, the structure of energy that was anti-life, collapses and there is no power to it any longer.

We will not detail Rwanda or any of the other areas in Africa that are suffering still these injustices, these imbalances. We do not seek for anyone to try to cause justice in these areas. Notice, be peaceable, be peaceful when you notice these things, peaceful when you go to those that know and learn of these atrocities, these horrors, these things that no other being in the universe concedes except the weakened human who lives in fear.

Forgive, not just those ones, but forgive the ones in your own life who have not done anything of that magnitude to you. Seek the knowledge. Do not become immersed in this. The family has a long way to go. It is on the right track.

I have heard in the past the large animals of the sea being referred to as a living library. Does that mean anything to you? Can you explain it a little?

The "Ones That Know." They hold the knowledge. No, there is no explanation for that at this time. Not from us. There are some that know this, some that are aware of this. It is not just the large mammals of the sea; large mammals of the land as well hold some of this information. It is not esoteric. It is not something that cannot be conceived of by the human mind. It is just not something that fits into the preconceived notion of life and vitality and the movement of energy, the movement of thought and the movement of emotion. Humans have conceived of the concept of telepathy as in exchanging thoughts, but there is telepathy of the heart as well. There may be others that speak clearer on that process. The Knowers, they like to know.

You talk about Gaia and that Gaia has changed already. Is it possible that she will change again from free will of what is happening in the world?

It is very interconnected, but the vital force is from Gaia, not the other way around. So the vital force, the free will, the mass of humanity, yes, can affect the vital force of the planet itself and it has. Will Gaia change again? Yes, certainly! It is in the nature of Gaia to change. Without that, well, what a boring planet this would be.

Stay out of the areas that change dramatically and you will not have to worry about lava, tsunami, and earthquake. Gaia is subject to all forms of energy. The planet itself is not in danger. The life force of the planet itself is not in danger. Again, there are those who choose to devote their lives to saving this planet. The planet is not in danger! The planet has taken much bigger disasters than humans can conceive or create.

The life force coalesces, changes, diversifies, evolves and moves from large saurian to small mammal. Gaia continues, the vital force continues, one of many in the universe. The life force has coalesced around the planet, around rock and stone and water. Gaia magnificently portrays the diversity of the universe. We have said before, "Touch the earth." Please, please, touch the earth. Hear it, listen to it. Contact it, communicate with, and be there with the planet. It is not just your home, it is you. You are an aspect of this planet. Love it. Love it.

Return to a phrase channeled many, many hundreds of years ago by a man misunderstood at the time and more so now. Listen and hear this one phrase, "The fruitages of the spirit," listen to this, "are love, joy, and peace. Against these things there is no law."

Love. Love is not weak, you see. Love is strength. Love is strong. Love does not abide behavior that is not conducive to growth. Love moves forward and grows. Love forgives when forgiveness is warranted. Sometimes love forgives because forgiveness is warranted on a much larger scale, much larger than the individual that was unloving.

Joy. Find the things that you enjoy that contribute to growth. And grow. Joy.

Peace. Not the absence of violence, no, but the cessation of against-ness. Yes. Stop being against things and you will find peace. Do not force anyone and do not attempt to force anyone to do anything you want them to do. Allow each individual to be an individual, including yourself.

Be at peace with yourself. Seek peace.

Things to Remember

- There are five energetic categories of mammalian life. Walker, Watcher, Knower, Grower, and Harvester. The Harvester category is increasing.
- The large mammals of the sea are holders of information.
- Forgiveness is the key.
- Know yourself and be clear in your communication with yourself.

Things to Come

- Over the next one hundred years, humanity will begin to come together, though not in a way that can be imagined now.
- There will be a return to agriculture and a reduction of manufacturing over the next one hundred years.

Questions to Stimulate Your Personal Growth

The true fruitage of the spirit has always been love, joy, and peace.

Do you act in a spiritual way?

Personal peace is found when we cease being against things.

What are you against?

An Amplification of the Five Energetic Categories of Living Beings

Onereon has provided the information on the following pages with the understanding that there are not boundaries between these types of human, simply strengths within each one of us. We, and to a lesser degree our animal companions on the planet, may fall into these categories quite easily. If, during your life, you have always been attracted to one of these paths, that is an indication of who you are at a fundamental energetic level. If you have not been following that path, the time to start is now.

The question that has been asked is if we can be more than one of these categories or switch from one to another. The answer provided during the live channels indicates that we can do these things, but it is not advisable. The recommendation is to play to your existing energetic strength. By trying to fulfill too many different roles, we may dilute the life we are leading and not feel fulfilled as an individual.

If you feel that you are not living your life according to what your strengths are, then this may help you to see the disconnection of your energy with your current incarnation. It may be that you will change the direction of your life.

Remember that these categories are broad and any dramatic life changes should be considered carefully and from more than one point of view. Ultimately you are the one responsible for any and all of your actions throughout your lives.

Walkers

"Those who Walk." The Walkers - The ones who move about and gather and explore. They are seekers of new paths in the physical plane, new approaches to life and existence. They are often the tinkerers and mechanically minded, the inventors and discoverers, innovators of dwelling lifestyles and alternate energy sources and transportation. These are the members of the family human that most often presage the next great leap forward in history.

Balanced Walkers:
You will know the true Walker by the intensity of effort and the perseverance of personal energy towards their project or goal. The true Walker is indomitable and unstoppable, their spirit and morale rarely fail them. Explorers, scientists, inventors, National Geographic types.

Unbalanced Walkers:
You will know the unbalanced Walker by the fervor of belief (without any real proof) in such things as "free energy" or "anti-gravity" or "alien technology" or the "exact center of the universe" or the "exact location of Atlantis." "Crackpots." People who "know the secret that the government has been hiding."

Watchers

"Those who Watch." The Watchers - These are the ones who keep the flock, maintaining an oversight and having supervision. They are often alone and as such may "hear" differently as much as they "see" differently. The bigger picture is often in front of them, though they are equally interested in the details, the individuals of humanity. These are the members of the family human who are most often concerned with the emotional balance of the tribe and often are the spiritual leaders or directors.

Balanced Watchers:
You will know the balanced Watcher, often only in hindsight. You may not realize the depth of spirituality while they are in your presence, though you will certainly feel a sense of peace and calm. The true Watcher is often a listener and other beings will find themselves opening up and revealing themselves in ways that they never have before. Shamans, ministers, priestesses, priests, guidance counselors.

Unbalanced Watchers:
You can tell the difference between a balanced Watcher and one who is not by the number of times they use the word "I" or refer to themselves as an example. Some self reference makes them accessible; too much indicates they spend much of the time watching themselves. They will be overly concerned about being accepted and will self-publicize their exploits and experiences, real or imagined. Roadside or carnival psychics, self-proclaimed healers, faith healers, TV preachers, anyone who spends an inordinate amount of time talking about your donations funding God's mission of which they themselves are an integral part.

Knowers

"Those who Know." The Gnosis - These are the humans that gather and collect knowledge, philosophical and scientific, and categorize it into usable forms or locations for the use of others. They could be referred to as librarians, but not limited to books or recordings in the traditional sense. There is an indication that they also have access to higher realms of thought, though it is not always apparent to them as individuals; they may believe that the knowledge is apparent to everyone. These are the members of the family human that most often play the greatest role in leadership of tribes.

Balanced Knowers:

You will know the true Knower by the ring of truth, what they say will sound correct. They will not have an axe to grind or position to promote. They will seek only to enlighten and educate, helping ones to find their own truth and to take full responsibility for their lives and growth. Librarians, historians, philosophers, advocate lawyers.

Unbalanced Knowers:

An unbalanced Knower can be represented in these ways, politicians and those who seek control over others. They will often be heard to say, "Knowledge is power" and indicate a moral superiority over those who do not have access to the same information that they do, and they will attempt to keep the same information from others. In the case of an unbalanced Knower, they will believe that the end will always justify the means. They will often be found as members of high level or secret societies and old boy networks. Politicians, ambulance chasing lawyers, developers, land barons, colonizers, clergy of long-standing structured religions, fundamentalists, and ultra-right wingers.

Growers

"Those who Grow." The Growers - These are the humans that institute new plans and ideas, germinating the concepts and potentials for using raw matter. This would include those who design and engineer projects (different from "those who walk" in that "those who grow" work with what is there, while "those who walk" discover new things), but also those who would bring life into line with the flow of the universal energies. Ones in this category may also be referred to as healers, those who promote health and vitality. There is some indication that arranged procreation is acceptable in the course of the continued evolution of the family human.

Balanced Growers:
The true Grower will have a strong charitable streak, a willingness to give of themselves at deep levels. They will be emotionally strong and feel deep compassion for others. They will feel a drive to promote health and vitality by helping to provide quality food and water and shelter for everyone. They will not give themselves away but will ask for a fair exchange for their efforts, thus teaching the principle of "every action has an opposite and equal reaction" by their example. Farmers, architects, teachers, doctors and nurses, caretakers, caregivers, emergency medical technicians.

Unbalanced Growers:

A grower who lacks balance will feel that everyone should get what they need given to them without effort. They will talk about the evil of money and wish that we did not need it. They will be ultra-idealistic but have no real solutions for humanity. If this course is followed, a welfare state will soon exist, often with the unbalanced grower first in line for bread. Ultra-left wingers, pseudo-spiritualists, advocates of, "Just ask deity and it will provide," school of thought.

Harvesters

"Those who Reap." The Harvesters - These are the humans that harvest and remove matter once its purpose has changed. This would include those who process and manufacture, but mostly is about those who assist life to advance it into the next stage. The purpose of the hospice worker is well defined using this category. They do not remove life, only assist one to move from life. There seems to be some indication that euthanasia is acceptable if extreme and special circumstances dictate it. This is a form of energetic efficiency in getting life forces back into a situation of renewal and regeneration.

Balanced Harvesters:

A balanced Harvester has a deep compassion for life and will often be involved in rescue shelters for animals of all kinds. They are certainly not wishing for anyone to die but are comfortable in the understanding that beings pass and will often be in the position of comforting the bereaved, those left behind. They are not fatalistic, merely practical in the face of reality. Often the calm in the storm of emergency situations and crisis, they will rise to the role of leadership in such moments. Farmers, funeral and gravesite workers, food and water processors, doctors and nurses and healthcare workers in ICU or terminal disease wards, garbage removal and processing and recycling personal.

Unbalanced Harvesters:
An unbalanced Harvester will feel that they have a power over life and death, that they are somehow more worthy of life than others around them. They will find nothing wrong in the might makes right philosophy and will bully and intimidate their way through life. Violent criminals, murderers, serial killers, terrorists, ethnic cleansers.

All life falls into these general categories. It is possible that you may feel drawn to more than one. It is advisable, and we remind you now, to follow the strongest path. This will allow your life energies to flow naturally, and your time spent on earth will increase in quality and in love and peace and joy.

Look to the examples of balanced Walkers, Watchers, Knowers, Growers, and Harvesters and seek to place yourself in that energy.

These are only examples. The variety of pursuits available to the family human is innumerable. Your imagination is a key to balancing your energy in any of these categories.

Imagination is the first action of creation.

Questions to Stimulate Your Personal Growth

Trust your perceptions, but make sure they are your own perceptions.

Why do you believe what you believe?

10
Global Polarity

Atypically, I was woken up one night with this brief communication. I have tried this exercise with several people. It is always thought provoking. It is not always satisfying. Try it. You might learn something about yourself.

As a human, an undivided one, it may be interesting for you to begin to use a globe.

Several times now we have indicated an area of energy on the surface of the planet, a place of significant activity that will affect all life. Each time we have also referenced the opposite side of the earth.

Polarity is a term that will become increasingly important to the family human. Being aware of the geographic concept will further assist you, the undivided one, in attaining, regaining or retaining your balance, and thus your growth.

Scientifically, we look at the north and south poles and find them to be significant. On a global or planetary scale, this is the most well known and easily comprehended example of polarity. It is not the limit of polarity.

Find a representation of your home planet; a spherical example will allow you to see things easier. Locate your geographical, physical home. Note the latitude and longitude to be certain of precision. Now look 180 degrees to the opposite side of the earth. Study this area.

For your physical self is one point of polarity. The other point of polarity is there, 180 degrees away. At first this will raise many questions. We will not supply the answers directly. This is an exercise in self exploration and self development.

We will say that this may be a significant key to understanding your future development. This may be a point of comprehension of your placement of energy not simply in the present, but also in the future as well as the past.

Do not jump to conclusions, only observe. We know that most of you will not take the time to do this. The ones that do are the ones that we are interested in the most, for they are the ones ready to move forward.

Do not jump to conclusions. This is a simple exercise.

The Question of Geography

Although it is not a necessary thing to go to any area of the planet to be in a sacred place, you may feel yourself drawn to a geographic location. There may be areas of the planet that have a vibration that is similar to your own, an area that seems more harmonious to your personal energy, where you feel stronger, more balanced, and more at peace.

Flow to those areas. At first you may only do this within your own heart or in your thinking. You may be able to travel there and, for a short time, visit. Test these areas out and learn if they truly hold a strength or power for you. Begin to gravitate to these places. Allow the planet to realign your energy with its own.

It may sometimes feel difficult or even impossible to you that you will ever get to that area. There may be things, jobs, possessions, friends and family that hold you to the place that you currently reside. You may be unwilling to let these things go. That is a choice. It is not right or wrong.

If, however, you begin to trust in the planet and trust in your own spiritual path and release a need to hold on to what also holds you, paths and opportunities will open up that you can not always see from the perspective of a member of the family human. You are a sacred place, and you can be strengthened by the planet.

Question to Stimulate Your Personal Growth

Humans are sacred places.

Do you act as if this is true?

The planet and all life on the planet is a filter.

What is in your life that you no longer need?

11
The Wave

This channel was the first after relocating from the Midwest to the West Coast. It references the proximity and the movement of the Pacific Ocean, and a surprise close encounter with the local dolphin pod.

Together; as above, so below. We can very quickly step out of our routine and into a new pattern, can we not? Many things may *seem* to interfere. You have been watching the waves. Let us tell you something about waves. They can be a challenge!

Affect

Whether it is a light wave or a wave of water or any type of wave of energy, one wave will affect all other waves of energy. Wave affects wave, and in the spiritual dimension there is the energy of waves as well. It is difficult for some to understand the action of waves in the spirit realm, and it will be until such time as science can teach it, demonstrate it, make it duplicable for the human eye to see, the human brain to comprehend.

You know, when you are in the physical realm, how wave affects wave. It is not really interfering, it is creating. It is creating and recreating. The resulting patterns are a natural expression of the movement of the planet and the movement of the system of planets and the sun.

Marking the Wave

In the physical realm, you measure waves from peak to peak or trough to trough. It is a perception, then, that waves are made up of peak events and trough events. It is a mistake to limit the energy of waves in this way. This perception is valuable only if you wish to measure the waves or their frequency, how frequently they occur.

If you wish to ride a wave, an important thing to know is where the waves are. It is also important to know that if you wish to avoid a wave! It is also helpful to be balanced as a wave approaches. This increases the possibility of remaining balanced once the wave arrives.

Waves are representations of energy in motion. If you wish to be still, then it is beneficial to get out of the way of the wave. If you wish to be in motion, and a wave is going the direction that you wish to move, it is a good thing to catch that wave.

To best ride a wave, it is good to be a part of it. This means that you do not attempt to control or shape the wave. You cooperate with it. You maintain your balance within it. If you fall, do not worry. Chances are that there is another wave coming close behind. That is the way of the universe as it moves energies. There are many waves to catch.

When a wave of water approaches land or a reef, the wave does not think that the land interferes. When the energy of the wave touches the land, the land allows the energy to flow through. It is altered, different, changed, but energy still, and the wave still continues in a form. The wave of energy has ceased to be expressed in water and now becomes a vibration through land.

This western coast is a land of waves of energy, a land of waves, not currents. The Midwestern United States is a land of currents. The area that you were in flowed in steady directions; here the waves come in many patterns, and there are many waves. It will not be like it was, similar, but not the same.

As humans living in the world of dimensions of height and width, length and time, you have concerns regarding events. That is a strength and an attribute. It allows you to mark progress and movement and direction. Do not let the attribute create the wrong type of wave. We are very specific when we say the wrong type of wave, because there is a flow. If you attempt to affect the flow, you may find that you have limited the energy. Better to pick the direction you wish to go and catch the wave going your way.

There are moments in the wave when things appear low. It is best to move with the peak of the wave, the crest. Sometimes you will be in the trough. It does not mean the energy went away. Perceptively, the energy is in a different place. The cresting energy is building up again. There are practical matters to be taken care of at those times. Be at peace. Take care of those matters. Notice that the energy has not stopped.

Waves of All Forms

The waves that you see in the water, in the physical realm, they echo. They echo in the spiritual realm, but they also echo in the mental and the emotional realms. The waves you see on the water are the physical.

There are patterns to be discerned and it is sometimes difficult to measure the patterns of the large bodies of Gaia's waters. It can distract from the strength and the action of the seas. Do not be distracted by measurements and the marking of times and distances.

When in the presence of the waves, allow the wave patterns to restructure your wave patterns, to restructure your energy, to restructure your thoughts and your feelings. Be open to the changes. Be accepting of how things are.

For many there is a concern, an attribute, regarding where the energy for living will come from. What direction will daily supplies come from? You are human.

The family human is a family of creators, yes. As such they often feel that they must constantly create a wave. It is difficult to create the wave, easier to ride one.

There is always the wave of money. There is always that wave. You know where to find that. You know how to catch that wave. It is not the wave of money that brought you to these words, to this point. It is the wave of spirit and spirituality, of purpose, of togetherness, of growth, of knowing who you are and where you are or where you are not, of knowing your energy and where you are at your peak.

Allow the light, the literal light, to touch you and change you. Many of you have asked for a shift. You have asked for the DNA change. You have asked for the emotional change, the mental change, the physical shift. You have asked for this, now allow it. Allow it now. You are not here at this point of linear time by accident. That weight may be heavy on you. You have concerns, a human attribute.

Waves of Words

These words represent a wave of practical spirituality. There are many who cannot catch the wave of these words. Their balance, their attention, their *intention* is directed elsewhere. That is not right and that is not wrong. If these words are not practical to you then find words that are. Find the wave that is moving in the direction you choose to go.

If these words are stimulating to you, if they inspire balance and direction, then flow with this wave until such time as your personal direction shifts. From our perspective, the work that we are doing is important work, stimulating work, stimulating for you. Stimulating for those that can hear and understand. Not all will hear and understand. That is not right, and it is not wrong. Do not waste these words.

Some will be stimulated to move away from this type of association. Some are seeking things they are not prepared for. The pattern of waves moves them differently.

Some will be stimulated beyond what they themselves could imagine. The human individual can often achieve goals far beyond what they believe. It is often that they must move in a completely different direction and their lives turn to a course they had not anticipated.

To understand if you have caught a wave or missed a wave, think back to what your life was four or five years ago, or ten or twenty. You may have had a desire at that time. Is it still a desire? Have you moved closer to it or farther away from it? Have you been riding a crest or sitting in a trough?

Trust us when we say that the waves will carry you. They will carry you quickly if there is harmony in the frequencies of the physical, mental, and emotional, and the spiritual elements of you, the undivided one. They will seem to be interfering waves if there is a division between the heart and spirit, and the brain and body.

The waves are moving whether you choose to cooperate or not. Why not cooperate? Your heart's desire is there. What you want is already in existence. How can you be certain? Because you can imagine it! Be aware now that other energies are in existence and factor them in to your course. Still, you must leave land to ride the waves of the seas. You must also leave what appears to be solid if you are to ride the waves of other energies.

The destination is already there. The journey awaits. Once you arrive you realize this. It is the faith that it is there that allows you to move in the first place. In the end you know, it was already done, already there, already here, already an accomplished situation. You simply had to move through it. We all move slowly through gravity!

Let light touch you now. Do not be afraid of it, cautious perhaps, but not afraid. The waves are still coming, and they will not stop. You may fear that some waves are causing interference. They are not. It is creation. It is a shaping. The waves are shaping you. They are shaping the people around you. Yes, even the people who are closest to you, your human family. It is good to recall that these are not things everyone will understand. Do not waste your words.

Do not look back. Trust that your lessons have been well learned.

Trust the New Things That You Know

Trust what you *know*. Also, trust that what you know from before has been changed and shaped by the waves. Trust the new knowledge, the new things that you know. Think of that statement, "Trust the new things that you know," and repeat it to yourself. Think of the things that are new that you know. These things are not based on anything except that you *know*.

It is not always a comfortable position to be constantly facing a newness of things. Listen to the other voices. They will have things to say, traditional things to say, and they will not be wrong, but trust the new things that you know. The traditional things may not be wrong for some. If you are hearing these words and understanding, you are not traditional! You are riding a wave.

There are paths now that you can go by. There are different paths. There will be choices that call to you, and you will be offered different things, some of them very traditional. None of these paths will be wrong. Trust your purpose. The comfort will be to go towards what is familiar and yet to ride a wave is not to stay with the familiar. It is leaving behind familiarity. It does not make sense to a physical perception to leave behind what you have known, what may in fact be working. It is not the wave of physical realms only that we are riding. You are riding the wave of spirit. Trust this. Trust this.

When we speak to you through our voice, the earth is very near to us, and we like it. We like the patterns and what we now know. We like the karma that has brought us all together. The wave we ride of karma, and the elements and the particles of a vitality of life that is Onereon now, we like. In the past we knew things. We learned and watched and explored and walked. We *knew*. That is really the secret of the Walkers and the Watchers, that at some point in time they simply *know*. The Walkers though, they are not content to know. They need to prove. To a strong Walker, life is new. Life is always new. Trust what is new. That you know.

You are good at creating, at manifesting. You created this place that you call the present moment. You did. You rode the waves that shaped it. It is not right or wrong. It is just what you have done. You know this. You do not need proof. You just know. Is it what you want?

Touch

We have said, "Touch the earth." You can carry elements of the earth with you. You have asked the question, "Is working with crystals and minerals touching the earth?" The answer is yes. Understand that the earth is not just the stones, the earth is more. It is also the light, and it is not just that the light touches you; you let yourself touch the light.

It is difficult for humans to understand because they always feel that something is happening *to* them! You touch the water, you touch the waves; it is not just water reaching out to touch you. Reach out and touch the light! Reach out and touch the wind! Touch with your eyes. Touch with your breath. Touch, touch, touch.

At the water allow your mouth to open, to sense the water through your open mouth. Sense the vibration of it, the feeling of it, the wave. You do not have to be in the water to sense that. Breathe. Let the energy flow. Open up more to the light, let the light touch you more and touch the light more. Do you understand?

As you allow yourselves to experience through touch in this way, you will become open to different forms of perception. You will be allowing your brain waves to relax, to open, to be less dense in the pattern of vibration. You will begin to sense beyond what you have known. Other waves then, other frequencies, will be able to harmonize with yours.

It may at that point you feel like you are hearing someone. Thoughts that are not your own may gather within you and become your thoughts. You will then know what you did not know before. Where did that knowledge come from? It was always there! You simply allowed for it to exist within you!

For some of you here today *[at the ocean side]* this will feel natural. You may question the reality of the thoughts and their source. We say, "How does it feel to be with others of your kind?" Because it is the mammals of the sea that you "hear;" it is those who know.

This is amongst the new things that you know. It is not an accident that you are here now. In a greater sense this is a greater purpose, to be with those who are like you. It is a following of the wave. It is a following of the vibrational pattern that you are currently on.

We have given you an exercise. It is not just with the ears that we hear. Are there questions?

How is it for you, speaking to us here instead of in the Midwest?

It is interesting for us. One would not think that geography would affect spirit and yet it does. Sense of place is important and at no point is it ever the same place. The planet spins and moves, and so one year from now the planet is not in the same place. The illusion is that it has rotated around the sun, one year. It is illusion only.

The sun has also moved. The planet has moved with the sun. It is nowhere near, on a human scale, where it was before. You are always someplace new. So, we are a family, we are together, a team, a group. We go our ways. We come together for these moments. Particles of us are here now but force of us is elsewhere.

I have heard it stated that for us, as humans too, that part of us is here and part of us is off existing somewhere else.

Like the tides, it is the energies, it is the field, it is the planet. The "Source That Is," is all of it, all of us. We have these moments where we are together. Yet we all are changing constantly. So it is that we may feel that something is missing or that we are scattered. In situations that seem familiar, we feel that we should know what to do, that we should know something.

It is because a part of us somewhere has done this all before. It is why the children being born are so aware. They are the ones that are coming together, coalescing. They are born *knowing*.

The Greater Light is all of the little sparks and so the Source is all of these little sparks of energetics. The Source is also the space between sparks. So from one spark to the next spark there is no difference. From one peak of the wave to the next peak of the wave it is still water, all the way through and all the way through, and the peak may be different water and will be, and all water peaks and all water troughs. It makes no judgment about it. It moves with the energy of the planet. It moves with the dance. It is Source dancing with itself.

The individual human, and sometimes, on the spirit realm, the individual being, really can begin to believe that they are undivided, and special. In fact, it is only the experience of the energy at that moment that is special and unique. Life can come and life can go, but life will always be life because that is the energy.

For this planet, life is clustered around this planet. For other planets it is not, not in the way that you can currently comprehend.

For the family human, a practice is often required. We have indicated that everyone channels. The channel is a form of communication but is not limited to speaking. Channeling is an expression of your connection with your spiritual aspects and sometimes with your spirit companions. You communicated in a particular way for a span of time. Some channel through a garden or their art, some through cooking or through service. How will you communicate your connection now?

The same energy that you put into your lives up to this present moment is here now. Go to the water and do the same thing. What will be the next step? You need to open your ears, open your mouth. Sense the mammals and you will be able to put the thoughts into words. You will speak English, in the same way that our voice speaks in English. The information that comes from us is not in English, not in any language that a human can speak and understand.

The advantage now for you is the information that comes from the mammals is in a language that a human can learn and understand, but not in the traditional ways of listening, thinking, and repeating. It is more a language of mind, not brain only, you see, but heart. This is where you practice. This is why we say, "Open your mouth, face the water, sense the energy flow down inside you."

At this point in time the question will always be, "Do I share this communication or not?" The answer is that the communication is always out there whether you share it or not. There are some that will listen and some that will not. For now, do not waste your words. The words come, communicate what you know, but do not waste the words. Stick with the ones you trust.

Your companions are here. You are here. Be here.

Seek peace.

Things to Remember

- Waves affect all dimensions.
- Waves create.
- It is best to catch a wave that is going in your chosen direction.
- It is better to catch a wave than to try to create one.
- Trust the new things that you know.
- Make the next stage of your life a choice.

Things to Come

- Communication with the mammals of the seas is increasing.

12
Echoes

As above, so below.

Echoes of Life

We wish to speak of the echoes of life and the echoes of humanity and the vitality of life. There are those that are still tied to the earth even though they have passed. This shows the fundamental sameness of life, whether it is in a human or another physical form, or whether it is in a spirit form. For some pass and they still believe so strongly and so they stay, as if that is what they are supposed to do. As humans, people become sensitive to that and they begin to think in terms of ghosts, haunting.

When things are out of balance with an individual human, you sense that about them, and the farther out of balance the stronger the sense, the stronger the vibration. We have spoken of vibration before and we will talk in terms of echo in a few moments, because the echo is also a vibration.

The echo of a human at the end of a life is retained by those who could hear the human, that could feel their vibration, that were in harmony with that vibration, that human. When they are gone, the harmony continues for a period of time just as sound continues despite the fact that the chord that has been struck is no longer being struck.

The harmonic, the echo. When the human is passed, the transference should be complete. They should understand, they should know, but there are so many misknowings in humanity at this point. Science now has all of the techniques to find what is true. They are not applying the techniques. They will. Someone will make the intuitive leap.

There are some humans who will tie someone who has passed to themselves and will not release them. You have made this observation as well. Sometimes the life force is tied to a space where the individual died, and it is very difficult then for that life force to flow away from physical existence. This will create a problem.

Let those that have passed, pass. Let them go, for in this way they do prepare a place for you. They then know your energy and they know. They know when your sound changes, they harmonize with you because their skill has increased, their vibration has changed. They understand how to change vibration on, what you would say, the other side, beyond the veil, though in truth it is not so much a veil.

They are not dead. Dead is no vitality. The body, in fact, is not dead until it has returned to the elements and even then, it is not dead, it is changed. It is transferred. Energy does not become destroyed. Energy does not become "not energy." Energy continues to be energy. Everything is energy.

This is not to devalue life. This is not to devalue perceptions of remaining alive, of being, the value of being alive as a human being, as an individual, an undivided one. There becomes a point where the child leaves the mother.

You see, growth and then death, so called dying, consider that as the child leaving the mother, not to be forever separated but to move on, to move forward, to grow.

The planet is a filter. Those that cause death, there is much filtering then, there is much haunting. For if you have the blood of someone else on you, much of their vitality then stays with you and your karma becomes heavy indeed. And there is no atoning, only cleansing and return and filtering and return and return.

In spirit we still feel the humanness, the humanity of our previous existences. It is much more diverse now and we speak of the coalescence. This will not take away the diversity; it will just take away the numbers. Diversity will remain. Harmony will unify.

Echoes of Humanity

The echo of a human can be felt by another human. Have you had the experience of walking down the street and suddenly you feel an insight, you feel a thought, you feel a perception that is different or foreign for you and you wonder where it could have come from?

Certainly, it may be an intuitive hit, but you may have just stepped into the same step as someone else that is having that thought, that feeling, that insight, that perception, who is recollecting an experience. When you follow in someone's footsteps and they have a moment of high energy, you may sense that vibration; you may feel that vibration for minutes after they have had that vibration.

For a time, the harmonic, the note, carries. The energy of sound carries, and the echo returns from the far side of the canyon or the opposite side of the wall. Like a footprint in the sand and a wave of water as it moves past, it becomes dimmer, dimmer, and dimmer until it is no longer there. Yet now you know that note. It is new to you and yet you have learned something.

All too often in this current time, this current moment in time, these years of time, we are trained to simply dismiss them. As a human, we dismiss that insight, intuition, perception, the idea of being in someone else's mind. It is frightening, is it not?

In the past histories of the family human, some diverse branches of the human race have been able to see into someone else's mind, to communicate without verbal skill, to think to each other. It was not invasive; it was extremely peaceful. It was beneficial for them at the time that they lived.

As time went on, lower vibrations came about and those born into that time became fearful of those that thought differently. They acted in fear and perceived these thoughtful ones, ones full with thought, as enemies. The policy became, "take off their head," so they could not get into yours.

You block their thoughts. You think of other things. You train your mind so others can not get into your mind. You wall off your mind, and soon the tribe is a closed-minded tribe, wary of anyone that comes to them. One, maybe two, are allowed who know these skills, these things that are natural, these things that are normal, these things that are now suppressed out of fear and out of a false sense of danger, and so your religions continue.

The skill is diminished but not lost, and at moments of high energy, at moments of close relation, at moments of togetherness, you get to the echo of your partners' energies, your partners, those that you trust, those that you are one with, undivided. Humanity has divided itself even within its own body and this is changing.

Vitality of Life

The sun is coming in, the increase of sun on the earth. You see, they were right. The scientists were right. People did not want to believe them. Interesting thing about science, it is difficult to lie but easy to ignore.

A disaster? A disaster for the planet? No. A change for the planet, merely. An adaptation thus will be forced to begin again, to kick in, to advance, to move forward in the same way as when the sun went away many thousands of years, ten of thousands of years ago.

Thus the echo of humans becomes purer as it filters. The vibration of life becomes purer as it filters. As it filters, it adapts.

Let the humans that have passed go. Let go of the perceived need to be in touch with ones after they have passed. Let them go. Do not seek to wake them up. Stay away from the places in which they have passed. It only serves to anchor and, for those who are already confused, anger.

Some would say, "Let them sleep." We would say, "Let them become fully awake, rejoining their Source. Let them come back to life, continue with life in a collective beyond your sight. Let them take their positions. Let them tell us their experiences and their knowledge, and their emotions, their feelings. Let us work with them so that they can return, so that they can prepare, so that they can do the welcoming work." You cannot talk to the dead. You can only talk to the living. There is no death. There is only continuing. Thus we speak, for we have died from humanity many times.

Are there questions?

You close with the phrase, "Seek peace." There is much talk about those in warlike situations; how can they choose peace? Is there a suggestion for the current situation in the Mideast?

Not so much the Mideast but everywhere. These events are not necessary in this form, but they are necessary. It is what the ones that have returned and passed from in that region understand. There are other solutions for changing the energy of the planet, but this is what the ones alive in that region have called choice.

Much hinges on the recognition of the rights of all groups to exist and to release the need to be in control of areas that have long since lost any holiness. The ones that are truly holy are yet to arrive in full.

Choose your personal responses to difficult events well. There will be a wave of beings. There will be a returning of energies, a returning of persons, and they will be strong in their pursuit of peace. Ones that know war but have been filtered and coalesced, ones that now know peace and have the balance of it are preparing to return. It will be a strong return, a wave of that energy.

There is no practical thing to do that we can say at this point save this, "Maintain your balance." Until people are educated out of their superstitions, by which we mean their religions, there is no changing these situations.

Will this group coming in, this peaceable group, will it come in the normal generational ways, or in what has been referred to as walk–in energy?

It has already begun in terms of birth. There is a swelling of this energy in terms of birth. There is something new that is going to happen, not so much walk-in as, a little more like takeover than walk-in, but not a forcing; it is going to be that they are invited in.

Events are going to cause some to say, "Won't someone please help us," and that will be part of the wave. There will be a general appeal to sources outside of humanity and, at that invitation, there will be a general stopping of, not a belief so much, but a dropping of the need to have everyone believe.

The coalescing will ease this by creating it. As energies of different individuals of differing experiences come together in one being, there will be a search for internal peace. Inner struggles will lead to inner dialogues and a kind of emotional consensus will build. Make no mistake, this is not about things becoming perfect. There will be struggles.

At present there is more of a "stop it" energy about the situations, an arresting energy and that is coming through in a higher form, not spiritual yet, but emotional. The mothers are the leaders of this energy and the children that they bear will be born into that emotional consensus of "everyone has to stop it." Something else will need everyone's attention together.

For the individual member of the family human, remove judgment from within yourself. Do not send anger towards leaders of any tribe, government, or religion.

Do not be opposed, opposite to any one. Be for something.

Start new growth for yourself. Act in a way that affirms life in all its forms, not just the life on the physical planet.

Honor those that have passed and release their energies from you so that the coalescing may continue faster and faster.

In this way, the planet moves toward a new age.

In this way we all seek, and, in the seeking, we find peace.

Things to Remember

- There is a fundamental sameness to life, whether human or spirit.
- The planet is a filter that cleanses the vital energies of life existing in and around it.
- The echo of a human can be felt by another human.
- Let those that have passed, pass. Let them go.
- Act in a way that affirms all forms of life.

Things to Come

- There will be an increase in the amount of solar energy on the planet earth. This will encourage an adaptation in life forms.
- There will be a group of beings invited in to assist in the resolution of conflicts and the completion of the harmonic coalescence.

13
Children of the Sun

As above, so below. We speak now to bring a clarification and expansion of some of the information that we hear discussed.

The Children of the Sun have already been born and are being born. The congress of vitality is being called and the ratio is approximately three to one. A third of humanity will change first. A third of humanity will be reborn and changed. The power of the sun will trigger the change, drive the change, and it may seem like a disaster to those that first go through the change.

Information and Intuition

Already the information bearers have begun their work and those closest to the seas may begin to hear them. Those that will be of the seas have begun their changes. Diversity is set, but what course is not. There are decisions yet to be made and we, above, do not make them. We will be on hand to continue to guide.

The genetics are not yet understood by your scientists. There is the leap of intuition that they have not made for fear of being wrong. There are those now alive that will and are making that leap. They are not being taken seriously because they tie themselves to many things that are not important. Be aware.

We have said before, "Do not waste your words." That is not simply a principle for the outflow of your concepts and intuitions, but also for the influx of concepts and intuitions. Allow your filter to be cleansed and to be clean, as there are many ideas whose time has passed being promoted as current reality. Two thousand and six thousand solar years past is not current and holds little use for you at the time of the change.

The change must be viewed with a cosmic and karmic perspective. Understand that, as above, so below, means we also will go through an equal change, for we are you and you are we! More about our change later, though we have already given some information regarding that.

The human species is linked in ways that are understood by genetics, but there are new discoveries to be made. It is larger than you know, and the complete scope of genetics may not be discovered before the change. There is information about this that cannot be believed by the scientific community for it has no basis in their physical world. Listen and you will know. It will always obey the laws of energy.

Do Not Waste

The change is growth. Growth for the vitality of the planet you are part of. Remember that the individual human is not that important. The actions that we take as individuals to become undivided, to filter out the impurities of energies that do not serve the karmic waves, that is what is important. Be aware. Do not waste your words. Do not waste your efforts. Do not waste your energy. Do not waste your life.

Many things are minor. Assign importance to things with an eye to reality. Ask what the karmic view is when you reach levels of frustration or fear or anger. Turn that energy around by releasing the need for things to go your way. Feel the flow and release the old patterns of thinking. Renew yourself by not being the old self. Move with the current of change and be a particle of the change. The individual atom does not judge the chemical change that it participates in, and you are the same, with this exception, the individual atom does not make a decision. The family human makes decisions. The individual human, the undivided one, makes decisions. Decide now to not be against things. Decide now to be for something, move forward.

It Is New

We have said these things many times. We say them again for it is a time when much is in existence to be against. We do not say condone; we do not say agree. We say accept where you are and who you are and what you are and how you are and especially accept when you are. Move forward and do not get entangled in the ways of the past.

We have said that you are truly on a new earth. Look around! Become aware! The earth is becoming new still. When you were first here, the surface and the climate were much different. You would not have survived in your current form, and your forms then would not survive the planet today.

When we all merged with the others, when guidance of Gaia's life forces began, we began the decision-making process, not as separate entities but together, as one and unified. In time, forces moved us apart and that was not in error.

Now we have begun the harmonic coalescence, the bringing together, the unification. Now is the time to be aware of the direction of energy, the flow of energy, and to choose to move forward and release the past.

An Increase

The filtering continues and you see its increase every day. Do not be afraid. Do not add to the fear. We have much work to do, and you can assist.

We speak of the increase in the class of Harvesters. These are the ones who aid in the changing of energies. Many of you are now being asked to do this work, not in the actual changing of energy, but assisting those who are passing to pass in peace. We have spoken of the reverse hospice work being done on this side of the veil. Ease those in pain out of the physical plane so that when they arrive above, they are at peace. This requires very little action on your part. Understand that not all are being called to this work.

Many remain as Walkers and Watchers, Knowers, and Growers; some hear their calling clearly. For some this will be a confirmation of what you have already felt. For some this may be a revelation! Rejoice in it and make the decision. There is no right or wrong, simply move forward and accept the who, what, where, how, and especially the when of your individual role in the coming together, the coalescence of Gaia's vital forces.

The legacy of the humans of the past may be discovered if the genetics can be proven. Look to the hairy men and the red men for the first wave of change. It has begun already, and you see it clearly in the ways of communication.

Soon will come a time of the Children of the Seas; they also have begun. The Children of the Sun are in motion. Be aware. For we are coming together, and we will come together in joy.

Be joyful. Seek peace.

Questions to Stimulate Your Personal Growth

Do not waste your words.

Are the things you talk about worth the energy?

14
Evolution

As above, so below. This is our agreed upon entry into channel with our voice.

Separation from Source

As Onereon, we are in constant stages of change. We do not define or delineate; all is one. There is simply distance from Source and then only if we choose limits and perceive limits.

Since the beginning, since the Source, there are forces that have shaped us and the forces are no different than us. We are all from the Source and thus, in a way, all the same, all the Source. Of course, the separation of the material of the Source, the energies that are and were and will be the Source, the separation is a belief and so the delineation remains. With delineation and markings of space and time and matter and energy, a common perceived disconnection from all else began and so exists until the perception is changed.

Life, on all levels, is affected by and has an effect on all perceived elements. We speak now specifically of the life of Gaia. The vital force that is a unified field, that is the stellar system, but specifically this place of earth and moon, this vital force is divided and that is no accident. It is what makes your portion of the energies from Source different from much of the rest of known and unknown space and time, the element of consciousness, the opportunity of choice.

Two Forces

In much of evolution there are two evident forces that drive the change: opportunity and necessity. On Gaia, the family human has worked hard to eliminate the force of necessity. In many ways this has slowed the evolutionary process down, especially for the family human, but for all life expression of Gaia's vital force.

Many opportunities now present themselves and the natural process is a deeply encoded imperative. The end result is not completely satisfactory for Gaia's natural process, however. Technologies will not replace for long what the natural order of energy can do more efficiently. The mammalian mind has capabilities that are repressed and latent. They will be expressed in the near future. Gaia will see to that.

Necessity, then, may become more of a force for evolution in the near future. The energy of choice is still available, however.

The Harmonic Coalescence

We have spoken of a change, a harmonic coalescence, that is upon the family human, but also upon the vital force of Gaia, a coalescence that will come in a natural way, though not always physically pleasant for the individual human. Yet it is a choice to participate in this way and on the realm of spirit there is much rejoicing after the matter is accomplished. There is much to balance out and the passage to and then from the planet earth, the filter, is an efficient cycle in the system of energy. You will soon know of greater forces that are also a part of the system.

We have spoken of the sun, the star that powers the planetary system. An increase of solar energies now is near. This will catalyze the process of evolution. We have spoken of the return to water of some and of the return of the wisdom of the past from the waters. We have spoken of the reclamations of lands by Gaia and the return of spirit to spaces upon the surface of earth. We have spoken of the fear of death and the fear of life. We have spoken of violence and of peace. We speak always of personal peace.

You have chosen. We also have chosen. Soon many will become "as above" and many that are above will again be "so below." We will greet one another in the passing and then the change will be upon us all!

In the next three generations we will all see the coalescing of vital force. Within one hundred years we will all be together in a way that is new to all of us. Those that are above us, those that we, Onereon, describe "as above" will then begin descent and the next full stage of evolution will begin in truth and in harmony. Have you been learning your song?

The Energy of Peace

Your personal peace has been tested for three decades. Ask yourself now, what am I against? Now cease being against that! For the energy of peace is not served by anger. The energy of peace is not promoted by protest. The energy of peace is not advanced by ideologies or useless philosophies or ancient dogma.

The energy of peace is served by the individual, the undivided one, taking full responsibility for their own course and no other. The energy of peace comes from the promotion of balance, and you have the opportunity to balance only one person in your lifetimes. The energy of peace is advanced only by moving forward with your own personal creation and connection to spirit.

It is the age of responsibility. Increase your abilities to respond to whatever situations may exist. The action by the collective family human to remove necessity from the equation of evolution has also had the effect of taking away personal need to learn anything truly new. The only thing that the family human in general is learning today, at present in linear time, is the newest form of distraction from spirituality.

The import of the new technologies is lost on the majority of the population of the planet, and they are in danger of falling in behind some who will appear to them as wizards or demi-gods, someone who will wield great powers that are inexplicable to those who are ignorant of logic, who follow only heart, and then only down pathways that others direct them towards.

In the past histories of the planet and its many cycles of civilizations, there have been seats and centers of great learning and advanced thought. Today these have become the target of those who protect the false histories and ancient arguments. Look to the youth and direct them to release judgment regarding their space in the political and religious arenas. Remind them that if they are against something they are merely helping to hold up the walls.

Look to the seats of learning and understand why the planet is turning to the force of necessity to advance the process of life rather than leave it for the force of opportunity. There are plenty of opportunities that have been offered and missed, or gone by unacknowledged.

There are no guarantees. Life may take a twist in a different direction due to any number of outside forces.

Conscious Choice

There is one force for evolution that we have left for us to discuss, the force of conscious choice. For this force to have the greatest effect we must, all of us, raise our consciousness.

Raise the consciousness of the body by being aware of the earth and all its systems, by being aware that you, the undivided one, are not the pinnacle but simply a particle.

Raise the consciousness of the mind by understanding things with a balanced heart and brain, by feeling as much as you logic and think, knowing that spirit cannot be found through logic but only through heart and that, in the end, spirit will prove to be the highest of logics. You have yet to know all the facts, though your science gets closer each day to the technology that will change the way you view death.

Raise the consciousness of your spirituality by approaching all beings as if they are a part of you, for in fact they are, and you are a part of them. You are an undivided one, an individual cluster of energy that is a particle of greater energies still.

Now make the choice, the choice to move forward in personal peace, the choice to sing your own song until you find the harmony that you seek. The choice to live actively, creating the life you desire and trusting in your own perceptions, not wasting words on those who choose to hold to the old energies, but moving in the direction of the newest of ages.

Evolution is not something that has ceased to have effect. The planet is in constant change as that is the law of the universe. Diversity continues and in your human form you cannot imagine the splendor of choices that the vital forces of original Source have made in the universe that surrounds and awaits you!

You are in the midst of it all. In time and in space there is a convergence of energy happening and it is happening to all local beings.

The vibration has been raised in and around the planets. The pitch and tone are purer, the notes sound cleaner and clearer than anytime in the long history of this system.

All vital forces now are raising their energies to match the song of the spheres. Will you not join in? You make the choice!

For us, for the beings that are Onereon, for the ones that hear and are Onereon with us, together, we recommend this course with great joy, with great love, and with great peace.

Join us now and know peace.

Book Two
Touch the Earth
A Path to Ascension

Touch the earth. When you are in physical form, you are of the earth. You are not on the earth; you are of the earth. You are of the elements of the earth. By this we mean, get in touch with who you are, where you live, and what you truly are. The aspect of you that reaches for ascension, we acknowledge that. Now also reach for decendancy. And touch the earth.

Do you want to be more spiritual? Then find more reasons to be joyful, to enjoy your life. When you enjoy something specifically, invite your spiritual companions to join you. In this way, you grow in your spirituality.

Regarding Inspiration

Inspiration is an amazing word. The root of the term is heard in many ways in our modern language. Most often it implies a connection to spirit. To be inspired, then, is to be of spirit or with spirit. What better way to be a spiritual person than to be open to the energy of inspiration?

There are many ways to be and feel inspired and many ways to express inspiration. Music, art, scientific discovery, or anything that creatively adds to our experience here on the planet earth can be classified as inspired.

Not every artist is a Van Gogh. Not every composer is a Beethoven. Not every musician is a George Harrison. Not every scientist is an Einstein or Hawking. Yet from my perspective, each of those people was clearly acting under the energy of inspiration at various moments in their lifetime. Many writings are clearly inspired as well. These writings do not have to deal with cosmic issues or deep questions. Simple poetry or descriptions of beauty can help us all to access that place within ourselves where we feel connected to the creative energies of the universe.

The words found within these pages were written or spoken from a spiritual space. Does this mean they were inspired? Not necessarily. But if a song or painting or scientific observation of the universe gives your spirit a lift, then it is something that inspires you.

I hope you gain inspiration from the words within these pages.

The quotes on pages 6 and 9 are from the book, The Art of Peace by Morihei Ueshiba, the founder of the practice of Aikido. A very inspirational book!

Jeff Michaels

Table of Contents

1. The Balance 1
2. The Yin and the Yang 9
3. The Four Paths and the Four Paths 15
4. From Body to Spirit 21
5. The River 37
6. It is All New Now! 51
7. Enlightenment and Ascension 59
8. The Totality 67
9. The Principles of Love 85
10. Touch the Earth 91
11. Endings and Beginnings 107
12. Within and Without 123
13. Are You Prepared? 137
14. You Are Not Alone! 145
15. Source 151

1
The Balance
(Channeled at the Winter Solstice)

We begin with the phrase: As above, so below.

The Equalizing

Now it is a time for balance on the planet, an equalizing of the light and dark. From differing perspectives this means different things on this day and days like it.

From one side of the planet, it means a long period of light. From the other side of the planet, it signifies a long period of dark. Both perspectives are correct even though it is still the same planet circling the same stellar body. No one in the family human questions this balance.

The family human does question the balance in many other ways. It is because their perspective is not fully informed.

The physical universe, where you are, is always in balance. It cannot be otherwise. It may not always seem like balance to the separate particles. For some that are in motion, they may desire stillness. For some that are contracting, they may feel a need for expansion. For some that are divided, they may believe that unity is a better expression of balance. Sometimes a fluid situation may seem unbalanced while a solid situation looks, from a certain perspective, to be better. Yet motion is good, contraction and division of energies is often necessary, and fluidity certainly helps when motion is in order. This, then, is the balance of the way the universe exists. Not just the physical universe: as above, so below.

For the family human today, these moments in linear time, this point in history may seem increasingly unbalanced. You may feel that you are divided from many others, and you will be correct in that perception. You may feel that events are too fluid and that a wave is rising very high and very fast, and you will be correct in that perception. You may actually feel the fast motion of time and see, with a correct perception, that there is little time for stillness in the lives of most of the family human. You may sense that the energies of the planet are closing in around you and you would not be wrong from a certain perspective.

Your perspective, however, may need some adjustment and informing. For it is not imbalance that you sense, it is only that where you exist as a particle of the universal energy, there is a great deal of energy in a state of change.

We have spoken of the wave before and the need for balance. Too often, the listener looks outward for the balance. We have spoken before of the energy of manifesting. Too often, the listener looks outward for the energy of manifesting. Once again, we remind you that these energies, balance and manifesting, are inherent in the family human, to be found in plenty within the individual, the undivided one.

There is one more energy that we will mention at this time that is inherent within each member of the family human, the energy of health. We will speak on this at a different time. Know this now. The energy to heal yourself is within you all.

The universe is always in a mode of balancing. It is why the harmonic coalescence is now in progress. First there was division of energies. This is called the variance. Now there is a movement towards unity of the vital forces. It may not seem like it from your perspective because you may be holding on to an ancient thought. Let go now.

The Centering

For a time, there was stillness in the movement of the evolution of humanity, then rapid motion of which you are a great part. Soon, stillness, a form of peace will approach as you move towards a centering of energies. To use the word centering is to give a linear representation, as if things are in a line and there is a pendulum moving from one side to another. We remind you at this time that the universe, the whole universe, moves in waves.

For a time, there was a solidity of society and science in the family human. Look back on that time and you will fully appreciate the fluidity of your lives today. Solidity does not need to be repression and much that you do as individuals, undivided ones, will impact how the life on the planet, the vital force of Gaia, expresses itself in the near future. Choices were made in the past and new choices are now being presented. Make a new choice if you are unhappy with the results of the past. Do this first on an individual basis. Do not look outward, but inward. That is the best use of your personal energy.

Begin to cooperate with the contracting of energies. Pull this energy into your field and strengthen and manifest and balance yourself. Heal and be healthy.

Extension of your energies outward will not assist the balancing of the universe in your area of physicality. We are in a coalescing.

Stop being divided. Stop being apart from things that are real. By extending your energies into the artificial you are no longer an individual but have become one of the mass and you have no control over your own path. It may feel safe within a mass and that is correct from a certain perspective. It is not personal growth within the mass, only growth of the mass.

It is in this way that you can understand that these forces work together and at the same time. Divide yourself from the mass by uniting yourself as the individual. Divide yourself so that you may be undivided, an undivided one.

Contract your energies together so that you may expand them in a healthy manifestation of your life. It is no accident that the word contract has become so prevalent in your world at this point in time.

Solidify yourself so that you may flow where and when you choose. Move so that you may find stillness and peace, not out and apart from you, the undivided one, but within. It is there.

The balancing will happen. You will be balanced by the universe. You have a choice to cooperate with the balancing or not. We recommend cooperation, a joining together with what is real.

If you are in a mode of motion and making choices, you are in a cooperating energy. If you are in a mode of striving to maintain the status quo, you are boring the universal mind.

The best way to gain and maintain your balance is to be in appropriate motion. What is appropriate motion? Look around at the way the universe moves, in waves and in spirals. Are you lining things up in a row? Are you trying to exist in a straight line? Do you believe that the shortest path from point A to point B is a straight line? Do you believe that the shortest path is the best path? If a planet were to travel in a straight line, there would be no opportunity for consistent life and, if anything got in its path, there would be little to recommend being in that vicinity.

Are you trying to balance by being rigid and straight? What in your natural world is rigid and straight? Again, we say this often, listen and hear now, "Touch the earth."

The Balance Point

The planet is your balance point for you are of the planet. If you want a balanced life now and in the future, you must spin with the planet and her companion. Touch the earth and touch the moon. How does one touch the moon? With your light, your eyes, and your consciousness. There is too much that is artificial in your lives at this point. There are too many artificial issues and too much information that is not real. Take a moment and look at your word "information." Do you see it differently now?

There is too much that is called reality that is the furthest thing from reality. We have said, "Do not waste your words." This means also the words that enter into your consciousness and your field of energy, not just the words that flow from you.

You have requested balance. This then starts with you. You must center yourself. You must take the responsibility for that and only you. Nothing, not one thing in the material or spiritual universal energies can do that for you except you and that is the joy of humanity at this time. It is what we all have been learning while incarnate on the planet earth. Enjoy the balancing of yourself and you will feel the naturalness and ease of life.

There is one thing then that will assist the majority to regain and maintain balance. This will be difficult to understand for many and so the balancing for them will be done to them and not with them. Let go of the need for control. Pay attention to the words as we have stated them. There will be many who disagree. Do not waste your words.

We close now and give you these words that were channeled before and from a separate source.

> *There are eight forces that sustain creation:*
> *Movement and Stillness,*
> *Solidification and Fluidity,*
> *Extension and Contraction,*
> *Unification and Division.*
> *-The Art of Peace, Morihei Ueshiba*

It is with this thought then that we bring you balanced peace.

The Balance

- Begin to cooperate with the coalescing of energies. Pull this energy into your field and strengthen and manifest and balance yourself.
- Cease being divided. Cease being apart from things that are real. Do not extend your energies into things that are artificial.
- If you are in a mode of motion and making choices, you are in a cooperative energy.
- Touch the earth and touch the moon.
- Center yourself. Take responsibility for that. Only you can do that.
- Let go of the need for control.

The Question of Being Tested

There are moments in your lives when situations seem intent on pushing you to and beyond your limits of endurance. Once past, these same situations may appear to be lessons for you, even beneficial. The swifter we learn the lesson, the quicker we pass the test and ascend to a new level.

We do not look to the past and easily say, "Those things were for the better. I am better for those things having happened." It is an enlightened one that can speak those words about the most painful moments in their lives. It is an enlightened one who looks to things that others would avoid and welcomes them. Having passed the test once, the enlightened one fears not the test. It is not that they do not experience tests; it is that they move through them very easily and very quickly, for they know the path.

It is easy to act in a spiritual way while times are good. It is necessary to act in a spiritual way when times are challenging. There will always be tests when you seek to ascend.

2
The Yin and the Yang

As above, so below. We have spoken of balance and the eight forces that sustain creation. These are:

> *Movement and Stillness,*
> *Solidification and Fluidity,*
> *Extension and Contraction,*
> *Unification and Division.*
> -The Art of Peace, Morihei Ueshiba

Let us now speak of the two forces that are creation. You know them as Yin and Yang, and it is this designation that we use at this point.

It is no accident that you have assigned Yin as the first word. Yes, you, the family human, have chosen the order of the words and you did so in the past when things were closer to reality.

You have associated the word Yin with the feminine aspect, and, at the time of the designating, that was a correct perception. Now it is not. For your feminine elements of the human expression of the vital force have become weakened and Yin is not weak! In some cases, the feminine element has abdicated their role. In some cases, they have been subjugated and repressed. In all cases this has been the result of a choosing and now we are in an age when the fruits of the choosing are ripe for the harvest. It is a poor harvest.

There is not a thing to do regarding this because the physical past cannot be altered. There is an altering that is available, and it is the past of the mind, the emotions, and the thoughts. We have addressed this briefly before and will expand on it in the future.

Yang, the second term, is not inferior. Its placement is one of support. Yang does not suppress Yin. Indeed, Yin cannot be suppressed when it is balanced, and Yin and Yang are always balanced for they are the forces of creation.

It is not Yin and Yang that are out of balance in the universe and on the earth. It is the human element that is out of balance with the Yin and the Yang. Our voice has said that it is not more Yang energy that will save the world, but a raising of the Yin energy that will save the world. Let us comment on that statement, for it is correct from a certain perspective.

The "world" is not the planet, in this case. What is referred to is the event of history as it is happening. It is then, not history that needs "saving," but the place of the family human within the continued history of the planet. The family human cannot survive without a balancing, an *internal* balancing of the Yin and the Yang energies.

Yin is strength, a force of creation, but only able to create when appropriately balanced with Yang. Yang is strength, a force of creation, but only able to create when appropriately balanced with Yin. This means that for balanced creation, both forces must work in harmony and in truth they cannot work any other way. If the family human chooses to be out of balance in this way, then balance will be achieved by the universe and by the earth in another direction. If one aspect of the physical world rises, another will sink. Look to the waves of energy for the fundamental truth of this.

If an attempt is made to suppress Yin, to weaken the force, then an equal attempt to suppress Yang is also happening. You cannot separate the two forces. There is no dividing of this energy except in our thinking and our feeling. There is no real dividing of thinking and feeling, only the choice to be unbalanced.

The Choosing

The future of the family human is not one of certainty, yet that is not reason to become unbalanced in fear. It *is* a reason to become balanced in hope! The future of the family human is one of coalescing of energies. You are experiencing this now. A balance will be attained that either includes or does not include the family human and it is this critical time that you are in. The *probability* is that the family human will continue. Adjustments will have to be made.

Within the time of the coalescence is a time of choosing. If the harvest now is not strong, then let us not plant those seeds again. If perhaps the seeds are not the problem, then perhaps a change in the soil or the method of cultivation is in order. We tell you now that it is a combination of these elements. The seeds are the energy of the Yin. The soil and the cultivation are the energy of the Yang. The seeds must fall on fertile soil in order for growth to occur, and seeds must fall in order for the soil to sustain growth. In this way you can perceive that Yang is not always the seed bearer and Yin is not always the carrier of the growth. In this way you can begin to sense where the imbalance is in the family human and in yourself, the individual, the undivided one.

Where are you fertile? Where are your creative seeds? If these questions are difficult for you to answer, then ask them in this way. Where are you barren? Where in your life is there no fulfillment or growth? Answer the last two questions and then turn around to see the answers to the first two.

You may have to turn away from what is in your life and head in a new direction. This will stop many. Balance is best achieved through appropriate motion.

You are both Yin and Yang. If one is weak then also the other will be weak. It is so with the world today, the history of humanity as it is happening. The feminine cannot dominate and thus balance Yin and Yang, any more than Yang domination has balanced the history of humanity. Yin will rise and is rising. Will you allow it to rise in you? Not by being or becoming feminine, but by being Yin and Yang together, equal and united within you, the undivided one.

Now is the time of choosing within the coalescence. It is a time of individual choosing, a time of balanced choosing. Before you make the choice, be balanced. To gain and maintain your individual balance you must be who you truly are, not who the world wants you to be.

Ask yourself, are you part of a mass, a collective grouping following a specific thought and giving it reality simply by agreement? Yes, you probably are! Even if you feel that you have separated yourself from others, did you simply separate yourself into a smaller mass? This, then, is the way of the past.

In the future, the way will be one of individuals working in harmony. The division of humans into separate groups will be a study of history past, not of history present.

The life span of the individual human will increase. At the present moment, many of the family human will be alive to see the changes begin, though they will not continue in their current incarnation to see the changes through. Do not be concerned. You have chosen to be the ones who walk between these moments of history, these "worlds." In the linear future there will be a coalescing of the energies that are you in the present moment, as you hear or read these words. This is being accomplished by choice. Are you choosing?

Let Yin lead you and let Yang support the Yin. It is what was chosen in a more golden era. It is what will lead to the future and a balanced family of vital life of Gaia. In this way and only in this way can you have a positive effect on the future.

Fear and anger are Yin and Yang out of balance. When you next feel fear or anger ask, "What am I choosing?"

Peace and joy are Yin and Yang in balance.

Love is the word you have chosen for the energy of the universe, the true name of the Source.

We say to you again, listen now and hear with understanding, "Love and joy and peace."

The Yin and The Yang

- Where are you fertile? Where are your creative seeds? Where are you barren? Where in your life is there no fulfillment or growth? Spend more time creating.
- Are you part of a collective group following a specific thought and giving it reality simply by tacit agreement?
- Let Yin lead and let Yang support the Yin. This is balanced energy.
- Fear and anger are Yin and Yang out of balance. Peace and joy are Yin and Yang in balance.

3
The Four Paths and the Four Paths

As above, so below.

It is time for the lesson and the lesson is basic. There are four paths to the experience of humanity. They are the body, the brain, the heart, and the spirit. There are four paths to the experience of the planet. They are the earth, the wind, the water, and the fire.

The body experiences the earth. The brain experiences the air. The heart experiences the water. The spirit experiences the fire. To live as a human fully, you must balance each of these paths. To live on the planet fully, you must balance each of these paths.

How then do you balance a path? How is it that we say to you balance four paths? Again, it is not a linear path that we speak of, but a path of energies. When you are physically vital your thoughts are vital also. When you are emotionally strong your spirit then is strong also. You become physically strong when you touch the earth, feeling the gravity and magnetics and minerals and all that the earth has to offer in a physical way. You become mentally strong when you listen to the wind, the air, and breath of knowledge, of words that hold true worth. It is not words alone that make one strong; it is the balancing of the heart and emotions as they seek the waters of life, the flow of feelings and experiences that combine to grant wisdom to knowledge.

Walk in Your Own Light

The path to spirit is a balanced path when walked in light of creative fire. What then do you create? You create that which is the truth and that is you yourself and no other. Walk then in light and make it your own light that you cast. In this way, you dispel darkness around you and become a beacon for others. Do not give your light away, however, and do not allow any to simply follow in your light, for in this way, shadows are formed. Better for each one, each undivided one, each individual, to burn their own fuel and light their own path. In this way, the light spreads and all who light the way remain illuminated themselves. None need exist in darkness as they have in the past, for none need to rely on others and their dim, poorly fueled light to guide them through dark ages.

Neglect the spirit and the body will suffer. Neglect the body and so the spirit suffers also. Become not entranced with your own form. Become your form and in this way be an individual, giving equal energy to all paths. This then is not so difficult. Be near water and also land. These things carry a vibration and give strength in proper ways and freely if you only take the time. There is much water and also much land.

Sit quietly and still your physical form and let your breath regulate and your thoughts will follow. The calm and peaceful mind is not one that has ceased thinking. It is one that has begun to think purely and in concert with the heart. The mind that has ceased thinking is going to give off a poor-quality light indeed, for the fuel will not be refreshed and the flame will obtain little air and be unsteady and the flame of creation will gutter and flicker. This one will continually need to be re-lit and trimmed and more care will be taken to keep the light going than light will emerge. Do not waste your efforts on such a one.

Though you are still, you may be in motion physically, for it is a stillness of the spirit that we speak of, not stillness in the way you conceive from a human standpoint. It is stillness with depth. An energy that is reserved and balanced and prepared for any and all that might lie ahead. It is a constant power in place, and it is strength held quietly. There are some today who possess this stillness.

You may know these ones, not by what they say or do, but by the feeling of energies that spiral about them. They will affect you in each of the four paths and you will see your way clearer. It is not their path that you seek. It is not their light that will serve you. It is their teaching and their lesson that will guide you to your own light and your own path and your own teaching. They will not call to you to follow, nor will they ask you to lead. This is their first lesson. Heed it well.

Light a fire, a candle perhaps, or something small to cook or warm yourself, perhaps in a stone ring or bricked place with chimney and mantle. Let the light wash you and bathe you and let the warmth sink into your physical form. Grow into the flame and dance with your spiritual energies. Let the flame consume what is not necessary and purify your spirit. In this way, the elements shape you and you are a natural person. In this way, you become a walker of the four paths of humanity and also a walker of the four paths of the planet. A balance is achieved then and without effort, save for what is natural.

Perfect health is not the goal and perfect knowledge is not the goal. A perfect heart is not what you will be striving for, nor a perfect truth. Yet all these things will begin to be attained by the natural one and without seeking and without effort. Only by paying attention, only by awareness of the elements and the paths of the planet and the human experience will you create a place within your own existence for these things to root and to take hold and to grow.

Act in Your Own Life

Your humanness is not in error. Do not let any describe this experience as wrong or failed or weak. Do not listen to words that do not motivate you to these paths in balance. Do not ascribe to limits or disciplines that seek deprivation as a source of growth. Does that even make sense to you at any level? Why would you deprive your heart or your thoughts or starve your body for passing fashions of valueless perceptions that originate outside of yourself? Do not accept others' judgment of you and do not seek their approval. If you do, in this way you will have become one who follows another's light.

Shine your light and do not look to see who follows. It is not from outside that validation arrives. It is a life fully experienced that is a life validated. The judgment at the end is only yours. Do not pass from this life with regrets and in this way, you will be judged worthy. Not by others, but by yourself and no other. It is different from what has been told, but listen now with the heart while watching water.

Ask now if what you are doing is worth doing. This does not mean to indicate that all actions must be grand and noble. The simple act of drinking water is worth doing. Do so now and be aware, feel the worthiness. A moment of relaxing is also worthy. Stop now and take a quieting set of breaths, closing your eyes if only for a moment. Feel the worthiness. Raise your face to the light of the sun or the reflected light off the moon. Allow the light in to your skin and cells just for a moment. Feel the worth and the value of the light that is always around you.

Touch the earth and feel or imagine the spin of the planet and the flow of the force of the magnetic field. Balance yourself as you glide through the space around the star and through the dimensions unseen and unknown. Feel the energies that exist all around all the time and everywhere for everyone. Feel the worth and in this way feel your worth and your value. *This is a life well lived!*

Judge yourself then and if you do not feel the worth of your pursuits, if your flame is not burning steadily, take some time to gather new fuel, clean and pure, the fuel of a new thought or of a new experience or a new place or a new message. Release the old fuel, for what has powered us in the past may be spent and wasted. Release it to be filtered and processed and it may become valuable again, though not necessarily for you.

Do not judge yourself harshly, for that would be burning fuel for the past. You cannot cast your light backward into your previous life experience, only forward to light your way. The brighter your light, the farther you may see, and this is the secret of many sages.

We say these few things again and again. Touch the earth. Invite us to be your companions. Be aware. Increase your ability to respond. Do not waste your words. In all of your life seek to be loving, joyful, and peaceful.

In this we mean be active in your pursuit of peace, seeking and finding peace in everyone and everything. For if you can find it in others, it will be in you. We have found you and we can say with love and joy, that we see peace.

The Four Paths and the Four Paths

- Sit quietly and still your physical form. Let your breath regulate and your thoughts will follow.
- Light a fire, a candle, and let the flame symbolically consume what is not necessary to your life. Purify your spirit.
- Shine your light and do not look to see who follows.
- Ask yourself if what you are doing is worth doing.
- If you are not burning brightly, release the old fuel, that which has powered you in the past. Take time to gather new fuel: a new thought, a new experience, a new message.
- Do not judge yourself harshly, as that is burning past fuel.

4
From Body to Spirit

We open with our agreed upon phrase: As above, so below. We welcome you. When we speak as Onereon we speak as a group. We say Onereon means "together." You are Onereon, not that you are necessarily in agreement with the words that we are saying, but you are in agreement with purpose. You are in agreement with direction. You are in agreement with spirit.

Centering

We will talk now in terms of body. We will talk in terms of spirit. There are some on the planet now who are very body centered. They are oriented towards their form, their figure and their health, their muscle and their mass. They are oriented towards these things for a very specific reason, for themselves. They look to themselves to be centered in a very physical way. This is not wrong. Those that are body centered often times have a sense of spirit.

There are some that are spirit centered. Now what we mean is not that they are centered in their spirit, rather that they are focused on spiritual things. The parallel with the body centered and the spirit centered is that they begin to follow rules. For a healthy body you must be this way. For a healthy spirit you must be this way. With rules come lines. With lines there comes a right and a wrong.

Let us talk about right and wrong; there is no such thing! Everything is energy. If you are moving forward, if you are fulfilling your goal, if your path is strong, this is correct; you are living a vital existence, life, vitality. Health is not the absence of disease, but the presence of vitality. Health is not just physical; it is also spiritual.

Let us look at spirituality. There are those who truly believe there is a right and a wrong, that there is one way, and all other ways are wrong. They are not happy people. Only when they are surrounded by others who say, "Yes, we are right" do they approach any form of happiness. Even then it is not happiness; it is agreement. Agreement to what? Not to their own spirit, but to someone else's vision of what spirit should be.

In the same way that people discipline their body, sometimes to the point of starvations, deprivations, and physical pain, some people will discipline their spirit, by depriving the spirit, by causing pain to the spirit. Do you enjoy pain? It is not conducive to vitality. There are some things that are painful. We work hard to avoid those things.

Let us talk about heart. Let us talk about brain. Here is where pain happens. When we struggle with a right and a wrong way, we cause our brain much mental distress. When we alienate those that we love, when those that we love can no longer be around us because they feel they are right and we are wrong or we feel we are right, they are wrong, where does it hurt? In your heart, in the area of the chest you call the heart.

As above, so below. We are not creatures, in spirit, in the sense of a physical creature as you might imagine. It is a peculiar thing to the expressions and manifestations of life here on this planet that you envision us as human looking. Cats envision us in cat form. Dogs envision us in dog form. The human species is one of three that can really comprehend a difference, a way of existence that is not human. In truth, dogs think all other things are dog. Cats think all other things are cat.

In Spirit

In spirit we believe that the Source must look a lot like us. We are probably wrong. As Onereon we are closer to the earth. We enjoy the earth. We enjoy our companions on the earth. We too can feel grief. We too can feel mental distress. So, it is not without pity, it is not without sorrow that we look down on the shape of the planet today. We recall the times we were on the planet. We recall when we felt strongly. We recall when we felt right. This can still cause us some distress, even from our perspective as above.

We say these things to you now so that you understand that we understand. We have been there. We say these things to you now as well because we understand that there is a higher perspective, there is a purpose, and there is a point. We are fond of pointing out that there is no point, in that there is no linearity. When we say there is a point, we mean there is a reason. There is a reason for things to be the way there are. There are choices that have been made. Some of them have not been the wisest of choices.

Raising Consciousness

Humans were not a forgone conclusion as an expression of life from Gaia, any more than the destruction of the dinosaurs was a forgone conclusion, but for the experiment to work there had to be a level of consciousness rising and rising and rising. That is what we are doing now. The family human is well suited for this. Now, during the harmonic coalescence, more, more, and more, you feel and see the consciousness raised. More you see people coming together, not in agreement, but in spirit. There is still much that is old energy. There is still much that is the past. We invite you to look closely at what you believe. Is it truly what you believe, or it is merely what you have been told?

You each have companions, each one of you. As you pursue your spiritual paths, as you walk, as you move, as you maintain a vitality of the spirit, that is Onereon. That is the energy of being together.

You each have your own spiritual group, your own department, your own goals, your own energies, things that you have chosen to work on. You have each been guided in the past. You will be guided in the future. You will be guided in the future not as children, but as companions. We invite you to really, truly comprehend this.

What is Missing?

The hierarchy as above, so below: it is a poor analogy. We are not above you. We are with you and your companions are with you. They wish to be with you at a deeper level. Where you all are, each one of you reading this, is not as a child. You are not walking as a child in the spiritual realm.

You are walking as a mature being in the spiritual realm. The coalescence has worked well with each one of you. Each one of you has felt perhaps just a little bit of a loss, just something missing. The next time you feel that, the next time you are at that point, rather than hide from it, rather than close that moment off, embrace that moment. Feel that emptiness, feel that gap, feel that moment of "Where is mine?" and embrace it.

Here is an experiment. Here is an exercise. The relationship of life and water is unique on the planet earth. Your scientists are discovering that as they probe the solar system. There is indeed water out there in the universe and even in the solar system. Water on earth is unique in this way: life depends on water. Not all life in the universe needs water!

Next time you feel that moment of wanting, or find yourself asking, "Where is mine?" pour yourself a glass of water. Just before you drink the water, invite your spirit companions. You may have known them in the past as guides. You may have their names; you may have a vision of them. Let us tell you now, they may have changed. Invite your companions to join you in drinking the water. Some of us enjoyed water on the earth. There is no drinking of water in spirit. As you drink the water, enjoy it, taste it, feel it, change it, make it hot water, make it cold water. Invite your companions to be with you at that moment and sense the clarity of that moment and then remember that moment.

You are the Sacred Place

It is not necessary that you kneel in prayer. It is not necessary that you sit in meditation to be in touch with spirit. You are in touch with spirit all the time, because you are of spirit. Yes, you are on the earth. Yes, there is gravity. Yes, there are all of these things. Just chose a few seconds to be a sacred place in a sacred space. You are a sacred place. Say to yourself, this is my offering to the sacred space, the water, the moment of time.

Watch and feel and listen and learn how you are sacred in that moment, at that precise moment, and then always remember that feeling. Remember how it felt, and make that moment larger, larger, until you are living your life in that moment, when you are the sacred space, and you are not just physical but also spiritual at the same time. Your companions are around you and you know what to do. You are fulfilled. You are whole and holy. The future of the planet will be made of such ones.

The coalescence will continue, approximately one hundred more years. At that point in time, the population will be significantly reduced, but the quality of being will be holy. You are the beginning of such ones. This does not mean to remove yourself from all things around you. Holiness is not solitude. Holiness is being vital in your spirit. If you are not in perfect health in a physical way, you are still a vital individual, each one of you, an undivided one, and yet you let yourselves be divided. If you want to be holy become an individual, an undivided one, one that is whole. Growth is there.

It is no accident that you are here on the planet at this time. It is no accident your experiences in life. If you choose, *if you choose*, everything that came before can be someone else's history. In the same way, when a human passes and makes the transference to spirit and then from spirit back into the planet, you do not remember those times for a reason. Why wait to lose all of those memories and pains of the past? Lose them now, drop them away.

Become new. Become alive and vital and you will be new. Your bodies will show it and your heart will show it and your brain will show it and people will say there is something different about you and they will be right. Do this with caution because everything that you know may go away. There are questions?

When you say we have the opportunity to move away from the pains of the past, what is the procedure? If we chose not to have that frustration around us anymore, what steps do we take?

It is easy to not have the frustration by moving away from it. Would it not be better to have the frustration move away from us? And so, in this way, as you open yourself up, as you experience more and more moments of holiness, of connectedness with your spiritual companions, those things that do not vibrate with that moment, they will begin to go away.

We know about vibrations. We have spoken about vibration before many times. Let us speak about vibration once more. You know when you vibe with someone, correct? The terminologies that we use, vibe, vibrate; we know when we vibrate with someone. We know when that makes sense, our sense, our senses are in agreement. We know when someone does not vibrate with us. We know when their vibrations are not working with our own.

Increase your vibration. Increase the frequency of moments of spiritual pursuits, of holiness, of undivided individual activity, not seeking approval of anyone else and allowing others to not need your approval as well. Take away the judgment of right and wrong. Focus on your own vitality and watch how vibrations that are not in harmony with you go away. Those people will go play their song somewhere else, because you are not listening.

Frankly, many humans' vibrations are way too high now. It is important to remain grounded. We began by speaking about the body and the spirit, that there is no difference. The body and the spirit are the same. The vitality is expressed in these ways. So your body is also your spirit and your spirit is also your body. There is no difference. There is no line. Spirit is the higher vibration; body is the lower vibration.

Since I was a little girl, I believed that since we renew ourselves every seven years, there is absolutely no reason to age. Would you agree with that?

Yes.

Then how come we are aging and how do we stop?

Belief is a powerful thing. But the truth, and again we speak of vibrations, in truth, the vibration of the human body does, because of the heaviness, eventually come to an end. The higher the frequency of the spiritual, emotional, and mental aspects of the individual human, the higher the vibration of the complete individual, the undivided one. Thus, the longer their life and the healthier their life. Why? Because the physical vibration then is raised as well.

Look around you, look around at the humans now and look at the humans in the past. There were some that were very long lived. They were very concerned with the spiritual things. They were very focused on "what is spirituality?" Not what is right, not what is wrong, but staying in harmony with the earth, the cycles and seasons of the planet and understanding that they did not rule, they were caretakers. They understood their place. They accepted it and still sought to be spiritual beings, not animal.

You are aging because right now it is natural. What is viewed as natural has started to change. In many cases an individual member of the family human can look at their parents or grandparents and see that they are aging slower than their predecessors. The generations now look and act in a more youthful way than any generations in the last seven thousand years.

The human, the family human, are starting to really comprehend that it is not necessary to age, disease, and then die. There are experiments in place now that may get you to a point where you do live on. Then belief can change. From our perspective we understand death in a different way. Death is growth. You get to a certain point in your vibration, you have grown past that, and the body cannot go any farther. The vibration is just that much higher. We do not advocate anybody seeking that before their time.

You are correct about the seven-year period, but that is deeper than you know. There is a deeper change that goes on every seven years. Imagine that the human, the individual human, is one ripple in a wave and that every seven years the wave is somehow strengthened and new. It is difficult for you to understand this, because what you are thinking is that the ripple is an effect, the cause of something dropped in the water and the ripple moves out from that. How could the ripple then, be renewed?

In spirit, the renewal energies are always there. In the cycles of the seasons, the renewal energies are there. It is human, it is the family human, that have limited the renewal energies by believing that there is a death that is an end, by the acceptance of a lower vibration.

When you begin to understand death as a continuation, merely a moment in your path in the movement of the energy that had happened to coalesce into the form you are in now, you will start to understand the renewing of the wave and now other ripples, other waves, begin to cross your path. Some are ahead of you, and some are behind you, and some come from the left and some come from the right and in spirit we would understand that they come from the top and the bottom and sometimes from inside of us. They are not ours, they are not our energy, but sometimes there is something inside of us and we wonder, "what was that?" To renew yourself, understand that you do not stop at your skin and understand that you also do not stop at your DNA. The energy that is the individual human is a much grander energy. The energy that comes from inside is inspiration and is from the Source.

In spirit, we experience the cycle as well. The expression of the seven years is very interesting, because there is an echo. As above, so below. The ancients knew this. It is one of the things that will be discussed and learned within the next one hundred years. There is much to come out of Egypt. The cycles of sevens, it is a universal law. Change your belief, your believing that there will be an end. Very ingrained this is.

You had said when we are feeling like we are missing a part of us, to invite our spiritual companions in at that time, to drink water and to share experiences with us. Will that help to fill the space of what is missing?

It will make you aware of it. It will make you aware of the grandness. It will make you aware and give an opening for the space to be filled. When we say "water," it is because it is a constant in the family human. The search for water is a constant in the family human and it is the easiest thing for you to do to connect with where we, as above, feel emptiness, a desire, a need, a want.

It will show you that it is not a lack. It will show you that it is not something that is missing from you that makes you less. It will show you where you can grow and give you the potential for growth in a very specific direction. In this way, your spirit companions may be your spirit guides, but also you may be a guide to spirit.

It is easy to say this to any human, "I feel that there is something missing, do you feel that there is something missing within you?" Every human feels that. We are speaking specifically to you reading and hearing this because you have the opportunity and the potential to realize that it is a growth from within and not something that will be fulfilled from without. It is the growth of Source energies.

Many humans today would say, "Yes, I am missing something, if only I had something from without...." You here today are higher. We want to be careful with this, because that is not to say that you are better. Your awareness is higher, your frequency is higher. Find the areas that feel empty and view them as spaces available for growth, not from without but from within. There is much growth available.

Can you speak of the many varieties of techniques that are supposed to lead to enlightenment or healing or ascension?

There are so many words and so many techniques out there, are there not? Let us speak simply of spontaneous activation. Let us speak of epiphany and revelation. Let us speak of that moment of genius. That is that moment where somehow your brain is out of the way and the logic does not need to be there; you just suddenly know something. This can happen not just with knowledge but also with the heart. You just suddenly know someone is going to feel very good about you. This also happens with the body. Less and less with the body because the belief is that it cannot happen with the body and the vibration is lower than the heart and brain.

DNA can be sparked and changed in an instant, but you have got to get the brain out of the way, you have to get the heart out of the way, you really have to get the body out of the way. Miraculous healings, well, they are more available than humans can believe at this point. They are more frequent than believed.

When someone is activated on any level, it cannot simply be body activation or mind activation, it must be everything. When you feel that moment of genius, that moment of awareness, that moment of totality, wholeness, holiness, everything is out of the way. That is pure connection at the moment. You feel it through all levels of your existence at that time.

There are many words, many names for techniques. There are many discussions, and many people discovering many things. In many ways, this is still in infancy. Follow a path to the point of your own understanding, but be prepared to leave the path. There is much more to know. The trouble the family human gets in is sometimes they think that they know everything, either as an individual, or as a collective. They think they have got it all. That is when we like to show them something and they get to say, "I did not know anything." You knew a lot. You just started to think that you had found what is exactly right and exactly wrong.

It is a fun world, is it not? There is so much. When you are in spirit...We want you to understand something, there will come a point in time when you will be as above and we will be, as below. That time is coming soon, because there will be a great change. There are many on the planet who will reach a level of ascension and really be higher and we, who have gone through the filter many times, will return. We want this companionship to start now. The reason we want it to start now is so that when we are below and you are above, we are already talking. We already know each other. It will be so much easier for us then. Would you not like it if it was that way now?

The point of activation is as simple as this: agree. Simply agree. Agree to your path, whatever it is, however scary it might seem and watch how all the techniques suddenly seem as one technique and watch how all knowledge suddenly seems to be one knowledge. Watch how wisdom supersedes all words and your life starts in the direction that it was always going to go anyway.

I am getting this image of when things start to feel like a struggle, running into a wall, or I run into a person who does not feel correct, just to breathe, to stop, to breath in total God energy and not be concerned about the event? Is that sort of what you are saying?

Think of things in this way: the body moves like the earth; the spirit moves like water. So it is a difficult combination sometimes. Yet water continues to flow, continues to break down earth and eventually earth moves. When water comes up against something very, very hard, it does not stop, does it? It goes over, it goes around. It may have to stop for a moment, pool and collect itself, before it finds a path around whatever has stopped it. Find the path around. As it flows, it flows past without any judgment, without having to change the stone, without having to change whatever has blocked it, and the water continues to flow.

It has changed its path, but it continues to move in the direction that it is pulled by the force of the universe. When you run into something, when you run into someone who just does not want to get out of the way, you can spend much time pushing against. But againstness, that is not peace, is it?

Our voice has a saying, "Peace is not the absence of violence, but the cessation of againstness." Stop being against things, and you will find peace. Water does not think of itself as against things. Water thinks of itself as moving alongside, moving around, moving through. To act in a spiritual way then, you would not put yourself against anything but move through, move around.

Conflict is truly rare for the truly spiritual person. It will happen in the family human because of the vibration, because of the gravity. The family human, the planet earth itself, is moving toward a situation where the energy and the gravity will change. It has happened before. It has happened in the past, and now we are moving towards it in a way of consciousness, that the vitality, the life force of Gaia, did not possess the last time we went through this cycle.

Coming up against people there is a lot to be against, but only if you chose to say, "They are right, they are wrong" or "I am right, I am wrong." You just are. So, as long as you are not interfering or attempting to stop life, as long as you are promoting growth, you do not have to be against.

When someone is against you, move out of their way, because if you push back, then they can stand up. It you do not push back, then they can fall over.

We speak of peace, and yet you see people who say, "We want peace" that are very angry. How can that be, to practice peace and be angry, to practice peace and shake your fist? How can that be, to practice peace and violently protest? How can that be, to practice peace and hate someone for not practicing peace in your way?

Be peaceful within yourself first. If you are peaceful within yourself, then you are causing the wave and the wave will radiate out from you. Peace is *not*, not doing. Peace is active. So within yourself, *within* yourself, be peaceful. Release the need to be connected to other people's problems. Release the need to be connected to other people's issues. Release the need to be connected to other people. People will find you attractive because you have become peaceful.

So, we close with these words now, channeled words from before that we enjoy, words from another author, another channel from another time. Spirit is made manifest in the family human in this way. You will know someone is spiritual by the fact that they are loving and joyful and peaceful.

So find a way to love yourself, find a way to enjoy yourself, find a way to be at peace with yourself. All other things then fall into place. The most important things for you to do is to find love, find joy, and find peace.

From Body to Spirit

- Increase your vibration. Increase the moments of spiritual pursuits, of holiness, of undivided individual activity, not seeking approval of anyone else.
- Release the need to judge right and wrong.
- Stop being against things, and you will find peace.
- Focus on your own vitality and watch how vibrations that are not in harmony with you go away.
- Change your belief. Change your believing that there will be an end. Believe that you will continue.
- Be peaceful within yourself first. Release the need to be connected to other people's problems. Release the need to be connected to other people's issues.

5
The River

We say, "As above, so below." This is our agreed upon phrase to enter into the moment of lesson.

Tonight, we will speak about a river, for a spiritual life is like a river. When a river begins, it is not always obvious. When a river begins, it is perhaps a trickle, perhaps a bubble from the ground, perhaps it is a gentle flow from beneath snows and ice, but the river will always follow a course that is natural. Gravity will draw the river. The river will always follow a path of least resistance in a channel. The channel will broaden and increase and shift and it becomes the riverbed and the riverbanks until sometimes the river becomes very, very mighty, and far from the river source may empty out into a lake perhaps, a gulf, a vast sea, or an ocean.

At no time do we say to the river, "The water at the beginning, that was old water and at the end, that is new water and so that is better." We say the river is the river and the water flows from the source of the river to the outlet. We say the river is the river and sometimes the river is going south and sometimes north and sometimes east and sometimes west. We do not judge the river. The river flows.

We use the illustration of the river to describe the action of spirit. It is the most easily applied situation for the family human to understand.

Spirit Moves like Water

In the physical realm, water is the thing that most closely approximates spirit and spiritual energy. The action of water will give you many, many spiritual lessons. Now again, do not say "old water" and "new water" or suggest that the old water would be bad, and the new water would be good. Yet, this is what we do as the family human here on the planet, in speaking of life and of knowledge. There is a conflict that is in motion today. Here is our lesson. Strive to flow through the conflict without becoming conflicted.

For there is water and by water we mean knowledge. The old knowledge, when it began, began as a trickle and it obeyed natural law and it flowed in a specific direction, the path of least resistance. The knowledge built, and the knowledge grew, and the knowledge continued to flow from then until the present time. Now there are people who say that the old knowledge is the best knowledge. It was fresh when the world was young. There are people saying, "Yes, but that is the old knowledge. What is the new knowledge? The new knowledge, it is the best knowledge." In reality, all of the knowledge is coming together.

The struggle, the conflict, is when people cling to the sides of the river, and say, "This is the best place for the river to stop, for this is the best water." So, we have many beliefs, people who tried to stop the belief, to stop the knowledge, and they built huge dams and huge structures to hold the knowledge back, to gather the knowledge, and keep it and store it. What has happened to the knowledge? It has gotten stagnant. It has become water that does not flow.

Let Knowledge Flow

It is the nature of the family human to gather things together. You are shaped like that. Allow yourself now to relax and let knowledge flow through you. We say knowledge and we speak specifically about the brain. The reason there is so much distress of the heart is because there is so much activity of storing of knowledge and there is little activity of expressing the heart.

We speak again about the rising of the Yin and Yang energies. The heart is your Yin. The brain is your Yang. Together, acting in concert, they represent your mind. Again, and we have said this before, "Lead not with the brain, but with the heart." Let knowledge flow through your heart. In this way, the knowledge that rings true, the knowledge that is true to spirit will be filtered and will become a part of you.

There is no need to store spiritual knowledge. It is all around you. You are capable and able to pull this knowledge to you at any point. Are you willing? Or is it better for you, in your brain, to hold onto old knowledge. Is that safe? Is that secure? It is an insecure world and so, as the family human, you seek security, you seek surety. You wonder, what is it that will not change that I can cling to and be safe? We say, "Nothing." The universe is change. The universe is not a noun, it is a verb, and a human is not a noun. You say, "A human being." So be in motion, *be in motion*. Allow things around you to be in motion and follow the natural path and allow the river of knowledge to flow through your heart.

Renew Yourself

We say there is a conflict, and you can see it. Let us reduce the conflict. Let us take this example of the weather. Suddenly everyone is at the same place and saying, "global warming." Yet this has happened many times before. The planet warms and the planet cools and the planet goes through seasons. Things that will be recommended are things that would be best for family human to do anyway, so there is no need to struggle with this. Simply *do* the best thing for yourself. Human life is a renewable resource. Renew yourself!

Expend a little extra energy with your body. Take a little longer to walk. Spend more time, waste less energy. Gain the exercise. Gain the power. Gain the energy from the earth and leave the energy that is in the earth, in the earth. The earth itself needs the energy.

We say again: is it a question of saving the planet? No. The planet has taken much bigger hits than humans can possibly imagine. Yet here you are. The planet remains beautiful. Is this a question of saving the human race? Perhaps. We are here to say now that the human race has a purpose. The human race is not a sure thing, but the probability is high that the family human continues.

For your part, do not get involved in the conflict. There is no need to protest. There is no need to take great actions. There is need to take small actions that, by your example, show others the small actions to take. This is true not just regarding this issue of the warming of the globe. This is true in all cases. First, yourself and then, yourself.

Allow others to view you, not to follow *your* path but to find *their* path. There are moments when you reach out in support of others and if you spend all of your time supporting others, whence does your own support come? Does this sound selfish? Focus on yourself first and then when you are done focusing on yourself, focus on yourself. Yes. It does sound selfish.

We are not asking you to take from other people. We are asking you to live your life in a clean way. Does that mean you do not get dirty? No, we have often said this before, "Touch the earth." Get into the earth. Stand on the earth, take your shoes off, and put your feet in the sand, in the soils. In this way, you will draw energy that cannot be measured into yourself. The consciousness of the planet communicates with you in this manner. The consciousness of the planet communicates with you through touch. Many, many areas of the planet have been covered over, but it is not that hard to find some grass, to find some sand and to find the sea. Touch the earth in these ways and let the knowledge of the earth flow through your heart.

Bodhisattva: The Potential for Enlightenment

We will speak of the concept of bodhisattva. In the great religions there are these concepts. Bodhisattva becomes misunderstood. It means enlightened one, certainly, but it means one who has the potential for enlightenment as well. It means one who is becoming an enlightened being and thus is also a verb, a form of action. Bodhisattva is one who assists others to find their way in the dark. How? By being the light. Not by picking people up and carrying them, but by showing them right practice through their own life.

Be cautious now, because we are not recommending dogma, we are not recommending precepts, we are not recommending vows, we are not advocating a religion. We are speaking of a concept. There are stages of enlightenment. Bodhisattva is someone who is on a path of enlightenment, first. They are not necessarily enlightened on their entire path. We recommend this concept to you here today.

Look to things that are light in your life. Look to things that are right. Look to things that speak to you in a natural way and follow the natural course. In this way, your spiritual energy of the body, mind, and spirit will find its way and follow its own natural course and flow like a river. Recall when spirituality was a trickle in your life, something barely even noticed. As more tributaries add to the flow, you feel more and more spiritual and you flow not necessarily faster, but steadier, stronger.

In the end, the river flows into the sea. So at the end of a human life, spiritual energy then returns to the source, to the vast body of water and the river becomes an aspect of everything else. This is what your energy does as well. Not to return the same, but to be taken from the sea in droplets and molecules and brought up into clouds, filtered and transformed and brought back down to the earth like rain: purer, cleaner, and ready to form yet another river.

In the realm of spirit where we exist, we like the idea of water because we do not have water. Water is a particularly physical experience and unique. We have said this before and we will say it again, "There is water throughout the universe." You will soon be finding water throughout the universe and understanding that the uniqueness of the earth is not based on the components of the earth.

The work that we do with the earth, with the planet, is a filtering work. It is a cleansing of spiritual beings. It is an opening to new levels.

We say, "as above, so below" and again, this is not a hierarchy. We are not above you as though we are greater. We are you and you are us. In this regard as you return in spirit, you have a greater understanding and as you become the spirit guide, as you become the spiritual companion to those that return to the earth, enlightenment becomes easier and easier and easier.

Flow

The children being born today are remarkable. Their children and their children's children will be stunning. Yet, we have this conflict, *the old energy is good, the new energy is good, the old energy is bad, the new energy is bad.* Do not be conflicted, do not allow yourself to be drawn into these arguments. We say, "Do not waste your words." There are those that have their opinions. Do not waste your words. Live your life. What an amazing statement! Live your life. You know those that are not living their life. They come to you and they say, "I do not know what I am doing. I do not know why I am doing these things. I do this day in and day out, but it just does not feel like me." They are not flowing with continuous knowledge.

Age does not mean aging. Remember that. Time will pass; it always has. New things will be discovered; they always have. Do not assume that you know anything. For what you know may be correct today, but in a new light it may look different tomorrow. The universe is a verb, the universe is change. Do not bore the universe; it will change you. Flow with the universe: spin, dance, sing with the universe and watch the universe favor you and grant you energies that you cannot yet comprehend through science.

As for the old energies, do not judge them as wrong. We have traveled far and to navigate a river near the end, based on its shape at the beginning, is folly. The old dogma, the old law, the old scripture, from every religion, is just that, the trickle at the beginning. We are much farther along. Spiritual energy is much more steady and yet, less and less people have climbed into the river of spiritual energy. More and more attempt to cling to a side; this side of the river is best or that side is better, and judgments are made.

When we say go with the flow, we mean it. Release your grip, release your hold. Allow yourself to flow. It is not secure, but this is what the universe does. It is the natural way. Get yourself used to constant movement and your life will move. It is a wonderful, wonderful world and we have seen many of them.

We will say one more thing. The old knowledge is not based on all of the facts. The old knowledge is based on a pre-supposition. Information that is available has been bent and warped and twisted to fit a preconceived idea. It will not be long now before people will begin to re-imagine. They will look at old texts. They will look at old sites. They will look at older civilizations and begin to arrive at comprehensive ways of thinking that are fundamentally different and will not support old beliefs. We have said there is more to come out of Egypt. Egypt was larger than they know, and Egypt was an outpost.

Your science is not so far from spirituality. Are there questions?

The River

When you were talking about the river, about it being dammed up, about people clinging to the sides of the river, I had two images come up, one of the dams breaking from too much force up against it at some point in time and one of a large wave coming along and scraping people off the sides of the river. This would cause much chaos, but it is a way the energy of the blocked-up system would be changed. Can you address this?

There was a decision made. The prophesy in many cultures was one of destruction and an end of time. In the western traditions it was the prophesy of Armageddon. For some the Kali Yuga represented destructive situations. The vision of that energy was not wrong. The interpretation of that energy was one of destruction. The destruction happened; it was just not as chaotic. Look at your histories, look at your recent histories and then look back two hundred years. What person two hundred years ago could have perceived this way of life around the planet today?

A dam rarely breaks because a mass of water hits it all at once. It is a continuous flow of more water than the dam is able to handle. It is a wearing thin of the material. There are many concepts and ideas out there now wearing thin the material of some of these entrenched belief systems.

It is not that the new concepts are correct. They are expansive and they give people an opportunity to have a different point of view. The new concepts may be even less valid than the old concepts, but the validity that they hold is that they are making room for new ideas. The dams will come apart. They always have, they always will, and that is part of the coalescence because before things can come together, they must be taken apart.

There will be more things taken apart. This can be frightening, and we understand that. It is why we reach out now as spirit companions because when we are below and you are above, we want your close support, in the same way that we have agreed to this in the past when you were above, and we were below.

You said Onereon's purpose is to act as a filter for the planet. Can you elaborate on what you are doing with that please?
Our purpose is to communicate the filtering process. The planet itself is the filter. As we all come off of the planet there are experiences that we bring with us. We need to return people to the planet to filter some of those experiences because they have been severe; they have been less than spiritual.

This is part of the agreement. Rather than one large destruction many small things have happened. They look large to you but in the scheme of things, in the reality of things, these are many small things occurring all over the world rather than one large thing. Rather than start over completely with only a few survivors of a great catastrophe, is this not a better way? Yet still there are some who have died, who have suffered in great pains and great agonies. There was a better way for that as well, but the family human does have free choice.

We ourselves do not do the filtering. We assist in the bringing together of those as they return either to the planet or to spirit realm. We sometimes say, "hospice." Hospice on the planet would be helping for some to make the transition into spirit. Hospice, above, will be the same things but bringing them from the planet into spirit, making that energy, that being, feel more whole, more comfortable. Sometimes in hospice on the planet, it does not work well. There is denial, there is anger, and there is fear. There is no making peace, and when those ones come through to the realm of spirit there is still denial, anger, and fear. They return quickly to the planet then to complete a cycle that may have been interrupted or, let us say, "to take the test again."

Exiting the planet is not necessarily a bad thing, is it? How many of us have had those moments when we have said, "Why can we not just go home?" Your spirit guides say, "You are at home here on the planet." It is funny about life. In the spirit realm we say, "We really like the planet." On the planetary realm we say, "We really like spirit." There will come a time, and this is what we are all going for, when physical and spiritual realms are close once again. It is something we have enjoyed in the past. Now there is filtering work as we raise the vibration of the planet and allow the planet to raise our vibration as well. As Onereon we are together. That is what we do, bring people together, people of like thought and heart. We do not ask for agreement. We only seek to expand thought.

Has the Onereon energy incarnated and walked on this planet?

We use the term Onereon as if we are an individual but there are many. We are undivided in our purpose and that is Onereon, together. Our voice is fond of saying we are the human resource department and so we accept that because we care about the rest of the company. When benefits need to be distributed, we enjoy that part of our job, distributing benefits. Making sure that people have what they need when they need it. Yes, we have been incarnate, some of us will again, but as above so below, and we have addressed this before: there is an above for us and some of us will go above. We have felt the earth beneath our feet many times.

We come together as a group to assure that no one's individual agenda is too focused and to give a broad perspective of the realm of spirit but also from a broad perspective of history of the planet. We choose not to come as individuals on a regular basis in this format because then people begin to say things like, "Could that one particular person help me out. Could I pray to that one?" You have your companions, speak with them. They are not to be prayed to; they are to be lived with. So be together with your companions. Again, saying thank you for what you receive from the spirit realm is good. Then ask, "What can I do for you?" On the planet, you can still do things for your spirit companions. How delightful it is when you invite us to share a joyful experience: a sunset, a good meal, the light of a fire and, in our case, water.

We speak of these things now and there are very specific reasons that we do so. We do so to bring people back to basics, back to the trickles of the river's source, so that they can understand where they have come from. We remind you of the Source, but we also seek to elevate your sight so that you can see beyond where you are, so that you can raise your head erect and look out at the horizon.

There are times when things seem very, very close and feel very cramped. Those are the moments that we suggest that you drink some water. Tilt your head back with your eyes open and watch how earth changes to sky, to heavens and see that there is no division. In the future this is how we will live, again. It is not that far from where we are now. Communication with spirit is just this easy.

We spoke before of conflict and said, "Do not be conflicted." Look for areas that are light in your life. Look for the natural things, the natural flow. Do not be concerned with what others think about you. You are fine as you are. As you flow, you will go where it is natural for you to go. You will get there by not being conflicted, by not being divided, by being together, within yourself first. This is the time that you find those qualities that we always close with…

Find joy. Begin to enjoy your life.

Find love, though first you must love yourself for no one can love you and fulfill you without that first.

We say, "Peace." Peace is not something we fight for. Peace is not something we strive for. Peace is something that is in existence. We step into peace, and we exist in peace. So now we say to you, "Step into peace."

The River

- Lead not with the brain, but with the heart.
- Be in motion. Allow things around you to be in motion and follow the natural path. Get yourself used to constant movement and your life will move.
- Touch the earth and you will draw energy that cannot be measured into yourself. Touch the earth and let the knowledge of the earth flow through your heart.
- Saying, "Thank you" for what you receive from spirit is good. Then ask, "What can I do for you?"

6
It is All New Now!

As above, so below. This is our agreed upon opening and we welcome you. To have an agreed upon beginning is comforting and indicates that what is to follow is something that in some way is familiar. Our presence is familiar to you, but our words, our perspective, is new. In this way, the agreed upon phrase is also an entrance into something unique. We take a moment to talk about this as an entry into a lesson for you.

Your Unique Perspective

Humans look at things from their experiences. Their personal perspective is unique. In this way history and stories take on importance, for it is a way for the individual human to learn from other's experience and thus not make mistakes that others made, or to choose to take an easier path to a goal. The communal experience of the family human then takes on a perspective as well and you begin then to experience an agreed upon reality. That reality, however, is often based on what has already occurred and leaves behind the possibility for something new to occur. In this way, the family human finds that they are often expecting the past to happen again.

As members of the family spirit, we also have a unique perspective and, from the point of view of the family human, it seems to be the superior one. We will not say that it is equal to the perspective of "as below." We will say that it is true that we see farther from our vantage point. We see the past. We see the future. From the standing point of the individual human, this must seem like a blessing and something to strive for. In this way, you call on us as guides and angels and seek the answers for questions and concerns. In so doing, you seek hope for the future and forgiveness for the past.

Path and Destination

Imagine that you are standing on the earth, and you are on a path. You have a choice of looking forward or of looking back the way you have traveled. Doing either of those things is not right or wrong, it is just something to do. What you cannot do is move the path behind to become the same as what is in front of you. You cannot make where you have traveled into where you will travel. You can turn around and go back the way you came, but even then, this will not be the same experience as the original journey. Now, hills that you climbed upward become slopes you must descend. Your original goal recedes, and your beginning becomes your new destination. Where you have come from becomes where you are going.

When you arrive, it may be familiar in shape and structure and in the people that are there, but there are differences. The people have continued without your presence and have changed things without your knowledge or input. Life there has continued without you. Your perception may be that it is the same, but the longer you have been away, the more changes you will notice. Your original goal is now the same distance away, yet farther from your unique perspective, for you were once closer and turned from the path.

Imagine now that you did not turn from the path, but merely glanced behind and continued on your way. In the glance, you may have taken your eyes off the path in front of you and in this way some small thing may have caused you to hesitate in your step or stumble a bit. Yet a glance does not take you from the vision of the path ahead for long.

At the end of the path, you do not expect to find the place you started from. It may be similar and there may be people that are in familiar positions and accomplishing familiar tasks. There may be structures and housings dedicated to the same purposes that you have experienced previously, but these things are not the same. You expect something new and that is why you have chosen to make this journey.

Vision and Future

Here in the spirit realm, we see the past and we see the future and they are not the same. We tell you now, your vision of the past as it has been handed down to you is in error. In this way, you look to the future thinking that it may be a certain way, similar to the past that you have been taught. We say again, there is more to your past, dear human, than has been revealed to you. It is not a case of purposeful hiding. It is a case of acceptance of a point of view that is invalid.

Time has lasted much longer, and civilizations have been in existence for greater periods than an artificial history has indicated. It may not be civilization as you expect it to be, for the way that you have created reality for yourselves today is based on an imagined right way of living. It is with regret that we say that you may not find any trace of the previous civilizations. Time has passed and the earth changes. In this way those that lived very naturally with Gaia have accomplished their purpose in returning all they used back to the planet. It is a lesson that you must and will learn again.

We see the future and it is not as you might expect. The agreed upon reality can only exist as long as you all agree. With your own eyes, you can see that this agreement is breaking down.

Turn your vision now from the past and the histories that some are trying to defend and make the future. Turn your personal sight forward and raise your eyes to a new level. Do not seek to make others turn their sight or change their vision; do this for yourself and only yourself. If you begin looking with intent elsewhere, then others will notice and wonder and make a choice to look in a new direction or to remain fixed on the old. It is their choice to make and also yours. If you begin walking in a new direction and towards a new vision or goal, others then have a chance to realize that there is something more out there than what is past. In this way, your vision can change the world and in no other.

Spiritual Explorers

Look at the future as if it is all new. This is not a safe or comfortable way of moving forward. If you think of the pioneers and explorers that roamed the earth and seas, they did not know what was ahead. The only thing they knew was what they would need for their personal comfort and survival. They took along the necessary tools to catch, hunt, or grow food, but they did not always know what or even if there would be anything to catch or hunt or even if the ground was tillable soil. They took their chances that things would be familiar and in many cases they were correct. But they did not know. They also did not take everything with them, but only what they could carry. They left many things behind. They were self-reliant.

It is not just land and sea that is something to be explored. It is also the mind, the emotions, and the logic. It is also the spirit, your connection to the Source. This is what many of you are: spiritual pioneers and explorers. In this way, you must turn to face the future. You must be prepared to leave things that are not necessary behind. Old concepts may have been useful in the past, but to cling to them now may prohibit your forward movement. You must walk farther than you have traveled before. You must keep your own balance and carry your own load. It is what the new ones are doing, and it is what you can do to advance in spirit.

We tell you now that it is all new! We have been your guides in the past and we continue to be your guides. We remind you now that guides do not carry the explorer. The explorer must walk their path and the guides walk with them. In this way, guides become companions and that is one thing that the future holds for us all.

Old Ways and New Light

The family human is capable of so much more than what has been taught to them. The civilizations of the old ways had much more freedom in their ability to communicate.

This ability has not been lost; it is merely unknown and untrained. Children retain this ability naturally and mothers can sense and feel this communication. It is soon trained out of the new human and so it is diminished or lost. The next generation and the next will carry this ability strongly and you are already seeing evidence of such ones.

Some will ask, "Should we then seek to learn and follow the old ways, the old paths?" We say now that the old ways are not new, and their validity is diminished by what is available to the family human in the present moment. It is not that they are wrong ways; it is that they are not in the current of time that you are existing in now. To look back at the old ways is to look back at the past as if it were the future. What is true and valid from the old ways is still true and valid and must be learned in the light of the present moment. What is natural now is not always what was natural then.

Energy has shifted and the darkness experienced in the written records is no longer capable of existing. New light is shining, and new ways are available. It is not that you need look to angels or guides for hope in the future. It is to yourselves that you must look, for hope is a human quality and an aspect that is intrinsic to the earthly experience.

We invite you now to look, not to the deeds that are written, and not to the faulty interpretations of what is absolutely right and what is absolutely wrong. We invite you instead to look at the planet and the patterns of growth and cycles of seasons and rebirth and seeding. We invite you to look at the harvesting of fruits and vegetables and witness the patterns. We invite you to observe the regularity of times and the passing of time and also note that nothing remains the same.

It is All New Now!

It is the way of all things, matter and energy and life, to follow the same patterns. The sooner we all comprehend this, the sooner we will begin the coalescence of the universe. There is enough time for that. Remember that every day is new and every day you are new. Manifest yourself into that day and the coming days in accordance with the patterns of growth. Create yourself from hope. In this way, the truth of the future will be one that is agreed upon in the essence of hope.

We remind you now that hope will lead you to love. Love will lead you to joy. Joy will lead you to peace.

We see the future and in it we see peace. So you, too, seek peace.

It is All New Now!

- Turn to face the future. You must be prepared to leave things that are not necessary behind.
- You must keep your own balance and carry your own load.
- Remember that every day is a new day and that every day you are new.

7
Enlightenment and Ascension

As above, so below. We enter into this session knowing that there are many who are seeking spiritual enlightenment and there are many who are seeking to ascend. We welcome you all with love in these endeavors and offer you guidance along your way.

It is a human path you are now on and so we encourage you to enjoy the physical beauty the earth has to offer. You are one of those beautiful things. It is a part of the human experience to seek spirituality. It is as necessary as water to the individual human.

Enlightenment and ascension are not physical goals, but spiritual paths. They are in the linear future for many members of the family human. If it is your choice to approach these qualities sooner, then our words will be of benefit. There are three ways for a person to move towards the future.

Looking Back

Many try to move to the future by looking backwards. They are concerned with their past and how it has shaped them. They seek first to rectify errors or misjudgments or karma from lifetimes ago. We say now that this way is filled with many stumbling blocks. As you walk forward, things that are natural and normal along your path are unseen and unobserved because you are focused not on what will be, but on where you have been. This is not as important as you may think.

The acknowledgement of the past and the acceptance of it is a step that you can choose to take in your search for ascension and light. To focus on the past for too long will lengthen your journey.

We do not say this is right or wrong. We point out the reality of walking without watching where you step.

Looking Ahead

Some attempt to move to the future by looking far ahead, seeking answers to questions before they may arise, seeking to see the end without taking the journey. They study and learn and prepare before they even stand up to take a step. In this way many will walk past them on the path to ascension and enlightenment.

Some will stop and ask questions of these ones who are studying. Some will greet the learner with enthusiasm and the learner will feel good about the learning. Some will stop and join the learner and then others may also stop. In this way the path becomes blocked and narrow and difficult to navigate for those who choose to continue to walk. Many who are looking backwards will stumble upon these ones and some will stay with those seated at the point of learning.

We do not say this is right or wrong. Some learning is valuable. When a person has learned all there is to know they must still walk a path.

Amongst these ones you will also find those that seek to know what cannot be known. They seek to see the future and know what is coming. They sit quietly and look far. From their perspective on the ground, they may see distant events, but also from their perspective they do not comprehend what is before and what is after the events they see. It is like seeing a mountain on the horizon. If you make the mountain your goal it is easy to move forward to that end. What is unseen are the valleys and deserts that may lie between you and your goal. Some looking ahead is valuable.

Looking at Your Own Path

There are those that search for enlightenment by walking a path. They see that ahead there is light and so they take a step. They are like the flowers that grow by following the sunlight.

There are those who search for ascension by raising themselves up and walking a path that has a higher perspective. They do not get involved in the events around them by saying they are for something or against something. They observe as they continue to walk and in the observing they learn what is constant and what is of true value. In this way they are a learner and also a teacher for they offer an example of one who is not to one side or another, but is in the center, a centered being.

They do not seek to ignore the past. They also do not seek to defend or repair things that are long ago. They accept that they have been born into this life. They take what is around them and create the best thing they can at that very moment. They do not attempt to carry what they have created, for then they would have a load and possibly a burden. What they have created is of the moment and when the moment has passed the creation is now the past. They do not burden themselves with the past.

Learning of their surroundings, they understand that if they move farther and away from where they are they must learn new things about new surroundings. In this way they do not study observations of the past to the exclusion of the experience of the moment.

They look ahead only as far as they can reasonably see, noting the horizon for any peaks, but keeping an eye on the path directly ahead of them. In this way they avoid stumbling and crowds that may limit their progress. If they come upon an area of the path to enlightenment that seems to be blocked by throngs of people, they may choose to take a side path or avoid what is holding others in place. They may also choose to join for a time and stay at the periphery. In this way they may gain some knowledge and yet not be caught in knowledge's net.

The future is important to this one, but they are willing to arrive at the future by moving forward and experiencing it in due time. Without thinking about it they are gaining the wisdom that they will need in their future incarnations. In this way they start out ahead of where they may have begun.

Their path is the same in many ways as all others, yet by keeping a clear sight and straight vision they avoid what will halt others' progress. They will seemingly be on a smoother path. It is in this way that an undivided one may move forward swiftly.

The future will arrive regardless of what you do. It is in this moment that you prepare for the future, and it is only yourself that you can prepare. Seeking to change what is before is an exercise and you will become known as one who lives for the past if you choose to do this often. Looking to the see the future is an exercise and you will be known as one who sees only what might be. Upon arrival, a mountain that is smooth in the distance is still a rocky climb. The sooner you get to the mountain the sooner you begin to ascend.

We speak of these things as a linear path and as one who lives in gravity you exist in linear time. Spiritual paths are best pursued outside of gravity, but this is not always possible for the family human. We now give you guidance in the pursuit of ascension and enlightenment.

Enlightened and Ascendant

Enlightenment is not the gaining of light. It is the allowing of light to enter within your life. To focus on darkness, your own or others, past or present, is to limit light within your own spirit. Judgment of right and wrong is a way of focusing on dark things.

Ascension is not something you achieve with effort. It is the releasing of all that holds you to the earth. This is not the releasing of all material goods. Some have followed that path and that is not right, and it is not wrong, it is only not necessary. To release what truly holds you on earth you must examine the thoughts and emotions you carry in your mind. Are they necessary or are they old stories of a life that only exists in the past? Releasing is not forgetting. Releasing is looking ahead without looking behind. It is experiencing things in a new way. It is a re-examining of life as it flows through you. It is growth.

Learnings have value, but can be a trap that holds you in place. Looking ahead has value, but can give a false perception of the future. What you see may be changed by the time you arrive.

The light is around you now! Open yourself up to it and feel it flow through you and carry you along your path. Let the light dispel dark areas of pain and fear that exist in your mind and allow the release of these thoughts and emotions to lift you higher.

In this way you shine light farther and help to enlighten the world around. You become a beacon for others to see clearly their own path. It is not for them to follow you. It is for them to also become beacons. You become light and in the becoming you ascend. Enlightenment precedes ascension.

Seek light. In the finding and following of light you will find your existence gaining balance and, in the balance, you will find the ability to love freely. If you are loving, you will be loved.

Seek light. In the seeking you will leave behind the things that pull others to one side or another and in this way, you will feel peace. Peace is not against anything or anyone. Peace is energy for growth.

Seek light. Feel love. Seek peace.

Enlightenment and Ascension

- It is in this very moment that you prepare for the future, and it is only yourself that you can prepare.
- Seeking to change what has gone before is an exercise and you will become known as one who lives for the past if you choose to do this often. Looking to see the future is an exercise and you will be known as one who sees only possibilities.
- Open yourself up to the light that is around you now and feel it flow through you and carry you along your path. Let the light dispel dark areas of pain and fear that exist in your mind. Allow the release of these thoughts and emotions to lift you higher.
- Enlightenment is allowing light to enter within your life. Ascension is the releasing of all that holds you to the earth.
- Enlightenment precedes ascension.

The Question of Enlightenment

Enlightenment is what many seek and yet few find. There are many paths to become enlightened. One is the shortest of all.

When you ponder enlightenment, often there is an image of one sitting very still. This is the one that can still their mind, the one that can quiet their own thoughts. This one remains calm of heart. This is the one that now communes with spirit. It is not that spirit is somewhere and they go there. They sit and spirit is there.

It is not necessary to be completely still physically. It is only necessary to realize that stillness will allow you to be enlightened. Be still in spirit and learn that you are already in light. There is no need to go or do, only to be and allow your own light to grow.

8
The Totality

We now enter with our agreed upon phrase: As above, so below.

We will begin by talking about a totality. We will speak of the globe first. The planet which you live on, the living planet Gaia, is where your vital force comes from. There is a level of energy about Gaia that translates into life. So the reduction of some species and the rise of the human species, the increase of the population, that is just the balancing of the vital force of energy.

We want you to be aware of this because some are concerned, deeply concerned, that some species will completely die off, will completely go away. Let us say now, that is possible. It has happened many times amongst the histories of this planet, but as the population of humans begins to coalesce, and quantity becomes quality, we will see how the vital energy then returns to other forms of life. These energies then begin to spread out once more.

The interesting thing about this totality, this vital life force around the planet Gaia, is that life continues to find a way to be different. Now, diversification of species, that is a given in most halls of science. What scientists do not question is why the human being, the members of the family human, have not diversified but have, in fact, gone the opposite direction from diversity.

We say that it is part of the experiment of the earth. The human has a consciousness, an ability to grasp concepts beyond simple life, simple living, simple vitality. The human has the ability to explore, to advance, to understand and to categorize. The human has the ability to delineate, to create separates, and to understand that some things belong here, and some things belong there.

As the coalescence energy continues, what we will see is less of a need of categorizations and more of an understanding of systems. In this way, many in the spiritual communities are far ahead of the field because of an awareness of the field of energy. It is a joy to you to be in this energy, to really understand this and to really feel the waves of the field of energy.

Let us talk about separates for just a moment. If you were to look at human-made representations of the planet, the living planet, you would see lines and squares. You would see two points, one at the north and one at the south, the north magnetic pole, and the southern magnetic polar region. The northern magnetic area is what allows the family human to draw lines on the planet and then say, "This direction and that direction and another direction."

The compass always points in one direction. You do not always follow the compass, but you use the compass for guidance. Despite the fact that it points in a single direction, you have a choice of what direction to take, of what direction to travel. By using a representation of the planet, in many ways you do yourself a disservice. You do not see the planet as a whole, you see it as separates, and you begin to think that the planet moves in a very specific, orderly and perfectly regular way around the sun.

What you fail to understand by looking at the representation is that the sun also moves. It is said everything, everything, everything in the universe spins. From the largest cluster of galaxies to the smallest subatomic particles and even below that, everything spins. But in truth, everything spirals. For as the sun spins and the earth spins about the sun, the sun is moving in an orbit around something you have yet to discover. The sun is being affected by things closer than you currently know.

The spiral is the nature of the galaxy. The pattern of the spiral is set because it is natural. You can observe this in things as simple as a shell. You can observe this in things as simple as a flower. But because you have a north pole you think that there is a point, and you think that point is somehow stable. This begins to affect your lives. You look for the north pole of your life, the constant of your life as you seek to create constancy in your life. This is not right; it is not wrong. But to seek to create a constant slows down growth.

Growth and the Cycles of Seven

You will grow, that is the law of the universe. You grow in these ways. You grow in body. The human, the undivided one, the member of the family human, grows very specifically and there is a lesson in the way the human grows, from child to adult and on to its passing. Let us tell you now that you do not begin as an embryo, and you do not end in a graveyard. This is matter and matter returns and matter transforms. But the energy, the spark of you that is part of the great experiment, is part of the vital force of the planet, the living planet.

Your experiences here are very specifically designed and they correspond with the spiral. They also correspond with the cycle of sevens. The cycle of sevens can be observed within your lives by observing seven-year cycles. The cycle of sevens is specifically tied to the star, the solar energies. It is not the same cycle for each person. Your cycles of sevens began based on when you were conceived. Events in your life and events around you can shift and alter the cycle. Something tragic, something extremely happy, can shift your cycle of seven. Look back to the last very important thing that happened to you and begin to note from that time the cycles of seven in your own lives.

The earth moves and the sun also moves and so the earth is never again in the same spot. You can never return. You can never go back. That also is part of the lesson of physical matter of the universe. There is a direction to travel and there is a reason for that direction. That is the matter of things. That is your body.

You grow also in the emotional and the mental realms. If you are a balanced spiritual person, your mental and your emotional growth are equal. If you are a balanced spiritual person, your emotional growth leads your mental growth. In other words, you follow your heart, but you keep your brain involved. You let your brain structure your heart's desire. How much fun is that! And how different then, from those who say that there is a law and there is a rule, and they give numbers to the rules, and they give numbers to the laws. Follow your heart. Your heart does not have numbers. Your brain has numbers. Follow your heart and find freedom. It is within your heart that you really truly find the cycles of sevens.

Let us talk about your spirituality, for this is the third way that you grow. Your spirituality must be forward moving. We say forward very deliberately. Source is constant and, in this way, you can use Source as your guide, but Source is constant in a tricky way for the family human to understand. Source's constancy is constant growth and constant change. You can be connected to Source, and you see change is indicated in your life. For you to seek permanency is a way for you to seek disconnection from Source. This does not mean you have to abandon your home and roam the world. No, what this means is continue to seek new spiritual thought, things that may be difficult for you to understand. Do not hesitate to look at the old spiritual thought but look at it with new eyes. Perhaps there is a different interpretation on old spiritual thought. They may not have been wrong. They may just not be applicable to your world today. Let us tell you now, they are not.

Old Thoughts

Old spiritual thought was valuable for the time in which it was written. Look at how old spiritual thought is currently transmitted. They put numbers in it, chapters and verse. Now what are we doing with old spiritual thought when we number it? Are we making it something for the heart to access or something for the brain to access? We have made it something for the brain to access and then the brain must try to prove a truth. In this way we prevent the heart from accessing the truth because there are numbers. It is a disservice to the old spiritual thought.

There are those, and they are many, who are still trying to build on old spiritual thoughts. What we mean by this is not what you may think. There are those in the leading spiritual community today which you would call the metaphysical community who are still attempting to prove the rightness or the wrongness of those who have written spiritual things very recently in linear time, the twentieth century. We want to be clear. We are not saying that this spiritual thought was wrong. We are saying that it was correct for the moment of perception at that time.

The energy of coalescence is one of bringing all of these thoughts together, not as a dogma but as the feeling in your heart. Bringing these things together not as dogma but as freedom to access Source and to filter yourselves into a purer access of Source. It may seem obvious to those that hear these words. There are many defending old thought, as if they found the one single thing that connects to Source.

It is our understanding as Onereon that the coalescence is a model and these times of bringing the family human together are a symbol of what is happening on a larger scale of time as Source brings Itself back together and takes all of the disparate experiences and energies of you, you, and you, takes all of those things back into Itself and then continues to create in infinite ways. Source creates.

Essence and Ascension

Let us talk about passing. When a creature, a being, a part of the vital force of this planet passes, the essence of the creature also returns to the energetic level of the planet. That has been the past model. Life returned to the planet. When the earth was chosen to experiment, to test things out, to be used as a filter for energies, spiritual energies, more vitality was brought to the earth. However, this vitality could not remain in physical form indefinitely while on the earth. Thus what happened to dinosaurs, they returned to the earth. What happens to humans, a portion of them returns to earth, the obvious portion. But the unobvious portion, rises, ascends. This is much on the minds of people these days, ascension.

We do not ascend, we become. In the same way that a child does not ascend into adulthood, the child becomes the adult. The family human does not ascend, the family human becomes. Becomes what? Becomes spirit. It is then the spiritual being's decision to go back down, to return to the planet. Remember that we are saying up and down, as above so below, not as a hierarchy but as a vibration. We decide while still in spirit form to lower our vibration until we solidify on the earth. That vibration, and you feel it, you feel the vibration, it feels a little trapped sometimes in that corporeal form. You feel if you could just meditate long enough you could release and you can, but after meditation and deep prayer you must come back to your physical incarnation.

There are some who have chosen not to return in the human form. There are also some that have chosen to return in an animal form. We are conscious of using the phrase animal. We must remind our audience, the human is also an animal, but an animal with difference, an animal with consciousness. You have noticed, have you not, a rising of consciousness within the animals. Some have noticed it within the horses; some have noticed it in the elephant. Many feel it in the dolphin and the whale. It is even true with the smaller creatures, the cats and the dogs and you know it. You have seen it. You have seen the dogs that are simply dogs, but you have also seen dogs that are conscious of their spirituality or are conscious of your spirituality and in this way you make conscious connections on a spiritual level, even though you are individual animals together on the planet.

You are an Integral Part

You come to the end of a life, and it seems that we can mark it and see a direct path, but really there are a lot of spirals in that path, there is a lot of growth. That seven-year cycle continues and continues, and it does not stop at the end of the mortal form. It continues on as you become Spirit. Why do we bring this up? Because the coalescence is important. You are here because of the coalescence. You are part of it, an integral part of the coalescence. We say that because there are some humans who are not. They are all part of it, but not integral. The bringing together of energies that you represent; it is something that you chose to do. This is why we encourage you to look at your seven-year cycles.

You will return to spirit. As Onereon we prepare this. We are among the ones who welcome those in. When one being of consciousness returns to us, it is joyful. But every reaction has an opposite and equal reaction and so the joy that we feel, the opposite reaction is the grief that you have at the loss of the one that you loved. The loss of one that you loved; it does not hurt in your head; it hurts in your heart. Even if you know intellectually that life continues, even if you have a faith in this, where does it hurt? Your spiritual connection with this other consciousness being has been pulled from you. This is not a permanent thing. There is no such thing as a permanent thing. The loss of love, the energy of the universe, the thing that powers us, the Source as it is represented through the energy of love that you have lost, you feel the grief of being separated from the Source. We say again, it is not a permanent thing. Lost things can be found. Are there questions?

You mentioned the earth as an experiment? Why?
So the humor is, why not? It is not the only experiment. There are other things happening throughout the galaxy.

Let us address that for just a moment, not to avoid the question but to say that it is our understanding, our perception, where we are at this present moment of the connection we have to the planet, we feel that within the next one hundred years this experiment here will be strongly connected to other experiments throughout the galaxy. That connection has already happened. It has already begun, but it is difficult because of the perception of the experiment here on the planet. Now, you are looking for things to be like you and to look like you. It is not that way. The difficulty also is that there are many out there who are not being truthful about their experiences. They are manufacturing experiences and selling them as real.

Begin to remove the model that all of the experiments throughout the galaxy are going to look like matter or human form, or even human thought. The connection is begun in the hearts and in the spirituality. We are not talking about ourselves here. There is life on other planets, and it has been going on longer than the planet earth.

You ask why. The universe is an experiencing universe. It is creative energy. So why do you experiment with things? Why do you change the color of a room? Why do you change the style of clothing or hair? You want things to appear differently. You want to see how things look from a different point of view. Now here is where an old way, an old spiritual path, is truth. The universe is trying to see things through different eyes. Source is an experiencing energy. It wants new things to love. Family human and family earth is something to love. How do you use this information? By loving the planet earth.

There is great concern about the earth. Will the earth survive? Let us tell you now, yes. We have said this before; it is not the planet that is in danger. It is not even life force that is in danger. It is the forms of life that are in danger, but this too is an expression of the energy of the coalescence. There is a great movement; you call it "green." This is not a movement that needs to be against anything. We caution people for taking action against things. We say take action for things. Begin with yourself. Begin with your home, with what you buy, what you own, what you throw away. You are integral to the coalescence and what you do has much power if you simply do it as an individual.

Why the experiment? Love. More to love. More to create. The energy of the universe is a creative energy and so if it is going to experience things it must create things to experience. Would you say that this is a planet with many wonderful experiences? There is a lot of fun to be found. In this way we miss the planet when we are in spirit.

It is amusing to us sometimes when we see those who are trying to ascend because there are those of us here that would like to come back down and feel the waves of an ocean, smell the pine on a mountain. There are those of us that would wish to feel the cold again. There are those of us that wish to put our hand in the hand of another human. So again, we ask you to remember us in these things. Not just us as Onereon, but your own spiritual companions as well.

Invite them in. Invite them in and if you say, "I am not sure who they are," invite them in anyway and this is how you get to know your neighbors. You invite them in and share a meal or share a drink, share a sunset, share some moments, share some time. Invite your companions in, not because you need something. By doing that, what happens? You begin to be invited in to share their perceptions as well. You want enlightenment? This is a way of doing this. You will become brighter in your light.

Are there physical manifestations of spirit that you can feel in your life?

There are rare moments in spirit when a being cries out and is in true danger or true need. You have heard stories of people who have done things that are seemingly superhuman. That is where spirit has really stepped in and really brought the human being, the human body, to a better conclusion than what might have been expected in the situation the human found themselves in.

Sometimes it is the action of a spirit being directly affecting the physical realm. This, however, causes an opposite and equal reaction in energy. A burst of energy in one area requires a lessening of energy somewhere else. In the spirit realm we work to balance energy.

This is why it is more common for the spirit being to swiftly assist the human in realizing their own full potential and to reach within themselves to access the energy that is theirs to begin with. A common experience of those who feel what is termed a miracle is that time seems to stand still or to slow down. This is an encounter with the spiritual realm.

In times past, there were many opportunities for people to have this experience and feel this way. Thus there were many moments where there was an imagined feeling of spirit assuming them and possessing their body. We say now, unless invited in, a spirit being will not do this. The forced possession of another being, whether physical or spiritual, is not an expression of love, joy, or peace.

We will say that the family human has a great imagination and will sometimes feel things that are not necessarily there. Often what they are feeling is assigned a meaning that is not completely accurate. If it is in your realm of perception to feel touched by spirit, then that is what can happen. If it is what you need as proof of existence of your spiritual companions, then that can happen. The fact is that if you are asking for this proof and perceive this as a possibility, then you already believe. Trust your perception, but be wise. As Onereon, a group of spirit beings, we ourselves are very cautious about these things and do not often enter into the physical realm, unless very specifically invited to enjoy and to love.

How do we know we are listening to our spiritual guides?
It often sounds like your own way of thinking, does it not?

How do you tell it apart?
It is a part of the Harmonic Coalescence. In truth, you do not need to tell it apart. You know it is your spiritual companion because it feels like you, only more so. It feels right in a way that is not in the realm of logic. It is not necessarily something that you had in your heart and your brain before. It is something that you *feel* is right and it may come through as a voice, it may come through as a feeling, it may come through as a song. You may just look at a color, a flower or a tree or a child's eyes and just suddenly

know something. This is your spiritual companion. This is them communicating with you in a pure way.

The barrier between us is artificial. It is perceptual and only perceptual. So when you ask, "How do you tell it apart?" There is no apart. The answer to your question is: if you feel that it is apart from you, perhaps it is not a part of you. But if you feel it is a part of you, then you know the truth of it.

Philosophers say that if perception is reality, what you perceive is real. It is real to you. Perceptions are fluid and they change from person to person. You must allow other people to have their perceptions. Perceptions change within each person as well. A spiritual being will constantly be experiencing new things and gaining new perceptions. If you find that you are continually reinforcing old thoughts or beliefs, then perhaps you are closing your heart to the communication from your current spiritual companions.

If you find yourself thinking new thoughts or feeling love and joy at new things or in new ways, this is likely a spiritual communication. It does not need to be logical. It is not apart from you; it is a part of you. It is growth. You do this very naturally as a child and now we say *you*, you felt this very naturally as a child. You felt connected and then, through training, through social environments, you began to doubt, not consciously perhaps, but you began to doubt, and you began to think, well, these other people know more than I do, so I will follow them.

Your spiritual companions also know more than you do in many cases, and so when you feel like you suddenly know more and it feels true, it feels as if it is a part of you, as if there was an area of darkness and then suddenly there was light in that area, that is truth. That is your spiritual companion and your guide. That is your moment to say, "Thank you" and that is your moment to ask, "Now, what can I do for you?" You are open. You are open to instruction at that moment. You are open to guidance at that moment. You are open to growth, to raising your own vibration.

Let us tell you about vibrations. The higher your vibration, there will be fewer beings around you. So as you allow yourself to vibrate at a higher rate, people may leave you. Old relationships may no longer harmonize with you. Raising your vibration sometimes can be noted by the things in your life that go away.

Are you referring to other people and other circumstances?

Yes. It is not right, and it is not wrong. It is not good, and it is not bad. Light is not good, and dark is not evil. People are people and they do what they do. If you continue to grow, as we believe you will, your continued growth will not be matched by all of those around you. Perhaps your growth will be in a different direction from others that are growing at the same pace as you. You may be found to be growing alone for a time. That is not right, and it is not wrong, although some may try to put that judgment upon you. So, be cautious with your growth. Be conscious about your growth. Remain balanced. Remain grounded to the planet and do not merely assume that things will all go away.

As your vibration changes, you will affect the vibration of other people and other beings around you. Because you opened to a higher vibration, often by simply asking a question, now you are already vibrating differently. Your spiritual companions then say, "Here we go!" and they begin to bring their vibrations towards you and direct it towards you and you feel that. The more you want to retain the lower vibration, the less you will hear the higher vibrations and the less affected you will be by the higher vibrations. If you open yourself up to it, the harmony gets clearer and purer the higher we go and also a little less intrusive. The lower notes, you feel them. Higher notes, you sense them. So there you are. You need to play a higher note. Trust your perception. Trust your guides.

(Author's note - Onereon will rarely give a personal channel, especially during live channels when there are many others in the room. Occasionally they will sense a common question or concern and address an issue beyond the original question asked. The following is a good example of this situation. They address the individual, but the response applied to the entire audience in attendance that day)

Can you speak to me about my visiting spiritual companion today and yesterday? I got a message from someone...

We will speak not directly to the question for that is a personal conversation. We will speak to your experience. Trust it, in all cases, when you feel that visitation. There are some that will fear that. Our voice was one of them. There are some that will hold back, they will withhold themselves. We use the model of the child meeting someone new. Sometimes they will want to hide behind mom. They get smaller, raising their hands to their face. They want to look but they do not want to be seen. In your case, you may want to be seen, but you might not want to look. So, for everyone, when you feel it, when you feel a visitation from the spirit realm, say, "Hello" for it is a very simple process. Do not consider the companion as something strange.

How many people believe in spiritual beings? And yet, how many people fear to have any contact with them? When we contact someone higher than ourselves, say in a business sense, they greet us, and they get to know us. What are they doing? Why? They look at us because they are thinking that they might be able to advance us in the company by giving us more responsibility. It is the same with a spiritual contact.

There is often a concern within the spiritual model, because if you are contacted directly, you may be asked to take on more responsibility. More responsibility in the business model, what does that mean? More of your time devoted to something and less of your time devoted to what you used to devote your time to. You may need to become more serious about your studies and much more serious about your practice when spirit approaches you, taps you on your shoulder and says, "Hello."

True spirit will never ask you do to something that you cannot do, and true spirit will always allow you the opportunity to say, "No, thank you." It is always your choice. By saying, "No, thank you," it does not cut you off from anything. By saying, "No, thank you," that means, "Not this. Not at this time." We in the spirit realm understand this. We are often asked the same things. We say, "As above, so below." What happens to you happens to us and sometimes those of a higher vibration to us say, "Would you like to move to this vibration?"

Do you understand that everything is a vibration? Understand that. We may say, "No, we do not want to go there at this time. We are really kind of enjoying this, where we are at." That is Source, enjoyment. It is another answer to your question, "How will you know your spirit companion?"

How will you know that it is truth? How will you know that it is a true voice of spirit? You will feel love, you will feel joy, and you will feel peaceful. You will promote love by your actions and by your words. You will promote joy by your life and your words, and you will promote peace in your life. Now these things are telling. They tell you what is true spirit knowledge, what is true higher vibration and again we say not everyone will accept the perception of love, joy, and peace.

So, energy moves in waves, everything is a vibration, all things spiral. If they seem to be spinning, they are, but they are also spiraling. We remind you about the pattern of the cycles of sevens. This is for you to observe, and it is a deep, deep spiritual pattern. Invite your companions to be with you. You all have them.

Understand that you are also their companion and that you have the same ability to guide as they have to guide you, because every action has that opposite and equal reaction. If you have a guide, you are also a guide. The teacher must also be a student. The student must also be a teacher for the systems to be complete.

We have enjoyed our time and now we leave with this admonition. We have used these terms throughout, love and joy and peace, and we remind you again. Peace is not the absence of violence; it is the ceasing of being against things. So seek in your life what you might have been against and begin to not be against that thing. That does not mean you agree with it, simply do not be against it and watch how room appears in your life. Watch how space appears in your life. Watch how peace appears in your life.

Thank you for being here. We say, "Seek peace."

The Totality

- Observe the seven-year cycles in your life.
- Begin to remove the model that all of the experiments throughout the galaxy are going to look like human form, or even human thought.
- Invite your spiritual companions in and share a meal or a drink, share a sunset, share some moments, share some time. Invite your companions in because you want them with you, not because you need something. By doing that, what happens? You begin to be invited in to share their perceptions as well. You want enlightenment? This is a way of becoming enlightened.
- Understand that you are also a companion to your spiritual guides and that you have the same ability to guide as they have to guide you, because every action has that opposite and equal reaction.
- Trust your perceptions. Trust your guides.
- Seek in your life what you may have been against and begin not to be against that thing. That does not mean you have to agree with it, simply do not be against it and watch how space appears in your life. Watch how peace appears in your life.

9
The Principles of Love

As above, so below. Within this greeting is great truth.

We greet you and express our admiration for all the efforts of those who hear and read these words. It is a difficult time for many, and, in each day, there are many possibilities for stumbling along your spiritual path. It is with intent that you move forward and in the realm of spirit we laud that and now express our appreciation for hard work well done.

To continue to love in a world of trial and struggle is a sign of true connection to Source. It is not something you must do perfectly, only steadily. In this way we say that some of you must go easier on yourselves for there are those that feel guilt that they are not doing more in a spiritual way. Guilt is not a motivator of love. Rather guilt will sap the energy of the bearer. So we say now, examine the source of any guilt you may have in your life. Forgiveness is an aspect of love and love is the true energy of the Source of creation. If no one else will, you may still forgive yourself for any perceived failings. The universe already has!

Stumbling Blocks

This does not excuse anyone from the work of spirit. This only clears a block that many encounter somewhere along their path. Accepting this as a block is unnecessary. Others may try to keep this block in your path, and we say let them then bear the burden and move away from those that would attempt to assign guilt to you in order to impede your spiritual path.

Move away from those that attempt to render judgments in any form. You are the sole judge of the truth of your path. Do not allow others to place their stumbling blocks along your way.

It is then a potential stumbling block when we experience this, for we may be tempted to anger and lose our love for these ones. We say again that love is the true energy of the Source and everything and everyone has access to the same energies from Source. It is like the sunlight which shines on everyone. It cannot be captured, and it cannot be limited. All have access to the light of Source. Only some choose to hide from the light.

You have chosen to be in the light and exist within the energy of Source. In this way, you have already succeeded on your spiritual path. Those moments of time when you have lost your balance are not moments of failure, only moments of opportunity to grow stronger. Ask yourself, "What is it that caused me to lose my way?" Now you are aware of issues or situations that may cause you to lose sight of the path of love in the future.

Remember this: nearly all stumbling along a person's spiritual path is due to judging or being judged. Release the need to be absolutely right or wrong about anything, especially yourself, and watch as your spiritual growth moves forward with increased speed and steadiness.

Principles of Love

It has been said that love is the answer to many questions. How do we apply this in the physical world of the family human? These principles may serve to guide you in your life and along your path.

> Love each other. There will be those that are different in their ways and so you must sometimes love on principle rather than from the heart, but love you must. It is the creative energy of the universe and thus must be the energy of a successful life.

> Love all the children in your life equally. They all should have access to the same opportunities though they will be different in their temperaments and interests. The success they enjoy in their youth will be the seeds of the success of the future of the family human.

> Love all children. Let discipline be approached with the same spirit as we all approach Gaia. Ask first, "Will this action promote growth in the child and those around?" Discipline is a teaching and not a form of judgment.

> Love your parents. There will be those that are of a different temperament than their parents, yet they do remain your parents. In this way you set

the pattern for how all children may see life and also for the way you will be viewed by all children.

Love all strangers for you do not know when they will be your neighbor or what gift they may have for you. In time you may find yourself or one you love as the stranger. Set the example and others will benefit. As others benefit so do all members of the family human. In this be reasonable with your resources.

Love life. It is what we know, and it is what we have. Live as if love powers your every breath. In this manner all other spiritual principles will be natural to your life.

Love Gaia. She is our home, and we belong to her. Ask always, "Does this action promote growth for others on the planet? Does this action serve the best interests of Gaia?"

The Path of Creation

These things are not commandments but principles to be applied as one on a spiritual path sees fit. Recall that you are a child of the universe and as such you are of the same energy of creation.

This moment, begin to create yourself. It does not matter the paths you followed in the past. It only matters the paths you choose from this moment on. Live your life with intention to love any and all without judgment, including yourself.

We here in the spirit realm love you there in the physical realm. Again, we ask that you invite us in to your presence, not just in times of need or decision, but also in times of great joy and beauty. We have all been companions in karmic times for longer than you can imagine while you exist in the lower physical vibrations of Gaia. We rejoice at your steadfast course in the face of a changing world.

Do you believe the world is changing for the better? It is if you are changing for the better! Look around you at the small things as well as the great and see the earth as it truly is, a beautiful place for us all to visit while we continue to move along our karmic paths.

Tell others of the beauty that you see, and, in this way, help remove the fears of others and begin a line of energy that is appreciative of the planet. In this way you create support and love of Gaia. It is not a campaign. It is only a noticing of a single thing of beauty and sharing it with a stranger or friend. In this way you strengthen your love also.

Smile and laugh often for these are things that move energy in a path of growth. These are things that we in the realm of spirit see the world of the family human lacking. These are things that we see lacking in those who are stumbling along their way.

We say again that we give thanks for your efforts and your love in critical times of great change. Stay steady along your path and do not concern yourself with speed at this time. Soon will come a time of greater growth and you are preparing for this time now.

As always, we exhort you to seek three qualities. Seek these qualities not outside of yourself, but within, and in the seeking find love of self, joy of existence and peace of heart.

The Principles of Love

- When you have lost your balance ask, "What is it that caused me to lose my way?" See it as an opportunity to grow stronger.
- Release the need to be absolutely right or wrong about anything, especially yourself, and watch how your spiritual growth moves forward with increased speed and steadiness.
- Live your life with intention to love any and all without judgment, including yourself.
- Tell others of the beauty you see around you and be appreciative of the planet.
- Smile and laugh often. These things move energy in a path of growth.

10
Touch the Earth

We enter into the lesson with our agreed upon phrase: As above, so below. By this we do not mean that what is happening above is exactly mirrored below. In the spirit realm actions happen differently than in the physical realm. When you are in gravity things happen much slower. When you are on the earth, things happen much slower than when you are in what you speak of as the realm of spirit.

Do you all understand that you have been in the spirit realm before? Not just once, but many times. You are recognized by those in the spirit realm as members of what you might term "families." You belong, each and every one of you, to a group that is not physical. How does that make you feel? You are not alone.

As individuals, humans who have been pursuing a spiritual path, your vibration may be higher than many others who live on the earth. We tell you this now, among those reading these words, the vibration is higher. So when you enter back into your daily lives, what you try to call your normal life, you may feel alone and in this way you are, alone.

Often around you the vibration is not as high. Do not despair. It is here you can turn to your guides and say, "As my guide, please guide me to others of like vibration." This is where it gets fun because you may not be guided to another human being. You may only become closer to your guides, and they then become closer to you, and you find yourself working together again in a spiritual purpose at a higher vibration.

Your guides then become companions to you. You come together with your companions in spirit. You begin to understand that spirit has more to do than assist humans in finding parking places. Spirit has more to do than comforting ones that have perhaps mismanaged their lives. Although it is true, however, that spirit will do this.

Guiding Spirit

We say, "As above, so below." In the realm of gravity there is a rule: for every action, there is an opposite and equal reaction. That is a true rule on many levels. As often as you ask for guidance, you must then give guidance and sometimes we, in spirit, appreciate guidance. This is where prayer comes in, this is where directed meditation comes in, and so we ask you to be aware of your prayers.

Pray for yourself, certainly. Pray for others as well. From a higher perspective, from a higher vibration, we respond to the number of prayers being directed to certain areas of the planet. You would not believe the number of prayers sent forth from all over the world. You would not believe the number of miracles that occur. Small miracles, invisible miracles, individuals pulled from the abyss of despair. Hope in the face of tragedies, strength in the face of loss. These are the miracles. This is the power that you have to guide us, by asking for help, for yourself certainly and that is not inappropriate, but asking for help in areas of great crisis. There is an account of a prayer, and the teacher says, "You must pray in this way." Let us talk about prayer now.

Let us use the example of a war. To pray for one side is an incomplete prayer. When two armies clash, this is an imbalance. To pray for one side to be stronger is to pray for one side to be more unbalanced. To pray for both sides to be balanced is an opportunity to lessen conflict, to increase resolve. In your prayer, do you pray to support a troop, or do you pray instead for a resolution, a cessation of things against? Do you pray for those you disagree with? Do you pray for wisdom to be given to those who are in positions of power at the higher levels of government? If everyone prayed for them to have wisdom, how much wisdom would they then be granted?

Touching the Earth

It is true we have much to do in the spirit realm and there is much joy in the spirit realm. Do you want to be more spiritual? Then find more reasons to be joyful, to enjoy your life.

Let us make a statement now and it is one that we have made before. Touch the earth. When you are in physical form, you are of the earth. You are not on the earth; you are of the earth. You are of the elements of the earth. What powers you does not return to the earth, it returns to spirit. The body does not return to spirit. The body returns to earth. In this way, you are not the same person when you return to the earth. Different body, different person, but an accumulation of energies, what you may term karma, is with you at that point. Not within the body, there is no room for it. It is connected to you via what you would say is your spirit self.

Your spirit self is not outside of you, it is within you. It is difficult to understand, but it is the connection to all of the energies that you have connected with along the path and this karmic line, this karmic lineage. You can think of this as a thread of a vast and beautiful tapestry. You are weaving that thread now, as you walk, as you move, as you visit, as you engage, as you converse, as you do all of those things that a social creature does. We do not simply mean human when we say, "social creature." There are other social creatures, are there not?

You are connected to spirit, but you are on the planet. You are here, not "as above." You are "so below." We laugh because it always sounds like a hierarchy to us when we say it that way. As below, so above. What you do impacts spirit. How you live impacts the realm of spirituality. You rejoiced when you returned to the planet because you were coming into a time of increased spiritual energy. It will be sad as the population of the planet begins to die off, but it will be happy as this energy begins to coalesce and come to a higher vibration and again return to the earth in the form of holy, spiritual human beings. Gaia will respond and Gaia will heal.

You are concerned with the planet. Please do not be. Be concerned with the fate of the human race. The solution is already in process. Touch, therefore, the earth. By this we mean, get in touch with who you are, where you live, and what you truly are. The aspect of you that reaches for ascension, we acknowledge that. Now also reach for decendancy. And touch the earth.

You can do this in many ways. You can literally get out and get on your hands and knees and literally touch the ground. Not the concrete, not the tarmac, but the grass, the earth. You can grow plants. If you live in an urban area where there is little ground, earth, grow some plants. Obtain some stones of beauty.

Take some time, each day, to remember that you are of the earth. In this way you will gain strength. You will feel it flowing up from the ground and into your body. Not holding you down, not keeping you from ascension, but balancing you, strengthening you, centering you so that your ascension can be orderly and practical. We have seen too many people ascend too fast and they are far too impractical to be of any use to anyone, including themselves. They are as imbalanced as those who are only concerned with the physical things of the planet such as food, sex, pleasure. There is a place for all of those things just as there is a place for ascension. Stay with your body. Enjoy your body. When you enjoy something specifically, invite your spirit companions to be with you and enjoy this with you and in this way you grow in your spirituality.

Touch the earth. If you were a dolphin, you would have named the planet "Ocean" because that is where you live. We say this now and we acknowledge the observation from outside of us, because the ocean is a part of the planet and you are truly of that part of the planet as well and some of you are returning to that part of the planet.

From above, when we look down, we do not see individual matter walking about on the planet. We see the glow, we see the light, we see the spark of energy that is each human. We also see the spark of energy that is each dolphin, elephant, and horse. If you were to see this, you would see that the majority of these lights are in close proximity to the oceans. Humans do not move far from their home. There is a returning of the human species to the ocean and there are guides waiting for you there. Touch the earth. Touch the ocean.

Raising Gaia's Vibration

The purpose of the coalescence is just this, to allow the earth to return to a vibration it enjoyed many more thousands of years ago than your historians believe humans existed at this level. There will come an increasing diversity of the human species. You will notice that science speaks of a great deal of diversity of humans in the past and now we are down to what, one species of human? Diversity is returning. It has truly been there all along. Gaia is nothing if not imaginative.

We tell you now that humanity as it currently exists is not the pinnacle of creation. So that we do not offend anyone, we will tell you this: we also are not the pinnacle of creation. We are all aspects; we are all particles of creation. The coalescence is a way of filtering out unbalanced energies, not bad energies, not negative energies, just energies that are no longer balanced. The coalescence filters these energies out and puts them back together in a way that is once again useful to Gaia. Gaia once again has a higher vibration. Does the planet become spiritual? Yes. Do you think Gaia does not have chakras? All other life forms do, including those in spirit.

Gaia is a life form as much as you are. Gaia is an aspect of creation as much as you are. Becoming balanced in your own physical life, that is your job. That is your task on this planet, if you were wondering. We tell you now, become balanced, in your body and in your mind and in your spirit.

You do not need to have perfect health to be balanced in your body. Health is not the absence of disease. Health is the presence of vitality. So become vital. Enjoy things vitally. Look at things consciously. Your life will improve, your life will lengthen, and ascension then comes more easily.

Touch the earth. Human society, human civilization, the human family mostly lived with the earth, touching the earth on a daily basis, touching it with their bare feet, touching it with their hands. Living upon the earth was a necessity and staying balanced on the earth was a necessity. It has all changed. It will all change again. This time it will be a voluntary change. A decision will be made to return from the large, dense, spiritually cold cities, to the green plains, to the green forests, the green lands. We have said before, we will say this again. In one hundred years, you will not recognize the civilization that will exist on this planet. Except that many of you will be back again.

Touch the earth. Are there questions?

You talk about us passing. Our energy goes up into spirit and then comes down into another form. Do we retain the spiritual knowledge, what we have learned, what wisdom we have gained in one life or in many lives. Is that within us and accessible to us when we come back?

The direct answer is no. It is not within you. For the life that you live is a life to be experienced. The indirect answer is yes, it is available to you. We spoke of the chain of karma, the karmic thread, the line of energy that has been the path that your energies have followed. Your energies have followed many paths and they have culminated in who you are at this point. Those experiences are available to you. When you think in terms of past life, some of you remember two lives at the same time. It is because two threads have come together in one, you.

The higher your vibration, the more accessibility you have to the threads that make up who you are at this point. The higher your vibration, the more accessible karmic memories are. We caution you about this. There are many who spend way too much time trying to remember the past. We say to you now, there is already an answer to your question. Ask your question and remember the answer. In this way, you do not have to spend much time striving for the past. You can then move to the future.

Your personal individual gravity-based experience, from what you call conception to what you call death, is an addition to the vibrations that make up your karmic threads. You do not have room to hold all of those other vibrations. Those that try too hard to attain those vibrations, those memories, are the ones that become spiritually unbalanced in many cases. They reach too high too fast, and they become unbalanced. It is not that they are wrong. It is that they have difficulty communicating what they now know, what is now in their perception. This is why we encourage you to touch the earth, so that you remain balanced. So that when you reach high and higher still, you are not going to fall over.

In what reference will the earth be changed in one hundred years that we would not recognize?

The mountains will still be there. (Laughter) When we say, "the earth," we fall into a pattern of speech. The course of life on the earth will be changed. The attitudes, the ethics, and the spiritual pursuit will be changed, purer. There is a necessity to get past the old ways of thinking. This is why there are wars and terrible things happening in the name of God. People voluntarily destroying themselves and others because the god of love wants this?

This is an archaic way of thinking. It is animalistic and to meet it with force because you believe your god is better is also archaic. The holy land cannot be holy with this much blood being shed. This is not a criticism of the first thoughts. They were pure. But people are trying to prove one thought better than the other and they are the same thought.

When we say that the earth will be changed in one hundred years, these conflicts will be exhausted. There will be an agreement within the family human to "just stop it." It will happen suddenly. It will happen swiftly. It will happen because something else gets the attention of the family human and you will say, "We need to pay attention to this, all of us, everywhere, right now." The old ideas of vengeful gods will go away. They just will not make sense. The idea of masculine gendered gods will also go away, and really, that does not even make sense to the ones that claim it.

The rivers, the lakes, the oceans, the valleys, the deserts, they will all be here. The earth abides. The earth has taken large hits and rebounded again and again. The form of life on the earth is what changes, again and again. The expression of vitality is what changes, again and again. Gaia has great imagination in this regard. You have the evidence. You have the proof. Go to the museums. Look into the books of science and marvel at the diversity of expression of life and vitality that Gaia can allow.

Imagine that energy is life energy, and that energy is also a part of your karmic thread. You go back far enough and the light that you are is no longer human because there are no humans. You go back on the karmic thread of that energy that has existed always. Energy cannot be destroyed, it can only be transformed, and you are transforming now. It is the way of the universe. What will you be in ten thousand years? The way things are going, you will be water based.

Can you speak to us about the shift from third to fourth to fifth dimension on this planet?

When we speak of these terms, we want you to understand something. There are higher vibrations and there are lower vibrations, and the shifting of dimensions is simply that, a shifting to a different vibration. We encourage people to remain within the vibration that they are in. Raise that vibration and do not seek to live in two places at once. You will naturally move through. Humans naturally see the boundaries of things. They think in terms of solid boundaries. Let us change that thought and say, "membrane." As you move through these designations, you are moving through membranes and not everybody in the same dimension is at the same vibration.

Maintain your balance in the physical realm. Then as you ascended, as you increase your vibration, and let us be clear about this as well, because ascension does not mean leaving the planet. Ascension means increasing your vibration while you are on the planet. We are not ascendant in the realm of spirit. We are life, the same way that you are life. We are just less bound by gravity. This is why we caution people about ascending too quickly. Ascend too fast and you may fall over.

Third, fourth, fifth dimensions, these are labels, and they are useful in some ways, but they are limiting in others. We want you to be cautious in using those labels because they are not hierarchical. It is not that the third dimension and the fifth dimension are different; they are the same in different ways. One human is not better than another human. They are different; yet they are the same in different ways.

There is a lot of literature on DNA activation. Can you talk a little on that?

Yes. Go ahead and do it. It is your DNA. Activate it! This is not a topic that is our specialty. There will be more information coming from another source on DNA and soon. Science, what they can see, is not all that is there. DNA strands have a particular vibration. Sometimes you can hear the vibration of music and sometimes it is called ultrasonic. Why is that? Because you cannot hear it consciously, but the sound is still there. It is the same way as when they observe DNA. They cannot see all of it because the vibration is too high.

You want your DNA to be activated. You have to pluck it. You have to say, "I am going to activate my DNA and the higher courses of it" and then do so. This is where the limitation comes in. The family human thinks, this is what we know about DNA so this must be all we can do with DNA. In the realm of spirituality, in the realm of metaphysics, we take the limitations away. We may still only see that, but we have given it room to grow.

You want your DNA to be activated, then activate it. It is a decision, a choice. DNA activates automatically as you raise your vibration, but your DNA can become unstrung if you lose your balance. The DNA starts down here with you on the earth and if you try to ascend too fast...What happens to a rubber band when you pull it too tightly? It snaps and goes off someplace else. I believe you know those ones who have gone off someplace else. They may be in their bodies someplace, but they are just rambling. It is unfortunate because they are not necessarily wrong, but they are not practical.

Your DNA is already activated. How do you know? You are here and you are moving around. You are walking and talking and growing. Your DNA is already activated. It you want it to be activated further, release judgment. Stop thinking in terms of right and wrong and watch how your life changes. There is more on DNA coming up. There is a program, a schedule, a delay perhaps. But more coming, and soon.

Help me to understand, how is it that our human actions affect spirit?

Because as above, so below. Because we are all part of the universe. Let us get cosmic for a moment. The seven sisters, the Pleiades, there are many that have an idea of the Pleiadians and how they influenced the planet earth. They are not wrong, and they are not quite right. They are trying to make it come from a certain perception. They are trying to make it look human. The Pleiadians are not humans. Nothing outside of the earth really looks like a human. But their actions affected the planet earth, without them necessarily arriving on the planet earth. Pleiadians are not spirit beings, but they are of a higher vibration, and they affected the planet earth.

The reason they affected the planet earth was that they sensed that something was happening on the planet earth. The vibration from the planet earth was also going out in that direction. Now, there came to be an interaction and the earth then became part of the experiment, the experiment of creation, of vitality, of the expression of life. Not all planets are alive. Not all planets have life energy around them. Not all stars have life energy around them, but many do. Things happening on the earth affected the Pleiadian and the Pleiadian then affected the earth and this interaction occurred on a vibration that you as a human will not sense.

Again, in the same way that there is infra-red and ultra-sonic there are higher vibrations of the physical realm that border on spirituality, on the spiritual realm. Pleiadians have been close to this for some time. If this little planet, this little dusty dry planet that received the gift of water, can begin to affect a higher vibration like the Pleiadians, it is just a little bit further before it begins to affect the realm of spirit, the creative energies. Then we all turn our attention to this little blue ball, and we say, "How cute is this child, this little baby and what can we do to help it grow. What can we do to help this planet begin to express itself?"

So now the history of the earth is one of maturity. It has grown up. How do we know that? Because of the level that you are at as humans and the enjoyment that we get of interaction with you on a personal level now at moments like this and moments of prayer and moments of meditation. So the vibration of the planet has risen. You are not near the Pleiadians, but we have a different system here and so we say, "As above, so below." So, sometimes you are above, in spirit, and sometimes you are below, on the earth, and it is the same for us.

What you do, what you choose, the vibration you choose to exist in on the planet affects us in spirit because you then return to spirit at a higher vibration. The higher vibrations are expressed in terms of love and joy and peace. In this way, we want to clarify that as above so below does not mean that if there are wars and fighting below, that there is an equal energy to that above being expressed in conflict.

There are opportunities to express love in those areas. There are opportunities to express joy in those areas. There are opportunities to express peace in those areas. That is the similar vibration above as below, because we then feel the opportunity to express love, or joy, or peace in a particular area. Those areas of disaster and crisis are holes in the spirit.

You have heard it said that nature abhors a vacuum and spirit does too. The creative energy of the universe, this is what we talk about when we talk about Source, or we talk about God, or we talk about divinity. It is the energy that created us and allows us to continue to create and to be creative and to be created. In those areas of crisis there is a hole in creation. The karmic thread that you are and the way that you weave that thread patches those holes in creation. This is why we encourage you to continue to move towards love, joy, and peace. These things alone will increase your vibration, help you maintain your balance, and you will rise, you will ascend in a very natural and easy manner and so it is that we leave you with those words now.

Regarding the challenging individuals in your life, recognize that they are challenging and love them anyway. You do not have to walk up to them and say, "I love you." It is not an outward thing. It is an inner thing, and so that inner thing, that love, is what you express inside to that individual. They will feel it, we promise. We know because we feel it.

If you are having a challenging day and things look bleak or rough, find something to be joyful about. It does not have to be much: a flower, a kitten, a breath of air, a glass of water.

Those moments when you feel like there is nothing but bad news, stop judging. Cease being against things and become a center of peace so that anyone in this entire world can approach you and be loved and enjoyed and feel a moment of peace. So we say, "Seek love. Seek joy. Seek peace."

Touch the Earth

- When you feel alone, ask your spiritual companions to guide you to others of like vibration. Do not be surprised at the outcome.
- Touch the earth. Enjoy what you do while you are in gravity.
- Take some time each day to remind yourself that you are of the earth.
- Enjoy your body.
- When you enjoy something specifically, invite your spiritual companions to join you. In this way you grow in your spirituality.
- Become vital. Enjoy things vitally. Look at things consciously.
- Do you have a question? Ask it, and then simply remember the answer. It already exists!
- Release judgment about the challenging individuals in your life. Recognize that they are challenging and love them anyway. Sometimes you must love on principle rather than from the heart, but love you must.
- If you are having a challenging day, find something to be joyful about. It does not have to be much: a flower, a kitten, a breath of air, a glass of water.
- Stop judging. Cease being against things and become a center of peace so that anyone in this entire world can approach you and be loved and enjoyed and feel a moment of peace.

11
Endings and Beginnings

We use the phrase: As above, so below. There are so many questions today! It is a world of uncertainty, is it not? It is a time of change. It is a time of endings and beginnings and so we address that today, the endings and the beginnings.

Death and Birth

The ending of life on the planet is called death and for many, death is a finality, death is an ending, a stopping, a ceasing, no more. There are faiths that describe death as the end and then they tell you what will happen afterwards. They make something up. "You will go to heaven, or you will go to hell." "You will cross a river." Sometimes it is a river of fire, sometimes it is a river of truth. Some say, "You are a complete entity, and you will come back as that complete entity, and you will remember everything completely." These are all observations; these are all glimpses, and they are all attempts to describe what you know is true. Your energy does not cease.

We have used the term "karmic thread" and so we would like to invite you now to think of your life force as a karmic thread, something that does not stop, but rather something that can be woven, something that can be used to create a pattern, something that can change color, something that can change direction, something that can be embroidered on the fabric of reality.

Reality is a fun word, is it not? Our perceptions are what create our personal realities and so as a human, a member of the family human, you have perceptions, and they are based on the limitation of being human. In the realm of spirit, we also have perceptions, and they are based on the vibration level we are at.

Death is not a stopping. Birth is not a beginning. The beginning of a human life is a continuation of the karmic thread. The coalescence is a weaving together of many threads into one human life, thus making it a stronger life form. The purer the thread, the purer the life. We purify through many ways. Much of the purification has been the process of raising and lowering your vibration. Raising the vibration to the point of being in the spirit realm, lowering your vibration to the point of being in the physical realm where you are more and more affected by gravity.

Gravity is why aging exists. An object in motion tends to stay in motion unless it is acted on. The karmic thread, the karmic energy, stays in motion unless it is acted upon. Gravity acts upon those things that are not of the spiritual realm.

Each one of you carries within you aspects of the spiritual realm and you can add to that and you can take away from that with each incarnation. That is your true choice. Your purpose on the earth is variable. To assume a single purpose in life is to apply limits to yourself that are completely unnecessary. To accept a purpose and then to accept a second and then a third and a fourth purpose is to show your variability, your ability to respond to different situations and, in this way, you raise your vibration, not only on the planet, but also in the spirit realm. The more ability you have to respond to situations on the planet, the more responsibility you have in the spiritual realm.

The returning to the earth, then, sets you in a different place than other human beings. It can be lonely to be a spiritual person on the planet these days. We have said this before, and we will say it again: Fewer humans are concerned with spiritual things than you may believe. There are so many beings with causes disguised as spirituality. This has not slowed down the ascension. This has not slowed down the raising of the vibration level. These things that appear to be spirituality, that are not, are merely purifying the field for those who are truly spiritually active. Large groups of individuals may feel good together, but a spiritual path is a solitary path. Thus you may feel lonely on your spiritual path. When that happens, understand that it is your personal vibration that is higher. Understand that you have access to aspects of the spiritual realm that others may not.

The assisting of ones to pass comfortably and peacefully from this physical life to the spiritual life is a way of accessing spirituality. The bond that you form with the individual as they pass into spiritual life remains. Feeling grief at the passing of an individual is a normal human situation, though it is not only a human situation. There are other beings on this planet, and they feel grief at the passing of one of their own. The family human is interesting in this way, in that they they can feel grief at the passing of any being, not just another human. Why? A higher vibration. This does not make the family human better than any of these other beings. It merely indicates a higher vibration.

As you help someone pass, you maintain that connection. You feel the force of them at a higher vibration and they may come to visit in spirit form and so we welcome some today. Their vibration, their path, now shifts and changes. They are not your guides. They are not your angels. They are still your friends, your companions. So we direct you to think in those terms, companion, not guide. You guide each other and we have said these things before.

Love Yourself

Endings and beginnings, as above, so below. From above, in the spirit realm, we watch people return to the planet, but we also watch them ascend higher than the location of Onereon and we do not vision them as missing; we vision them as moving forward. All things will coalesce. It is the way of Source to separate and return and to separate again and return. It has happened this way many times. It is an experiment, an experiment in creation, an experiment in love, and it is a way of Source expressing love for itself.

Do you express love for yourself? One of the ultimate goals of all vitality and all vibration is to harmonize with itself. Do you find yourself not at peace? Do you find yourself seeking something to approve of you, outside of you? Approve of yourself, love yourself, and then you will be closer to Source.

Endings and beginnings. We watch as an entire society has ended. There was no definitive date of ending; it merely is no longer that society. From above, we look, and we see the change, the dramatic change, in how the family human was living and how the family human is now living. There are certain pivotal points where things turn, and sometimes take a dramatic turn but, from the perspective of the family human, it may not be as dramatic as you might think or expect. It may simply be a raising of the vibration of the planet. It may simply be a speeding up of the harmonious vibrations. It may be a coming together of harmonious vibrations.

Simply love yourself more and more. Treat yourself with love, more and more. Find your center, more and more, regardless of what happens around you, regardless of the rest of the family human. Maintain your own center to the best of your ability and take this time now to increase your ability. In this way you will be the energy of these times and not merely a reaction to it. You will be the cause. There are already some who are close to this.

Your association with your spirit companions, your association with those that have passed from this life, this earthly realm, helps you to raise your vibration, helps you to have a truer vision of what it will be like when you yourself take that step from gravity into the realm of spirit. Your guides change, your companions change. They change based on their needs as much as yours, so be aware of that. There are many responsibilities at whatever level life exists. The simpler the life, the lower the vibration, the less responsibility, until sometimes it is just a matter of being still so that other things can grow. If perhaps things around you are still, it is so that you can grow. Stillness is an aspect of the creative energies of the universe.

Appreciation is also an aspect of the creative energies of the universe. When we say, "appreciate," what we want to indicate is to look at things and understand the value of things. Be in gratitude for everything that is around you. Be grateful for those that have been with you. In this way, as your life transforms, it becomes easier. You will find that your energy is now in cooperation with the rest of the universe, for Source is grateful. Source is appreciative, appreciative of the differences, which is sometimes where the family human has some struggles. We are not always appreciative of the differences while in the realm of gravity.

The Cycle of Sevens

Endings and beginnings are not necessarily only births and deaths. The cycle of seven indicates an ending and a beginning. It is a universal law and we have said before to note how your life moves in cycles of seven: seven rotations around the planet, seven circles around the sun. In this way, there is a true rhythm to your life and, by noticing these things, by noticing where you are within the cycle of sevens, you can adjust your patterns, you can become balanced, you can look forward to the energy that is moving your direction and meet it with joy and with gratitude. In this way, you can handle what is coming at you. By not paying attention to the cycles of sevens you will constantly be surprised when things are low, when things are high.

So learn now where you are within those cycles. It is different for each human. The cycles can alter. The earth was reset the day of the tsunami and the cycles of seven for all of humanity were re-set, though not to the same cycle. Events in your life change the cycles of seven and you could say there is an ending and a beginning because within a seven-year period there is an ending, but it is also a beginning. So it is with birth and with death, there is also an ending and a beginning. You are birthed from death into the realm of spirit. You die from the realm of spirit when you are birthed into the human realm.

Endings and Beginnings

We address these things now because it is a time of endings, but it is also a time of beginnings and so there is no need to mourn what has passed. There is an opportunity to be grateful, to be joyful, to be thankful and say, "We got through this and now, what is new? What do we get to explore? What areas do we get to cast our light? What new thing do we get to enjoy and observe along our path?" We encourage you to do these things. Look for new things. Look for new experiences. Take courage and live by your heart and your heart's desire. Take today as a day of change for yourself. Consciously reset your cycle of seven. Start something new. This does not have to be a dramatic change. You do not have to have dramatic physical things alter around you. It can be a change in attitude, a change in belief, a releasing of judgment, an appreciating of things that may be puzzling to you, such as disasters and wars. It is difficult to say thank you for war, is it not? Move forward now and enjoy life, a new direction, a new pattern for yourself. Are there questions?

You mentioned we are in gravity and because of that we will always experience a passing from this realm, an aging. While we are here, if we increase the spiritual aspect of our self, do we then increase the possibility of the time we spend on the earth?

With the raising of the quality of humanity, the level of life rises, and the vitality has a stronger ability to retain its shape, its form, and so you already notice this. You live longer, not necessarily by year, but you remain healthy and vital and younger looking longer. So the answer to your question is yes, the higher the vibration, the younger you will feel, the younger you will look, and the younger you will stay. There is still that action of gravity and so the continuation of life eventually slows and processes in a natural way. Will there be an end to death? This is sort of our point. There is no death. There are only stages. You do not mourn the fact that you are no longer a toddler. You do not mourn the fact that you are no longer going through puberty. Why then would you mourn the fact that you are no longer human? They are stages of a repeating cycle.

I have been hearing messages about further destruction on our country. Is that something that will happen or are there changes that can come around…

More destruction is a certainty. It is difficult to describe this choice and why it has been made. The decision to allow humanity to take the course that it has taken is a much more human decision than a spiritual decision. It is not one that was agreed upon by all involved. It is not an irrevocable course. It is not an irreparable course. It is something that has almost run the course, however.

Will there be more destruction? Yes. Will it be manmade? Yes. The rise of vibratory energies around Gaia is shaking loose long entrenched energy and sometimes that energy is so deeply entrenched that the only way to shake it loose is to literally shake the earth. You will see an increase in destruction in that way. The positive aspect of this message is that you can be aware of the location, you can prepare for eventualities, you can balance yourself. You cannot protest against this for it will not do any good. It will merely support the energy of a particular form of destruction.

Two sides, opposing one another, support each other because they press up against one another and give credence to each ideology. When an opponent steps away from another opponent there is space, there is room to consider, and the opponent, the opposite, is farther away. It is easier then to see the center, the middle way.

Gaia has much to say about the energy that surrounds her at this point and yet she loves herself. As Gaia shakes, she reforms. In this way, Gaia always remains beautiful. Look at areas of Gaia that have been eroded, destroyed, and you will see great mountains. You will see great grand canyons, you will see rocky shorelines and everywhere you look, you will see vitality and life in an infinite variety of forms and how does Gaia experience these things? By adapting an aspect of herself into the form of humanity. Clever, intelligent, resourceful, so that an aspect of her personal vitality gets expressed in an individual that knows how to survive in the coldest, the hottest, the highest and the lowest of climates and continues to adapt and continues to evolve and continues to learn and continues to move forward. Source notices this and says, "Let us experience this as well and let us combine our energy with the energy of Gaia at the point of this being, this human." Not just the human, there are other creatures that are at a level of sentience as well. It is the human part that chose this course of destruction. It is the vitality of Gaia that will shake things up and change the course.

Is Gaia interested in shaking things up in the area we are in now? (Southern California)

Where do you scratch an itch? If your shoulder itches, scratching your knee does not help. There are systems and the shaking of, and we use this term loosely, the shaking of a particular area may simply be a reaction to the shaking of another area, or it may be a way of building energy or directing energy to another area. The area of the planet where you reside is the starting point for many things. That is what we will say about this.

Does the divine feminine energy have a role to play in the future adjustments that Gaia needs to make?

In so many ways Gaia is, what you would call, feminine. We speak through our voice, and he feels the Yin of Gaia and identifies Gaia as her and, in truth, most of humanity has identified Earth as mother for this is what Yin energy does, it nurtures and grows. So Gaia is identifiable as Yin energy. The divine feminine is just that, it is Yin energy, it is that vibration. So your question is, "Will Yin energy support more Yin energy?" The answer is yes. The vibration of Yin energy is increasing, and we believe most people would say it is about time. It is not that the Yang energy is wrong. It is that there has been a rebalancing of energies. The spreading of life in the way that it has across the planet has been a Yang energy. This was a necessary thing for the survival of Gaia.

We are not talking decades or centuries. We are talking hundreds of thousands of years ago now. For there was a moment of impact that brought a different form of energy to the planet, stimulating the planet but also throwing her off balance for there was a great deal of destruction at that point in time. For the life forms on the planet this was a catastrophic situation. In the realm of history, this was a catalystic opportunity for the planet.

The bringing of sentience to Gaia has allowed all of this to happen and has allowed Gaia to become a spiritual being and to express her spirituality through these sentient beings that are populating her now. The notice by spirit came through other beings throughout the universe as they noticed sentience in this location. So what was viewed as a catastrophe by the smaller life forms was viewed as opportunity from a higher perspective and there are more opportunities to come.

The Divine Feminine, the Yin energy of spirit, is certainly increasing. Gaia vibrates to that energy well and always has. The Yang energy now becomes balanced by the rise of Yin energy, not passive, but peaceful. We have to say to the Yang energy, be active, not aggressive.

So the shaking occurs, the same way you might scold a small child. You say, "Stop that!" If the child does not respond, what do you do? You take them by the shoulder, you say again, "Stop that!" and sometimes, "STOP!" So Gaia says, "STOP!" All of humanity then says, "We have to pay attention," and they do and you have seen it happen. Regardless of the cause of the disaster, the tragedy, for example, the buildings collapsing upon themselves and many people dying, the purpose of that is minuscule compared to the actions taken by so many, praying, "Please divinity, be with those people."

Spirit becomes extremely focused then, not just to those but to everyone that connects to that event when they ask, "All of those people that died in a wave, please, be with those people and now, spirit." The raising of the vibration, spirit, happens then. Spirit us? No, spirit Earth. The connection becomes stronger and stronger and the ascension of the earth, the vibration of the earth, rises and rises.

We then say, "Why wait?" Why wait for the disaster, the catastrophe, the cataclysm? Why not institute the catalyst by speaking to those areas now, speaking to those individuals now. It is so easy to do. It is a reflex in times of cataclysm. The higher vibration will make it a reflex in times of peace. This is a way that you can now gauge your spiritual growth. The paths are easy, and the paths are varied: a prayer, a meditation, a simple good wish, perhaps a charitable donation of money or of time. All of these things are very simple, and they take little time.

Here you are existing within time, and you get what everyone else gets, a rotation of the planet, a cycle around the sun. What do you do with your year? What do you do with your day? Within that day, can you find a moment to wish wisdom upon your leaders, those of you that have chosen to take the difficult position of power and governance? It is any wonder that they are unbalanced?

Look at your planet and look at everyone that is pushing against someone else. Send a good thought now to every one of them from every ideology, every faith, every belief system. They can use your good thoughts, your prayer, your meditation. By sending a good vibration out, it is like the plucking of a guitar string. The sound just goes out and the guitar string does not dissolve, it continues to exist. So you will continue to exist. Unless you pluck the string of the guitar, it has not fulfilled its purpose. Unless you send out vibration, you have not fulfilled your purpose of harmonious vibration.

Is there any over-reaching purpose or intent that I should be with my mom when she may cross over? Am I meant to be with her or is there something more about that?

We have spoken of the five energetic categories of humanity, and we indicate that we are speaking specifically about humanity, but we are also talking about other sentient beings at some level. The categories Walker, Watcher, Knower, and Grower are the common ones. The category that increases is the fifth, the Harvester. We will speak directly to you, out of character of these sessions.

You are powerful in the energy of the Harvester. You may experience these situations at various levels, not so much for your life now. As you return, you may have the opportunity to be a very powerful influence in the harvesting work, in assisting the transference and transformation of energy to a higher and higher vibration.

A greater purpose with this individual situation would be the experience you gain, the perspective you gain, the opportunity for learning empathy for others as they go through this same situation. Is it necessary for you to remain extremely close? As the Harvester, you need to learn to make that decision and that judgment for yourself. How do you feel about it in your heart? That is your truest answer. You will not find your answer in your logic. If you feel the need to be away, then that is a true answer. If you feel the need to be close, that would also be a true answer. In this way, you already know the answer to your question. True?

You began by speaking of the Harmonic Coalescence. Is it something off in the future or have some of us here and in the past already begun to experience a coalescing of the energies?

That is true. We are marking this as the time of the Harmonic Coalescence, but now is not the only time that it has happened. It also occurs in cycles of sevens but in levels different from the ability for the human to currently understand. This current coalescence, however, is more integrated with the ascension of the planet earth. The history of humanity at this point and the reduction of species in other areas of the planet is a way of preparing a very different and very new vision of the earth.

The lack of diversity in the human species indicates that you have been in a time of coalescence for many thousands of years. The family human was once many branches. Diversity of humanity begins again through this coalescence. This is part of the greater coalescing of energies, the point of all of that. That is why we speak now. It is not simply the coalescing of energy on the planet, but energies around the planet as well. This is the higher vibration, what you might call an increased angelic presence, where companions in spirit realm and companions in physical realm are so close that moments like this will be unnecessary. We will just all be together.

The passing and the birth will be celebrated equally because we will have a clearer understanding from the perspective of the family human and the rejoicing will not be limited to those that are of the species of human. There is an approaching closeness and some of you feel it now with other aspects of the beings on the planet: cetaceans, elephants, and the horses. They all have something to communicate, and you see the rise in humans that communicate with the animals.

The rejoicing of life, it is part of Source. It is part of true Source energy, and we pull all of our words close to us at this point now as we close our session. We remind you that rejoicing is an expression of joy. These are the things that we speak of at the closing of these sessions.

Source is love. There is no other word for this, that unconditional acceptance of all life and the complete harmonious vibration of all things. Love. Source expresses itself in joyful ways. The more joy you experience, the closer you are to Source. Love coupled with joy produces peace. Have no argument and no position against anything. So we say now, in this way, love and joy and seek peace.

Endings and Beginnings

- Think of your life force as a karmic thread, something that does not stop but that can be woven, something that can be used to create a pattern, something that can change color, something that can change direction, something that can be embroidered on the fabric of reality.
- Love yourself more and more. Treat yourself with love, more and more. Find your center, more and more, regardless of what happens around you.
- Look for new things. Look for new experiences. Take courage and live by your heart and your heart's desire. Take today as a day of change for yourself.
- Wish wisdom and peace upon others in times of trouble, certainly, but even now, every day, send out a good thought.

The Question of Prophecy

The desire for absolute knowledge is strong. There have been those in the past who have seen from a higher vibration what the potential for a future course has been. Many then believe that this is something that cannot be altered. Generations begin to fear the outcome. In fact, the opposite is often more truthful.

If you learn that a road is under construction and traffic is backed up before you get to this point, you seek alternative routes. It is this way with foretelling the future. A prophecy may be given as a warning. One then has the option of changing the possible events to a better outcome. There is no need to fear the future.

This, then, is a prophecy for you. Beings on the physical realm and those that exist in the realm of spirit will begin to communicate with greater ease and frequency. Together we will get better at seeing and adjusting the probable future. We will act in a manner that brings about greater spiritual action all around the planet.

12
Within and Without

We always begin our session with the words: As above, so below. Today we add these words: As within, so without. We are going to step back and take a look at, "within you and without you" and "above you and below you." These are called correspondences, above and below, within and without. We will also add affinities today and we will begin to describe things in this way.

The Egg and the Nest

We will talk about the nest and the nest, as you know, is someplace that holds eggs. Within the egg is the creature to be hatched, let us say "bird." Within the egg is the bird but within the bird within the egg is another egg. It is a probability, and it is a potential. The bird that laid the egg within the nest returns and continues to upkeep the nest, strengthening it where it is weak, protecting it, and the nest also protects the egg when the parent bird is no longer there. Think now in terms of the solar system as a nest and the planet earth as an egg. Are we saying then that within the earth there is another system? Another potential? That the earth will reproduce?

As we look around, we see the children of the earth, the species that is connected with spirit, the species that has tapped into the creative energies of Source, doing what? Reaching out from the egg to other planets. In this way, the earth is not just the egg but also the nest, within and without. The system that we call the earth we also say is Gaia, the living planet. Are we saying then that Gaia has consciousness or that Gaia directs life? In a fashion, yes. There is much about Gaia that will be understood as time goes on, clearer and clearer, and it will follow this concept of the living planet, of a mother planet.

Let us not make the mistake that Gaia is simply Yin energy. Gaia is also Yang energy. That also becomes clearer as Gaia takes action to expel from the nest things that threaten the eggs, things that threaten the potential for continuation, things that threaten the continuity of creation and life. The signs are there for those that are aware, for those that see. The signs are there. For Gaia to eliminate threats, Gaia then takes actions. For some these are fearsome, fearsome because these ones try to maintain the status quo. They have no respect. It may not be that they are purposely fouling the nest; they are simply not paying attention.

This is not a matter of simply recycling. This is not a matter of changing what you eat. This is not a matter of any of those small things. This is a matter of changing what is within you, as an individual, an undivided one. The internal change must look like this. It must look like Gaia. It must look natural. It must cooperate with the natural forces that are out there, that are present, that are within sight of everyone. The concept of straight lines in a person's life must go away. The concept of curves and irregularity must be embraced and encouraged.

As within, so without; as above, so below, and we have spoken this way about the spiritual realm and the physical realm. Now we speak about the undivided ones and apply the concept of as within, so without. Who you are within must be clear to those that are looking upon you from without. No artificiality, no hiding, no masks, no lies. Where is it that you see Gaia lying, covering, masking? Nowhere. If the solar system is the nest and Gaia is the egg, if Gaia is also a nest and the family human is the egg then what is within the family human that makes the undivided one the nest and what is within them, the egg? The answer is the future of life on the planet.

Let us be clear about this, for each species on the planet also holds the future. Parts of information have been spread amongst all the species on the planet. Some of the species hold more important information than others. Some of the species communicate the information in ways that you as members of the family human can not yet comprehend.

Let us look at the bees. They act as a unit. Without the bees, life would begin to decay quickly. No bees, no pollination. No pollination, no plants. No corn, no wheat, no roses. The bees themselves do not have information in the way that your brain has information, but without the neural network of your brain, the sparks and the synapses, your thoughts would remain locked in the individual cells. The bees are like this. They carry the thoughts, they carry the ideas and as they pollinate, the ideas then grow within the new plants. The residual of the bees, the honey, then carries new ideas. These are all particles that the life form that devours and absorbs the energy of the plant, the energy of the honey, then has an opportunity to put together in terms of new thought. In this way the bees carry energy of the future and spread it around the lands. There are bees in every land.

The larger mammals of the planet are the memory. They hold the things past and when it is time for Gaia to recall the process of evolution, they bring this forward.

A Time of Change Approaches

The time is close. The planet is shifting. The Yin energy has nurtured and cradled civilizations and allowed the family human to grow and multiply and spread. In this way, knowledge has also spread about the globe. When an egg hatches, the shell goes away. Its usefulness has ended. We want to be clear here that we are not speaking of great destruction, but we are speaking of great reduction. The energy of life on the planet remains the same. The levels of energy remain the same. The form that it takes alters.

We speak now of the next one hundred years and the current energy of coalescing. This coalescence brings together many disparate energies that have spread and separated over tens of thousands of years now. As these energies come together, there is more opportunity for greater variety and greater expression of variety upon the planet. Once again, we are not saying that this is exactly what will happen in exactly one hundred years. We are saying that we will see the beginning of this change within the next one hundred years.

The change begins within. The change begins within you as you address yourself, as you use your brain, as you use the synapses, as you speak to yourself of what the future will be, not specifically your future. As the energy that powers you, that drives you, that moves you, the anima, the vitality, as that leaves the matter of the body, that energy continues. The purer you make that energy; the purer life becomes in the future. Once again, we are not talking about purity of the body. We are talking about purity of energy.

As within so without, and in this way you begin to affect those around you. For within the solar system each planet affects each other planet. It is a measurable effect. The family human has devised ways of measuring this effect. It is so great, how could they not? It is more difficult to measure the smaller energies, so it has been difficult to define the subtle energies of spirituality and yet the family human gets closer and closer each day. More and more people claim they can feel the subtle energy of spirituality and the weight of the numbers of people that make that claim make it necessary to pay attention. So science begins looking and, in their way, stumbling around. This is the child learning to walk and so we are amused, but amused in a pleasant way as the child learns to walk but fails many times before succeeding. We encourage the child, and we help the child.

There is a large energy coming to an end, the energy of expansion. As the tide comes in, the tide also goes out. As humanity has been looking without, thus their tide starts to go within. More and more we find people pulling within themselves. Some seek guidance still. Some are simply lost to themselves. Here in spirit, we follow this energy. We note it, we comprehend it, and we encourage the child to continue to walk, to continue to move forward. There are those that stumble and fear getting up, lest they stumble once again. We try to comfort those ones. There are those that resist all help. They are going to walk without anybody helping them at all and they find their own means of support and they find their own direction and they are willing to try anything and the best we can do is to stay with them as they begin to go up and down the stairs.

We have spoken about the energetic categories of the human beings, the Walkers, the Watchers, the Knowers, the Growers, and the Harvesters. Certainly, the Harvester class is growing. The generation coming in, the generation that has arrived, is going to be rich with the Harvester class. They are beginning to have children now. Walkers, and the category of Walker, then begins to grow next.

First there will be the harvest and the reduction of the presence of humanity on the planet. Not the elimination, merely reduction, and then the variety begins again. Diversity of species is common in every form save one, humanity. That is about to change. As above, so below, as within, so without. We encourage you now to go within. Are there questions?

Since we are a particle of the creative source of the universe, what makes us forget that right after birth?

As within, so without. The more distractions without, the less you notice the within. You do not forget that after birth. You know that right after birth. You feel it. It is very frustrating, and it is one of the things we find amusing as a story we tell in spirit. We say, "In my last incarnation when I was a child, I remembered and then I got distracted by..." and in this way we learn from each other what distracted us, how did we lose track, how did we get off base? Then we marvel at the randomness of life, that we still managed to fulfill our purpose, our agreed upon contract (we use that term contract very loosely).

We say, "I was distracted by...and then this happened, and Source kicked in and helped me achieve anyway." In this way, the vibration of humanity is getting higher and higher and higher because we do share these stories and we do laugh about the distraction of without. As the vibration becomes higher, it becomes easier to be within.

So, when you go within, do you then remember? What is it that reminded you? It has been there all along. As a particle of Source, as something that carries creative energy, you are different. Because of the linking of the higher vibration of spirituality and the lower vibration of life in gravity, you now get to make decisions as to what vibration you will pursue.

There comes a point in time that you start to realize that there is no wrong vibration. Just pursue it purely, without judgment, without harm to others wherever possible, with support for others wherever possible, but maintaining your own energies and your own strengths.

It is always there, and nothing reminds you, you simply remember, and you remember best when you go within. In this way, as above, that is, in spirit, so below, that is, in the physical realm. As above, we mean the higher vibrations. As below, we mean the lower vibrations. When you are in the below, we can also say, as within, so without. Without is the lower vibration. Within is the higher vibration. In this way, you are closer to the as above when you are within.

If the purpose is to be as pure as we can be before we cross over to assist in the coalescence, if, as you have stated, there are fewer individuals seeking spiritually now than we suspect, how will that energy be encouraged, inspiring people to become purer?

In some cases, it will simply be the passing of that energy and the coalescing of it back to the planet, bringing some of those back together to learn their lessons together in one singular form. Coalescence is a purification process. Life on the planet is also a purification process. Life is a filter. The planet is a filter; it is true. They may not come back in the sense that they come back as members of the family human. Their vibration may be lower in terms of their consciousness and so they may be rewarded a life more suited to their level of vibration, their level of consciousness. This is a blessing in the same way that a human that is promoted to a position that they are not suited for feels relief at the demotion back to the area that they were good at. So the spreading of the vital energies has served a purpose. Now the raising of the vibration of the energies of the planet has become the purpose.

As those ones return to spirit, there will be new agreements made. No one will be forced; this is not punishment. It is also not reward; it is simply energy seeking its own level, its correct level. The energy around the planet has maintained for longer than the energy of any other planet within the solar system. There is a reason for that. It was a decision made. Not a conscious decision in the way the family human understands that, but similar, an agreement with all of the diversities of energies that this is optimal; this is the prime opportunity for all of us to continue to be alive. This is all energies from the smallest algae, from the earliest of the oxygen-dispensing beings, and in this way the planet made small decisions that lead to larger opportunities for larger opportunities. The process has not changed. Gaia continues to make these decisions.

There is no pinnacle to life. The family human has made a mistake in thinking that they are a pinnacle, that they are the end of an evolutionary system. They are a point of evolution, and they too will evolve and that is a constant. The decision to reduce the diversity of the planet was not necessarily solely based on the planet. There was information from off of Gaia that came through. This is why humanity has the level of appreciation of spirit that it does and the access to the creative energy of the universe. This is merely one way to express a life form that appreciates the creative energy, the Source energies. Source appreciates itself in many forms and it does not always look like a human.

It just seems like it would be more efficient to the coalescence if we all worked towards becoming purer now. Is there any potential of energy encouraging that?

The mouse might always think that it would be more efficient for the cat to eat a fish. Change of energy is sometimes very, very difficult. Transformation of many beings at one time is difficult to comprehend and yet it happens repeatedly all throughout the planet. It is why we exist in the form that we do. It is why we welcome ones who have transformed from harsh and hard ways, through battle, through disaster. Here in the spiritual realm, as those ones end their physical existence, we welcome them, we treat them, we bring them back to life. For truly their life never ended, merely transformed.

Efficiency, now there is an interesting concept, because it is not necessarily what you will see throughout the universe. What you will see is movement. Sometimes that movement causes collisions, but the energy of movement never stops. It is why there is sentient life on the planet today. The collision was not advantageous for the life that existed on the planet at that time. Could there have been a more efficient way to do this? Perhaps.

Once again, the family human, because they can be logical, imagines that all things must be logical. We have said before, give up the straight lines. Begin to think of spirals and curves and irregularities. There is an aspect of love about this, and it is hard to tell, when loved ones are lost, that there is an aspect of love. Many of these decisions have been made prior to your incarnation and yet Gaia decides.

When the mosquito bites you on your shoulder, you do not slap your knee. Where there is a problem, Gaia will scratch that itch. Why do people cling to life in the desert? There is a stubbornness about that. Perhaps Gaia does not want life there any longer in the form of humanity. Perhaps there is a desire to allow that area to relax, rest, and recreate. The reduction of a population will, out of necessity, free the planet up to recreate the areas that are tired and worn. The remaining population will then go to where the life is easier, where food is more plentiful and more natural, and it takes less work to acquire food and water. We speak of the seas. This has happened before. It will be happening again.

You have mentioned a destructive course that is coming. Is that close on the horizon and is there anything we can do as an individual and for the higher good to prepare for that?

As we hear our words, we want to be clear and remind all those that also hear our words that it is not cataclysmal, but catalystic. It is not a single point of destruction, but many, many smaller points of destruction. Single points of destruction do not happen that often within the experience of the universe. It is really not destruction. It is really just change. Will there be an increase in moments of catalyst? Yes. You have already seen that. You have already charted that as members of the family human. You look to the increase in the earthquakes. Look to the increase in the strength of the natural occurrences on the planet.

These things are natural: hurricanes and tornados and earthquakes and floods. They are natural things. They happen all the time. They are Gaia's way of shaking things up, stretching. You do this yourself. Stretch, shake your hands, move around, stamp your feet, all to reinvigorate and redistribute your energies. As with Gaia, so with Gaia's life forms. The increase has already begun. There is a wisdom available to the family human and yet we see how the family human does not follow the wisdom en masse. Why would you buy a home built on a fault line? Why would you create a home below sea level? Why would you create a home on the side of a muddy mountain? Why would you create a home on islands of current volcanic activity? There is no clear wisdom in these actions. The wisdom in the action then becomes this: let us return to the "above" so that we can come back in a lower vibration.

There is wisdom in some countries, some ancient lands, and it seems harsh, but the level of wisdom is there, a reduction of the birth rate, reduction of the use of resources, reduction of populations, stability of numbers of population. Are there better ways to go about this? Yes. From our perspective we say yes. But the wisdom is there.

There are ancient lands that have forgotten to touch the earth and although masses of the population there still touch the earth, those that are leading, those that are conducting the logic, they are not, and so they have lost the balance of Yin energy. Other countries allow a population to grow and continue to grow and they call it spirituality as this population starves in the streets and there is no wisdom.

There are areas of Gaia where she is tired. She needs to rest in those areas and so those are the areas that will be affected first. There are areas that are blocked, where once energy flowed freely, areas that are now blocked or dirty. In a sense, this is an efficient form, is it not? If you feel blocked in your digestive track, what do you do? You cleanse. It may not be the most natural thing for you to do, but it works, and you feel better. For life to continue, Gaia must feel healthy, and life will continue.

When you speak of wisdom and logic, would wisdom be "within," the higher vibration and logic be "without," the lower vibration?

There is no wisdom without logic, but logic does not bring wisdom, logic structures wisdom. Wisdom comes from the higher vibration, it is true, but it is the heart's vibration connecting with spirit where wisdom begins. Someone who is strong in their heart is not necessarily wise. They need to be practical as well, so we need the balance of the lower vibration.

So wisdom is a combination of those things, but wisdom is a perspective as well. It is not just the heart, it is not just the logic, it is not just the emotions in the brain, it is also the experience that is garnered by moving, by travelling, by watching, by seeing, by observing. Thus, we say there are the Walkers and then there are the Watchers and then there are the Knowers and after that there are the Growers.

In that sense, the heart and the brain do not produce wisdom, the heart and the brain merely provide the field for wisdom to grow. They need to get out into the light and test what they feel and test what they think and test it together. In a sense you were correct, wisdom is the higher vibration, logic is the lower vibration but again, wisdom must be the heart and the brain working together and adding the experience of life.

Source gains wisdom in this way. You as a particle of Source, as an aspect of the creative energy of the universe, walk around and experience. Source then takes what you experience to its figurative heart or its figurative brain, its Yin energy or its Yang energy, and thus wisdom is created. It is such a higher wisdom and to speak in terms of heart or brain when we talk about Source is so limiting. So again, we refer to the Yin energies and the Yang energies for Source is both of those things in balance. Equal and together, they cannot be separate and that is ultimate wisdom. Separating activities lead you farther and farther from Source.

Sense the freedom that you feel as you consider yourself an aspect, a particle of Source, as you remember that. We sense that as what we say are the three energies to move things forward and so you represent that. We say, "Love" and truly that is Source energy in ways that cannot be comprehended by the family human but are felt never the less and then we say, "Joy" because that is the idea of being alive, of being in existence, and in this way even the planets of the nest, of the solar system, express joy because they exist and they are varied and they have their tasks and they have their purposes and they protect and balance. The sun expresses its joy, providing light not just to the earth but all around equally, up and down and left and right and north and south and east and west. The earth receives such a fraction of the joy of the sun. So rejoice in the sun.

Along with love and joy we say, "Peace." Peace is the balance. Peace is the cessation of struggle. Peace is the stopping of being against, the ceasing of striving, the acceptance of what is and the feeling of flow. Peace is not passive. Peace is motion, free and easy. Peace is following your true path. If you find yourself struggling, perhaps you have stepped off of your true path. Where do you feel the flow the most? Return to those areas. In this way, find peace, both within and without.

(Author's note – The Five Energetic Categories of Human Beings are described in the Harmonic Coalescence section, Chapter 9)

Within and Without

- We encourage you to go within.
- Pursue your path purely, without judgment, without harm to others whenever possible, with support for others whenever possible, but always maintaining your own energies and your own strengths.
- Sense the freedom that you feel as you consider yourself an aspect, a particle of Source

13
Are You Prepared?

As above, so below.

An exciting time is upon us all! It is no secret that we are in a time of change. This is a beginning for you all. It is important for you to now take a look at yourself and your activities. Are you prepared for change?

Much is being said regarding the coming years. We raise the question again, are you preparing or are you merely waiting? Will you be in motion at the arrival of this time, or will you be swept away? Will you be part of the activity?

We note for you that this time is not an event that concludes, but an important part of a process that will continue. It is not a time where true spiritual beings will be still. Rather it is a time of increased activity, and this means you! That is, if you choose to be a part of the changes that have begun in earnest.

A great swell of energy is now building. Are you balanced? There is no time like the present moment to make the decision to be balanced in your mind and in your body and in your spirit.

Make the Decision

If you are feeling some difficulties with this part of your life you have only to ask of your spirit companions and help will arrive. This is not a promise of rescue nor is it a signal that you will not have to make an effort on your own behalf. Your spirit companions are there to help you make wise decisions and choices for yourself. They are there to guide you and not to carry you. This is a time to intensify trust in your inner voice, your intuition. Is this something that you have difficulty with? Let us give you guidance. Begin with little things. This is the way of the universe.

Make the decision to decide. Start with decisions that do not matter all that much. Ask yourself what is right for you. Do not listen to the voices outside of you that say what they believe you *should* do. The change that is coming is about your ability to clearly communicate with spirit. Your intuition is your key to that clarity. Soon will come a time when you will decide things that matter in great ways. A wave of energy has been traveling towards the earth for some time now. It will propel you towards a cleaner and clearer connection with Source.

Make the decision to be healthy in your physical form. Begin with the small things. Understand that the human form is limited, and the existence of the human form is finite. There is much about the physical aspect of humanity that can and will be improved with the coming change.

The energy that is you in this incarnation is borrowed from the universal Source. How are you taking care of it? Much of your future depends on this simple concept. If you choose to grow and purify, you will be given more energy to work within the next incarnation. If you waste time or pollute the energy entrusted to you, much will be redirected away from you.

To help you to understand this principle, ask yourself this question: would you continue to loan money to ones who never pay it back? There are some on the planet who will take whatever they can and squander what they receive. They do not accept guidance. They are a burden. They ask to be carried. They move only when forced from their comfort. The universe does not accept this. All things move in the universe, or they become assimilated into other things. All is given. All is given from the Source. In this way Source gives only to itself and it does not take. Source grows.

We are not speaking of charitable donation. That is a different energy. In some cases, an abundance of energy can be used to assist others to gain motion and momentum. Freely doing so is a sign that you are in concert with Source. It is a sign that you value life, not just your own but also others. It is an attribute of Source. Do you display this attribute in your daily life?

The Value of You

The things you do with your life have value because you do them. They identify you both to yourself and to the creative energy of the universe. A strong identity is a sign of a spiritual being, an undivided one, an individual. The more active you are in spiritually valuable things the stronger your identity will be. If you find no value in what you do, why should the creative energies invest in you? The change that is coming will ask us all to re-evaluate what we do and who we are at the very core of our ongoing existence. This is a karmic adjustment in the universal energies based on decisions made by many beings in both the spiritual and the physical realms. There are many who will find that the paths they have been following will now alter and change. It is not that what you are doing is wrong; it is simply that more opportunities will now arise. The old ways will become less efficient in the pursuit of spiritual goals. This change will affect you from within.

There is no inherently better path, only a better attitude in following your path. As you shift your attitude your path will naturally shift, like a ship trimming sails gains speed or maneuverability. The purer your attitude, the more value your actions, the less time you spend your energy on things that do not move you forward, the faster you will go and with greater accuracy. Your growth and progress along the karmic lines of energy will increase.

At first it may seem as though nothing has happened. Remember that the physical realm is the last to notice the changes. It is affected by gravity and so moves with linear time. Spirit is least affected by gravity and so things seem, from your perspective, to happen nearly instantaneously.

Do not lose patience at this time! For many the changes are already occurring. Have you felt out of place with people around you? Have you had opportunity to question the motives of those you once trusted? Have the old ways of your spiritual practice seemingly failed you? Have you pondered the seemingly senseless actions occurring around the sphere of the earth? You are not alone!

The Change

You asked for the change. It has begun deep within you at levels that human science is not yet comfortable discussing. It is happening deeper than your known levels of DNA. The shift in your vibration is, of necessity, very subtle on the physical plane. If it happened all at once your bodies would be unable to handle all of the sudden changes and your minds would shut down with all the new perceptive abilities. Yet these things are inherent within you.

Nothing and no one outside of you can raise your vibration or change your DNA. It is all something that you will do, and you will do it by your actions and activities, by how you act. You are doing it right now simply by perceiving these words. It is not a matter of agreement with these thoughts; it is the portion of your mind that you are using at this moment.

Take a lesson from the action of light. Turn towards the light and the shadows will fall behind you. There will be some who will be uncomfortable with this for it means that they will be fully exposed to the light. There are some who, by their actions in this incarnation, will continue to seek the shadows. You may find that there are some who wish to stand in your shadow. The change that is coming will not allow for anyone to be anything less than responsible for their own lives. Your attitude in doing this will go a long way in assisting your growth.

What qualities should you then display? We have said these things before and many times and in many ways. We say them again for they are wonderful words and the truest path to pure Source energy possible.

Make the decision to begin to enjoy your life now. Wherever you are, whoever and whatever you are, make the decision to accept the place you are at and the shape you are in. Begin here and refuse to look at the past or current difficulties as anything but the guidance you have been given. If it is difficult then perhaps you have not been listening to your own guides. Perhaps you have not been a participant in the constant flow of communication between the spirit and the physical realms. Perhaps you have passively accepted other humans' viewpoints of what spirit means and not explored your own personal nature. Act now to bring joy into your life. Begin in little ways. This is the way of the universe.

Make the decision to love your life. It does not matter if love was lacking in the past. It is present and available now. The coming change is all about love. It is an expression of the Source towards itself. You are an aspect and particle of the Source and as such you must love yourself if you wish to grow in spirituality and thus in human life. By doing this you will have made the decision to be pure and we have said this before, be purely you!

In doing this you will have found a way to practice peace. You will not seek outside validation for there will be no need. In this you will also not have a need to alter or change anyone outside of yourself. You will experience the peace of being centered. In this way, you will be balanced and thus prepared for the coming change. In this way, you will give to Source the gift of things that define true spirituality, those wonderful words, love and joy and peace.

Are You Prepared?

- Make the decision to decide. Make choices for yourself not based on what voices outside of you feel you *should* do. Begin to re-evaluate what you do and who you are. Begin to be valuable.
- Make the decision to be healthy in your physical form.
- Make the decision to enjoy your life now, today. Spend less time on energies that do not move you forward. Turn towards the light and the shadows will fall behind you.
- Make the decision to accept the place and shape you are in now. Begin here and refuse to look at past or current difficulties as anything but guidance.
- Make the decision to love your life.

Waves

Can you handle the waves of change? It is our question to you, and we say, "Yes you can." Will you, and will you release judgments? That is a choice that you have to make. In all cases as the waves flow, as the waves move, it is best not to fight the wave. It is best to steer through the waves. Navigate to areas of calm and peace.

Remember who you are in this incarnation. Know your core energy. Act in this capacity first and all other energies that you need will come to you naturally. A river does not seek water. Water flows to the river and then to the sea.

14
You Are Not Alone!

As above, so below. We enjoy the light that we see here. We are much appreciative of your presence, each and every one of you. Each of you in your own way has sought enlightenment and we tell you now that you have achieved your goal.

We also will point out to you that enlightenment is not a place of arrival. It is a word that indicates a path or a journey. When we say that you have achieved enlightenment, we mean that you have found this path. You have taken on the role of a being of light. By your actions you now guide others to also find their own way. It is a solitary path, but you are not alone.

Enlightenment is rewarded in many ways and at many stages. Recognize the rewards as you view your life. Some of you have said that you sometimes feel alone. Understand that those are moments of reward, for it is then that your spiritual companions are taking you away from energies that may batter you, that may wound you, that may smother you, that may seek to dim your light. Those moments when you feel alone are those moments when you have the opportunity to fuel your light.

These are the spaces between, and it is where you will find the opportunity to raise your vibration, unhindered by the energies of others. You can create these spaces yourself, these moments of respite and comfort. Some of you have done this through prayer, some through readings, some through meditations, through practice of lighting of candles, recitation of mantras and affirmations. All of these are tools. All of these do the same thing. They allow space and yet connect you closer to the spirit realm. They help to raise your vibration, higher and higher, as you get closer and closer to the spirit realms.

Still, there may be the feeling of heaviness at these times. You feel this. You feel the weight of the lower vibrations. You feel the trap of being in physical matter. We remind you now, it is not a trap. It is an agreement. We request you now reexamine your agreement and honor it. To be here in the physical form in the physical realm is not a mistake.

Gratitude Is Power

We in the spiritual realm are honored by your presence here. Please accept our deep thanks, our gratitude. Gratitude is power, it is an energy and so for each one of you, we express gratitude and give you power and energy. To keep? Certainly not, for energy flows, does it not?

Do you know what you are grateful for? Do you contemplate what you have? It does not have to be something great or grand. Be grateful for small things. Are you grateful for water, clean and pure and readily accessible? Are you grateful for the ease that food and nutrition comes to you? Some have asked for clearer communication with their guides, their spirit companions. Gratitude will open you up to channel, gratitude for being alive, gratitude for having been alive, gratitude for the opportunity to continue being alive in varying forms at varying rates of vibration. Gratitude will allow your vision to expand, and you will more readily sense your companions in spirit.

Let us tell you now, some of you will ascend and will not return quickly to the planet. Some of you will ascend and transform and transform yet again back to the planet quickly. You all have work to do. For some of you it is in the physical realm. For some of you it is in the spiritual realm. We ourselves will return to the planet at some point.

There is a strength within each one of you that we admire. There is a hope that is available to each one of you and we sense that hope is dim in some of you. It is difficult to have hope in times of great change and, make no mistake, you were chosen to be here at these moments, you were chosen to be here at these times, and the one that did the choosing was you. We say again that we have great admiration for your strength.

Your Spirit Companions

We are happy that you have found our words. Seek also to hear your own companions. We say our name, Onereon, means "together" and this is something that we do, we bring beings together and so our purpose is being fulfilled. Each one of you please, if you will, take just a moment now, take a nice deep breath and allow your eyes to close if you choose and think to yourself these words, speak them aloud if you choose, "I am fully aware of my spirit companions." Take another breath.

We have brought with us those that wish to connect with you and there is someone here for each one of you. As much as you wish to hear from them, they also wish to hear from you. In the course of the next three or four days, take some moments out of each day. The moments do not have to be long; they do not have to be formal. Sit quietly and repeat to yourself, "I am fully aware of my spirit companions." Then begin the dialogue within your heart. It is within the heart that you will hear spirit. Speak out loud if you need to. Ask questions, ask for names, ask for personalities, ask how long you have been together. This is all information that is available to you. Ask your purpose.

These things will then be revealed to you but not necessarily in ways you will find to be direct. You will have a change of heart about situations. You will find that subjects and topics appear to you, things that you have never considered before. Please, look at them seriously. We recall to you now the words, "Be careful what you ask for." Nothing will be thrust upon you. You will all have the choice.

You are all near to spirit. Over the course of the next four days, you have an opportunity to grow closer and closer and clearer and clearer in your communication with us. Not "us" Onereon but "us" your own companions in the spirit realm.

Do you know that we, in the realm of spirit, feel alone at times as well? There are times when we are near to you, and you do not observe us. Do you know how alone a person can feel? From the perspective of spirit, we feel alone, but not lonely. For we know the value of solitary practice and solitary walking and so we encourage you to find solitary time, and those are the moments that you become very, very close to your companions, to spirit.

Laughter

We delight that your presence is here. We delight in the way some of you arrived at this point. We delight in how some of you were motivated to be here. We remind you now that there is much humor to be had in the world, the world of the physical realm and the world of spiritual realm. Much of the humor involves us, you in the physical realm and we in the spiritual realm. You see, we are funny. We do funny things. We have funny perceptions, both human and spirit. If you want to become close to spirit, laugh, find something funny. Find something that brings you joy, that you enjoy deeply. Listen to other people laugh if you have difficulty laughing yourself.

Laughter is one of the purest expressions of the energy of joy. Laughter is one of the best forms of releasing old energies. It is balancing. Those that take things too seriously lower their vibration and increase their gravity. They slow down as weight grows. Life feels heavy. Laughter shakes it all loose.

And so we bring you the energy of laughter, the energy of gratitude, and we remind you of these words, channeled a long time ago by a man quite misunderstood. And if you are misunderstood, understand that great spiritual men and great spiritual women are most often misunderstood during their lives. Funny, is it not?

Spirit is represented by humor, by gratitude, and by laughter. Spirit is represented by three qualities: love, joy, and peace. Love, and that begins with yourself. You cannot be centered unless you are in love with yourself. We have mentioned joy. You cannot be centered unless you have the energy of joy swirling around you. When all of these combine, the energy of peace arrives. Peace is not stillness. Peace is activity. Peace is your vibration, rising higher and purer, cleaner and clearer as you sing your note, as you form a strong identity, not for anyone else, but for yourself. We wish this for you now. Seek, in this way, peace.

You are Not Alone!

- Create spaces for yourself of rest and respite, through prayer, meditation, and other practices.
- Reexamine your agreement to be here, on Earth, in the physical form at this time and honor it.
- Be grateful for small things such as clean water and easily accessible food.
- Take some moments out of each day and sit quietly and repeat to yourself, "I am fully conscious of my spirit companions." Begin the dialogue within your heart.
- If you want to become close to spirit, laugh, find something funny. Find something that brings you joy, that you enjoy deeply

15
Source

As above, so below. It is a changing world. There are those among you that feel they are experiencing loss. It is the way of things to advance and gain and mature. It is the way of things to move through the cycles of life and existence, to come together and then to be apart.

We have spoken of the times that we now exist in as the Harmonic Coalescence. When we are not coming together, those times are what we phrase, the Variance. In each of these phases we are still aspects of the Source energy.

Return to Spirit

For many today, you feel strongly the call to return to spirit. This feeling will increase for the family human in the coming years. It is important to remember while you are incarnate upon the planet that you live your physical life fully and honor the energy that is given you. We have said before and repeat now, the energy that is you in this incarnation is borrowed energy from Source.

The drive to reach for spiritual matters is a sign of maturity, both in the individual and the also in the energy of the planet known as Gaia. As Gaia matures and raises her vibrations, you and all life upon her will also gain and mature. Some of you have chosen to make the shift in vibration a conscious thing and you actively pursue a spiritual path. Some have chosen to not live a spiritual path. Their vibration will be raised in time. It is inevitable. Those that chose to live the spiritual life now will precede the others. In no way does this make you superior or better, for you all are of Source energy and one particle of Source is not better than another. Perhaps we could say that some are more efficient in some respects than others.

Source is often described as light. In many ways this is a true statement though not what you might see in your mind's eye. Source is a higher vibration and light is just that. Source is the highest vibration and light is not that. The highest vibration is what we refer to as love. It is accessible to all things regardless of where they exist in the vibrational realms. It is the desire to increase the energy of love in your life that drives you to seek Source.

A Loss of Individuality

Many want to get closer to Source while in their human form. This is like getting too close to a flame. You can and will become consumed. As an individual human this will require you to lose your personal identity. Most members of the family human are not prepared for this eventuality, though it is what happens to all energy at some point. We all return to Source, and we all lose our individuality at that moment. It is not the moment of physical death, that is, the transitioning from lower vibratory humanity into higher vibration of spirit. Here in the realm of spirit we stay as distinct personalities for many levels. However, we do coalesce more and more the higher we go. We must first get used to the increase of knowledge and emotion that comes with such a rising.

We speak of levels and rising, but it is not as crisp as those terms may indicate. There are many of a higher vibration amongst us and we ourselves at times walk amongst you. We do not always incarnate in human form. Perhaps you know of someone of a higher vibration that is not in the form of a human. Rather they exist as an equine or canine or feline. It is often easy to sense the emissaries from the oceans and we remind you now that when we say, "touch the earth" we also acknowledge the great repositories of knowledge that is the oceanic mass.

These levels may appear to you as better in some way, but in truth there is no level that is inherently better. All comes from Source and there is a purpose for all. That there is one Source is not in doubt. There are many perceptions of Source. In this way, Source looks as if it is many different things. All things emanate from Source and so all things are particles of Source.

It is only when someone attempts to raise their personal perception above all others that you begin to lose connection to true Source. The promotion of an aspect of Source wisdom above all others leads to a greater distancing from the center of Source energy. There are those that set themselves up as emissaries from Source and ascribe to themselves a form of deification or godlike status. This is distracting for others. There are some who are weak in their vibrational patterns, and they seek strength. In this way, followers of another person's perception begin to separate themselves from true Source.

The farther they go in this direction the harder it is for them to withstand the light of Source. It is why there is darkness in a spiritual sense. They seek to retain themselves without changing. This is contrary to Source energy which always grows and changes. Look around at all creation and see what does not change. Nothing! All things grow and change and alter and pass and continue in their particles, yet they do not stay static. All things change. Source changes always and in all ways.

This, then, is a strong lesson in spiritual maturity. If you attempt to stay still and change nothing, you are acting against Source. If you seek change and growth, you will be found to be acting with Source energies. We have said before that Source is a creative energy and now we point out that if you are not actively creating your own life, you are not following a complete spiritual path. Spirit is a not a passive thing. It is peaceful. Spirit is not an aggressive thing. It is active. If you are peacefully active in your life, then you are a balanced spiritual person and growing. Note that we speak not of events outside of you, but the inner life of the undivided one.

Return to Source

Your return to Source is, in a sense, an illusion, for you are never anything but Source. You cannot return to anything that is not absent from you! Your return to Source is simply acknowledgement that all is Source.

It is the level of variance that affects us the most. The more aware we become of the truth of Source, the more aware we become of the moments we act in non-creative ways. These times cause us to be dis-eased or not at ease within the flow of the creative energies of the universe. We may struggle to gain control of our lives in our current incarnations. In truth, we can only release and then feel the flow to gain true access to Source. We remind you now that this is not a call to be passive, only peaceful, and peace is an active thing when it is balanced.

It is now a time of coalescence. This is not the first of these times nor the last. Before the coalescence completes its cycle, you must still experience the variance of your incarnations, not just on the planet, but also in the realm of spirit when you are here. As we all purify the energies assigned to us, we will continue to grow together in peace. The swifter we all move towards this, the faster time will move for us all. You have likely felt this increase in time passage.

It is not loss that you feel. It is the removal of lower vibrational situations. As you raise your vibration, you will find that you are in a more spacious place, quieter and more peaceful. The concerns of the planet will transform for you, and you will not feel the need to be involved with things of little value. As you adjust and look ahead you will find more comfort in your life and also more peace. It is inevitable for all the life of Gaia. Accept this now and be on the leading edge of the coalescence. You have been before!

In this way we say to you, "Be love, be joy, and mostly, be peace."

Source

- Live your physical life fully and honor the energy that is given to you.
- If you are not actively creating your physical life, you are not following a complete spiritual path. If you are peacefully active in your life, then you are a balanced spiritual person and growing.
- As you raise your vibration, you will find that you are in a more spacious place, quieter and more peaceful. The concerns of the planet will transform for you, and you will not feel the need to be involved with things of little value. As you adjust and look ahead, you will find more comfort in your life and more peace. It is inevitable.
- Be on the leading edge of the coalescence.
- Understand - You have been here before!

Book Three
Beings
A Journey to Joy

There are new beings on the planet?
Would you like to know who they are?

They do not fear the coming days.
They know that difficulties will pass.
They enter the future with:
Love for each other under all circumstances.
Joy for living no matter what is happening around them.
By acting in a peaceful way, they act in a spiritual way.

Are you willing to be one of the new beings?

Regarding Self

It is in the unique nature of members of the human family to seek meaning to their lives. This is often a search for what is termed "self" and many times it is a looking outward. This is exactly the wrong direction.

Placing our trust in outside influences and teachings to give us a sense of purpose will generally result in being true to someone else's philosophy, ethics, or ideals. However, it is necessary to begin somewhere and before we find our self-confidence we need to listen and learn from others. The trick is to avoid being restricted to and by those early voices and lessons. They are valuable when we are young, but all knowledge and tradition needs to be examined in the light of the present moment in which you currently exist.

It is this willingness to step away from all familial and tribal wisdom that marks the beginning of the journey to your true self. Questions such as, "What do I believe? Does this tradition make sense? Is this belief valid to me personally?" all lend themselves to the release of the fetters of the past.

It is not that the beliefs and convictions of the past are necessarily in error. It is that we are not moving into the past. Rather, we look to the future, and here is where the human family touches on the spiritual aspect of life.

It is the inner voice that we must find and learn to listen to if we are to grow in a spiritual way. Following another's path will allow you to learn much about that person, but little about yourself.

The seeker must first believe that there is something to be sought. At that moment they can be lost if they are convinced that it is something other than themselves and their true essence. The light that exists within each being, all creation really, is the thing that directs the seeker. Too many times people turn away, fearing that the light is too bright. The seeker does not fear the light. They use it to examine all the dark areas of themselves and adjust, without judgment, their lives.

In this way, their future is brighter, and they find their personal truths. These truths may change as time passes. Continuing to listen to the inner voice is a choice. It is also a skill. When we feel inspired, it is often that same inner voice that provides direction for acting on the inspiration.

Being who you truly are is a gift we are offered in life. The actual act of being human, fully interacting with all the varied experiences available to us, is a choice. The process of creation continues. Your opportunity is to create your own life and exist as your true self.

If you knew you could not fail, what would you do?

Jeff Michaels

Table of Contents

1. Happy Beings 1
2. Choice Point 7
3. New Beings 13
4. Imaginary Beings 19
5. Being Abundant 27
6. The Future of Humankind 33
7. Communication 39
8. A Wave of Change 45
9. Loving Beings 51
10. Community 59
11. Comparing Vibrations 65
12. You are a Nexus for Change 71
13. A Gift 77
14. Harmonic Coalescence 83
15. Comfort and Truth 89
16. Are We There Yet? 95
17. Seeking the Future 101
18. Seasons of Life 107
19. Appropriate Faith 113
20. The Action of Charity 119
21. The Power of Love 125
22. The Decision of Peace 131
23. The Purpose of Joy 137

1
Happy Beings

And so we begin with our opening phrase: As above, so below. It is an interesting phrase. The phrase itself is our lesson in a way. We do not arrive today with a specific lesson. We just simply arrive with a feeling of joy, a feeling of happiness. We ask you all now to pause for just a moment and feel happiness. Each one of you has had happy moments, so feel happiness now. Recall those moments. When we say, "As above, so below," understand that we feel happy right now. So below, on the planet earth, feel happy.

Growth in Spirit

Each one of you has your guides. We ask now that you elevate yourself from needing spirit guides to accepting spirit companions. Ah, now that requires you to reevaluate yourself and to find value in yourself that you may not have seen before. You must understand that feeling happy and feeling joy indicates to you that you are then close to those who have been your guides, but now are offering themselves as your companion, your friend. Let us say one more word, "partner." A partner in what? A partner in your spiritual growth, certainly, but also a partner in your companions' spiritual growth.

Even though we are in spirit, we can still raise our vibration. We have chosen a certain path. We have chosen to be here with you, and this required us to lower our vibration. Were we to completely retain the high vibration of spirit and communicate from that level to yours it could hurt your physical forms, so we stay in a lower vibration as we communicate.

The vibration we now chose to communicate is joy and happiness, and the vibration we ask that you choose to communicate back is companionship and partnership.

Each one of you is ready to grow. Have you requested spiritual growth? Do you acknowledge that you have asked for this in your prayers and your meditations? You have said this to others and so now, grow! It can be as simple as this - feel happy.

Understand that your guides, your companions, are feeling happy now with you, with who you are, with where you are, and with your personal achievements to this point in time. Now, there have been mistakes. Do you know that we too make mistakes, yes, even in spirit? We do not call them mistakes, we call them experiments, because we try things and sometimes they do not work. So we release the energy and we allow that energy to become something else, something new.

In your lives you have made mistakes. You have tried things. Now release the energy of feeling that you failed at something and understand that you had a lesson. Now you can take that energy and turn it towards something new.

A Test of Spirit

Here is a spiritual test for you: Feel happy and return to that feeling of happiness. Now shift your perceptions and feel happiness about a mistake that you made in your life. This is a little more difficult, and yet your guides are happy that you made those mistakes because those mistakes have brought you to this point. In some cases, they propelled you, they motivated you, and they drove you to get away from situations that were not beneficial to your growth.

We see something. It is true that for some of you there was a direct intervention, what you might call an angelic deliverance, something similar to a rescue or a saving. This is not weakness on your part; this is something that represents your value. How can we say that? If you were not valuable to spirit, there would not have been that intervention. So feel happy about that situation where your angels saved you.

Our lesson is happiness. Our lesson is simply to be happy. This draws you closer to your guides, your companions. It is difficult to be happy all the time, is it not? There are many, many things that seem to take our happiness away from us. That is often a choice.

Our thoughts turn to the many conflicts and wars that are now being engaged in around the planet. These are not things that make us happy, and these are not things that we can be happy about. Yet, we can find things around those situations to be happy about. There are good things that are happening in the world and some of them are in connection with these conflicts. Was there an easier way to change this energy? Yes. There was an accumulation of lower vibrational energy, however, and so sometimes a wave of energy just forms and there is no changing the way of the wave. There is only enduring the wave; there is only getting out of the way of the wave. This wave will soon pass and so, for that, be happy.

The Feeling of Spirit

Do you feel your guides? Do you know them by name? Do you have a description of them in your own mind? This is not required, but it will help. To believe in something that is unseen – how do you do that? It is good to make things real. Allow yourself to know these ones by the feeling that they bring to you. This is why we have chosen the term "happy" this day. Your guides are happy. They are happy beings. They find pleasure in many, many things. Again, we say to you, "Feel happy!"

We ourselves feel happy but it is not what we are known for. We, Onereon, tend to be known more for our compassion, our willingness to help others. This is a strength of ours and so our channel, our voice, also holds this strength, which is a similar vibration. You each have a strength and the guides, the spirit companions that you work with, have a similar strength. Notice what we say here, "those that you work *with*." You work *with* them, not *for* them. Perhaps you are a nurturer, perhaps you are a scholar, or perhaps you are a gatherer. Your guides, your companions, will match that energy.

We speak to you now so that you can have a different perspective of who is around you, who is keeping company with you, who is there for you, and who you are there for. Because it is as above, so below. And it is not just that if your guides feel happy then you feel happy. It is also if you feel happy, then your companions can also feel happy. In this way, you are also are a guide to those who exist around you in spirit. We guide each other. We walk hand in hand and not simply through this life, which you see from your birth through your death.

Let us say this about birth and death and we have said this before: Your life did not start at conception; your life does not end at death. It is a continuous thread, and we are all woven together in a fabric of spirit, a tapestry. And just like the thread, sometimes you go over another thread and sometimes you go under another thread. Sometimes you go above and sometimes you go below.

The Feeling of Earth

It is a natural process, then, to come alive on the planet and then to shift the life force off of the planet into the spirit realm. Let us say this now, when in spirit we may be considered off of the planet, but we are not far off. We are connected to this planet in the same way that you are. We are *of* the energy of this planet, the same way you are.

The planet is a crystalline structure. Just as you know that you do not end at your own skin, that your energy radiates out from you, the planet also radiates energy outward in an ethereal way. You exist within this energy, and it forms you. As the energy of the crystalline grids clarify and purify the planet, so do you become clearer and purer. This is happening now. All through the planet there is a raising of vibrations. All around the planet there is a shifting and adjusting of vibrational energies. We feel this too! More and more, people seek spirituality as an answer.

If you want to be more spiritual in your life, look for things to be happy about. If you want to be happier, look for the ways that spirit is active in your life. And so we say again: As above, so below. We enjoy our times in discussion. We see you in ways that you cannot see yourselves. We see the purity that is all around you, the holiness and the light of Source that shines from within you. You may only see the physical matter in which you exist. The matter is important, but it is not what matters. Please know, as you go about your lives, each one of you, feel happy. Perhaps write this down on pieces of paper, *happy, happiness,* and place them in areas that you frequent, such as your bathrooms, your kitchens, your bedrooms, your cars or where your work, so that you remind yourself, because you will need reminding. This is the quality that your guides are bringing to you, happiness. This is the quality that you also, naturally, exude from within. For it is a quality of Source.

Thank you for being here at this present moment. We rejoice in these moments. They are interesting to us, and we learn from these times as we observe your energies. We rejoice and this is a form of joy. We relax and we feel peaceful when we see like ones, ones like you. Because we know that things are on a path and that things are working. You see, you are the proof. You are the spiritual evidence that things, that vibrations, are rising. We feel love for you, and we hope you feel love for us. And so, we close now with simply those words: love, joy, and peace.

2
Choice Point

As above, so below. We always welcome the presence of those who seek a wider vision of life. There are times when your existence may seem narrow and cramped. There are many who have this feeling, and we tell you now that it is an intensifying of energies that you sense. Changes are upon us all! It is to those that desire a change in their lives that we now speak.

A Lesson on Variety

First, then, a lesson on variation. We again note that the universe does not promote conformity. The universe does promote diversity or variety. It is this that makes the way of linear life fascinating and endless. It is what creation is based upon. You are an aspect of creation.

At the beginning of all things, that is, things of the material, physical universe, Source chose to create a vibration. As the vibration expanded, other vibrations came into play and into being. These were in harmony to Source and the original vibration. Each vibration separated and expanded into the way of the universe and on to this moment in linear time. You are each an individual vibration, an action of the universe that is a direct result of the original moment of Source choosing to create. As a result, you have within you the ability to create a new and varied vibration. By making that new vibration a harmonious one to Source, your opportunity to achieve your desire is increased.

We ask you now: What is within your life that you would change and what is outside of your life that you would choose to add? It is a time of change, and you have the opportunity to direct this energy for your benefit.

Choosing to Change Your Life

The universe that exists at this point is a series of possibilities. The possibilities are endless, and you are one of these possibilities. The difference between the matter around you and you as an individual is that the family human has within its makeup the ability to access the energy of choice and choosing. You can choose how you wish to display variety in your existence.

A key ingredient in this is the actual moment of choice. A desire on your part sets the energy of creation into motion. If you find you are not within the realm of possibilities that are comfortable to you, you must choose to move to a new set of potentials and possibilities.

There are many around you who would limit your potential. There are many who have a belief in the way things should be, who feel that the world is a certain way and there can be no other. These ones have limited their own vision and seek to have others agree with them and offer support to the limitations. They have chosen to not grow. They have chosen to dampen any attempt by others at reaching a higher vibration. It is imperative for you to remove yourself from such ones for your growth to begin and continue.

When we say remove yourself from them, we mean just that. Do not make an effort to free them from their thinking or limitations. This will only limit you further by engaging your energies in unwelcome pursuits.

We do not put a judgment on such ones. We do acknowledge their place in existence as holders of energy. These ones keep a level of stasis so that others may take a strong step or leap into new areas. If you are comfortable staying in place, then make that decision and become still.

We feel that if you are reading these words you are seeking to move to a different level. We address those ones now. The choice point is within each one of you. It is a point of power. It is the moment of realization that there is more available to you, that the universe is large and abundant.

All too many people let this feeling build up until they are forced to change their lives. They continue to exist in patterns that no longer suit them. They wait until their life is close to being unbearable, until stress presses them to a point of breaking and the decision is forced upon them.

We invite you now, this very moment, to make a different path for yourself. Choose to re-evaluate your position in this incarnation. Ask yourself large questions and do not be afraid to answer them honestly and aloud.

A Desire for Life

This, then, is a second key ingredient, the strength of desire. The more you want something, the more likely it is that you will receive that potential. And now we say, do not waste this creative energy on mere accumulation of things. Objects will not bring happiness. This is not to say eliminate all of your possessions. It is a truth that while you are physically incarnate you will need physical things around you, some for survival, but some also for pleasure. Pursuit of mere objects, however, will interfere with your ability to raise your vibration.

Pursue the feelings you wish to exist within. Here is another truth. Spirit connects to you primarily at the energy of the heart, the emotions. If you are following your heart and you are feeling emotional satisfaction in your daily life, you will not need to strive for spiritual growth. It will simply occur, like a seed flowers when well-watered and in rich soil.

A trap that many fall into is one of goals. The setting of goals may make someone believe that once they have achieved a certain position or possession, they will automatically experience spiritual growth or a higher vibration. They may believe that there is a point at which they can stop moving. This is opposite of true spirituality. Rather than set goals, set markers for yourself. These will indicate progress rather than an ending and you will then continually set new markers for your journey. In this way you are in constant motion and energy will flow through you.

Move Continuously

Here, then, is a third ingredient. Allow energy to continually move through you and you will always have what you need. Stop energy flow in your life and you will start to struggle. This requires that you let go of old expectations and beliefs and it is here that many of the family human stop in their ability to create what they desire. There is an expression that states, "A ship is safe while it is in the harbor, but that is not what a ship is built for." A ship's purpose is to travel and experience, explore and trade, learn new things and visit new places. When was the last time you personally travelled or explored or learned something new?

This is a way to bring your physical being, the energy that you have borrowed to use while incarnate on the planet, together with your heart and brain. This, in turn, connects you to your spiritual aspect, what might be termed the essence of Source that connects you to all other beings.

Simple Actions

It all begins with the simple action of you making a choice. What do you want in your life? What do you want to see or do? What do you want to learn or experience? Who do you want to meet? What do you want to achieve while on the planet? What do you want to achieve after you have left the planet? What do you want to achieve when you return to the planet? These are not questions that can be answered with logic. They must be answered from the heart.

The degree of your willingness to do so determines the speed that your desires become realities. It is not an easy thing to trust the unseen in the realm of the physical these days. That is why it is called faith. That is the action of spirit.

There is, then, one more element in the creation of your life. As a member of the family human, you are subject to gravity and so you exist in linear time. When you are aligned with spiritual energy, things will occur much more quickly than you may have been taught to believe. Yet time still must pass for the creative energies to shape and bring into existence your desire.

Patience, then, spiritual ones! You have the assurance that you are an aspect of Source. You know this inside of you where there is no logic. Stillness is not inactivity. Stillness is a feeling of peace and calm, a knowing that all will be well in its own time. Once you have set out on your voyage you must continue to chart and navigate. These are simple actions. Your destination will appear in time. And then you choose where to travel to next!

Move to your own decisions and journey your own path. Act in the manner of a spiritual being. Be bold in the love that you feel for life. Enjoy every day. Support peaceful relationships with all that you encounter.

3
New Beings

As above, so below. There are new beings on the planet. Would you like to know who they are?

They act in different ways, and they think in different thought patterns. Their goals are not what many humans seek or have sought in the past. They approach life in ways that make the world around them better each day.

They do not get angry at political events. They do not despair at financial changes. They do not react to created fears. They do not get involved in the mundane dramas of other people.

They walk their own path. They create their own life. They seek to improve themselves first, to make changes to their own perceptions. They look at the world through their own eyes and make their own decisions. They look for things of real value.

For these ones, life is always good. For these ones, every experience is a purifying one, a lesson that will only improve their energies and prepare them for the next days or even the next moments. For these ones are constantly renewing their energy. They are in continuous growth.

They are not always happy or joyful. They are subject to the same stresses and pressures of daily life that every other being on the planet faces. Sometimes they too may feel overwhelmed. It is then that these new beings step back. It is then that they ask, "Are my attitudes and my actions adding to or releasing the stress? Is this a situation that has true value, one where I need to engage my personal energies? Or is there a better use of my life, my thread of karmic existence?"

They feel sadness. They feel loss and grief. Why would they not? We here in the spirit realm also feel sadness when one of our companions suffers. We do not allow ourselves to stay in sadness. We look for ways to improve the situation or to exist in a balanced way as the sadness runs its course. These new beings on the planet also face tests looking for the balance. They will often ask their spiritual companions for assistance, and guess what? They will often receive it!

When judgmental statements are made, they will ask, "Why does this one need to make that statement? What do they lack within themselves that makes them try to remove balance from others?" These new beings will not engage in countering the judgment nor will they agree with it. They will simply continue to walk their own conscious path.

Spiritually and emotionally, these ones will seem to be consistently calm. It will seem as if they walk in a meditative state, not oblivious to the world around them, but aware of what is all around the world.

Mentally and physically, these ones will seem to be always growing more vital, seeking new thoughts and ideas and information. They will look for ways to improve their physical situation and apply themselves to healthy and wealthy ways of living.

These new beings will not announce themselves. They will not ask anyone to follow them. They will not claim any lineage to old ways of thought or belief. They will not seek approval from outside of themselves.

They will not seem to belong to anyone or anything. They may be very wealthy, or they may be of very humble means. They will not look to see what you wear or where you live. They will look at you as an individual and find the value that is at your core, your very essence. They will see what is golden about you. They will see your light, your spark of vitality, and then they will fan that flame!

Who Are They?

Where do they come from? Where have they been? How will you find such a being?

They come from where you are. They have been here all along. Cease looking outside of yourself for these ones, for they are YOU!

The world around has become new. We have gone through several changes in our recent history on the planet and we will have the joy of experiencing yet another in a matter of years. It is all new now, yes. Soon it will all change again. If the world is new, then so are you!

From our perspective in the realm of spirit, we see clearly the preparations that many are engaged in and it is good. Yet some are approaching this time with a sense of fear or foreboding. This is often simply a feeling that they may not be worthy, that somehow they are not acceptable. This is often due to a comparison to others who seem to be doing so much more. We tell you now that there is not one person on this planet that is unworthy of spiritual growth.

Source asks each one of us to do only what we are able to do and no more. Some are called to walk in front of others, and they are given the means and power to do so. Most are asked to walk simply through their daily lives, acting in a manner that balances the world around them.

How do you balance the world? By balancing yourself first, of course, but there is more that can be done. Smile at people. Speak words of value, words that lift others' spirits. Do not look away from those in distress. Look them in the eyes and speak consolingly and with hope. Do you have hope?

Help someone without being asked or seeking reward. Help them directly. Do not simply contribute funds or supplies to an agency, rather do that and then help distribute what has been contributed.

A Wave of Energies

This is not a call to preach or proselytize. There is no agenda to promote. It is a call to feel compassion for everyone. All beings on the earth will progress through the coming wave of energies. Some will not be prepared. You cannot prepare them. You can only prepare yourself. Are you prepared?

The wave may seem like destruction to some. Those that seek to maintain old systems and patterns will despair to see these things washed away. Are you clinging to old patterns within yourself? Do you still identify yourself with what you once were? Have you grown in any significant ways in recent years?

All will have the opportunity to participate in the new ways. Are you holding animosity towards anyone? Will you be able to work side by side with anyone on the planet? We are not saying that everyone will be or must be in agreement. We are saying that everyone will be in existence together. We are saying that old boundaries will dissipate and fade. You have seen walls fall.

What will these energies bring? We will tell you now that there will be an opportunity to become closer to the planet, to partner with Gaia and live fuller and more vital lives. In fact, "opportunity" is the best word we have at this moment. Much that we have all desired for so long will begin to return.

It will be a challenging time, to be sure. Many will accept a transformation during this time of change. Many from the realm of spirit will then be returned to the embrace of Gaia to join you again. Are we prepared? We prepare every moment and when we feel a need for assistance, we ask Source and our own guides and companions for help. And guess what? We receive it!

How Will You Act?

Do these words today bring you fear or hope? Do have a desire to protect yourself, or do you feel a growing joy opening inside of you? How attached to the old patterns are you? It is no fault to be attached to them at this time. It is the way of things. Are you ready to release them?

It is good to think of the future. It is good to imagine, to create an image of what you would like to see for all of humanity. Do this not with a spirit of what you do not want, rather with the idea of possibility and potential, of what could be. Do not limit yourself. The universe is vast and contains much energy and also much space. Dream large dreams, for you are an aspect of Source and Source is a creative energy. If you begin to create this future now, the transition will go along that much smoother and with greater swiftness. Much depends on the beings on the planet. Are you willing to be one of the new beings?

It will be a spiritual world, but it will also still be a physical world. Pay attention to yourselves in this regard. There will be no changes to the aspect of time, only ways that we deal with gravity. Health will come will more ease, but it will not be automatic. Effort will still need to be made in all things. Become vital now and do not wait. It will not be easier to catch up. Be in motion now.

Imagine what you want for yourself in the physical realm. Apply those principles that we speak of so often. Create images of the physical world in terms of love, a loving planet of immense beauties and experiences. Create images of living life in a continuous state of growing joy. Create images of yourself walking in peace and serenity.

As above, so below. We, here, in the realm of spirit, act in these ways. If you too are acting in love and joy and peace, then you are walking with us and we with you, together as it has always been. As it will always be.

4
Imaginary Beings

As above, so below. From above, we see clearly the energy of manifesting. It pools all about each one of you. It is a creative energy, and it is abundant. It is yours to use.

We bring this to your attention at this time for a reason. Many of you still believe that you must call on beings outside of yourselves to gain access to the creative energy of the universe. We tell you now that YOU manifest! YOU do this creating. You are an aspect of the creative energy of Source, and you can bring into existence the life that you want to live.

For many on the planet these days, there is a drive to create or manifest money or objects to possess. This is one possible use of the manifesting energies, but it is not the most efficient use, nor the most beneficial. We see from above that many are trying to recreate lives that others are already living. This puzzles us, especially at the point of time that we all exist. There is a great awakening that has been underway for some time. A spiritual maturing of the family human is evident. Why has the next step been so difficult to take? What is the next step? It is the responsibility for your own personal actions and peace, the movement of the individual away from following someone else's path to forging their own way.

Life on the earth is ever increasing in speed and complexity, so it can be a little frightening to some who have not learned to gain or maintain their balance. Life on the earth has also increased in opportunities for each member of the family human to become their own person, to live by their own ethic and belief and to express themselves in their own unique way. First, you must be willing to learn who you really are, deep inside of yourself. Not who you have been, rather who you can become!

How to Become

What is it like to be the first to imagine a different way? Rather than look backward and expect things to be the same, what if you choose to look forward and try to create something new? It is then that you are close to being Source itself. Although you are only a small portion, a particle of Source, you have access to great energies when you do this.

The first thing that must be done is to create an image. This is done not by logic, for logic will give you only what has come before, what is a known fact. This image will come from your heart and emotion for it is there that there are few boundaries. It is there that desire arrives. It is there that inspiration occurs. This is a form of spiritual communication.

Release the need for structure, at least at first. That will come later, and it must. When you are in gravity, the creative energies of the universe will insist that something holds things together, so structure will grow. There is life that is not vertebrate on the planet. There is intelligent life that is without vertebrae in the universe. Still, there is structure and support for such ones. Not in the ways that a being with bones can easily imagine, for your reality is one of solidity.

The image that you create does not need to be detailed. It needs to be satisfying. It needs to be something that makes you smile or feel content, joyful or at peace. Does an image of currency or precious metal make you feel this way? Likely the answer is no. Does an image of a beautiful sky or mountain or sea create this feeling? Likely the answer is yes.

So start with place. Imagine that you are in that place that touches your heart. Do not be concerned as to where it may be exactly on the planet. Only imagine a place that feels right to you as an individual. Imagine that you are in that place. Next imagine a task or project that brings joy and happiness to you. This does not need to be something altruistic or charitable. We are talking about your fulfillment at this point. The imagining of a project is essential. Creative energies are energies that are in motion. Something must be accomplished, or they will not function well. Imagine that you are accomplishing this project.

Being Still

Although activity will be required for the realization, the making real of the image, we say now that the best way to create and imagine is to be in quiet meditation and focus your intention on these images. Solitude is beneficial for you are creating your life. No one else need be aware of your intention. In fact, a sure way to lessen the energy of creation is to share your images with others. They will, with good intentions, attempt to adjust your vision to suit their own. We have said before: Do not waste your words.

Stillness will come to a conclusion. As you focus and create, energy must begin to move in a specific direction. This may take some time. Others are also creating all around you. Your manifesting must take its turn and also flow with other energies. While you wait, take time to connect to your spirit companions. Share your intentions with them for they can see from a different perspective and may have beneficial guidance and ideas for you above what another human may be able to observe.

There is no set goal for you. There is no script or pre-destined life. There is only what you decide to be. Do not fear! Imagine! Imagine yourself as how you want to be and the creative energy of the universe will begin to act as if it is already true. Soon, reality will catch up to your imaginary self and you will find you are a different person than you were and perhaps even more than you could have imagined.

Techniques

There are many manifesting techniques available. Explore them until you find something that feels natural to you. The simple fact is that within yourself, within your heart, is the best place to create your life. Do not accept someone else's opinion of what technique or procedure is the best for you. Only you the individual, the undivided one, can know what is best for you. It must feel right to you. It must give you a feeling of joy and peace.

A spiritually enlightened being will not need to use someone else's techniques for long. Once the energies of manifesting have been accessed, they will begin to be integrated into your consciousness. You will begin to manifest and create your life without thinking. It will become as natural as breathing. Here is a secret of sages from all history: Your breath is an integral part of your connection to spirit and thus to Source. It is why so many traditions emphasize breathing techniques in varying forms of meditation. Notice your breath.

Participation

There will come a time when others around you will know that something is changing. We may be individuals, but we do not exist within a vacuum. Others are affected by what we do or do not. We have loved ones or those we care for or care about and these ones need to be taken into account.

The reason we caution you about involving others too early in your creation is to ensure that you manifest what is purely in your heart for yourself. It is an interesting aspect of the energy of manifesting that it will never cause an outcome that will damage others. It may appear that way in some cases, but if you examine closely you learn that others resist change and so damage themselves. Or possibly it is that others resist taking responsibility for themselves.

Your creation of your life may require others to walk their own path rather than rely on your strength to carry them. Creating your own life carries with it the connotation of letting others face their own consequences. It is a spiritual law that you will reap only what you, personally, have sown. This is a truth.

It is likely that, once begun, others around you will feel the wave of potential and decide to join in and create their lives as well. Allow them the same space that you gave to yourself. Once the energy of growth begins, you will find that you naturally grow together or apart. The important thing is not to interfere with another's growth. Doing this is taking you away from your own creative path.

The Risk

The universe is a constant surprise. You may find yourself being asked to change your life in astonishing ways. You will always have the choice to say no, but we recommend that you say yes whenever possible, especially if you are the one who set the energy in motion that created the opportunity presented to you!

Will there be risk? Yes, absolutely, and every single time you use the manifesting energies there will be risk! Source has accepted the risk of spreading itself out through the universe. It has not always taken an easy way. Yet there is great opportunity for beauty and wonder everywhere in the cosmos and on every level of vibrational energy. Acting in this way, you will feel yourself rise in vibration.

It is a choice of some to stay where they are and strive to maintain a level of sameness of energy all around themselves. It is a choice of some to stay where it appears to be safe. There is risk involved in this path as well, but there is little reward available in staying safe. Acting in this way you will remain at a lower level of vibration. This is neither right nor wrong. It is simply a choice.

If you try using the manifesting energies and perhaps things do not work in the manner you expected, do not become discouraged. Try again and again. We see from above that the creative energies are all around you! What do you risk by not using them? Life is a creative process from the moment of conception to the moment of transitioning and beyond. The more you are active in the process, the greater your joy will be and the greater your peace of mind. The more you take the initiative to create the life that you want and desire, the greater your connection to Source energy, and we remind you at this time that Source energy is also called love. Seek Source. Seek yourself!

Companions

Engage with your spirit companions now. Do not despair if at first this is not easy. Practice is necessary and time will bring you closer. The distance is not from the side of spirit. Your belief in your own abilities and worth is where the distance occurs. We are here! Speak to your spirit companions right now.

There may be tasks ahead of you that you will find difficult. Your spiritual companions will assist and guide if necessary, but no task will be given that is not within your ability to complete. All tasks will relate to your growth. All tasks will relate to increased harmony, not with other humans necessarily, but with your own self, the integration of your body with your heart and brain and then with the element of spirit that is you.

5
Being Abundant

As above, so below. You are aspects of the universe! You are particles of the Source of all being. You are connected to the creative energies that formed all things seen and unseen. Do these words thrill you? Do they give a sense of belonging? Are you aware of these concepts in your daily routine?

For so many, life becomes a series of moments that are just like the days that preceded them. For so many, life has become an exercise in endurance, waiting for the next day off or the next social event to break a cycle that is very small. It does not have to be this way.

You are an aspect of the creative energies. You are not simply connected to them. We cannot emphasize this enough. There is an aspect of awareness that you must gain regarding this information. When you make a simple statement, you are inviting the creative force to action. Become aware of how you speak. This may answer some of your questions regarding your life at the current moment. Do you say, "I am tired," or "I am bored," or "I am without resources," or similar statements? Do you speak in terms that visualize life and the planet as growth oriented and vital? Or do you speak about problems and shortages? This is where the creation of your life begins.

Become aware of how you speak, and your existence then begins to change. Say what you want, not what you fear.

Co-Creating

Part of this awareness is that you are not the only being who is creating. This means that you will find it necessary to navigate through other beings' creations, that is, their lives. When you use the term "co-creation" remember that you are not just speaking of another being creating with you. There are other beings creating their existence without even knowing you. These other beings have thoughts and opinions of their own and a unique perspective as well. You must remember that they are also aspects of the Source, as are you. There will be times when it is necessary to be patient while other beings pass by on their journey. In the broadest sense, all creation is a co-creation.

We focus now on the concept of co-creating with someone else. Sometimes that will be a physical family member, other times that may be someone who is a business partner. Sometimes you may find yourself dealing with someone who is not on the physical plane at all. Let us speak of this latter situation.

If you are co-creating with a being of higher vibration, then you may want to allow them to express their perspective, for they have a greater sight. This does not mean that you must accept their sight as best. Your opinions are valid in the creation of your own life. There are three aspects to your life. They are body, mind, and spirit and these are not separate from each other. They must be equally fulfilled and balanced for happiness. You must pay attention to each of these areas as you create your life. Your spiritual companions are aware of your spiritual needs most of all. They are least aware of your physical needs. This is where you must place your attention to achieve a balanced and healthy life while you exist on the planet.

Prosperity, Wealth, and Abundance

There are three interlocking energies that provide for a happy physical life. We often find ourselves using these terms to discuss money, but in truth there is much more that contributes to a happy physical life. As we have said before, money is a symbol and nothing more. It is a symbol of energy, your energy, and you would all do well to learn what other energies impact your life and affect your relationship with money.

The three energies that provide for a happy physical life are prosperity, wealth, and abundance.

Prosperity is the energy of increase. It is applicable to many areas of life and should begin in each of those areas to be the most beneficial to you. Be prosperous in health and in your intellectual pursuits and in your relationships, and then prosperity will come more naturally in terms of wealth.

Wealth is the accumulation of energy, generally in the form of possessions or money. The goal of a prosperous person is not to accumulate vast sums, but rather to create a flow of abundance that benefits many, not just oneself.

Abundance is the use of energy to create a comfortable place for growth. It is similar energy to that of sharing. You do not need many things to create an area of growth, so there is no need to wait until you have amassed wealth to act in an abundant way. In fact, if you act within the energy of abundance, wealth will come to you easier, for wealth is an energy that needs room to grow.

Being abundant, then, is not simply about having more. It is about growing or creating. This requires you as an individual, an undivided one, to take certain steps and actions on your own behalf. You must be clear in what you desire and state a specific and attainable goal. Do not set small goals!

Setting Goals as a Spiritual Work

Once you have stated your goals clearly, you must act in a manner that is in harmony with them. If you wish for a peaceful family life, you must act in a peaceful, not passive, way. If you wish to have a higher quality of home or clothing, you must look and inquire and act as if those things are available to you. Even if you do not clearly see the path that will take you to your goals, you must take steps toward them.

The setting of goals is a spiritual work. It is a spiritual work because it affects your karmic thread. The setting of goals begins on the physical plane, however. Many believe asking for something physical is somehow against their spiritual path, as if lack has some hidden virtue. Does the universe lack anything? No, the universe contains everything! Again, you are an aspect, a worthy aspect of the universe. The universe wants balanced energy. If you lack something or deny yourself something needed, then you may find that your personal energy has become imbalanced.

In fact, if you are in accord with the energies of prosperity, wealth, and abundance, you have an opportunity to assist others to gain their own balance. We remind you now that you can only balance one individual in your life and that is yourself. No one can do this work for you; they can only assist you. That is why you have spiritual companions, so that you can have opportunities to become spiritually balanced.

Your existence on the physical plane offers you a potential that your spirit companions cannot easily access: the potential to assist other physical beings. This places you in good company. It also gives you access to more energy for creation, for the universe wants energy to flow and move. With more energy you will find that prosperity, wealth, and abundance follow easily and steadily. Your goals then begin to appear more readily. In this way, you will begin to achieve a more spiritual life.

Physical Life

All around the planet, life has been and continues to be abundant. Are there challenges currently? Yes there are, but the earth has faced challenges in the past and always it responds with abundance and creativity. Place yourself in line with this thought and concept now, today, and watch how you begin to feel abundance grow within you.

It is not a mistake to desire or to possess. To skillfully create an opportunity to have pleasant physical surroundings is an integral part of the universe. Why not do this on the scale at which you currently exist?

There are some who would want to limit what they should expect. We remind you now that the universe is vast and plentiful. Think big. Set big goals. Make plans and set a purpose for your life that exceeds what others expect from theirs. Look to the future by raising your eyes. You will see things in the distance, great things, and you will pattern your feelings and your thoughts in such a way as to expect to always see and experience great things.

It is easy, once you have started, to see the abundance all around. It becomes easier, then, to feel the energy of Source in all things and in all beings. Once you begin to feel this energy, it becomes easy to express love towards others and so create a space for them to experience prosperity as well. This is a cycle of the universe, and it is repeated many times and in many ways. It is the cycle that brings harmony and peace.

Become abundant and prosperous in your life and, in this way, you will seek and spread peace.

6
The Future of Humankind

As above, so below. We greet you in the here and the now. It is where we all dwell. It is where we all make our decisions and start the next step or stage of our karmic path. To look ahead is natural. We will always encourage you to pay close attention to where you are, but we also want you to begin to think of where you would like to be. This is the manifesting energy that is available to you as a member of the family human.

The Future

As Onereon, we are a not a predictive energy. We seek to assist you to adapt to your current circumstances. In doing this, we sometimes find it good to look farther ahead so as to give a better perspective and help you to be prepared for what lies in the future.

Many of you are already aware of the coming wave of energy. We tell you now that there are many more waves to follow, and time and life on the planet will continue well after that year. The change that arrives is one of decision, and not just for the members of the family human. This wave of energy affects all life in this section of the universe.

For many of you, there has been a feeling of stillness in recent times, as if nothing is moving forward. For some of you, it has felt as if you have been stuck with no way to progress. This perception is very true. Many things have been lining up and a stage has been set for the future. This next year will continue to solidify the course we have all chosen.

When the wave of energy arrives, it will be channeled in certain directions. We have done this several times in the past decade and a half. It has changed what was once believed to be destructive into something beautiful and constructive. It has strengthened and harnessed the energy available and used it efficiently. Systems changed and altered. They will continue to do so. If you should desire to cling to a system or belief from the past, you may find the coming wave uncomfortable.

Global Change

You are seeing what has been foretold happen. Financial and governmental changes are occurring. This will continue for the next four years before things really begin to settle down again. When the changes have been affected, your societies will be linked closer, and you will understand other cultures better.

This is not simply about the North American continent, or the society and governments found there. This is a global change, and all will be influenced. There are many around the world who are much better prepared for this change than those who live in the North American region.

For many, society has become a "take care of me" proposition. This is one of the things that will change. We have long recommended defining yourself as an individual, that is, one who is taking personal responsibility for their physical, emotional, mental, and spiritual growth. Ask yourself, "Do I have basic survival skills?"

In case of a natural disaster, would you be able to fend for yourself for a time until resources are restored? We do not wish to preach fear at this point. It is only practical that you learn to sustain yourself in times of great change. There are many skills which have been lost in recent centuries. In fact, early humans were much more skilled at simple survival than many modern beings. You were once among the life forms that lived in history. Do you remember what you knew then?

The Harmonic Coalescence

Society will change. That is an easy statement to make, for it is a constant. All societies have changed, all throughout history. Soon a more global society will exist.

We speak of the time that we live in as the Harmonic Coalescence. This energy is well underway. The very term is a hint as to the future of all humankind. Look now at your technologies and see the influence of this energy. For the past two hundred years humankind has brought things together, closer and closer. In cities and in towns, through the use of increased transportation and communication, we see how quickly you can get around or contact someone. For the most part, this is a knowledge that you take for granted. In the near future, and in fact the technology exists right now, you will begin to carry more information around with you than actually existed two hundred years previously.

This is in the form of music and entertainment currently, but soon it will be even more. Within the next few years, your personal information and history will be available to be carried like you now carry your identification cards. Much of your life will be dependent upon these forms of information transfer. This may seem scary to many, but it is part of the coming together of humanity.

Old systems will continue to erode and fall. This includes belief systems. Many of the old concepts of the end of the world have been altered or abandoned. It will be difficult for self-proclaimed prophets to find a following. There will simply be too much knowledge available to the ones that may have fallen under someone else's influence.

New information regarding the nature of life continues to appear. You already understand much of this from a spiritual standpoint. Soon it will fall within the realm of science, as they explore and map more of the brain and heart connection. The reality will be difficult to disagree with.

Your Spiritual Life

The extent that you are ready to release the past will be key to the speed that you enter the future. As things change and old familiar ways disappear, there will be many who try to bring those days back. We caution against nostalgic feelings. The past has passed. They will only impede your growth. There will be times when life is uncomfortable and uncertain. We remind you now that your guides are here and ready to assist, but you must be ready to do your part and face the future in a spiritual way. Are you strengthening this connection now?

Have you felt that it was difficult to get in contact with your spiritual guides? That may have been true! There has been much activity in the realm of spirit. Now we will see the meaning of the phrase, "as above, so below" become more clear.

Talk with your guides now, this instant. Greet them in love. Welcome them as kindred spirits. Hear them greet you in return and understand the shift that is occurring. Soon we will all be closer and clearer than ever before. We say soon and we mean this in terms of solar cycles. The change is not instant. It proceeds for the next century and even beyond that. But it begins with you right now.

This is why we, as Onereon, focus so much on you, as an individual. It is why we continually remind you to remain balanced. To be caught up in a political opinion or to involve yourself in trying to prove a belief system is right or wrong is not an efficient use of your energy at this time. To act in a balanced way in an unbalanced world is to set the example for others. It is a way to create the future as you want it to exist. It is the only way to promote true peace. It is the thing that sets you apart and on the leading edge of the wave of energy that is approaching.

Are you a spiritual being having a physical experience? If you are reading these words, you probably believe this to be true. We say now, continue to have that physical experience first and foremost, but do not forget that you are a spiritual being and that you have companions in the realm of spirit. We will soon be below, and you may soon be above. We wish that our relationship with you be strong and our communication clear. This, also, is part of the change that is occurring.

Do not fear these coming days. Difficulties will pass. A new age is not simply approaching us, it has begun. Entering this time with love for each other under all circumstances and joy for living no matter what is happening around you will set the proper course for all beings in existence. To act in a peaceful way is to act in a spiritual way. This, then, is the future for you if you choose.

7
Communication

As above, so below. We speak today of life in all its variety and the connections that can be made. We speak of potentials and communication.

Gaia has manifested life in many ways. Countless creatures and flora and minerals exist and expire as we look at the complete energy of earth from the beginning until the present. Vital forces of the planet come together to adapt and flourish. Some remain, some change and evolve and some simply cease to be. In all cases, Gaia welcomes the energy and elements back within her, utilizing the atoms and molecules to create something new. Life proceeds, the earth abides. The family human has differences.

The Time of Communication

The family human has traveled through many phases in their long history. These phases correspond to the concept of the chakra system. You began at the root chakra of basic survival and procreation and grew to be creative and individually self-defined. There is no clear and clean delineation of when in the stream of time these stages begin or end. We tell you now that the majority of the earth is in the energy of the throat chakra. This is the place of speaking and communication. It is also the place where the heart attains its voice and so becomes the chakra of choice and intent.

There can be little doubt that you are deep within the age of communication. Simply look around you and see the amazing technologies that exist, allowing you to create connections across the planet in nearly instantaneous fashion. In fact, the communication devices created spend much time and energy communicating with themselves and no human is actually directly involved. The exchange of information is on a scale that most choose not to comprehend. For most beings, there is no need to have an awareness of this information or even its existence. This, then, is a major aspect of the society that you exist within.

Despite the great ability to connect, many of you find you are often left with an empty feeling. The interconnectedness lacks useful energy and the exchange of your time and efforts is not returned. Much of the information transmitted is meaningless and simply allows time to pass in a person's life. You have participated in an event, but only passively. The meaning of your life may become defined by what you watch or listen to, and thoughts become dominated by outside voices.

Allowing such outside energy to barrage your consciousness leaves little time for a person to engage in communication with themselves. It is an abdication of one of the basic responsibilities in life, to be fully aware of your personal growth and to approach this growth with full consciousness.

We do not say that these other outside forms of communication are somehow wrong or lack value. The opposite is true. These devices are a marking and a model for the future of humanity. The imprint of speaking to another human being without being in their presence or connected in any visible or physical way is changing the consciousness of the societies on the planet. This sets the stage and pattern for a new phase of awareness and communication between you and all other beings.

True Communication

You must bring into balance the energy of the chakra of communication. This means restoring elements that are being neglected by many. Passive communication is an imbalance of Yin energy. Always seeking the center of attention is an imbalance of Yang. The centering and balancing occurs within you.

Let us speak for a moment of a different form. This seems new to many humans and in a certain way it is. You have done this in the past, but for a different purpose. Interspecies or animal communication is becoming more common. The information being exchanged is still limited. This is because the family human is still learning how to listen.

To truly understand what another person is saying to you, there needs to be an observing. Relying on mere words is not enough. To listen requires active awareness of the other individual. This often means silence on your part while the other being speaks. When was the last time you truly sat in silence?

To learn and communicate outside of your species requires this as well and more. You must acknowledge that your frame of reference is at variance with the other being. You must let them instruct you. You must release preconceived notions about the other being and observe them as they are.

We will give two examples. First, the dolphin, and in doing this we also include many of the other mammals of the seas. There is a way of storytelling within the family human that makes all beings speak and think like humans. You must release the notion that your experience of walking on land informs any being that spends its life floating and gliding through liquid. The sheer multi-dimensional ability of these great beings, the continual ascending and descending through various shades of filtered light, changes the way they perceive, and thus the way they think.

For you to communicate with these ones you must release the concept of being verbal. You must think in a way of ascension and descension within an expanse of fluid. You must be quiet and still if you are on the land near the ocean. You must be peaceful and steady in your motions if you are in the water. Relaxing the thought process is essential to hearing the thoughts of these ones. We tell you now that they have been with the planet longer than you and have long ago traveled through the energy of the chakra of communication and choice.

The second example is the horse. Your experience with walking on two legs is fairly unique and we say this not simply in reference to the planet on which you live. You are a puzzle in this way to the equine beings. That they choose to carry you is more in the way of mercy sometimes, as if you are limited in your ability to move. To communicate with these ones, you must observe them and learn of their heart and emotions. The joy that they feel is not always an obvious one. They truly enjoy a partnership with a human, and it is based on moving together. You must allow your hearts to be close and do not let logic get in the way of your communication.

We give you these two examples to allow you to receive a lesson about the most important communication of all, the internal communication. To learn about yourself from yourself is to act in a way that pleases Source energy. All existence is Source seeking to gain new knowledge and experience about itself. To go within is an action that raises vitality. It is a healthy pursuit for the body, mind, and spirit and adds energy and balance to life.

Spend time pondering the way of your life. Look to see the levels you have existed at, the moments of good feeling and the times of sorrow. Observe the way you rise and descend emotionally. Stand quietly and listen. Allow new thoughts to form by releasing the preconceived notions of the past. Things you were taught may have little import to your life currently. Allow them to float away and let fresh concepts enter into your mind.

Notice your heart. Allow your heart to speak to you not with words, but with emotion. The heart does not rely on logic and words to communicate. The heart does seek joy. In this way you connect with the higher self, the spiritual aspect of you.

The Inner Voice

This spiritual energy is not something outside of you. It is the part of you that notices and nurtures the connection with all other aspects of creation. It is here that true and meaningful communication begins. It is here that you begin to commune or feel at one with the things outside of your physical organism. It is here that you realize your true aspect in all creation. It is here that you hear Source speaking from within you.

Many seek meaning to their lives. They often look outside of themselves and thus miss the place of true meaning. Validation of your existence is inherent in the fact that you do exist. Moments of stillness will assist you in finding this truth.

There is much that will take you away from these times and many opportunities are lost each passing day by the population of humans on the planet. There will come a time when humanity begins again to communicate on a more complete level. This requires great changes, and this has begun. The ones that find the voice within now will be the ones that hear the new voices first.

The aspects of spirit are a key to this pursuit, but this is not only a spiritual matter. This is about the vitality of Gaia. She is shifting and great new knowledge is coming to all life. It is about the physical manifestation of energy and the experiencing of Source. Always remember that you are a particle of Source and all beings that you choose to commune with are also aspects of Source.

When you find others that you enjoy, this is the completion of energy. When you find others that you love, this is the meaning of all existence. To find these things you must first find peace within yourself.

We say to you now as always: Seek peace and, in the seeking, find yourself.

8
A Wave of Change

As above, so below. Your guides in the spirit realm know you. We know what you are feeling. Through you, we see the present and through us, you see the future. We are companions in this life. We sense the anxious feelings you have had, and we see the hopeful feelings you strive to attain. Now let us offer you comfort and perspective.

The Sense of Change

All things change. What you are experiencing now is a greater change than has happened in two thousand years. You are not simply experiencing it; you are an integral part of the change. You represent the link between the old ways and the new ways. The difficulty that you feel is that you are neither of the old ways and not yet of the new. You are between. You are the transitioning beings. Your example leads the way for others.

The difficult path that you follow will be an easier path for others. The way that you mark will be easier for the coming ones to discern. This is your choice, to be in this path of service for others in the future. Your effort and love on behalf of all that will live on the earth in the future is a great work. This incarnation of yours is pivotal to the advancement of all life around the planet.

In this way, you may often feel out of place. Yet some of you are beginning to feel that others around you have grown. You are beginning to sense that others have raised their vibration. You have begun to notice the change in tone of the political leaders. You are hearing consistently the words of many who are dissatisfied with the old spiritual ways. Still, those ones may seem few and far between in your daily lives. Many are still distracted by the mundane things, but that does not mean they lack a spiritual connection. You become distracted also. The connection is getting clearer for many.

There is a wave of change coming. You sense the wave of change. You hear the word "change" being used often and in many contexts. You sense this energy. It takes time for a wave to build. It is building now, and you feel it.

As you observe the changes around you, and there are many, you must remember that you want things to change. It is why you are here in this present moment of the stream of time. You have chosen to be a part of this. It is part of your karmic thread, and you are the weaver.

Reminders

More changes are approaching. To many, it looks like turbulent times. These coming days will require great courage from you. You will need to face your own doubts and beliefs. You will need to look inward. You will need to feed your own light and work to keep it lit. We remind you now, you are not alone!

As society shifts and alters, your light and example of pursing peace and balance will help to set the tone for the new wave of energy that approaches. You have already seen much of what can be called "weakness" in the family human. We remind you now to avoid judgment. You are responsible for your life and others are responsible for theirs. Work out your own karmic path the best way that you see fit. You do not know the inner life or karmic agreements that others have made.

What looks like turbulent times are, in reality, a massive restructuring. The world needs this, do you agree? Then why fear this change?

Become an active part of the new structure. Raise your vision beyond the things that disturb others. This can be very difficult when all the debris from the past is swirling around you, clouding your sight. It is then that you call on your spiritual companions. It is then that we happily take on the role of guides. It is what you have done for us when we were incarnate on the planet, and you were in the realm of spirit. "As above, so below," is a principle that reaches deep into our shared karma. Your growth is our growth.

In these critical times, we invite you to remember that we are in the energy of coalescence. Things are being brought together after a length of time in the energy of variance, when things were separated. We will enter the energy of variance again and then return to coalescence just as a wave crests and troughs.

The current set of waves is larger and more powerful than what is normally experienced in this section of the galaxy. It will leave the planet cleaner and refreshed. The family human will be stronger for this wave and more balanced. No longer will the pursuit of material goods be a primary focus.

Connection

Your connection and your willingness to be connected to a higher vibration is the key to much of this change. This means that you must let go of old thought. Here is where many struggle. You continue to find value in these old ways. It is true that there is much of value there, but it is also true that gold can be purified. Now we are purifying spiritual thought, and so some of the ideas and concepts that worked for tribes in the deserts and family groups in small communities must be let go. You live in a world they could not imagine. You imagine a world better still. Now is the time to stretch your focus away from the past. The principles that are still worthy will remain clear. You will feel them in your hearts.

Much of the change that you are experiencing is one of noticing. Much has already shifted, and you have not noticed. You have been too close to the old ways. We now invite you to step back and see, from the perspective of your spiritual companions, the purer light ahead.

Do this now. Sit quietly and invite your companions to join you. Perhaps make a cup of tea and, as you sip the brew, invite your spiritual friends to join in the tasting. Or find a space of warm sunlight and, as you observe the way the colors exist, let your companions see what you see. Then ask, "What else is there? What am I missing?" Then sit in silence and simply observe.

These are simple suggestions. This can be done in many ways. What do you enjoy? What quiet activity or peaceful place do you attend to that you might invite beings of a higher vibration to witness through you? In the exchange, you will be offered the opportunity to see beyond your own level. Would you enjoy this?

You will be taken past the concerns of the present moment. It is not that you will be removed from your body. It is that you will see how your physical life is connected to the realm of spirit. You will see how you are a spiritual being having a physical experience. You will see your place and your responsibilities more clearly. You will see that you are not alone. You will see that millions are waiting to be connected to what you already know.

Light Dispels Darkness

The light of spirituality is everywhere. It takes on many forms. Light waves combine. This produces a pure light. Shine your light in all situations. Maintain calm and balance no matter what is around you. If all seems dark, then shine your light. When others speak in terms of hate, distrust, or division, maintain thoughts of love, trust and connection. You do not need to counter anyone's words. We have said often: Do not waste your words. Simply do not give attention to the energy of fear that so many choose to exist within.

Your thoughts have power. You know this. Create a space of peace within yourself. Let the energy of peace radiate out from you. Become an oasis of peace and calm.

We tell you now that those who live in fear do not want to stay there. They want to have peace, but they lack the skills to see the way. They believe that peace comes from outside of themselves.

You are ones who work within light. Help others dispel the darkness and find their path by simply existing in a place of peace and light. You know that it is easier to say this than to do this, yet you have the power to continue. You are the ones who are steadfast in your movements to peace. As the waves continue to build, as we are all carried to and past the year of 2012, you are the ones who light the paths that others may find. Do not wait for them to follow you!

Your life here and now is one of seeking. What you represent is a hope that all life can and will achieve the spiritual connection that you are learning and enjoying. Focus not on the external strife of changing politics or economies or even belief systems. Focus on the inner life of spirituality and healthy emotions.

In this way, you will not only seek, but find, peace.

9
Loving Beings

We begin with the words: As above, so below. True spirituality is a matter of personal experience, not belief, and so we accept experiences and form our beliefs when we attend spiritual moments and events. It is less the words and more the emotion that makes us feel spiritual, feel our spirit, the element that makes us up. We feel spirit through the heart, as the heart is true. We do not feel spirit through the brain. Spirit is not logic. We look for structure in spirit and we find none, and so it is easy to reject spiritual things from a logical point of view. It is best to seek spirituality from your heart first.

Allow spiritual principles to guide your heart and let your brain structure your life according to those principles. These are not new words. We have said these words to many people before. We say them now as an introduction, so that you will open your heart, so that you understand what we will be talking about today.

Love Transforms

We are going to talk about energy. We are going to talk about love. It is a broad category. It is a broad terminology. Love, like everything else, is ultimately an energy. Like all energy, love changes. Like all energy, love cannot be destroyed; it is merely transformed. We say "merely," but for anyone who has ever had a love transformed, we understand, as you do, how difficult that transformation can be. But the transformation, the passage from one form of energy to another form of energy, it is a temporary thing.

In the future, relationships will be looser. Love will be measured not by length of time but by moments of experience together. Choose to be near those whom you love. In the choosing, it is better to base your choice on the feeling of love than on artificial rulings.

The difficulty now is that relationships, in the old thoughts that are defining relationships, are often based simply on physical actions and procreation. This is so limiting. This is so limiting for the family human. To be able to open up and allow two people to become three, three people to become four, this will go against the grain, but it is a natural way. It goes against thoughts that have been promoted, but not against the natural way. Families will form and tribes. In this way, the family human will develop a new society.

Less and less will be focused on the individual. Right now, that sounds perhaps like you will lose rights. In fact, what will be gained is an integrity to society that is lacking. A responsibility to other people will grow. There will be smaller groups, but tighter. They will be more focused.

The energy of love must take on the broadest of meanings. It must become the *acceptance* of others. Not necessarily the agreement with others, but the acceptance and the allowance to come closer and closer and to be near each other, to be open and caring in a physical way. We speak of a closeness beyond basic primal urges. We speak of creating a more communal spirit, a true community. Begin to reach out for each other.

You saw the wave of change. You felt the wave of change. You asked for the wave of change. And now that the change has come, what do you do? This is a good wave of change. Like love transforming into something else, it may be a difficult wave. It is a difficult process and will continue to be difficult for some time. But like love, the conclusion of one loving relationship does not mean no other loving relationships. In fact, the opposite is true. You have been at that point once. You will be at that point again, *if you allow it*.

You have asked for the change. It is here. It is happening. Accept it. Be a willing participant of it. Create it. If love is an energy, and you also are energy, then you can channel this energy. You can consciously choose to love. So who will you do this to? Only those that you already love? Only those that are already within your small circles? Only those that are easy to love?

Love is the Energy of Coalescence

Coalescence will be completed. It will be completed by the drawing together of energy. Love is the action. Love is the energy of that. Do you want to draw together? Do you want the family human to find levels and measures of peace upon this planet? Then begin to love. Love when you come up against something that you do not like. This is your test now. We in the spirit realm have great confidence that everyone with pure intention will pass this test. Think of what you do not like. Now, love that.

Love is an energy, and the universe likes when energy cooperates. Please understand, this is not walking up to a stranger and saying, "I love you." This is looking at a stranger and choosing: I will love that person. A conscious thought, a conscious decision: I will love that person. Then go into your heart, because it does not happen in the brain. Say to your heart, "love." It is an action.

Love Radiates from Within

We want you to feel this now. We want you to go to your heart. Feel that. You see, you cannot *think* love. Let your heart love right now. Where does it grow from? It does not come from anywhere outside of you, does it? It comes from within you. So, what does the energy of love touch first? It touches you. You are now loving yourself first. Let the energy radiate out from you. You cannot run out of this. The energy of Source is love. It is the closest thing we can say of this. What started all of this, what you feel when you love, is a particle of Source, right there, pure. Feel love. Be that energy. Be love.

Now, please, do not think it is going to be easy. There will be many challenges. Already you are thinking of some of them: How can I love *that* person? Just do that. Just love that person. It is not agreement. We are not talking about agreement. We are not talking about loving that person and accepting them for all of their faults. We are just talking about loving them, wishing them the opportunity to create a strong, balanced, and healthy life. Now, there is a reaction, because every action has an opposite and equal reaction. If you love, what happens to you? You know the answer, because it is an opposite and equal reaction.

Loving Beings

Love's Challenges

Things pass. Life transforms for us as humans and also for our animals. When we say, "our animals," understand that is not a label of ownership. It is like when we say "our" friends, "our" partners. Sorrow is a natural energy in the course of life. Sorrow is an aspect of love. If we did not love, we would not feel the sorrow. When you feel sorrow, you are touching love. So, feel the sorrow. Feel the grief. If you did not care, it would not hurt. When you feel sorrow, reach inside for the gratitude as well. Be grateful for those moments that you had with individuals. Do not ask, "Did I love them enough?" Love them enough at that moment. For energy cannot be destroyed, it can only be transformed. Take the energy of regret and transform it into love.

You may or may not know your karmic path while you are incarnated on the planet. Let us not worry about that so much today. What we will tell you about your karmic path is that it can only be improved if you seek this energy of love. Increase that. Remember, every action has an opposite and equal reaction. We are not talking about toleration here. We are not talking about someone who is rude being tolerated. For the loving thing to do is not allow actions to be continued that are to the detriment of others. The loving thing to do, also, is to avoid the urge to put that person in their place. The loving thing to do, starts where again? Within you.

If you do not feel you are in a situation where there is love, love yourself and remove yourself from the situation. Walk away whenever possible. Do not waste your words. We have said this phrase so many times. Do not waste your words trying to convince someone of anything. The energy of love, it will affect them. They will grow. But the most important thing to remember is, where does love start? Who gets loved first? Love yourself, first and foremost.

Is it difficult for you to love yourself? This often has to do with regret of beings and things passed. You are alive in the present moment, not the past. That is gone. What happened there, just let that be there. You are here now. Understand that in the present moment you are accepted. You are accepted at a higher level. Everyone reading these words is accepted at a higher level. Everyone alive is a part of a team. You say guides, you say angels, and we say companions. Because you are in physical incarnation does not mean you do not have spiritual responsibilities. The spirit realm is a continuation of the physical realm. You are of that realm even when incarnate on the planet.

There are times when your worth, your self-worth, your feelings of value, are low. Those are the times when your companions have difficulty getting through to you because you are not looking at them. Here is a physical thing to do to help in a spiritual way. You are body, but you are also mind and spirit. And so, with the body, look up. When you are feeling low, look up. When you are working at your desk, look up. It is not really "above." We are not really "above." We are right here. When we say, "As above, so below," this is an illustration. It is an example to you. When you are feeling down, your tendency is to look down. Look up. Raise yourself up.

Accept Love

There is no judgment about the past, you see. Not any more than if you were in school. Think of third grade.

Think of the spelling test you had. Could you pass a third-grade spelling test today? Yes, probably. Was it difficult then, when you were in third grade? Maybe. Why? Because it was new, it was fresh. Perhaps you always got perfect scores on your spelling test, but likely not. Do you carry with you the idea that, "Oh no. When I was in third grade, I did not know how to spell the word 'friend,'" for example. You do not. It was third grade, and you are beyond that now. You know so much more. Do not carry your mistakes with you. They are just part of the lesson.

Although it is common in human society to teach to the lesson, that is not how it is in the realm of spirit. In the realm of spirit, we do not teach to the lesson. The lesson comes and goes. There is no final test, only continued growth and learning. The human grows. In this way we do not have lessons in life. We only have opportunities of growth.

So, accept that about yourself, accept that you grow. It is as simple as that. Again, go back to the love, the love inside of yourself. Accept that love and continue moving forward, loving yourself first. There is nothing outside of you that you can give someone that will replace love. Whatever mistakes that other person has made, love them for who they are now. If they insist on continuing to make the mistakes, remember - we are not saying that love is an agreement. We are saying love is love. Help them to grow. Sometimes, helping them to grow means leaving them alone to follow their course. Sometimes, growing for yourself means being alone. Accept that aspect of it too.

So, love. It is an energy. We speak of these qualities: love and joy and peace. We speak of them often. Joy is a direct link to spirit. Peace is a result of spiritual pursuits.

Love is spirit. It is the main ingredient, and we wish you these things now.

We wish you peace, spiritual peace. We wish you joy. Above all, right now, we wish you love. Please, extend this out to the world, extend this out to everyone you meet. But remember, love begins within. Love yourself first. It radiates from there.

10
Community

As above, so below. We communicate to you now in a form that is common and a language that is well known. Our message is for those that choose to grow healthy in body, mind, and spirit. We have spoken often about how the individual, the undivided one, must take care to achieve balance within themselves first. Now we speak about a greater connection.

You are an aspect of the universe, a particle of Source. By being the best you can be, you raise your own vibration. This comes from within you. In doing so, you also raise the vibration of everyone and everything around you. In this way, you strengthen those with whom you are connected. Do they also strengthen you? This question is more important now than ever before.

Commune with Spirit

When you commune with spirit, that is, when you sit in meditation, contemplation, or prayer, you are open to receive communication from your spirit guides and companions. This should not be a one-way conversation. You may express yourself freely to those you are related to in spirit. Cares and concerns, requests and questions all may be asked and explained during this time. Many of you are mastering the ability to remain in this state of communion with higher vibrational realms throughout your days and nights and still accomplish all things necessary to physical life on the planet.

Many have discovered that the secret to this form of communication is a stillness of being. It is easier to commune with spirit when there is quiet and stillness around you, but you can cultivate stillness within and be equally effective. It is recommended to regularly find quiet areas for your personal communing. In this quiet, you can truly hear, and this is a part of the secret to raising your vibration, the action of listening. This always begins with your physical form and your relationship with the life energy of the planet.

Connect with Gaia

Are you aware that Gaia has chakras, energy centers, just like you do? They are not the same in their purpose, but there are areas of the world that possess specific energies, much like the chakras within your own physical form.

For you, the members of the family human, you communicate with the aid of the energy center called the throat chakra. Here you breathe air and change the vibrational patterns using lips and tongue. The sound travels and is received by another being's ear, which then translates the vibration into thought.

Gaia does not have a throat chakra in this way, but she communes, nonetheless. She is constantly vibrating, and different areas of the planet vibrate differently and for differing reasons. It takes practice and skill to commune with Gaia. Some have found it easy to achieve this communication through the use of crystals and we recommend this method to you, but anywhere that you find a peaceful place or sense a level of power will be an opportunity for you to receive communication from the planet. Any place where you can sit and touch the earth with all your senses is a place to commune.

For many humans, there is a separate feeling. They do not feel connected to Gaia. Ask yourself, "Where does Gaia vibrate the least?" Likely you will answer, "Where she is covered over by buildings and concrete. Where there are too many other vibrations that cover over the natural ones." It is not impossible to commune with Gaia in urban areas, but it is easier to do so in natural places.

Communication Choices

It is often thought that one needs to be solitary to achieve a proper communication with Source. There is much to recommend this idea. Yet communication indicates a community, others to commune and share energy with. Here is where it becomes difficult for many, for it is sometimes hard to find like-minded and like-spirited persons. There are many on the planet who do not communicate worthy thoughts. There are many who do not promote peaceful pursuits with their words and actions.
We have said before: Do not waste your words. In this way we also say, "Do not let others waste your energy with their words."

Understand who and what you commune with is your community. Are there worthy thoughts being discussed within your community? Worthy ethics, ideals, and peaceful moments? Or are there stressful, troublesome, fearful words being used and pressed upon you? Compare how you feel when you listen to comments about growth and flow with words about fear and loss. Choose which community, which communication, you feel better within. Choose what energy you commune with.

The time is coming for spiritual ones to establish greater connection with one another. It is happening already, though slowly. You may have felt alone for some time now. This may possibly extend a short while longer. Soon, though, you will feel the draw, the pull to gather together. This will not be in the traditional places. New ideas and new ways are upon us all. Your willingness to leave behind the old thoughts and enter into new understandings will guide you through the coming years of changes.

It is important now to commune, to communicate with the earth. Gaia is telling you something. This means sitting quietly more often. Do not expect literal voices to arrive in your ears. Simply listen for new thoughts and concepts to grow within you.

Dare to Be Still

We offer a challenge to you of silence or quiet. Stay quiet for one day. This does not mean do not talk or respond to others. Silently observe what others say and communicate. Is it worthwhile? Do not fill the silence with noise like communications from certain devices. Do not judge these things. Only, accept a day of quiet. Notice, what forms of communication do you regularly accept into yourself? What do you allow to commune with you? If you find that there are many things of little value, ask, "What am I communing to Gaia? Why should she listen to me? What do I unintentionally communicate with my vibrations to both the realm of my physical home and also the realm of my spiritual home?"

A community is forming, one of higher vibration. This is not a community dedicated strictly to spirituality. It is one that seeks to create a harmony of all levels of life. This community will search for truths about Source energies. It will look to remove the old traditions that hold back knowledge and learning. It will be different in that it will be accepting of everyone that is alive on the planet. All beings will be able to communicate equally with one another, and across time and space. This community will be one of easy technologies and mobility. This community will be less concerned with possessions and more concerned with learnings. This community will be one of worthy and effective communication. Together, they will commune with Source in a manner that is new. The beings that exist within this community will not always be in agreement. There will be differences of opinion. Yet they also will not need to commit violence in these situations. It will be a community of peaceful resolution and tolerance.

The wave is nearing. You can sense this. It is not a simple marking of time or a specific dating of a year. It is an energy of change. Many may leave the physical realm before all of this comes to pass. You still have an important role to play in this change. Free yourself now from judgment. Look ahead with hope. Commune with Gaia and your spirit companions in the energy of love. Find joy in the connecting with others of like spirit. Understand that peace is approaching. A peace beyond your comprehension.

Enlightenment

You do not look to past troubles or illness with hindsight and say easily, "Those things were for the better. I am better for those things having happened." It is an enlightened one that can speak those words about the most painful moments and subjects in their lives. It is an enlightened one who looks to things that others would avoid and welcomes them. Having passed the test once, the enlightened one fears not the test. It is not that they do not experience continued tests; it is that they move through them very easily and very quickly for they know the path.

The one that can still their mind, the one that can quiet their own thoughts, that is the one that communes with spirit. It is not that spirit is somewhere and they go there. They sit and spirit is there.

11
Comparing Vibrations

As above, so below. There are deeper similarities between the realm of the physical world where you dwell and the realm of the spirit where we and your spiritual companions exist. If you are observant of your world, you will understand more clearly what the realm of spirit is like.

You already use terms like higher and lower vibration and indicate that you comprehend that spirit is higher. Yet within the two realms there is a spectrum of vibration. Now, what in the physical realm is a higher vibration and what is lower? A pursuit of things higher may allow you clearer access into your spiritual nature.

We are not saying that things of a lower vibration are wrong or less valuable. For example, many of you are fond of crystals and minerals and sense their vibrational qualities. Understand that these are a way of co-operating with directional vibrations. Though they may be of a lower vibration, crystals are structured in unique ways and can bring benefits to you, should you choose to use them as points of focus.

Let us speak of sounds. Many of you are fond of music. The lower vibrations created through the use of certain instruments or voices are often pleasing and provide a support for the higher notes and chords. It is sometimes a relative thing to experience a lower vibrational tone.

For members of the family human, you sometimes hear low tones and feel that perhaps danger is near or approaching. It is why many go to fear or anger when experiencing heavy vibrations of music or loud chanting.

The earth itself will emit vibrations that are relatively low, and you will often associate this with earthquakes or strong winds or masses of water moving swiftly. You use the word "roar" and seek shelter. Sometimes a higher vibration will have the same effect. Too high of a vibration may be discomforting. A constant keening of wind may set nerves on edge.

This is less about the experience of danger, however. It is more about a relentless action that you may have no control over. In these cases, a calming breath may take away the feeling of nervousness. Rhythmic lower vibrations will actually be felt within you and breath may become difficult to regulate.

A balance between the higher and lower vibrations is most pleasing to all life on the planet. Allowing higher vibrations to be pure and clear while the lower vibrations support the structure is generally a pleasant experience. What does that tell you then about the spiritual realm?

The Earth's Higher Vibrations

Some of the creatures of the planet also emit higher vibrational noises. Bees, dragonflies, and hummingbirds are amongst these, and we will use them as examples now. By no means are these the sole beings that we are referring to, only the most common.

We tell you now, you are *of* the planet. We tell you that the planet is alive, and you are an aspect of the life of Gaia. Do you as a living being communicate with others? Would you expect Gaia to do anything less? It is not necessarily outward communication that we speak of here. You think and speak and write, yes, but you communicate so much more at all times. Your level of vibration is a communication to everything around you.

A person with a calm, peaceful spirit is a being of high vibration, and they help others raise their level. This calm comes from within and holds no logic. It is a way of existence that encompasses the physical form. It begins with the smallest levels of the being, the DNA, and connects to the cellular structure and beyond into the nervous system and the muscles and skeleton and organs and finally radiates outward from the visible aspect of the physical form. You enjoy being in the presence of such a person, do you not? They are harmonious and balance the higher vibrations of spirituality with the lower vibrations of earthly life.

Gaia herself communicates in many similar ways and we will speak of this in more detail in the future. For now, let us focus on the concept of neural pathways, that is, the impulses or vibrations that carry a message within the physical beings of the planet. These are not conscious things themselves, are they? Yet many neural impulses help to make up a conscious thought. Many are used to simply create an action or movement of the physical form, helping the body to function in a direct and progressive way, walking and talking and performing various tasks necessary to physical growth and life. The subconscious neural vibrations cause you to breathe and your heart to beat without you needing to think about the actions.

In the same way, Gaia has a way of sending messages around her own physical form. The hum of the bee and hummingbird and dragonfly are, in a sense, Gaia's neural message. It is from these vibrations that she learns of the state of the environment and atmosphere.

The Message of the Bees

Many of you have noted the bees recently. They are seeking something, are they not? They seem to be vanishing or decreasing in numbers. Should they disappear altogether, life, as you know it, will alter dramatically. It would be good for you to direct your attention to the message they carry, for they carry the same message to Gaia, your home.

Exercise caution with the bees. There is a potential danger when placing yourself in close proximity to bees, for they can and do sting, but that is not their purpose. Begin to understand this first. A bee does not seek you to sting you. A bee seeks to create a hive, a cooperative home, and produce a food source. In doing this, they also pollinate and assist with the creation of crops and flowers. They are an integral and vital part of the ecosystem. You depend on them more than they depend on you. Now, however, you can step in and learn a message about the world that you all share.

Speak to the bees. This may sound silly to you. If you see one or two, pause and express a friendly greeting. Express gratitude and offer assistance. Of course, communication also requires listening. Encourage the bees to be around you by planting flowers. Tend the flowers as if they are a solution to some of the larger planetary problems you see. Start with the smallest things and the larger things will begin to be solved.

Plant flowers that will encourage beings of higher vibration to come into your personal sphere of influence. Sit and watch hummingbirds and listen to their noises. Observe the motion of the wings of dragonflies and watch how light shifts across their small, fragile forms. There are lessons here for the one who is patient enough to observe.

Thinking with Gaia

By doing this, you will find that you are feeling peaceful. You will find that you become less nervous. You will find that you are touching the earth in a unique and thoughtful way. You will feel the strength and balance of life around the globe. And the earth will be touching you as well.

You will be putting yourself into the stream of Gaia's consciousness and so will become aware of her intentions in a greater way. You will be acting with her. You will understand clearer your place in the stewardship of the earth. The bee does not believe it owns the earth. It does not even believe it owns the hive. The bee acts and does what it is designed for, as does the hummingbird and dragonfly. Pause and listen. You will be amazed at what you might hear!

This is not a hearing of words. This is a noticing of thoughts and ideas. Not from within you but from outside of you. You will understand your place in a more complete way and realize that, as important as you are as an individual being, you are more important as an integrated being, consciously listening to the greater things around you.

Your vibration will rise. You will become peaceful deep inside. You will radiate outward calmness and balance and you will feel better and healthier. Your life will become more productive and thus all life around you is improved.

Some of you may take this to heart. Some may listen and allow the message to pass by, just as you allow the bees and birds to pass by you daily and without note. There is no right or wrong and no rule to obey. By placing yourself within higher vibrational situations, you will become a being of higher vibration.

Your physical existence is small at this moment on the planet. The earth and all life in and around it is preparing for a shift in energy. A strong wave of energy is approaching. We have experienced several such waves in the recent past. Look how life has changed in a short time!

Do not fear. In the future, life on Gaia will be of a higher quality, longer, and stronger. You will experience this. All life will.

Pay attention now to the small things around you. When you return to the realm of spirit and your existence within the higher vibrations, you will feel a deeper connection to all things. You will be more prepared for the tasks that lay ahead. Doing this now will bring you closer to Source and, as you travel your karmic path, you will find balance and peace more readily available to you. In this way, then, we continually advise and communicate to you all the thought: Seek peace.

12
You are a Nexus for Change

As above, so below. Our lesson may seem direct. Please read on and find the love within our words.

Have you called for change? It is here. Have you called for an end to old things? New things are on the horizon. Have you requested a more spiritually enlightened time? The light is growing.

Do you see these things? Perhaps not, but they are happening. How do you occupy yourself? Are you keeping your senses open? Are you remaining aware?

The change is upon us all. All levels and vibrations will be affected, physical and spiritual. Make no mistake; this is not something you on the physical plane have no power over. It is something you are *doing*. We are facilitating action from the spiritual realm, but you are acting on behalf of the physical realm. In fact, your contribution is the more important one. You are acting as a nexus for forces of change.

Consider this to be something akin to spring cleaning. We, in the spirit realm, have provided space. We have assisted by removing energies that may impede things. This makes the times you exist in seem sparse. The opposite is true. You now have opportunities to find the things of true value and place those energies in a more prominent position in your life. Doing so sends waves of energy out to the others alive on the planet now. These waves are eroding the old ways of belief on the planet.

Beneficial Choices

Assume neutrality in political issues. This does not mean non-participation, only that you approach each issue with a balanced mind, choosing for yourself and allowing others to do the same. In fact, involvement in the issues of your community is becoming more important. Being aware of the facts and the details behind others' concerns, and understanding effects that the choices offered will bring, is a way of practicing the physical path completely. Maintaining a neutral or balanced path in these things is to bring spirituality to yourself and thus the community. This wave of energy, then, emanates from you.

Make the action of love your first response, rather than fear. Looking for a way to express love to others who appear to be intent on causing conflict is a spiritual wave. This is a difficult thing in these times. Many are acting from fear, and this leads them to behave in unbalanced ways. You can remain centered by first asking, "What is the loving thing to do?" Too many are still acting on preconceived notions based on archaic religious beliefs. Release the old thoughts and enter the new ways. There can be no argument against loving behavior. This, then, is a wave that moves from the center of your heart and flows out into the world.

Redefine prosperity and abundance and recognize what is of real value. The collapse of economies you are now seeing was an inevitable thing. Many of you felt the imbalance, the top-heaviness of the structure. It only took a small wave to push it over, but it was a wave of choice. Too many have had the idea that possessions bring happiness. You are moving towards a time when possessions will be shared by communities. This is not to be confused with an old political idea. This will be a new way. Think of what is happening to information now and you will have a hint as to the future of art and science.

Grow yourself in ways that are truly beneficial now. Practice patience before seeking acquisition of products that may be obsolete soon. In this way, you will understand that there is little need for many items, or for great spaces in which to store them. In this way, you lessen the impact your life has upon the planet. In this way, the energy of the earth grows, and the vibration of every being is raised equally.

Be on the leading edge of this movement, but do not be fooled by some who seek only profit for themselves. Be aware of what is true by applying your mental powers to the study of new technologies rather than acting only on heart emotions. This, then, is an area where we will tell you to lead with logic.

Embrace Changes

There are many large waves washing upon the earth at this time. There are larger ones to come. You know this, yet some of you do not act in an appropriate manner. Ask yourself now, "Am I clinging to an old thought? Do I truly expect and welcome a new age of existence for all life on the planet?"

Several key steps need to be continually made. One is acceptance of others regardless of their beliefs. This means politically and religiously! We are not asking or even suggesting that everyone agree on everything. Variety of thought is an integral part of the experiment of the earth. Can you accept what you do not agree with? We in the realm of spirit practice this constantly.

The greater wave that approaches will provide a more complete opportunity for adjustment. The things that are being argued now will be irrelevant soon. Why waste your time? There are many things to be accomplished in your life that are much more important than mere political or religious agenda. Act in a way of growth and movement. Leave behind those who would hold each other at a standstill. If you engage them, they will hold you still as well.

Forgiveness is necessary to this wave, but is not the wave itself. Forgetting is not a part of this action. Do not forget; simply cease acting on old assumptions. You say you have changed. Have you? Or are you merely acting as if you are different while holding all the same prejudices and old patterns of thought. Do you believe that others have changed their patterns? Do you believe they can? We tell you now that in a short time everyone will be changing their patterns. Begin now and truly be on the leading edge of the wave of change.

Do you find yourself in a frustrated state? What is the appropriate action to take to cease this energy and move you to a productive state? Remember, you create what you focus on. You are part of the active force of the universe. You are part of a family that extends beyond the physical realm. We see the great work you are all doing. We also see the pressure you face daily.

Do not despair. Do not give up. Many of you have chosen to be incarnate on the planet at this time in history. Some of you are specialists in dealing with the type of energy being experienced at this time. Some of you are among the ones that helped chart this course for the family human. It is succeeding. A change is approaching. A higher vibration will be achieved for all life in the very near future. This change does not come without struggle or effort.

Stay the course. Remain in the light of spirit. Stretch yourselves when necessary, but maintain your center as much as possible.

We Are With You

Do you feel as if sometimes your guides are distant? Be aware that we have not left you alone. It is not possible for us to be separated from you. We are very busy at this time. It is up to each one of you to stand up and take a more complete responsibility for your own spiritual path. Do you realize how spiritually advanced you are compared to previous times?

There is an intensity building, a power that we have not seen for many eons. If you are truly practicing a strong spirituality, you will remain balanced and feel this as intense love. Should your spirituality be less than genuine, should you happen to follow others rather than walking your own path, you will feel this as an intense time of testing. How do you feel about the times you are living right now? The intensity is still building.

Be assured that you will find a way through. You are loved. Each individual will experience the intensity. Prepare well. Maintain your balance and you will maintain your joy. With joy will come peace. If you feel peaceful, it will be only natural to find the love in these words.

These, then, are the forces for which you are the nexus. They are what emanate from you. They are what will change the world. You, then, are a force of change and you are creating a world of love and joy and peace. Remain constant. We are with you. Are you with us?

13
A Gift

As above, so below. There are many questions in the world at this time. There is much occurring that is difficult to understand in a spiritual way. For many, it is seemingly more difficult to act spiritually now than just a few years past. There seems to be a lowering of vibration in human society rather than the expected raising of vibration. These perceptions are not inaccurate. We cannot, in this forum, answer every individual question. However, we can offer some general observations and thoughts on the nature of the times. We can also offer a gift.

The Universal Mind

First, we remind you that each of you is an aspect of the universal mind, the consciousness that is expressed by the physical universe. With this one thought, you can find yourself connected to unlimited resources. When we use the term "resource," what are we saying? It is an indication that you can return to Source. You can access the primary energy of all creation.

We know that in saying this, we make it sound easier than it is. It must start as a thought but, before it becomes a personal truth, you must also feel the concept within your heart. This is where the difficulty lies for most of the family human.

You are now alive at a time of great change. There is a stressing of the energies of the universe in the vicinity of the earth. Many things have altered, and they will not go back to the way they were before. For many of you there has been loss of physical resources, often through no fault of your own. When this occurs, you begin to seek a security that has its root in the physical realm. This, then, lowers the general vibration of your life. This is not wrong. We merely remind you of this so that you can examine where you are at in the stream of time and perhaps raise your vibration again. For most of those reading these words, you know well how it feels to operate at a higher level of spiritual existence. We say now that, after having been there in the past, it will be easy to achieve a return to this level.

The Energy of Tides

The second observation we will give is this: All things are energy. Energy moves in waves. In a sense, your section of the galaxy is experiencing a very low tide. Do you feel that you lack energy for necessary tasks? Do you sense this emptiness or imbalance in those you are close to? Do you see how the entirety of human society appears to be running out of things that represent energy? Have you noticed the great surge toward finding new technologies and sciences to gain or create energy in a clean or more efficient manner?

We tell you now, be cautious. The tide may be out, but tides return. It is better to sit away from the edge at this time. Many of the ideas and industries will be swept away when the tide of energy flows back into this area.

There is a time to be active and a time to be still. Now is that time for stillness. Take advantage of this as best you can. It is difficult when you feel your life is lacking. There will be a time for activity. Quite soon, many things will have changed. We are in preparation for a phenomenal time in all history. Be preparing yourself now.

You will likely observe surges. You may convince yourself or others that the tide has returned completely. We caution you: There will be surges, but the tide does not return all at the same time. Look to the oceans and recall the principle of as above, so below. If it applies one way, then it must apply the other. There is much you can learn about the action of spirit through the study of the movement of water.

If you are an aspect of the Source, if the level of energy is low in this portion of the universe, what then is the wise course for the spiritual being? To remain alive, we must sometimes ration ourselves. It is easy to see how this happens in a physical way. It is more difficult to understand how to ration oneself spiritually.

This is where the concept of re-sourcing becomes important. Much of what you need spiritually is inherent within each individual. There is little needed from outside of you for enlightenment. We have existed in a time of abundant energy for quite a while. Now that that energy has lessened, we perceptively may view this as a lack. We assure you now that there is no lack in spiritual energy. Change the way you think, and you will find everything you need to be very close. How can Source be distant from itself?

This is a truth. It is a primary truth that you, each one of you, is an aspect of the Source. Each one of you is complete. You have the inherent ability to manifest and to heal. You each have the ability to connect with your own spiritual companions, to learn your own spiritual histories, to discover your own karmic thread. Each one of you knows who you are and with what contracts you have entered this incarnation. You are body, mind, and spirit and there is no separating these things. In this way, there is no separating you from Source, there is only a blocking of the flow.

Clearing Blocks

We offer this third observation: A part of the great experiment of life on the earth is to clear away blocks that prevent energy from flowing freely. The things in your life that seem to hold you back, the moments you feel as if you cannot succeed, the times you feel alone or misunderstood, these are often your moments of opportunity and promise. You deal with the energy blocks from a physical vantage point for a reason. It is easier to identify these blocks when you are in a lower level of vibrational existence. Conversely, it is harder to deal with the blocks when incarnate on the planet. This is why you are being taught to operate at such a high level of spirituality. This is why you chose to be here at this time.

We tell you now that the times may be difficult, but you are succeeding in ways that you cannot fully comprehend while in the physical realm. The approaching period of 2012 and beyond is not meant to be easy. It is meant to cleanse and clear away old thought and practice. These old blockages are being broken down now by all of you. The old assumptions and rigid beliefs are being made smaller and being worn away. Continue to look for the new ways and thoughts. Approach your life everyday by asking, "What can I do that is new to me? What can I learn today that is different for me?"

Freedom from Guilt and Fear

Let us make a final observation for you: The blockages that we all experience are usually identifiable by the emotions they elicit. For example, if you feel fear, you must ask yourself, "What am I truly afraid of? What harm can actually happen to me if I act?" If you feel guilt, you must ask yourself, "Who is the one that created the belief in guilt? Am I justified in accepting someone else's judgment of my perception of right and wrong?"

Look to the old religions and see what fear and guilt have caused, a nearly complete moving away from true spirituality. Fear of punishment is never going to help anyone gain a closer understanding of their place in the universe. Feelings of guilt will never help one gain a higher vibrational existence. These emotions do not build you up. Rather, they tear you down and weaken you.

The approaching period of 2012 and beyond is also not meant to be hard. It is meant to assist and raise, not just human life, but all life to a higher vibration. It is a time of returning to the Source. It is a time of beginning and coalescence. And now we tell you that to gain and retain your strength in this time of great shifting, you need to remember and practice the above three things: a connection to the universal mind, an awareness of the tides of energy, and the action of clearing blocks. You do not need to be an expert in these disciplines; simply thinking about them will help. Acting on them will produce a life that will strengthen your entire karmic history.

We have said these words many times before. We repeat them now for emphasis, but always speak them as a reminder of true spirituality. How can fear exist if you are filled with true love? How can guilt survive and continue to block the flow of energy if you are acting as a living expression of true joy? In what way can energy be blocked if you are flowing with the quality of true peace?

Yes, it is a difficult time for many. You have a choice. We have provided guidelines and answers. Act in these ways and see the times you are living within become easier and brighter. In this way, and only in this way, can you affect the conflicts existing now upon earth. We thank you for your efforts during this era.

We send you love and joy and, above all, peace. We invite you to pause and take time now, this very moment, to receive this gift from the realm of spirit.

14
Harmonic Coalescence

As above, so below. We sense the weariness in many humans. It is a global situation and not necessarily limited to the planet.

We have all been very active for some time and the work is not over. The effect of things is this: what began in the higher vibrations of the realm of spirit moved through the lower vibrations of emotions and then into the realm of thought and finally has reached the realm of the physical. What place does spirit still have in your life? Are you ready to walk away from your belief because times have gotten more interesting and challenging physically?

Easy to Doubt

From the human perspective, it is easy to begin to doubt. Perhaps it may appear that all the spiritual techniques and practices you have learned are failing. This is far from true. It may seem that you have lost something spiritually. Be cautious now. There are many seeking to profit from you in this time of low energy.

There are those who may seek to return to old times and old ways. They may become filled with nostalgia and seek comfort in things past. Some will return to old ways of belief. This is not a wrong action, but it is not the wisest of courses. You left the old systems of belief for a reason and the reason has not changed. We remind, and we have always said, there is no need for a system of belief. Why try to structure spirit? Why not approach life with open eyes and acceptance of what is? Here is the beginning of many people's difficulty.

Expectation for a peaceful future is yet to be realized. Many had and have a vision of what things *should* look like. We tell you now that expectations are not wrong, but they can become a trap. If you are too detailed in your expectations, you will likely experience some disappointments.

Your vision is one of many. The vision of your community is one of many. The path created is energetic and knows no certainty. An expectation of a timeline, a list of moments and events where certain goals are met, is not realistic in this spiritual work. Time is an aspect of gravity. Spirit is not ruled by gravity.

You, in human form, exist in gravity and are therefore affected by time. It is natural to look for a timeline, especially when things get heavier, that is, when matters and events take on weightier importance. Your spiritual practice allows you to see farther and from a higher perspective. Do not abandon your spiritual practice now. Rather, adjust your priorities to the physical things in your life that need attention. This is balance and you can do this. You have done it before.

Recognize Miracles

You may feel your bodies breaking down. This is a very important effect of living within gravity that is concerning many now. This is the way things have been for a very long time. From a spiritual perspective you may ask for a miracle cure. Miracles do happen. You have likely experienced many in your life. Do not forget that you live in an age of miracles. Are you appreciative?

The very technology you live with, the abilities of modern science, would have been considered miracles two hundred years ago. Allow the miracle of technology to work with the physical body when necessary. Do not forget the miracles of spirit. Learn that the two are not separate. Miracles are science, even if you do not comprehend the science.

The difference is in gratitude. If you remain grateful, you observe and realize the miracles and wonder in your life every day. If you take these things for granted, you will find these times more difficult.

We come to you with these words to encourage you, to give you strength of heart. We are aware of the challenges you now face. We in the realm of spirit are facing these challenges too. In our own way, we see the work that is being accomplished. We thank you for your willingness to be realistic now and give you an assurance that all is moving toward a conclusion that will benefit all life in this section of the galaxy. That may seem like weak compensation when you are individually pressed from all sides.

We tell you now that you are stronger than you know. You are of the same energy that we in spirit are. You have chosen the more difficult assignment at this time. Ask for support, but remember that you are a manifesting being.

Facing Reality with Joy

Let us take one more moment to face reality more completely. Where is your joy? If you respond to that question with a list of physical possessions, then you learn that your joy is outside of yourself. We tell you now that joy cannot exist outside of a living being. Health does not exist outside of living beings either. Taking joy in life and maintaining a positive attitude in the face of daily stress will assist in experiencing the fullest vitality available to you at this time.

Life on the planet earth is difficult right now. You are living through very difficult and trying times. You have been for several incarnations. We have joined you throughout those cycles of incarnation. We recall the times of violence and strife.

These times are balanced though. As difficult as some things are, many things are vastly easier. When was the last time you had to plant, tend, and harvest your own food? When was the last time you had to repair your own house? When was the last time you had to dig your own well? When was the last time you had to leave your home and travel on foot? When was the last time you were forced to abandon your family to seek a better home elsewhere? When was the last time you had to live with a crippling injury because the technology was not available to repair your physical form?

One hundred years ago these were common occurrences, and you were there wishing for a solution to these troubles. Humanity was imagining a future, and now you are here.

What are you imagining now? Do you still image a future of peace, a time when sickness is lessened, and stress is reduced? Your ability to imagine these things is vital. Creation comes from imagination.

Take some time each day to imagine what you wish, not only for yourself, but also for the entire planet. Do not spend time on explanation or detail. Do not concern yourself with what is the right system of government or societal structure. The future will be far different from what you can imagine anyway.

Harmonic Co-Creation

There are energies approaching. They have been en route for a very long time. They are gravitational energies, and they will join with you and you with them. That time is still in the future. Now is the time to prepare the family human for a different way of life. Let loose the old ways and ideas and continue to reach ahead with your emotions and thoughts.

You have experienced a convergence and a concordance. Now is the coalescence and you are deep within the cycle. Each of these waves of energy is a movement towards harmony.

We remind you again, the achievement of harmony is accomplished through the action of love for one another whether you agree with each other or not. It is also achieved through the action of joy, which we have discussed briefly here within these words, and which grows from gratitude and awareness.

In the pursuit of harmony, there is no one element here that is more important than another. All elements act together to create harmony. Of these elements, we have chosen to leave the action of peace for the conclusion. Peace seems to be lacking in many lives today. We tell you that it is the striving for the old ways that causes the energy of peace to dissipate. The future may seem uncertain, but that is not to say it is not peaceful.

Imagine peace now. Begin the creation of peace within your life this way. Imagine peace. You have heard these words before. Be aware of the power of them now.

Imagine.

Peace.

15
Comfort and Truth

As above, so below. We bring an observation about beings seeking spiritual energy and a higher vibrational existence.

There are generally two things the spiritual seeker pursues. The first thing, and the hardest, is a search for truth. The second, and more common in the present day, is comfort. Very often if you are seeking one, you may not find the other. This in no way means one aspect is better than the other. Each is a legitimate and worthy path to achieve a higher vibration.

Ask yourself now, "Do I seek comfort or truth?" If your answer is truth, you must be willing to learn the truth of your own self first. This will not lead to immediate comfort. The search for your own truth will take you out and away from your comfort zones. It is an active path.

Comfort is given to those who need or chose to remain still. This can be a decision made to sit in quiet contemplation. A life of meditation generally is physically still. The one who engages in this practice reduces the need for physical things and in this way reaches for spiritual energy.

There are other reasons a path of comfort is sought in the present time. It is a discomforting world. Many find themselves in positions of physical need. They see no clear way to attain what they perceive they need and so they seek comfort from a higher power. From the spiritual realm we see and hear these requests more often.

Offer of Comfort

Much can be done by the individual, the undivided one, to alleviate their own situation, but your companions are always here to assist when you are feeling a lack of strength. Comfort is offered to those who are un-easy or dis-eased. We note that many diseases in the current times are stress related. This in no way makes them any less serious. However, stress is caused when a being lacks the skills necessary to deal with life or situations that arise in life. Improving your life skills will relieve stress. Relief of stress will make life easier, and dis-ease often vanishes.

If your dis-ease is manifesting in a physical way then you face a lack of skill in the ways you think. Examine your training and begin to question what you have been taught. So much is old information and much of that is based on older information. Sometimes it is not information at all, merely an old story that has never had many facts to it.

If your dis-ease is manifesting through your emotions then you are missing a spiritual balance. Oddly, this is often treated by examining the brain or is called mental illness. The brain is connected, but the heart is the source of this imbalance. You must examine your relationships with others, all of them throughout your life. Do you feel that you are a victim? Learn to strengthen your own power. Cease giving to others what is not theirs to take. In reality, it is not yours to give. Your power is given to you for a reason. The universal energy that exists as "you" is a borrowed energy in a way. This energy will return to Source at the end of your incarnation. What will you have done to improve and balance this energy?

By maintaining the energy within yourself you will feel stronger, more capable, and the stress upon your heart and brain will diminish. You will see clearly your responsibilities on the planet. You will see that it is you that you must take care of first and foremost. Attempts to fit in with old concepts can only lead you to de-forming your life in the vain hope of finding comfort in too small a space.

Do not look to others' achievements or possessions. Do not seek approval from anyone outside of yourself. Certain principles of society will apply at any age. Anti-social behavior has its consequences. Balanced behavior will never intrude or impede on others' lives. It is your own balance that you must seek, however, and there is no one outside of you that will grant you permission to fully and completely follow your path.

This is often viewed as a lonely way of life. If you need others' approval then, yes, it is. A solitary life is a spiritual life. We are not talking about being curmudgeonly or withdrawing from society out of disapproval. You see, the approval principle works both ways. Do not seek approval from others, but also do not seek to have others seek your approval.

Learn to improvise. Learn to release. Learn to cease judgment. Learn to see the opportunities offered in any situation.

Attaining a Path of Truth

From the realm of spirit, we offer comfort. Often it comes in forms that may surprise you. A spiritual epiphany can be one of those ways and, like the pursuit of truth, this may not lead to immediate comfort. Epiphanies, those sudden moments of realization, are infrequent. Do not rely on them as markers of your spiritual growth. An epiphany, however, is a way of making energetic room in a person's life. When you attain a realization that things are much more open and that there is a much bigger picture available, you often immediately relax. You no longer feel cramped in your own life.

Your spiritual guides, your companions, can also offer to show you truth. Again, this will be a truth about yourself. Each person and being in the universe carries their own unique perception. In this way, there is no true universal truth.

With truth may come moments of dismay. When you recognize the limitations you may have lived under or within, when you understand that you can alter your reality, you may wonder why you have not done so before. You may ask, "Why did no one explain this to me before now?" It is tempting to place blame outside of yourself. The truth is, you alone can accept truth for yourself as an undivided one.

Once seen, it is no longer possible to re-enter the old limits and boundaries. Once you know the amount of space you have available to create your life, you will find yourself feeling more comfortable. In this way, both paths will lead to each other.

A Path of Service

The paths of comfort and truth are not the only paths to a higher vibration. They are personal paths. They center around you as an individual. It is important to follow this and balance yourself first. Another is a path of service. This may be the most difficult way of all.

Choosing the path of service is less a choice and more a calling. It is ultimately a path of personal balance. It involves radiating energy from your center. This is why it is necessary to first achieve your own balance before embarking on this path. Some cautions are in order regarding this way of spiritual travel.

It is always a solitary path. Not that the one following this way is alone. There can be and often are many others surrounding a being following the path of service. Family and friends are integral experiences on the planet and, to a degree, in the realm of spirit.

Some are motivated to pursue a path of service as a way of avoidance. In serving others they do not strive for their own truth or comfort. They rely too heavily on outside sources for support. You can recognize such ones in the way they speak. Continued requests to angels and guides for help, or requests for constant material donations to a cause identify an imbalance. They are not-self-reliant.

Some choose this path as a means of support. In this way they seek to serve others for a price. Maintenance of a lifestyle becomes a primary objective, and the path is lost.

A path of service is, by its nature, its own reward. It is the path of the Bodhisattva. Few are called to this way and never before they travel the paths of comfort and truth. It is possible for one lifetime to contain all three of the paths we mention. It is not probable.

The path of service is one that entails an intimate wisdom. The attaining of this wisdom comes from knowledge and experience. A path of comfort can bring you the knowledge you need. A path of truth can bring you the experiences necessary. A path of comfort can bring you the sense of peace all spiritually minded beings seek. A path of truth can bring the joy that we desire. These things must also be rooted in the energy of love.

And so we conclude by saying, if you seek comfort and truth, search for ways to manifest peace, joy, and love within everything you do. You are not alone in your seeking, and we walk these paths with you closely. Open your sight and witness your companions now.

16
Are We There Yet?

As above, so below. We come to you with more information on an approaching time of change. We tell you that it is good to direct your attention to a moment in the stream of time but caution you not to attach yourself to a moment that will pass.

Some feel that this should be a time for fear. We tell you that you create the world you inhabit. Acting out of fear is not productive. Fear is the absence of the energy of courage.

There have been many significant markers throughout history. Many have sought to instill fear in others and always the world continues through these times. These are times to prepare for and consider, just like the time of planting or the time of harvesting. You must be ready, and you must act. Unlike the simple cycle of seasons, the approaching wave of energy is special. It is an opportunity

Many Markers

Some were present for and aware of the events called Harmonic Convergence and Harmonic Concordance. These were precursors to the action of energy that arrived in 2012. The times of Harmonic Convergence and

Harmonic Concordance were times of awareness and realization, times where many left old lives and relationships and came together in the idea that things could and would be new and different. Many of you recall the dramatic changes that you made and the better lives you created for yourselves during these days. If you look back now, you may wonder at your own strength! But where, you may ask, is the reward for all of the spiritual work you have accomplished? Where is the healing that you requested?

Some have become jaded by these many markings of time. Could this all be something imaginary, something that someone else made up, a nice story, but with no basis in reality? Perhaps, they may think, 2012 was simply a date with no importance, just an old prophecy from an ancient culture that meant nothing.

Notice now that over the past thirty years there have been an increasing number of these marked times. Notice too how more people are feeling compelled to speak about the energy and the lightwork that is being accomplished. Perhaps you are one of them. Have you asked yourself these questions? Have you felt "called" to some higher purpose? You are clearly not alone!

The energy leading up to and beyond the year 2012 could be called, "The Harmonic Coalescence" for that is what is occurring, the continued harmonizing of energies. Recall that first these energies converged, that is, they came near one another. They were not yet in agreement. This was the next stage, becoming concordant. The energies came to be in harmony with one another. This set the stage for true growth of all life.

Now it is time to coalesce, to merge together and move in a single progressive direction. This is not simply a time for humanity to evolve, but for all life on earth and in this section of the galaxy.

Many Messages

It seems like there are many new books and articles and even many new ways of communication, each filled with concepts and ideas regarding the future. There are so many messengers with so many words. How do you know who is a true messenger? How do you know if someone is not true? What is truth? Are these truly messages from the realm of spirit?

The easy answer is, yes, many of the words you read are channeled from beings beyond the physical realm. Notice that we did not say, "beyond the earthly realm," for many spiritual beings are closely involved with the planet now. They are as much bound to the earth as you who are in corporeal form. Understand that we all have tasks and responsibilities, just like you.

In human societies, there are many levels of existence and many occupations. Each member seeks meaning in their life and validation for their perceptions. Each has experiences that vary, based on the number of interactions they have in life. These experiences affect the way in which one communicates with Spirit. Your ability to respond to these communications affects how you hear and comprehend the messages.

The messages you read and hear from various individuals are all valid, from their perspective. Their value to you as an individual is based on your personal experiences and willingness to be open to such thoughts. It is not necessary to judge the messages or messengers. Simply seek the ones that sound like truth to your ears.

You will notice that many speak of very similar subjects and events. Not all agree in details. That is simply a matter of perception. From different views amongst different spiritual guides and translated by different humans, you may see things in differing ways. This does not negate one message or another. Ask yourself, "Which one sounds like the correct path for me at this time?" Also ask, "Can both be true in some way that is beyond human comprehension at this time?"

These messages are for the benefit of all humanity. It will not serve to edit or censor words that you personally do not find accessible at this time. It is possible that you will grow into these very words in the future.

Creating Better Spiritual Communication

It is possible for someone to exit from the stream of the family human and sit in solitude to gain great spiritual wisdom. At one time, this was an optimal way to do so, but no longer. The simple fact is there are far too many other humans for someone to truly remove themselves from the energy of other beings.

This necessitates a new approach to communication between spirit and humanity. Ask yourself again, "Why so many messengers?" We say as above, so below, and the true meaning is this: As diverse as human society can be, the realm of spirit is equally diverse. You may ask, then, "Is the spiritual realm equally contentious?" In a sense, yes, it is. We have great ranging discussions and debate. However, there is never a breakdown or contesting of wills that result in coercion or an attempt at subverting another's free will. Always the purpose of the discussion is to further the experience of life.

You can always test the message that you hear by asking, "Are these words that promote unity? Are these words that motivate peaceful action? Does this message make me feel joyful or help me find patience with the world as it currently exists? Am I motivated to greater kindness or gratefulness?"

A few moments of solitude after reading or listening to spiritually based material will assist you in accessing your own truth and finding the precise inspiration that will benefit you to continue along your path.

The Present and the Future

We, in the realm of spirit, communicate to many in the family human. In the future, this communication will come more and more directly. It is a time of coalescence. You are being brought closer to us and we to you. Our tasks are going to become clearer and more specific as the years continue.

Where is your reward? It is said that the reward for a job well done is more work! Do you feel as if you have more work to do? If so, then you have been doing well.

What is truth? You are truth! Act in a manner that reflects the unity and harmony you so desire. Think of the strength it took for you to change your life during the past decades. Realize how your determination to lead an authentic, spiritually fulfilled life brought you through and away from relationships that did not honor your true path. Recall that strength and know that it was assisted by those you call angels and guides. Recall that feeling and reach out to them once again, not as a mere spiritual child, but as a mature spiritual being.

It is the nature of some beings to seek a goal or a stopping point where all problems are solved, and life attains perfection. This is not what this energy is about. The marker of 2012 was about the bringing together of strong forces and preparing to align them to create a more powerful and complete race of beings.

Do not waver. Continue in your desire for peaceful coexistence. You are the ones that are creating the energy of peace and vitality in the physical realm. You face powerful blocks that will not be removed by force. They will be eroded by steady effort, like stone in water.

Be aware of the prevailing energy. If you are in a time of stillness, be still. If action is necessary, take direct, positive action. This is the yin and yang of all the universe and is true in the physical realm as much as in the mental, emotional, and spiritual aspects of all existence. Be balanced in your life and harmony will arrive.

We remind you now and tell you that you are amongst the strongest of beings to exist. You may seem meek to others. There are words that have been spoken before regarding meek ones.

We have said these things before. In the same way that you honor those above, you who are below are honored. Great times are upon us all. Great moments of history are being written. How will you choose to remember these days? As a time of strife and decay? Or as the time when the energy of love, joy, and peace rose and spread throughout the planet? Actively choose how you will think and feel. Actively choose how you will be remembered.

17
Seeking the Future

As above, so below. The future is of interest to those in the realm of spirit and so you in the physical realm also search for knowledge regarding coming events. We offer you some glimpses and also some perspective concerning both the visioning of the coming days and guidance for how to think and feel. In terms of prophecy, we must remind you that the future is malleable. Your personal choices affect not just your own future course, but also those around you. Choose your life wisely.

The Shift Toward Harmony

Many spiritual beings made positive choices during the Harmonic Convergence and the Harmonic Concordance. Now, as we move through to the peak of the Harmonic Coalescence, there is a greater tension on the planet. Emotions especially are running high, and many are not open to speaking in a clear and fair fashion with others of differing view. This tension will translate into action throughout the globe.

Rather than an escalation into large scale violence or social unrest as has happened in the past, the result will be more subdued, and the effect will be more immediate. The direction that the planet is heading is one of greater peace and unity. There still needs to occur further reduction in old thought patterns and belief systems. Events will unfold within the next one hundred years that will ensure this occurrence. The choice of the family human is this: Be surprised by and forced into change, or look forward with anticipation and embrace the new world.

From the realm of spirit, we see that the latter choice is the more probable one at this time. This may be difficult to believe from the standpoint of the family human, especially in light of current events. We remind you now that you have chosen to be here at this time. You prepared for this eventuality. We acknowledge that it is more difficult than initially visualized. This demonstrates that there are limits to vision even within the spiritual realm. However, there are few limits to what can be accomplished when humanity teams with their spirit companions.

Changes Coming

We will offer you some specifics for the near future. We again remind you that the future is changeable, but these few examples are more certain than most.

Several nations on the African continent will begin to come together in a unified way. Old tribal differences will begin to erode in the light of new thought. Much of this will be motivated by economics, but the underlying force will continue to come from the women in these regions. We point you again to Rwanda. This area holds a source of much of the energy of the history of the family human. This societal change will be health-initiated as well. Knowledge is spreading in this region, and we see a different light re-emerging from the women and their children.

The unity will be challenged and may not succeed at first attempt. Other nations will continue to fail to act in support of the populations there. It will be left to strong new economic entities rather than archaic governmental systems to further spread the energy of growth to these regions. Wireless communication will be instrumental and there will be new systems that arise from the actions taken.

Wireless systems have already begun the changes that you will observe in China. A collapse of sorts will begin within the interior of this vast nation. This is not a rebellion in the old style. This is more a separation of old ways. The vision of the Western culture gives rise to many questions in the population of this region. They do not seek to duplicate the consumerist approach to life. They do seek the abundance that can become available when unnecessary rules and restrictions are eliminated. There is a theology regarding the State. Like the old religious theologies of Europe, this too must undergo scrutiny and adaptation when exposed to new light.

Changes in You

What was once revered and worshiped is now being surpassed by truly spiritual beings. We do not speak of anyone in particular. Instead, we simply say that you should take a moment to look in the mirror and reread that phrase, "truly spiritual beings." This too is a prediction: the realization of your innate spiritual power and the acceptance of the responsibility that you have to continue the creation of the future. We do not invite you to take this action. The truth is, there is nothing that can prevent you from acting on this fact.

Let us take note now: you are not spiritual leaders. You are leading spiritually. The difference is the same as the old ways versus the new light. In the past, people looked for someone to follow. They sought rigid rules and responded to punishment as if these were something that a god or gods would do. The new way is experiential. It is personal and no one can instruct another in how they commune with the spirit realm. Judgments are put aside in favor of exploration. Rules are taken down and examined. They are replaced by spiritual principles.

In each of the changes that we predict, you see the guiding energy is one of unity. There is a seeming lack of this force in the earthly realm today, but this is simply an indication of how entrenched the old archaic rules are.

We do not speak of an apocalypse here, not in sense that it has come to be known. We do speak of an apocalypse in its original meaning, the bringing of light or the unveiling of truth. This points us to one final prediction.

Changing the Past

Do not be caught up in the many words that attempt to give fear. Many will seek to capitalize on this and draw others to them with promises of secrets to be revealed. Many will seek to acquire financial gain on the basis of claims of understanding of ancient thoughts. We tell you now that no one knows the full import of the civilizations that left the markers for this time.

Those that speak truth do not seek to explain old ways. Rather, they guide you in paths of peace. They do not ask you to follow or recreate old beliefs. Rather, they encourage you to find great joy in the present days. They do not require the study of old cultures that acted in primitive, lower vibrational ways. They indicate to you the opportunity for self-examination and powerful spiritual growth based on loving yourself and radiating love outwards in all directions.

Even the past is malleable. How we view different events changes as we gain distance and perspective. Some thoughts and ideas have been hidden and suppressed, while others have been promoted as absolute right. These are the thoughts that are in transition now and they are the most difficult for people to release. Understand that "that is the way things always have been" is not a true statement. Those words are designed to justify stasis. In a Universe where diversity is the only real constant, any effort to make things stay still will not be met with success. Maintaining old orders or behaving as if new thoughts or recently attained knowledge does not exist or have value will ensure that a person will have a difficult time in the coming years.

Willingness to re-examine and alter your perceptions strengthens your ability to grow. A being who will look forward is more likely to avoid obstacles and stumbling blocks than one who only looks to the past for guidance. We have said, "It is all new now." A brief scan of recent years will quickly demonstrate this when compared to a century ago. Yet this does not invalidate all that has come before. There is a continuum, and all events build to other actions.

Seeing the Future

The Harmonic Convergence and the Harmonic Concordance replaced the concept of a destructive Armageddon. They instead revealed the true meaning of the term "apocalypse." The shift that is occurring will finish the energy of those times and leave things altered beyond what can be imagined. Would it surprise you to know that this all began some two hundred years previously? Look back to the time numbered as the 1700's. Note the attempt by many to release themselves from old ways and old thought. Note the rise of technologies that supported this energy. Note how during the latter portion of the 1900's, personal freedom fueled the developing technology. This has not ended; it has intensified.

The vision of what spirit and spirituality meant was slowly replaced and altered from vast hierarchies to personal vision. This must proceed. It is something that moves faster with each passing year.

We remind you now that the future begins with you. If it is to be a future of loving, peaceful beings, then you must love yourself and feel peaceful within. No exterior force will grant you this state of mind. Being in a physical form may limit your spiritual power, but it does not prevent you from the exercising of your true spiritual nature. The actions of love, joy, and peace are the key to energizing your spiritual life now and always.

18
Seasons of Life

As above, so below. We speak from the perspective of the realm of spirit. Now let us focus on the human experience, particularly the passing of time. Consider the process of physical aging. It is a necessary thing, when you exist within the realm of gravity, to observe and mark the passage of time and seasons. Cycles of life are often referred to as seasonal, particularly the latter days of a human's lifespan. It is *not* a necessary thing to accept the current limitations of the passing of time or the process of aging.

We remind you now of the perceptive ability of the family human and also of the concept that perception is reality. For many centuries, when an individual human observed that they were getting old, the common belief has been that they must also be losing power or strength. In believing, this became a reality. Observe humankind in its present state of existence and you will see far fewer individuals believing they are in the autumn or winter of their lives. You will observe far fewer weakening physically as their lives progress. Are you one of these people? You can be!

A Separate Reality

One of the strongest accomplishments of the last several generations is to learn and begin the practice of creating a personal reality. This is a process with a great deal of momentum. The next step is the lengthening of vitality by using inherent power rather than outside techniques. The idea of belief in vitality and self-healing is not new in history, but you have all been removed from it through the advent of medical science and advancing technology. We speak now of necessity to an older generation, but our message is for a younger one as well.

The generations achieving adulthood at this time are the inheritors of this process and they are the ones who will build upon it in ways beyond the imagining of the generations just prior. They will integrate the two approaches of physical technology and energetic healing. They are creating the partnership from all angles. Many are pursuing the healthcare process in what is considered a traditional way, the way of hospitals and pharmaceuticals. Yet many of those ones are practicing such disciplines as tai chi, meditation, and yoga and are aware of the inner power of self-healing. Others who have grown up with parents who avoided the medical profession and focused on right eating and healthy lifestyles now find themselves less bound by the prejudices against medical practice than were their parents.

The result is an approach that reflects personal responsibility in caring for an individual's continued vitality. They will understand that many diseases exist due primarily to belief or stress and they will eliminate the need for them. They have begun to alter society around the world, making the potential for peaceful and harmonious relations stronger and closer than at any time in all existence.

Concordance, Convergence, Coalescence

Cycles are essentially regular, but they are not exact. Many elements and forces go into the action of the cycles, causing sometimes wide variations from predicted models. In the lifetimes of the generations here now on the planet earth, you have experienced some of the widest variations in the history of humankind. These large swings will continue for some time, though the peak is near. Soon the Harmonic Coalescence will come to a completion and a cycle will begin to wind down, allowing life to settle in for a straighter and calmer period.

Yet there is no going backwards to previous times. There will be movements to bring the older concepts to mass awareness. The goal of some will be the return of certain eras. The result will be a forward motion, bringing old and new into a concordance and convergence and finally to a coalescence of new ways of existence. Not simply for humanity, but for the planet as well. Indeed, this is an energy promoted by Gaia herself. It is why we recommend touching the earth and getting in harmony with the planet. It is why crystals and herbal solutions have become so prominent in the practice of health and wellness.

A balance is being achieved. It is the season for such a thing. Begin to think of yourself in a balanced way. Create the concept of a balanced life within your physical form. You will find that wherever you are in the span of your lifetime, your vitality will grow, and you will move in a straighter and calmer way.

Those of you at the end of the cycle of earthly life will find more fulfillment and activity than previous generations believed possible. Those at the other end of the spectrum will find a level of enlightenment that previous generations took years to achieve. In fact, the generations now being born are the conclusion of a bridge from one style of human living into another. Your life is an element of that structure. Your life is important in the vast vision of the purpose of the earth. Believe this. Believe in your personal importance and that of others.

Harmonious Generations

Now that the concept of harmony has been conceived and passed through the unique process of the concordance, the convergence, and the coalescence of human consciousness, it can progress and be assimilated by all incoming life. The planet has been prepared. There is still much work to do, and no one is to now sit still as if their job is concluded! Life is a continuing process and while you are incarnate you must continue to filter yourself and grow. We tell you now, these times are wondrous. Your works will not soon be forgotten.

When speaking of cycles, it is helpful to recall the concept of earth, air, fire, and water. The children of the near future will be more concerned with air and water. The past generations have seen earth and fire as a primary means for progressing the family human. Possession of land and the transformation of elements into power will be of lesser importance to the ones that are just beginning to take stewardship. They will focus on water and air, not just in terms of cleanliness, but also in the harmonious use of these elements to power future society. A time will come when earth and fire will be of concern again, but that is further away than we care to address at this time.

The accent, the underlying motivation of human endeavor for the next generations, will be to exist together not just with one another but also with the planet and all life. In the future, it will be difficult for them to comprehend the conflicts and divisions of these current times. It will be these things that are forgotten. Why not begin that process now within yourselves?

This will be true for all elements of society. Politics and religion are changing daily. You are witness to the wild swings and radical works that represent old thought trying to be viable in the face of a new age. It is the defining of what is actually human progress versus what is merely the desire for personal political power. It is the understanding of the difference between abundance and greed. It is the realization of true spiritual connection beyond rigid religious dogma.

Just as the old empires have faded, and monarchies and ruling classes have been replaced with a spirit of equalization amongst all peoples, the foreseeable future will be one of strong individuals combining in conscious choice to create communities of growth in many areas of interest. No borders will divide them and the very idea that such things once existed will be a puzzle.

Once, the idea of possessions and power over other people was believed to equal happiness. This has proven to be a hollow concept. Now, the belief of equality for all life has taken root and will not easily be removed. Humanity grows in this area constantly, fitfully at times, but growth is seen everywhere.

Just as spirituality and its shadow, religion, were dramatically different at the end of the twentieth century than at the conclusion of the nineteenth, so too will spirituality be eminently different at the close of the twenty-first century. No longer is the belief apparent that one need to have an intercessor between you and the Source of all things. Personal relationship with your spiritual guides is a well-known, though not always well accepted, thought. In the future, it will be an inescapable fact. Do you know your guides?

The Season

On a large scale of generational history, we note for you that you have passed through a winter. For many it has been severe. The ones alive now are seeing signs of spring, the sign of growth. Soon a new season arrives. It is the season of planting.

Now is the time to look to the fields, to decide what seeds will be used and what will yield the most successful crop and harvest for the future. The fertility of the future rests within each one of you. What you sow, you will reap. You know these words well. We add to them now. You are the seed and you are the harvest. What fruit comes from you? What have you provided that nourishes others?

As always, we emphasize the greatest of all fruits, those of love and joy and peace. These are the signs of a successful season and cycle of life. Take stock of your existence now. Prune away the things that do not yield this fruit. Strengthen yourself now and gain the nourishment you need. When the harvest arrives, you will be bountiful.

19
Appropriate Faith

As above, so below. With the world in a state of great change, do you have a personal faith in a balanced future for the family human? Do you feel that you have a place of peace waiting for you? Are you pursuing your own spirituality and ethics in a faithful manner?

What is Faith?

It is said that faith is an assured expectation of realities not yet seen. This means that there can be no such thing as blind faith. Faith requires vision. It is the ability to see past current difficulties and move towards a time when problems have been solved. Faith is a form of optimism. It allows you to see the optimal outcome, regardless of current realities.

Faith is not fantasy, a hopeful wishing for security and abundance. Faith is rooted in reality. It is a vision of reality not yet seen. The farther from reality your expectations are, the less real is your faith and thus the less appropriate.

Recorded history demonstrates that the family human and the earth itself have faced many difficult times. Whether it is societies out of balance, clashes of cultures due to errant belief systems, or ecological and geophysical challenges, there have been many times where danger was a common way of existence. However, there have been far more times when life on the planet is peaceful and abundant. Despite current societal challenges, you exist in an extremely pleasant and prosperous time of earth's history.

There will come shifts in the near future and for many this will appear to be a fulfillment of ancient words poorly interpreted. They have what they feel is a form of faith that great suffering will occur for those who do not share their belief. This is an inappropriate faith. It is a faith not grounded in reality, but rather based in fear and a desire to strengthen a weak system of religion.

True spirituality approaches the future with a vision based in love, joy, and peace. The adherents of true spirituality are noted for their ability to be kind, patient, and mild. It is not based on a vision from the past. It is rooted in a strong vision that the future can be and is being created today by each and every individual alive.

The Source of Faith

Faith is a belief in yourself first, an acknowledgement of your own value to receive what you need. It is also an acknowledgement that you can tap into higher energies to receive what may not be easily available to you. Remember always that you are an aspect of the Source of the creative energy of the universe.

The universe does not exist to destroy itself. That is not a reality that can be observed. The universe does exist to create and diversify. The universe never stops creating. It never takes a rest. It is a universe filled with experimentation and variety. A simple walk through a garden or forest can demonstrate that as reality. A glance at a globe showing the variety of climates or a visit to a zoo will demonstrate the very real concept of constant creation.

Do you believe in your ability to create a future for yourself? Do you believe that you not only have access to this possibility, but that it is a reality expected of you?

To be a person of faith, you must first believe in yourself. But it is larger than just a belief in yourself. Appropriate faith is a strong belief in humanity. It may be an easy thing to feel cynical about the current state of human action. Faith does not always take an easy path.

In the near future, there will be events that bring humanity together in a common goal. Those who are already in a state of optimism and willing to join together with others will find themselves in leadership positions. Having faith in yourself and those around you will strengthen others' ability to put their faith in you. In this way, you may become not just an aspect of Source energy, but a source of faith for others.

Do you speak in a manner that demonstrates faith now? Do you speak of reality? We add a caution here: this is not a position of superiority; this is a position of service. Look to your current leadership and ask, "Who is serving the greater good and who is seeking or promoting divisions?"

Balanced Faith

Faith is a power, an energy. You act in faith. Where can you best place your action? Act in appropriate movements to support continued growth and knowledge of Gaia.

Without Gaia you have no home, no direct source of energies.

This does not mean that you need to engage in protesting against things that may appear to be harming the planet. A peaceful person is not actively seeking to go against anything. A peaceful person, one who acts from a spiritual basis, will always seek to work for growth and balance. There may be times when acting in a stopping energy is necessary, but those times are far fewer if more people begin acting in a progressive way.

Acting in faith is acting as if the optimal vision of the future is already in existence. It is the creation of a reality that benefits *all* of the family human. The details may shift and alter as time passes, but the principles sought will be attained.

It is said that faith without works is dead. We say again, faith is not fantasy. Do not rely solely on faith. Action coupled with faith is an appropriate and powerful use of energy. In your personal life, it is better to create for yourself than to constantly ask for assistance. If you are in need and find you must ask, first ask, "What can I do to provide for my own needs? What path is available to me to add balance to the universe rather than take energy from it?" In this way, you demonstrate that you possess the vision of abundance.

Acting in Faith

Appropriate faith is a balancing. Source supplies, but Source energy also creates. You are an aspect of Source. You create. There are times when Source adapts energies to balance other aspects of Itself. How can you duplicate this natural action? How can you adapt your own energies to balance yourself? It is this self-reliant attitude that will assist you in personal growth. It is having faith in oneself that creates strong individuals, undivided ones.

To have a belief in something unseen or unexperienced by others is a private form of reality. To seek to proselytize others to your personal reality is to demonstrate a weakness in your own faith. Your belief within your self should be enough. To do otherwise is to invite division within your own heart.

The action of trying to adapt others' viewpoint to match your own is a seeking of outward confirmation. It is an attempt to prove what needs no proof. The greater the number of beings who follow a specific dogma or system, the less thought is actually going on. It is an abdication of individual responsibility for one's own spiritual connection to Source.

There are many who speak of faith as something to possess. We tell you again that faith is an energy that you use. It cannot be kept. It can be private, but it must be acted upon. If you say you have faith and take no action, then this indicates that the strength of your belief in yourself is weak. Your confidence in your own perceptions of the future must hold great value within you or they can be of little value outside of you.

This is not a judgment, only an observation of reality. If you are unhappy with what you see currently, have faith in yourself that things can and are changing and that you have a say in the matter. Build your self-confidence by placing small tasks for yourself. Place an element of faith in your ability to do something that you have never done and watch how greater opportunities to express faith will appear.

Faith comes from your intellect but is powered by your emotions. It is an intersection between the realm of spirit and the physical realms. It is where the future begins. Create an optimistic attitude within your own mind. Look for ways to see the future in an optimal way. Focus on the qualities of true spirituality: love, joy, and peace, and this path to your future will grow naturally within you.

20
The Action of Charity

As above, so below. Life is uncertain. There are no guarantees of comfort while in existence upon this planet. We speak of the needs of others and the opportunity for you to act in a way that creates a flow of balancing energy. We have often spoken of the movement of energy, how it will rise and fall like the action of a wave. In your life, you will experience times of abundance and times of need. We do not necessarily mean this in reference to physical things, but we will specifically address the aspect of generosity regarding physical resources.

The Reason for Charity

In times of extreme weather or natural geological actions, members of the family human may be adversely affected. Calls for aid can and do rise. As natural as it may be for a hurricane, tsunami, or an earthquake to occur, it is equally natural for the family human to respond with the power of compassion. From our perspective in the realm of spirit, we see clearly that the opposite and equal reaction to those events that are termed disasters is the immense outpouring of one of humanity's greatest powers: the love of strangers in need. This action of charity sets the family human apart from nearly all other life on the planet. It is the *conscious* action that sets you apart from *all* life. Other life forms may act in an instinctual way, but you *choose* to behave charitably. It is a spiritual thing and evidence of your spirituality.

There is often never even a request for assistance. You witness an event, and you respond with the question, "What can I do to help?" If you are close enough, you can assist directly. Rescue efforts are often made more successful by volunteers. Shelter is often provided by those living nearby. Food and water are carried and served first by ones who are in proximity to the event. Even if resources are stretched to a limit, there is a generosity of spirit that rises in these times. Emotions can and do run high. Tears of sorrow can swiftly turn to tears of relief when efforts of others arrive on scenes of tragedy.

When requests do begin, when the word spreads of the condition that some are left in, direct action is not always practical. Professional organizations often take on the majority of the work of moving large quantities of supplies into the affected areas. The individual at a distance then contributes in their own way through donations of supplies, but more often through funding. Many small donations grow into large sums and the work of recovery has the opportunity to move faster. A restoration of balance is sought by both those who are affected and the ones who seek to assist.

Being Charitable is Beneficial for You

We say that charity is a spiritual energy. In the giving, you intend for charity to flow. It is an energy that may be interrupted. The closer you begin the action of charity to

The Action of Charity

the space of need, the more energy will arrive to your chosen destination. The larger the organization, the more levels charity must pass through, the more diminished the final effect. This fact should not prevent you from acting on a charitable impulse. It should simply increase your discretion at the use of your personal resources.

Simply thinking about the opportunity for charity creates the space for a change within you. Once the thought is in place, it is difficult to return to a self-centered position. It makes you aware of the flow of energy around you. Are you moving your energy inward or outward? Like a wave, sometimes you are doing one, sometimes the other. Awareness of your own needs will help you in expressing charity. You must remain centered to be effective in charitable action.

The action of charity begins to weave karmic threads together. It is this that begins to bind the family human tighter together. The action of response to another's misfortune is an energy of the heart. The actual movement of resources toward that situation is an action of the brain. It is therefore a decision that strengthens the mind, which is the heart and brain acting in concert, and allows the brain, the intellect, the opportunity to connect strongly to spirit. Here is where spirit welcomes logic.

Charity is not something given in expectation of a return. Gratitude is an energy, and you will feel this in subtle ways. If you are less directly involved, those affected by the circumstances will likely express their appreciation through prayer or meditation. It will return to you in ways that likely will not be directly relatable to your original action. If you are directly involved, the gratitude will be powerfully felt.

The action of charity is a self-less one. It can be mimicked and used in self-serving ways. The person who does this will karmically receive equally what they put into their actions. Still, any charitable action, however it is intended, has the potential for greater benefit to those in need. Charity is a spiritual power that can rise above initial intention. Charity can alter the giver in powerful ways.

Guard Your Resources

A caution, then, is in order. You must not give to the extent that you put yourself in urgent need. There will be times of desperate need. Choose your actions wisely. It does not serve a situation to attempt to rescue someone who is beyond your ability to assist. It does not serve to create a situation where two people are in need of help instead of one. If you cannot swim, do not try to rescue another who is drowning by jumping into the water.

A clear mind is important in the action of charity. We emphasize the need for you to remain centered in your charitable efforts. Even as we say these things, we know that the heart will often draw ones into a self-sacrificing action. You may decide to reach out beyond your current means for the greater good of the family human. This is a spiritual decision. Choose wisely, kind human!

You are connected to and an aspect of the Source of all things. Having access to Source, you have some power to control energy around you. These energies can be tangible objects. You might use some of this energy to depletion. However, energy never is destroyed; it is only transformed. When you are finished with something physical, it can often take on a new purpose. The more natural the physical product, the easier it will be to recycle the energy of the object. You then seek more aspects of Source energy for yourself. You seek to "re-source" your life. Here is where you choose wisely in exercising charity. The stronger your spiritual connection to Source, the more desire you will have to provide Source energy, the basic life sustaining things, to those in need. By channeling such power, you will be re-sourced yourself. Charity is an opportunity to re-source or regain connection to the primary energy of the universe.

Charity Across Time

Charity is a supplying of needed energy. In many cases, an anticipation of need may influence some of you to stock extra supplies. It is a familiar idea, but it can go well beyond just the thought that you personally may need fresh water in the event of a natural catastrophe. It can spread to the organizing of groups of neighbors or family members into small units of balancing energy.

It can go even further into thinking of the future, not only of your family, but also for the coming generations of humans being incarnated in the coming years and decades. What does the future look like now? What will those ahead deal with by way of resources?

This goes well beyond the physical realm. If you are creating more debris from your existence, how will this action then translate into karmic energy? You need not become extreme in your efforts; only seek to do what can be done. It is wise, though, to look beyond what is already being done in your life. Look for ways to minimize intake and the unnecessary creation of waste. Look also for creative opportunities to re-use what already exists. The energy that makes up each and every human is a creative energy. Exercise this in reviewing your daily life. It is not necessary to live an austere existence. It is beneficial to live in awareness and consciousness.

If possible, view the future with the action of charity in mind. Think and act as if you might be alive one hundred or two hundred years from now. What do you wish the future to look like? What are you doing to get that reality started today?

We often speak of the spiritual energies of love, joy, and peace. It is these powers that allow the energy of charity to exist. They are all aspects of your spiritual life and each feeds and supports the other. Charity is an individual choice to serve others. The action of charity is an evident demonstration of your ability to express love, joy, and peace. Together these are powerful forces, not simply for humanity, but for all life in the physical and spiritual realms. Express these qualities and feel the strength of Source grow within you.

21
The Power of Love

As above, so below. We choose to speak of the energy of love.

We have said that love is one of the primary aspects of Source. Love is not simply an aspect of Source. Love is the quality that demonstrates Source energy to all beings. It is a common energy amongst life throughout the universe in both physical and spiritual realms. All things in existence are aspects of Source, but love is a binding power. Love will motivate a person to accomplish greater things than any other power in their life. When love is placed at the center of your life, balance and harmony become your natural state.

Paths of Love

Many search for love in their lives. They often seek it outside of themselves, someone to complete them. Their quest is external. We tell you now that it is better to learn to love oneself first. By loving yourself, you acknowledge the value and worth of your existence. You empower yourself by making a direct connection to Source energies. Loving oneself brings immediate balance to many difficulties you may be having in life and provides a new sight and perspective to your individual path.

This is not to say all problems will instantly vanish. You are still subject to gravity and thus also to time. The solutions will find a clearer path when the way is opened through the energy, the power of love.

Loving yourself will allow others to love you in a purer way. Partnerships will develop with more ease and regularity. You will attract others of a higher vibration. Relationships will intensify and emotional expression will flow steadily.

Many struggle with love and yet it is the easiest thing in the universe. In a sense, love *is* the universe. The degree by which you feel loved is the same as the degree of loving that you radiate. If you are not feeling loved, you must reach out and begin to practice your connection to Source. It is the realization that you are a valued aspect of Source that you must seek. At the same time, you must look for ways to express love to all others. Each action will strengthen the other. It is the feeling of being loved and the loving of others that pulls the purest, healing energies to you.

Many believe that they will only be capable of achieving balance through a relationship with another being. They seek a "one true love" style relationship. We tell you now, the idea of a single love for a single being is nonsense. Does Source only love one aspect of itself? The promotion of this concept is a limiting one. You may experience a primary relationship with a single partner, one that is strong and exclusive. However, there is such a great variety of beings that to believe there is only one person for you will result only in your unnecessarily rationing the inherent energy of love that belongs to you. Love will come slowly then and carry with it many limitations.

Love as a Spiritual Power

Many understand that true spirituality is rooted in unconditional love. Spiritual activities will help you open naturally to strong loving feelings. The release of judgment will allow an opening for spirit to enter your life. Again, becoming more aware of opportunities to express love will assist in realizing a truer spiritual life. Each action, taken together, will strengthen the other. The results may be felt instantly.

Love can approach any time during life. You must be receptive to it as well as a channel for it. If you put limitations upon love, imagining that there is only one true love, then you will find that you have created a greater gravity regarding love, and time will affect the process. If you become open to love, then you will not need to wait. Remain light and love will flourish.

The restrictions that are placed on love reflect the restrictions that one places upon spirit. If you place unnecessary restrictions upon spirit, you likely place them upon Source as well, but these restrictions begin and are wholly encompassed by your belief in and about yourself. Source is infinite. How, then, can love have limits?

Source energy can respond instantly to requests. Spiritual enlightenment occurs in a flash of inspiration. Love can happen in a glance, "at first sight." This happens when least expected and no limitations exist. If you can believe and accept moments like this, love will occur more and more often.

The Risk of Love

Love is an action. It is active and not passive. You cannot sit isolated and express love fully. You must risk your personal self, the deepest parts of you, in contact with others who are also risking themselves to make emotional connection. Without first making emotional connections, how do you expect to create spiritual connections? It is from the heart that humanity connects to the realm of spirit. Do not fear to feel!

If you have risked your heart in the past and have been hurt, you may be reticent about taking another chance emotionally. We tell you now that all life is a risk. This is a true statement in the spiritual realm as well as the physical. The truth is that your heart is willing to risk again and again. Your thoughts will seek to logic you away from such an action in an effort to protect you. Do you wish to be protected and unloved, or do you wish to have your heart fulfilled? There is only one course of action that leads to emotional fulfillment and that is to follow your heart's desire. Love is not brought about by thought.

When we say that all life is a risk, we do not mean that all life is dangerous. Certainly, the pursuit of pure love is not something that will put you in danger. We use the word "risk" in the way we would say that a seed must take a risk and grow. Once the seed has opened there is no going back inside. It may be safe to remain a seed, but it is not the seed's true and ultimate purpose.

Love, then, is a symbol of your growth. If you are active in life and in motion, you are growing. If you are not in growth mode, then where is your energy going? Are you playing it safe? Are you limiting your life? Are you limiting your love?

There is No End to Love

At some point, we all transform. As beings of energy, we all are subject to the laws of energy. Transformation is not destruction. If you, as a human being, are in the process of growing when you transform from this current incarnation to the next stage of your energetic existence, then your path into and out of the various realms of spirit and physical will be that much smoother. You will experience the joy of a life well lived and a path followed.

The opposite is true. If you are not in growth mode, you will experience resistance as you move along your karmic thread. You may ask, "Why do so many resist so-called death?" Even ones who claim a faith or belief in some form of afterlife will fight well beyond reason to remain, even at the cost of quality of living. It is because they do not see the inherent nature of the universe. They have placed limits on Source and thus on their own ability to connect to other living beings. They may not feel love in a strong way. They may feel unfulfilled and thus unwilling to leave this incarnation.

Comprehension of the power of love is crucial to growth and thus to the movement from one form to another. This is not to say that anyone should seek death from a human life. That would be a waste of energy. If life is somehow unpleasant, it is the task of each individual to focus their energies on making and balancing life around themselves to the best of their ability. The first step in any effort to improve life is to seek ways to express love. It is not common for anyone to reach the end of their existence and regret expressing love.

Love, as an aspect of Source, is a power beyond time. It is an energy with few limits. If you personally encounter limitations on your love, do not seek beyond yourself for the reasons. If someone does not seem capable or willing to express love to you, then redirect your energy, your love, elsewhere. Do not waste this commodity.

We have said that love is a primary aspect of Source. The practice of love brings with it commitment and purity. It is the power that connects all things back to the beginning of all things. It is not the only primary aspect. Love in a life will bring along with it joy and peace. These three things, these three powers, will create in each of us a strong sense of true meaning and purpose. They will fan the fire of passion for being alive. They will supply to us a limitless energy that will allow each individual to grow and experience strong spiritual connection.

We do not simply speak to you of love. From the realm of spirit, we send to all of you our love.

22
The Decision of Peace

As above, so below.

We greet you now and tell you that we recognize the difficult nature of remaining spiritual in such trying physical times. We also see how many are not simply coping but thriving in a spiritual way despite an apparent lack of physical means. We tell you again, you are among the strongest of humans to ever exist. As a group, you possess more spiritual potential now than at any previous time in recorded history.

Around the globe, the past decade has been one of testing and purifying. This testing will continue a short while longer. Do not let this information cause you to fear or despair! Those pursuing true spiritual practice are past the more intense times.

There are still many who will feel an increase in the intensity as energy shifts. They are unprepared for what is occurring and will find themselves off balance and uncertain. Their ancient dogma and pursuit of archaic thought will offer no solutions for the coming years of enlightenment.

Beneficial Skills

What skills will bring you through the increasing wave of change begun in the late 1990's? Is setting your intention enough? Is manifesting abundance enough? Is a positive attitude enough? Is it necessary to continually call on your spirit companions for help?

Positive thinking is not enough, but it is a good beginning. Those who expect things to turn out well are less likely to fall prey to ones who profit by the creation of fear. Without a doubt, there are things in existence to cause fear, but not nearly so many as you might believe.

You, as an individual, do not exist in a vacuum. The actions that you take affect many others, sometimes beyond your knowing. Setting a clear intention helps in the focusing of your energies, but there are many energies in existence that may press your intentions in different directions. Attempts to manifest abundance must be scrutinized to see if, by gaining personal abundance, others lose precious resources. In your personal pursuit of an orderly existence, be careful not to throw others off balance and into chaos.

Entropy and Order

We can describe two forces within the universe: entropy and order. To many, one of these energies may appear preferable to another. The search for order often defines the human experience. The creation of an orderly life or community allows for a feeling of peace to exist. This state of peace allows for a continued spiritual growth.

The search for order can be seen as a search for peace. However, too much order can create a rigid society. Too many rules can remove the freedom that allows for spiritual pursuits. It is not always a threat of violence that removes a feeling of peace.

When entropy enters into a community, there is often the feeling of a need to be aware and on watch for danger. Too much entropy can breed violence, yet entropy is not merely random violence. Entropy also allows the opportunity for freedom of expression and new thought.

Some alive on the planet believe strictly in entropy. They feel that all things are an accident or are random occurrences. At times, they are correct in perceiving entropy as a dominant energy. The universe possesses much that is entropic.

Some alive on the planet believe in complete divine order, that all things are purposed or fated and thus must be accepted. There is much in the universe that is orderly. But is one fundamentally better than the other? Should one be dominant over the other? The fact that both exist simultaneously indicates that they are necessary for the universe to continue. Together they balance the creative energy of the universe.

Creation is an ongoing process. We see the action of creation every day. It occurs when you make a decision to move toward a goal and set the steps in motion to make the concept a reality. This consciousness is a part of the human experiment on the planet earth. The drive to create an orderly life needs to be balanced with the ability to deconstruct old thoughts and patterns that no longer prove valid.

There are humans who exist in a state of deep imbalance and do not act in an ordered way. There are also those who act in a manner that seeks control of others' ways of thought and belief. Many among the family human have difficulty comprehending these extremists. This difficulty in comprehension is a signal that the human experiment is becoming more successful as time proceeds. A pursuit of freedom of thought is growing. You will soon observe an increased intolerance for war and ideological violence.

Increased Appreciation for Life

Is it possible to eliminate the death of an individual human body? The short answer is no. It is possible to prolong the life of the physical being and increase the quality of that life by a conscious effort. Is it possible to eliminate the desire for war and death to others? The fast answer is yes. This is one of the goals of the experiment of earth. Can the energy of entropy be brought into a cooperative state with the energy of purpose and order? Can life cooperate with other life successfully? Can balance be achieved?

In many cases, the survival of various species happens through the mechanism of predator and prey. The family human has arisen from this mechanism. The family human has also done much to rise above this mechanism. In doing so, it has lost certain survival skills but replaced them with other abilities. A higher consciousness and more acute awareness of their role in the larger order of things is one of the many blessings that the family human has bestowed upon themselves.

It is the continued rise of consciousness within the family human that brings you to these words today. You can be an agent of order or entropy. It is a decision. Before you can make a conscious choice, you must realize that both exist, and both exist within you. Understanding this will help you comprehend that you cannot subdue the entropic energy, only coexist with it. It is your actions and the setting of personal goals of order that bring these energies into alignment with one another. Random events in life can be dealt with easier when you are rooted in the creation of order, but never will there be enough order to foresee all random events.

Preparing for Future Decisions

Making better decisions is what you and all humanity strives for, but it is often still rooted in the action of gaining individual goals first. The decision-making process must and will rise to a higher vibration as the family human continues to raise their vibration.

When you set your intention, ask first for what you need personally, but then also consider the true needs of the community around you. When you seek abundance for yourself, make certain that you are not using or acquiring resources that are necessary to others. Ask first, "What is the true value to the goal I seek?" The practice of looking for the most positive outcome possible, not simply for yourself but for all others around you, will help encourage a cooperative spirit. You will find a certain synergy growing and feel a greater fulfillment and connection between your physical life and your spiritual goals.

Seek to do more for yourself and rely less on the concept of miracles. The idea of spirit accomplishing something for you is not incorrect. The absolute reliance on spiritual beings doing everything for you is far off balance. This is a fundamental misunderstanding of the order of things. First, you must realize that *you* are a spiritual being. As such, you have the power to create not just for yourself but also for others around you. Do you take this power seriously? Are you using it responsibly?

Miracles can and do occur in individual lives. When there is an absolute need for them, miracles happen with surprising frequency. Lack of preparation or the failure of taking responsibility is not necessarily a need for a miracle, however. You contain a power of order and a consciousness that is higher than any other form of life upon the planet. *You* are creators of miracles.

Action is necessary. Spirit helps you by showing you how to help yourself. Ask yourself, "Do I really need a miracle?" If the answer is truly, "Yes, I need a miracle" and is not simply an abdication of responsibility, then expect the miracle! But be practical and do not wait for it. Seek positive solutions and make the effort to assist your spirit guides to a swift completion of the task at hand.

Remember, you have been here before; you will be back again. In the interim, you will find yourself in the role of spirit guide. Seek a positive practicality now while incarnate. Make decisions based upon true spiritual thoughts and principles. Recall always in your lives that there is no energy that can ultimately overcome that of love, no better way to live than in joy, and no better decision to make than to live a life of peace.

23
The Purpose of Joy

As above, so below. We often point to the feelings of love, joy, and peace as necessary to true growth as a human being while incarnate upon the earth. Understand that these are actual energies, not mere concepts. Just as it is necessary to eat healthy foods and drink clean water, it is essential for spiritual growth of the individual human to seek out these forces to gain strength. In these times of low energy, many feel weakened. Finding joy in life will allow for a considerable gain of strength physically as well as emotionally, mentally, and spiritually.

Seeking Joy

Where does a person find joy? It is not an item that can be purchased. This means that mere acquisition will not satisfy this need. The gaining of a physical object may bring some small level of pleasure, but pleasure is not joy. Pleasure is when you have been pleased. Look to the words "please" and "thank you" and you will find the beginnings of greater pleasure in your life.

Joy comes from appreciation, it is true, but it grows when you begin appreciating things that are more simple and natural. A cool glass of water on a warm day, the simple observation of color in flowers, the noting of the sun or moon showing through clouds, the glimpse of an animal in a wooded area or even just the feeling of the woods or forest itself, these all are gateways to the simplicity of finding joy.

Notice that these are things that you experience personally. These are moments when, if you are by yourself, you can take the observations at your own pace and fully inhabit the moment. These are times that can be meditative. These are things that can point to the richness of daily existence.

This, then, is a key to joy: the encompassing observing of each day's natural occurrences. It is the slowing down of the external forces of society and the re-entry of your energies into the natural rhythms of the planet you currently reside upon.

Joy is not something that needs to be sought out. The smile of a child or a baby's laugh can bring joy to you unbidden. The glimpse of a dolphin or whale surfacing for a breath, the sight of a hawk, the light of a rainbow are all things that occur with suddenness and bring a moment of wonder to us all. They are all things that cannot be planned. They are things that you can be prepared for and encourage.

Many simply allow moments of joy to occur. They wish for more joy in their lives but do not act in ways that promote or increase this energy. They may place themselves with people who are argumentative or closed-minded. They may go to films or read books of a disturbing nature. They may consistently focus on what they perceive they lack in life. They may hold on to old wounds or continually identify themselves with diseases or disorders. They may look to others and find flaws, real or imagined. All of these things are ways of seeking to pass judgment. Passing judgment will never promote joy.

If you are faced with an illness, it is something that must be observed and tended to. It is not something that needs to be dwelt upon or communicated to everyone you encounter. It may be difficult to maintain a level of joyous energy when your physical body is in distress. We tell you now that by seeking joy in those circumstances, your physical body will gain strength and vitality. In this way, health can be seen to be a byproduct of joy.

If you feel that the world around you is failing or heading towards some fearful destruction, the practices listed above will remind you that the earth has been in constant and beautiful existence for longer than the family human has resided upon it. The earth has seen many things change and alter and will see many more changes. Observe for yourself the way that seasons pass and arrive, the way foliage blooms and then returns to dormancy, the way water polishes rock. Let these lessons be absorbed into your emotional core. Pay more attention to reality and less to fear-based commentary and you will find that joy comes to your life with more ease and swiftness.

This is not to say that you should ignore all that happens around you. It is to say that you can be a balanced individual by seeking joy first and letting fear get worn away like a stone in a river.

Choose your associations with wisdom. If you do not feel joyful with your companions, then seek different companions. If you are not enjoying yourself where you are, move to a space where you can feel joy. This is not to say abandon everything in life that may be a challenge. It could be that your purpose is to bring the energy of joy to some of these challenging times. You must be joyful first before you can bring joy. Do not let outside energies weaken your joyful nature. It is a natural thing to be in joy. What happens when you take time away from your daily routine to relax and re-create? Does not joy begin to grow quickly?

The Cycle of Joy

Joy is not a logical energy. It is not something to be processed in the brain. Yet joy can still be considered and meditated upon. When the feeling of joy is achieved, the brain will respond by becoming clearer, more decisive, and forward thinking. It is then that the physical body will respond with greater vitality. It is then that the individual will be able to seek their higher purpose with more vigor. It is then that paths will become clarified.

Seeking joy is not simply appropriate, it is a spiritual pursuit. Have joy on purpose. Joy begins in our emotional center, our heart. It is not a thing that can be thought, it is an energy that will be felt. By starting within the heart, joy then links us all to spirit and thus to Source. The greater your spiritual life, the more joyous your physical life will be. Conversely, the more joy you experience, the higher your level of spirituality will be. Each will feed the other.

Joy will also feed us in other ways. The more you enjoy your life and existence, the more you embrace your full reality in joyful anticipation and appreciation, the more love you will feel. It is here that we see how joy brings us closer to Source, for love is the great reflection of the original creative energy we refer to as Source.

There is no set equation, but we can see easily that adding or multiplying any element of love or joy into our lives will help us to achieve, in all areas of existence, a higher feeling of peace. Peace is the strong symbol of balanced living.

You see clearly that the world is out of balance. You see clearly the lack of peace in human life. You can then see how this makes it more and more difficult to find and achieve joyfulness. It is imperative for each spiritual seeker to find joy and allow it to grow within themselves. It is the way, the *only* way that the world will be brought into balance, by individuals, undivided ones, finding and maintaining their own true center.

Joy is not a passive energy. It is dynamic and active. Joy brings vitality and growth to every being that allows it to take root within their heart. Joy spreads. Joy heals. Joy enlightens. Joy is the key to enduring peace and love.

In the same way, then, peace and love are not passive energies. You cannot simply wait for these things to arrive in your life. They must be sought, cultivated, and tended until they grow strong with deep roots inside your very core. Doing this will benefit not just this life, but all aspects of your energetic existence. It is a way of empowering your entire karmic thread.

It is not lightly that we greet you with the phrase, "As above, so below." It is not lightly that we end our messages with the thought, "Seek love. Seek peace. Seek joy." It is this that will bring to you greater spiritual light and, with you, the world.

Life

Life is Joy. Sometimes you need to fight for your joy. Life is Love. That may be a truth closer than any other. Life is Peace. We remind you; peace is an energy of action as well as stillness. We invite you to be at peace to the best of your abilities with full knowledge that it is not a peaceful time. Let others find within you an example of peace.

What brings you joy? Do you see how in times of energy depletion, we sometimes let go of joy first and so spiritual connection becomes difficult. Strengthen your heart. Find the joys in life, even the small ones.

The more joy you bring now, the more joy you will have later. Love and joy and peace. These do not come from anything outside of you. They only come from inside of you and when you open those gifts up, they will immediately attract love and joy and peace to you.

Do what you love. Do what brings you joy. Do what grants peace. In this way, you are fulfilled.

Book Four
Light
The Reason for Existence

Think of yourselves as elements of light.

When the darkness the world is experiencing is deep, imagine that you are the stars that guide others. The stars themselves do not ask for others to follow them. They do not seek to be worshipped. They do not call attention to themselves. They only shine in the dark in a natural way.

You are a being of great light.

Regarding Enlightenment

Amongst those that are spiritual seekers there is often talk about enlightenment. Many speak of "reaching an enlightened state" or "becoming enlightened" through some practice or discipline. The idea is sometimes discussed as if there is a single place of enlightenment, almost like it is a physical destination, a place to travel to and arrive, like Chicago or Paris. This way of thinking reveals a linear way of perception. It is the way we live within the physical realm of gravity. Yet enlightenment is not a physical thing, is it?

The nature of spirituality is to see beyond the physical, to gain a greater perspective of events and actions. One might say it is a higher perspective, or vision of what is truly important, looking beyond the matters of the day and seeing the broader picture of history past, present, and even future. Of necessity, spiritual quests ask, "What can I do now that will make the future a better place for others?"

Thus the quest for enlightenment is not a goal. There is no stopping point. It is a continuous process. There is no real point when a being is assigned the title of Enlightened and receives a certificate that proclaims them to be a spiritual master. This does not mean these states do not exist. It only means that some get themselves sidetracked by seeking a qualification or marker to demonstrate where they are on a path in relationship to others. This misses the mark of the enlightenment.

No one becomes a master through learning or will. No true master ever claims mastery. The Dali Lama says, "I am like you, a simple monk." Religious leaders who adorn themselves and appoint themselves in highly public and lucrative ways bring little to the table for others. The titles they create for one another are often empty, and void of any true spiritual nature. They are more interested in what they can gather than in what can be spread. This is not the way of light.

Light spreads. Light continues until blocked. Even then, light does not cease to act. There may be darker areas or shades where the light is not as bright. This does not mean there is no light. It only means there is diminished light. To become personally enlightened is to move out and away from things that block light. To become enlightened is to begin to spread light.

A true master will shine with their own inner light, helping others dispel shadows simply by their existence. They understand clearly that there is no marker or comparison to where others are on "the Path." They know that there is only their own path, and none can walk it with them nor can one being ever truly be ahead of another. We all take our paths at our own pace. In this way, we are all personally responsible for the future.

Ask the questions, "Do I cast darkness, block others' light, or deepen the shade of the world around me? Or do people look to me as a beacon for direction, a guide through perilous passages of time, as a person with a reflective nature?"

Others may polish you, but it will be in the nature of abrasion or a testing. This is polishing through force. How much better it is to act in ways that invite a brighter personal path, than to wait to be clarified by external forces. It may take some time to polish away what inhibits your personal light. No one will do this work better than you. You are the one who chooses how much light you shine.

Jeff Michaels

Table of Contents

1 - Light 1

2 - The Nearness of Heaven 7

3 - A Vision of Dying 13

4 - Going Home 19

5 - The Sense of Existence 25

6 - What Will You Fear? 31

7 - Remaining Spiritual During Difficult Times 37

8 - In Dreams 43

9 - A Magical Universe 49

10 - The Wave of Creation 57

11 - Sense and Spirit 65

12 - On the Matter and Meaning of Prophecy 73

13 - Becoming Whole 81

14 - A Vision of Current Events 87

15 - A Time of Light and Unparalleled Growth 95

16 - Regard Source 101

17 - Do You Love? 107

18 - Essence and Existence 115

19 - Time and Change 123

20 - Return to the Light 131

1
Light

As above, so below. We speak in illustration. It is often easier to speak in specific form and be direct in our instruction and lesson. Now we choose this illustrative way, for the subject matter is not specific or direct. It is radiant.

Light presses out from a source, moving at a measurable speed and without discrimination. Light touches all things. It is not the action of light that creates shadow; rather, it is objects that impede light and create shadow.

Light is ambient in nature and will seek to fill space. Light has limitation. The further from its source, the more diffuse light becomes. The larger the void, the more light sources will be necessary to illuminate an area.

The Existence of Shadows

The more non-illuminating objects within a space, the more shadows will be formed. This is not the fault of light or of the objects; it is merely the consequences of the nature of two things interacting.

Should a space be filled with items that do not provide their own light, many sources of illumination will be necessary to dispel darkness. Conversely, darkness is not necessarily a thing to be dispelled. If, however, one is seeking a brighter condition, many sources of light must be brought into play, or many objects must be removed from the space that is to be illuminated.

The objects themselves could have a value attached to them. They might have a reason to exist. In this instance, the value must outweigh the desire for enlightenment. One must accept a certain amount of shadow when choosing to retain objects.

In an illustrative way, we say now that objects are not always physical. Objects can be and often are remainders of energies long past. Memories or patterns once forced upon a life will echo throughout the vibrational existence. A seeker of enlightenment will then find these objects of energetic memory casting shadows on their path.

Dispelling Shadows

How best to dispel these shadows? Often, seekers will find ones who emanate a certain light, and then gravitate towards such ones. This can be an effective way to gain a clearer vision of one's path. The complication is this: as a seeker, you might not clearly see the illuminator's own shadow-creating objects. You might be unaware of the depth of shadow in another being, especially if you, the seeker, are focused on your own shadow-casting objects. What looks like a pure light at first might, in fact, be simply reflective.

Shadow-creating objects could actually be hiding other shadowy energies within the darkness they cast. From your perception as the seeker of enlightenment, it might feel as if all the world is in darkness. Others might bring a level of light to you, but once they pass from your presence, darkness returns: unless, of course, you have found a way to sustain and radiate the light for yourself as a seeker.

This, then, is the way to effectively dispel shadows from your path. By *being* a source of light, shadows are now cast away from you, and you begin to exist in an incandescent world. All things will look bright to you, the seeker, at this time. Even objects that once cast shadows will be illuminated; they may actually appear to convey a light of their own.

This is a matter for meditation now. Just because the objects might not appear shadowy to you any longer, it is not only your perception that must be taken into consideration. If you begin to be a source of light as a seeker, the objects of energetic memory and pattern you carry will now cast shadows outwards from themselves. This could leave others bearing the darkness you are causing.

No matter how bright the source of light, when objects remain, shadows will be cast. Enlightenment might be effective for a seeker, but it could actually cause more difficulties for others following their own karmic path.

What is the answer? What will allow light to flow fully and evenly? It is clear that a seeker must first examine the objects, patterns, and remainders of ancient, forgotten, or misunderstood perceptions. Remember, the farther away from the source, the less likely for the light to be pure or bright. So this is the way, then, with teachings and structured learning. The farther from their original source, the more likely the teaching is to be tainted or affected by shadow-creating objects. First, tend your own light. Re-evaluate what you believe and carry by way of objects of memory and pattern.

Light: The Reason for Existence

There is no formula. All proceeds at its own pace. For many seekers, an incarnation might pass in its entirety, without any clear evidence that more light is being shed upon their path. It is enough that they become aware of the shadows they cast, for it is then that decisions can be made regarding what to carry and what to release.

The more focused a light source, the better one is able to direct illumination towards specific areas of darkness. The more focused a seeker of enlightenment, the swifter the action of dispelling shadows in specific areas. A focused light is not as ambient in action. Much will remain dark, especially that which is behind the focused light source. There is not a right or wrong in this observation; it simply recognizes that there is a decision to be made on your part as a seeker of enlightenment.

A Source of Light

How does something become a light source? First, fuel is needed. Some things are better suited for fuel than others. Some fuels can release things that are toxic or irritating to life forms. Some fuels combust swiftly, leaving a flash of light that could blind more than it illuminates. The proper selection of an energy source determines the quality of the light that is produced.

The next aspect necessary to create a source of light is ignition. This is something that, in combination with fuel, will produce a reaction that brings light into a seeker's life. The better the fuel and the more efficient the ignition process, the less likely it is that you, the seeker, will need light from other sources.

Ignition can and often does begin with a borrowed light. Fuel can be found through other sources. It is best when you, as seekers, realize that you yourselves are the best fuel for the creation and activation of your own enlightenment.

This is the lesson then: true enlightenment never comes from an outside source. It is always an inner process that radiates outward from the being seeking enlightenment. The fuel is the life of the seeker. The ignition is that person's passion for life and all the elements that make up their karmic path.

The objects that create shadows are judgments passed on or made by the individual being. Enlightenment allows for a true sight that releases not just old prejudices, but the need for judgment itself. The concepts of separation begin to fade. The realization of Oneness, of a unified existence, a Uni-verse, becomes clear.

It is then that you, as seekers, can fully embrace the reality that you are an aspect of the Source of all light and energy. It is then that peace enters into you at your very core. It is then that love radiates outward from you, providing light for others who also seek to dispel their own shadows.

Karma

Your future approaches. You will be there. For now, continue to seek peaceful things. Do not be against what you hear or see. If you know that an idea is incorrect or that there are misperceptions of what has been said or instructed, remember it is not to you that correction falls. You are not an agent of karma.

See things clearly and in a spiritual perspective. Act in a manner that does not require outside validation. Walk a path that is uniquely yours. In doing this you set a quiet example. Do not seek others to follow you. Join with others and they with you in a fluid movement. You will find that you are progressing without effort.

You have your own karmic thread to weave. Pay attention and understand that to weave this thread means that you need other threads. If you are to be strong, then you must entwine with others' karmic threads.

There is no better way. There is only this way, your way. No one can cleanse your karma. No one can heal you. No one can purify your life in any way for you. Only you can do these things for yourself. The model of a priest or priestess being your spiritual master is old and outdated. You are more mature as a species than you have been in many cycles of years. Your growth should reflect that.

2
The Nearness of Heaven

As above, so below. We take you now to a vision outside the recognized boundaries of human senses. In doing so, we seek to show that boundaries are often a perception that is inherited and no longer valid. We will use the term "heaven," but we seek to demonstrate the reality of the concept rather than a perception created to control others. It is a beneficial thing to re-evaluate what has gone before. It is also beneficial to perceive where and when you truly exist. We tell you now that waiting until you are dead to glimpse heaven is like waiting until you are dying to appreciate living.

A Sense of Heaven

Heaven is not a place, a geographic location. It is a state of existence. It is not always bound by gravity, but it still responds to the physical laws of the universe, only in ways that you do not comprehend while you are incarnate. It can be sensed by physical beings, but it cannot be literally seen. This is the thing that separates most people from heaven; reliance merely on actual vision, physical touch, or sound will create a distance of perception, and the actuality will become vague to the perceiver.

In truth, and we have said this before, there is only one sense and that is the being, the individual, the undivided one themselves. All elements of your being human, acting in concert, provide for a much higher awareness of all existence around you. The division of the one sense into five is limiting. This perception can be overcome. Techniques like meditation, chant, prayer, or simple movement done in repetition will assist in creating a state of mind that will allow the observation of heaven.

Yet heaven is not simply a state of mind. It is a state of wholeness, of oneness. It is a unified existence. The higher the level of ascension, the more unified you become with all things. Merely exiting the physical realm does not enter you into the highest levels of this state of existence.

Even in the realm of spirit, there is a vast space where we continue in a perceptually separated state. It is a more peaceful existence, true, but we still continue as individual entities. There is a reason for this in our present continuum. This will change as energy flows toward what is called the future. There is no future or past, only present moments. It is part of the separating accomplished by gravity that creates the concept of time moving forward. Gravity, then, also carries a purpose. By creating a separateness, we can appreciate the parts of the whole.

While in the realm of gravity, it is easy to get caught up in the belief that there is no wholeness to be experienced. Yet the Universe is all around, and the effect of gravity is what gives great beauty to the senses in their individualized forms. In this way, the separating of the senses is not an error or something to be overcome and eradicated. It is to be appreciated for what it accomplishes. However, it is good to note any limitations and practice an expanded way.

Levels of Heaven

Heaven, then, is not a separated state of being. The levels of heaven are not delineated or numbered. The realm of gravity is not a separated existence from the realm of heaven. Some imagine that a set of stairs may take you from one floor to another and that each floor carries a higher purpose. This is a way of seeking to understand heaven by comparison to existing structures artificially crafted by religions. It is a way of limiting others by not granting access to all levels for all individuals. A better way to illustrate heaven is with the idea of many beings acting in a variety of purposes. The more specific your purpose may be, the lower your existence in life. Those who seek to serve only themselves or be served by others are in the lowest of places.

Those that seek a path of service are looking to attain a oneness of existence. This raises the level they exist at and allows for them to work in cooperation with other elements of Source.

Like all things, there are aspects to the unified energy called Source. Source is a consciousness, true, but that is itself a limiting way of observing Source. Source is beyond consciousness. This is beyond full comprehension by the family human. At the lower levels of the realm of spirit, it is also beyond complete comprehension. That is not a judgment.

The Constancy of Change

Growth is the essence of the Universe. In all of your life on the planet, you are offered opportunities for growth and for the purification of your energies. It is no different before you enter or after you depart the planet. When you make the passage from gravity into the realm of spirit, there are often tasks along the way. In a sense, this is unfinished business from the incarnation. Many view the entry into heaven as one of pure bliss. By comparison to life in gravity, it could be perceived that way! Yet life in the realm of spirit continues to carry responsibilities and tasks.

You must understand that while in the current state of things in the realm of gravity, you are often bound to tasks that are essentially meaningless in the grander purpose. You participate in economic structures that are designed to support a way of life that may soon phase out. This is necessary for the individual to continue a certain style of life, but it is never fulfilling in and of itself. It is not wrong. It is simply the way things are at this present moment. There is an agreement about this way, and this agreement is soon to be concluded. That is the way of consciousness on all levels, and at the highest level there is a completeness of agreement.

In the area where the realm of spirit and the realm of gravity are the closest, events are under close scrutiny. New agreements are formed. In this way, you might say that there is sometimes a new heaven or a new earth. In the physical realm it takes time for new agreements to get into motion. Some fear the new ways and possibilities, and they will strive against them. You see the increased resistance to change even now.

We say again that the only thing that is constant in the universe is change. The best way to cope with change is to be a part of it, and the best way to be a part of it is to instigate change. This starts within you first if it is to be effective at all. Seeking to change outside matters first is often a way of avoiding the need to change and alter your personal ability to respond. The river does not seek to change the rock. It flows according to the natural path of gravity. The rock changes as the river passes, and it does not resist. In this way, the seemingly immovable mountain travels to the sea. In this same way, you travel to the state of existence of heaven. It is resistance that slows this process down. It is clinging that ceases progression in yourself and also in that to which you cling.

Traveling to Heaven

The observation of heaven, the realm of spirit, is a thing of certainty. There is no true need to seek it while upon the planet. You are an aspect of that state of existence. You know of it because you come from it. The separateness you feel is an illusion of sorts. The parts are being examined by the parts. Only when you see how all parts form an ever-changing partnership will you again sense the nearness of heaven.

The tasks that point to this state of consciousness are the ones that become the most fulfilling. They might also be impractical to a contemporary existence. These tasks will be similar to those conducted as your energies transform. They include centering yourself, forgiving others, peaceful action on behalf of the planet, support of future generations, and a seeking of personal growth, including the taking of responsibility for one's own past and future. You will be asked to do all these things at the time of passing. You have all done them before.

This, then, is an aspect of the filtering of energy and a force of the evolution of life on Gaia. As you learn to adapt to new ways on the planet, you can bring yourself in closer harmony with the realm of Spirit. A restructuring of priorities is necessary for all members of the family human. Those who are practicing a higher spiritual pursuit feel this need already. It is still difficult to step away from old ways. That is the pull of the realm of gravity.

Like the stone, do not resist. Like the river, continue to flow along a natural path. Allow your consciousness to dwell on the aspects of spirit that can easily be applied to life, here and now. Heaven is not a place to seek; it is an awareness to acknowledge. The aspects of heaven that are inherent within each member of the family of human are love, joy, and peace. Seek these things in yourself and acknowledge them in others, and you will find your life near heaven.

3
A Vision of Dying

As above, so below. In living, there are few things that are certain. This can cause an element of fear to exist in each being. Fear is not a wrong emotion, but often fears are not necessary. A small amount of thought may allow for a better reaction to certain situations that exist in life. Fear has a purpose, but it is not a thing that should control you. Fear of a bee sting is appropriate, but once you recall that a bee's purpose is not to sting, but to pollinate, you are more apt to see the beauty of this creature. The bee does not want to sting. It wants to live and fulfill its purpose.

In this same way, a balanced member of the family human is at their best when they are allowed to live a fulfilled life. One fear many have is the fear of death, yet death is one of the few certainties that everyone faces. Let us apply a small amount of thought to the idea of death and bring some insight into the action of passing away from life in the realm of gravity.

We all know that there will be one journey we must make: the passage from earthly life. If you plan a trip, there is a certain amount of preparation that precedes the event. Sometimes there is an emergency that may force travel. A natural disaster or perhaps an illness of a family member or friend will send a person hurrying from one place to another. The difference between being relaxed and feeling a sense of panic or urgency is often found in the amount of time available for preparation.

There are many belief systems regarding what comes after life on earth. Obviously, they cannot all be true. We will attempt to speak in a way that allows for your personal perception to remain intact, for there are many truths to be found in the variety of observations. One truth is this, you cannot truly know until you arrive. Faith must not be blind. Faith must be flexible. There are those that believe that one human life span is all there is. We tell you now that you will see. Our words are for all, but they are not meant to change a cherished belief.

Practice Dying

If you consider that dying is a form of travel, you will instantly see the value in the idea of practicing the act of dying. This exercise will allow you to sharpen your current existence as well.

A way to appreciate your current life is to imagine yourself in the space of death, that is, the transition from the physical realm of gravity to the realm of spirit. It is not a necessary thing to become morbid in this exercise. Simply imagine that you are taking your last breaths.

What do you ponder at this time? What is the strongest emotion or thought? Who would you like to be with you at this instant, the last face you see with your physical eyes? Are there any regrets, any unsaid words? Do you recall pleasant things, or is your memory filled with matters that caused pain?

This is not a time of judgment. It is a time of passing, and all life performs this transition. It is the family human that does so consciously. This is a gift, but many seek to avoid thinking of these moments. We tell you now that there are only two times when our consciousness is truly alone: the passage into and out of the realms of spirit and gravity. It is better to be prepared and we will explain this now.

In an ideal way, there should be a sense of acceptance in this final time. There will come the moment of a last breath, a last sound heard and a last glimpse of light. Loved ones may have gathered and you will see them for the very last time. Will they be sad? Most likely, but how much nicer would it be if all are prepared, and they can smile at you and you at them in this final gathering?

At this time of last bits of physical life, you will likely feel a new sense of motion. This is commonly reported by those in near-death experiences. It is the release of gravity on the energy that has been you. A sense of weightlessness begins because there is no longer an attachment to the physical form. You have now entered into the first stages of the realm of spirit. It is not an instant transition.

During the passage, there are tasks along the way. Although your body has ceased, your personality, your thoughts and your feelings are still strongly rooted in the reality you just left. Now comes a time of forgiveness, review, and release of memories. There will be a strengthening of focus on the present moment. Time as you knew it will change, or rather, there will be a change of view of time. No longer will perceptions be based on past experiences. In the realm of spirit, perception is based on potentials.

Light: The Reason for Existence

A Form of Birth

Some may view death as an escape from responsibility. It is really the opposite. In the realm of spirit, you take on more responsibilities, but first you are born back into a more complete awareness. A form of hospice is necessary for some who have died in accidents or disasters or some other seemingly premature way. They are often unprepared for the transition. The new reality, pleasant as it may be to others, is a shock. There sometimes remains an energy of injustice and a sense of incompleteness. These ones who feel this way often desire to return and finish their plans or at least to communicate with ones they loved. It is not an improper emotion. The reality is that energy does not return in this way. If the body functions cease completely or even if major aspects of the physical form are damaged beyond repair, there is no return possible.

Many have perished in violent action. These are often youthful and very vital beings. For them, the desire to be alive on the planet is still strong after the passage. Others have died with a particular belief system entrenched within their energy. The reality of the spiritual realm is different than what can be fully imagined by those who exist in the realm of gravity. The hospice action for them is a way of assistance to fully access the continuance of life force. Here is where you are cleansed of fear. Here is where you are comforted. Like a newborn child that is cast into a world of light and space from a womb, warm and close, those newly arrived from the realm of gravity are bathed and, in a sense, swaddled. Here is where we first experience the intensity of the wash of love.

The wash of love is a powerful thing. The feeling of weight and the pressure of time can pull a person away from the higher vibrations. The release of those energies allows for a cleansing feeling. The refreshment felt at this time is sometimes felt by those in near-death experiences. The clarity of mind associated with this moment is sometimes accessed by ones in deep meditation. Yet, it is not a sustainable energy while on the planet. This is not in error. The purpose of the planet is to experience the lower vibrations and harmonize them with the higher vibrational aspects of Source.

The wash of love is a purifying action and serves to separate any remaining fears that may have been carried by the being making the transformative passage. It is now that the energy that was human enters fully into the realm of spirit.

Reunions in Joy and Love

Many believe they will be re-united with loved ones. This is true, though not quite in the sense that many are taught. Their reunification is with all beings. You will first re-unite with ones of similar vibration. This will surprise many, for they are not always aware of why others have been in their lives on the planet. Some who have caused great difficulty in your life may be amongst those who, in a sense, greet you. The difficult times will then be understood, and the higher purpose revealed. Instead of anger or recrimination, there is often great joy and love shared at this moment. It is an even greater sense of joy when energies that loved one another are brought together in the harmony of the realm of spirit. It is not possible to exist in anger in the spirit realm.

The grief felt at someone's passing from gravity is countered by the joy experienced upon their entry into the realm of spirit. This is in harmony with the principle that every action has an opposite and equal reaction. This is not simply a physical law; it holds true in all energetic forms. Will people feel grief at your passing? This, then, will grant a view of how you will be received. Make no mistake; all will be welcomed. It is the individual who will decide how he or she will accept the welcome.

Consider your life, then, by way of your personal approach to death, your vision of dying. Will you have lived a fulfilled existence? Will you leave behind great sadness at your passing? Have you created joy and love in the people around you? Will the world be the poorer for your absence in some way, no matter how small?

Rather than approach the subject as morbid or with a level of fear, seek now ways to improve the life at hand. Do not accumulate for yourself items of value only to those in the realm of gravity. Rather, seek to create times of peace and joy and love. In this way, your final breath will be a sigh of satisfaction, and your final act can be a smile.

4
Going Home

As above, so below.

This planet is your home while you are in the realm of the physical. It is not a place of security these days, however. A home should be a haven of sorts, a place where you can relax and enjoy personal time with loved ones or even private quiet moments alone. This does not always describe the planet earth at this point in time.

Many of you long for and can sense the powerful feeling of home that awaits your return to spirit. This longing can turn to thoughts and even actions of escape.

The World Today

We see a great sense of questioning on the planet these days. Many wonder at the nature of life and death. Many ponder their nature and reason for existence. In the face of many disasters, natural and man-made, some openly ask, "Why continue?" when pondering the matter of being alive. Some are considering the possibility of returning to the realm of spirit early. Let us speak plainly of life and death.

Light: The Reason for Existence

In times of turmoil, it is often difficult to see that the future is brighter. We tell you now that things will be better, that life on the planet will attain a greater level of peacefulness and security. This is not a straight line and there are and will continue to be points of dramatic change.

The world you inhabit is one that holds strongly entrenched views. These do not easily alter their shape. Many prefer to envision the future as a return to yang-dominated ways. This will not occur. It is not in the nature of the universe to have one form of energy dominate another. Balanced yin and yang is a constant force.

Much of the purpose of the planet you inhabit has been to create this balance in this area of the galaxy. This is a reason for such an extended period of struggle. A strong wave of change is occurring at this time. You exist in an era of change. For many, those that carry strong spiritual energy, this translates into a difficult time, and they find it hard to deal with what is happening. Even strong spiritual beings can succumb to a depressed feeling, a lowering of personal energy. Some lose hope and the desire to remain alive. This is an understandable reaction to such desperate times. We speak now to give perspective and help you regain a true vision of the state of events and your role.

We are imparting wisdom to you, but it comes in the form of knowledge. With this knowledge, you must gain personal experience before it can become *your* wisdom. Never fear. You are not alone. You may be disconnected for a short time. This will not last. There is no need for you to pass to gain this wisdom. Death does not automatically confer any wisdom. The process of rebirth would be unnecessary if this were true.

Who Are You Now?

Earthly physical life is a very valuable thing. If you are reading these words, you likely understand that you have chosen to exist at these times. Did you imagine that it might be easier? Did you comprehend fully that you would be a leader and example for the future? In the rush of energies swirling about the planet today, it is hard to even recall the decision-making process. Much of life is simple reaction to random occurrences caused by those who have no clear spiritual connection.

In this time, you are the path; you are the guides for those who did not enter this incarnation with strong spiritual goals. You are the ones others can look to for guidance in conducting a spiritual existence in difficult times.

Many do not believe in the realm of spirit. They have confused the reality of existence in a different realm, a higher vibration, with the erroneous command to worship those that dwell there. We in the spirit realm are fellow beings, not rulers. We are companions, not royalty. To believe in a deity separate from your own self is to miss the entire point of life.

We are all aspects of the creative source. We are not different at our most fundamental elements. The heart of the atom is the same as the heart of a star which is, in turn, the same as the heart of the galactic cluster. You are the same as all of these.

You are composed of ancient energies. There are beings that are older than you can easily imagine. Even these ones have no clear memory of the beginning of all things. It is not a necessary thing to know all there is to know to realize the inherent creative power you carry within.

The Reason for Existence

Life on the planet carries a level of responsibility. We act in certain ways to advance the balancing of the energy of Source. In this, we take on certain tasks, much in the same way we have duties when we are off the planet in the realm of spirit.

Many are here to heal themselves from past trauma. Perhaps that is a portion of your mission as well. Stay the course; it is getting better. You are getting better, more complete, more whole. True, you may be feeling drained of strength and energy. Thoughts and attempts to exit from your current incarnation must be questioned thoroughly. They are not necessarily wrong, but the decision will affect your future existence. Ask yourself, "Have I truly exhausted all avenues of balance? Is there truly no other path to follow? Is there no lesson left to be taught by my example of spiritual endurance?"

Often the feeling of weakness is brought on by the individual's attempts to do all things themselves. The expending of all your personal energy is unnecessary. True spirituality encourages cooperation and synergy. In the realm of the spirit, this is a natural way of existence. When it occurs on the planet it also feels natural. Humans are happy when all cooperate for a greater good. Knowing this, you can see why there is a general feeling of weakness in the world today.

The idea of returning to spirit, or as some say, "going home," is appealing, especially now. So much strife from so many small areas is something new on the planet. Such intimate, personal knowledge of every tragedy, every battle, every disease, and every personal trauma has never been experienced before. You can literally know what is happening along every curve of the earth. It is overwhelming. Yet, now is the time that true spirituality is needed the most. Exiting the planet is counter to the actual purpose of your existence at this time.

Completing Your Life

Could you have predicted the events occurring today, the societal changes, or the technological advances? From the time you were born up to now, more information has been gathered and disseminated in new forms than in all of recorded history. Soon another great change will sweep the planet. We tell you now that you have helped prepare the way for this adaptation. Power will shift. Energy will alter. Communication will require truth.

This is vastly different than what you knew and the way in which you may have planned your lives. The course you wanted may be unavailable to you now. This is a time to access your creative strength and press yourself forward into new opportunities. If you are older, this may cause some sense of despair. Be alert for the vision of elders to shift. Seek ways to influence the way that others regard the aging process. Set new goals and priorities. Stay healthy and vital as you age. You may live longer than expected.

An inventory of what you have accomplished up to now is a way of ascertaining what current priorities may exist. It is not necessary to hold on to old goals. Changing times and personal growth will alter the undivided one's vision of life. This inventory, taking stock in what is important to you, may not be comfortable or easy. It is an action that requires a certain boldness. Not all have the strength to do such a thing. The true spiritual being will embrace such a task and embark on this quest for information with a level of joy and happiness.

Do not berate yourself or others for perceived failings. What was not finished may not be considered a valid use of energy now. Creating something that will stand the test of time is not necessary at this point in history. Understand that many things will be going away. Place your sight on things of true value, qualities of life. There is no reason to abandon or renounce physical things. Only comprehend that they go away and act accordingly.

Create a Vision of Home on Earth

Create communities of caring and cooperation. Strengthen the higher values. Do not seek ways to repudiate others' behavior or conduct a moral inventory on others. Set the appropriate example in your own existence. Create a vision of home that others can emulate. It is not necessary to leave the planet to find home. Earth is a significant part of our home as spiritual beings engaged in a spiritual work.

Do your part to make this home a joy to live on; there is already much here to be joyful for. Strengthen a vision of peaceful life by your efforts and example; there is much pleasure to be derived from peaceful action. Above all things, love everyone you possibly can, even under stressful circumstances. The expression of love will always relax times of strife and tension. In this way, you will return the feeling of home to the planet.

5
The Sense of Existence

As above, so below.

In times past, there have been many who contemplated their own existence. They questioned the meaning of their lives, and they considered the implications of all other things from the perspective of consciousness. They questioned whether or not there was any importance to life. We tell you now that there is great importance to all life. In the seeking lies the seed of the reason for existence.

In the realm of gravity there is often a natural creation of hierarchy or caste within the family human. Some individuals seem to carry more importance or power than others. In a sense, this is energetically true. Even within plant life some seeds yield larger life forms. This does not mean that smaller, more humble plants are less important than large trees. Each form has its place in the system. Witness the small nature of the bee and understand that, without it, propagation, and pollination of plants you rely upon will cease.

Some view life as a struggle. In nature, this is not an observable phenomenon. It can be interpreted this way, but life continues under great adversity and without regard to the question of existence. Only the members of the family human contemplate life in this way. A plant does not cease seeking light if a larger tree begins to shade it. The plant does not give up or despair. The shaded plant grows toward light. It is not a struggle. It is what a plant does.

The Measure of Life

What prompts the family human to contemplate existence is an awareness of the passing of time. A day may pass, and you may wonder where the time went. If you are pursuing an absorbing distraction or are engaged in fruitful work, the sense of time is not a priority. The difference between distraction and accomplishment is found in the setting of goals. If you are aware of a time limit, you will structure your life in such a way that completion of tasks is finished first. There is a time for re-creative activity. What is your life goal? Work toward this first.

Awareness that you have a certain time upon the planet needs to be balanced with the idea that you continue past this human life. Knowing you are mortal is an advantage. In a balanced human it produces a desire to achievement. Knowing your energies continue may cause some to become spiritually lazy, considering that there is no urgency in the raising of vibration or harmony. They may take the attitude that it can all be taken care of at a later date or incarnation. Spiritual procrastination is a choice that has its consequences.

Anything that does not contribute to growth can be considered to be spiritual procrastination. Understand that there are seasons to growth, and, like plants, each individual needs a certain amount of rest. Life on the planet is not a race that must be completed in the fastest amount of time. It must be a life of satisfactory activity. The awareness of time does not need to be translated into urgency. It is a factor that needs be considered. It is not a necessary thing to count the seconds or minutes of your life. It is a good thing to review time spent and refocus your energies on a regular basis.

The abdication of individual responsibility in personal growth is common in history. Many times simple survival took precedence over advancement of personal spiritual development. Today there are many things that may look like they are necessary actions, but in reality they distract from what is true and natural. This is not to place a judgment on any activity, merely to create an opportunity for self-examination. Too many activities of little worth will lead to a spiritual malnutrition and you may find yourself weakened.

Actions of Quality

It is good to remember that you are human. The freedom given to the family of humanity is a purposeful energy. The ability to affect the world is powerful. In recent past centuries this has been an energy of expansion and variance. Now, this energy is of coalescence and harmonizing. What does this mean for you?

Look to your life first and search for ways to bring energy together. Look to see what is truly necessary and what can be removed. There are things needed in life and this is not to say that possessions are wrong or unspiritual. There are many who need much to continue their current lifestyle. It is good to review your current life and determine if it is one that you have consciously chosen or if it is a reactive life, one based on the actions of others.

Choosing your own direction and where you best can expend your personal energy will lead you to a less stress-filled existence. The less you have to carry, the easier the journey will be.

Remember that life is a journey. It is a personal one and your story is written daily. Act in such a way that your story is one of higher purpose and you will find that the energy of the Universe opens many doors for you. A guiding question for you can be, "Is the action I am engaged in one of quality and oriented toward my personal growth?" If the answer is yes, then you are acting in a way that is in harmony with the natural flow of energy. Remember that this does not mean constant activity. Rather, it means balanced action.

Re-Creation of Energy

A living being nourishes themselves and replenishes their energy from a constant and universal source. This is part of the continuance of existence and all life participates in this action. The opportunity that members of the family of humanity have is to actually change their course, improve themselves, and pursue different avenues of learning. This, then, is true re-creation. As an energetic being you can choose to move beyond what you once were and into a state of higher vibration. This will require the action of leaving behind what once was, including old beliefs, relationships, expectations or even possessions. At the conclusion of your current incarnation, you will leave these things behind in all cases.

Growth will be the key to determining appropriate decisions. Does something contribute to your growth? It may have at one time, but does it still? Because something or someone held value in the past, that value is not inherent. Because that same thing or individual does not carry the same value in your life at present does not mean they are of little value, however. Allow growth to be your guiding factor in your continued existence. Grow towards light. In so doing you will find the shadows are behind you.

Life is growth. As long as you are in existence, you can choose to be active in your own personal growth. You can also choose to do other than this, but why? We exhort you now to press forward and envision your existence, not from a daily aspect, but rather look at the larger picture. Time given is finite. What you receive will directly reflect how you honor the energy given you. Look to your inner thoughts and emotions and seek a balance with the outer life you are leading.

A purification is in progress. Every human is an active participant in this, and it is larger than existence upon the planet. That there are frustrations and setbacks in life is a part of this process. Rather than attempt to make sense of these moments, look to your own internal work. Act in a balanced way and move forward on whatever levels possible. Use times of frustration as opportunities for self-examination. Use setbacks as times when you can re-create yourself and your life.

These are points when the action of love or joy may seem distant and not applicable to current life. It is at these times that you can create a way for these spiritual qualities to resolve issues in life, not just for your own benefit, but also for others. Finding peaceful solutions to the challenges of existence is a large part of the reason of human existence. This resolves larger energetic actions that, in the past, needed to be worked out in more catastrophic ways.

A time approaches when the action of humanity will potentially alleviate strong natural energies. Are you looking at the larger picture of existence? It is fine to contemplate one's own place in the cosmos, but also consider the reason for the cosmos you exist within. It is here that you can sense the value of all things in harmony. It is here that you can sense the power that exists all around you. At this point of awareness, you can make powerful changes that will affect not just your own existence, but also that of others. It is here, then, that the reason and importance of your personal existence finds validity and sense.

Express that sense in the actions of love and peace and witness your existence from a higher state. In so doing, you will increase your personal strength and experience the joy of all existence by being an active presence in life.

6
What Will You Fear?

As above, so below. In the societies of the earth today there is a prevalent feeling of disquiet that more and more often ranges into fear. Is this a necessary emotion, one that is somehow correct for the current time? Or is this a manufactured feeling, one that interrupts spiritual growth? Can you avoid fear?

The Source of Fear

In times past, there existed men who sought to control by fear. Their purpose was to create a perception of a common enemy and unite others under a banner so that they could gain and retain power. In a broad sense, the fears created centuries ago have taken on a life of their own. We tell you now that the time will soon come when created fears from the past will have expired. Timelines have been given and dates for disaster and destruction have been predicted. You are seeing those dates come and go swiftly now. All are passing and proving to be moments of change rather than devastation.

Superstitions and poorly interpreted prophecies have held much of the family human in a sort of stasis for well over two thousand years. There are those who wish this to continue. However, the timing of the fear-based elements of those prophecies and the false understanding of the prophecies themselves now concludes. The reasons for fear are dissipating.

The Erosion of Fear

The energy of coalescence is upon the planet, and it is an energy of harmony. This is not an instantaneous point of change. There will be many elements to this era, and you have seen the beginnings. It will not always be easy. The end result will be a society that differs greatly from what you exist within today. Even if your present incarnation passes before these changes take firm hold, you must take individual responsibility in this time of change.

Your personal decisions affect the speed and smoothness of this transition. To view the future with fear is an old pattern that is eroding away. To envision the future in hope and love is the energy that will assist its birth. To continue to live in fear will erode away your spiritual power. Alter your vision now, and you will sense the opportunity for growth immediately.

The world is not without problems. Today there are many situations that need solutions. To fear the situations delays the implantation of the solutions. To be angry regarding these situations also does not help the process of resolution. To think in a rational way, to look ahead with thought as to how action taken today will affect the future, to seek a way that will create a path into a unified community all about the planet, these are the quintessential preparations for a fertile field in which the family human can continue its growth.

Division along political lines for the purpose of retaining or regaining power is one area where fear and anger are currently being cultivated. The coming energy of coalescence will be one of personal decision and responsibility. The energy promoted by fear is one of blame and abdication of personal power. In this you, as an individual, have a choice. Which path do you choose?

Clarity of mind is necessary. Without clear thinking, it is easy to be swayed into believing certain elements of fear are necessary. The reality is that fear serves an instinctual purpose. At the lower levels of vibration, it is beneficial for survival. When higher levels of vibration are attained, fear no longer serves the greatest good. In a structured society there is little use for instinctual fear. You have a luxury of time for sharpening your minds. Do you do this?

The Greater Good

The concept of a common enemy is similar to the principle of a common goal. When beings have a common goal, they will carry more energy together than apart. Animals that hunt in packs or run in herds can often be more successful and live longer than if they are solitary.

It is an easy thing to switch from thinking there is an enemy to fear, to realizing the tremendous amount of work that can be accomplished by co-operation towards the achievement of a common cause. Synergy of purpose will carry the family human very far. A common goal of progress, now, will redefine the future.

The idea of a created commonality through the energy of fear is one that does not serve the greater purposes of life. Where is the aspect of peace in such a thing? Those who create the feeling of fear will tell you that it is in the future, that once the perceived enemy is conquered or destroyed, you and your family will then live in peace. They will also add that, "sacrifices must be made." Generally, the ones that create the fear are not the ones who will be doing the sacrificing.

Always, when a being acts in a spirit of againstness, peace will be driven further away. There are times when presenting a unified front to destructive force is necessary. The goal should always be to attain an accord or understanding. In this way, some are better suited at leading in certain situations than others.

Be cautious that those who lead are balanced in both yin and yang energies. Those who are imbalanced and rely solely on yang energy will be aggressive rather than active. They may accomplish certain goals but will have no restraint or see no need for attaining harmonious reconciliation. Strong yang energy is necessary in leadership, but it must be equally balanced with strong yin energy. Allowing yin energy to lead and letting yang energy provide structure will accomplish more growth for all beings.

Appropriate Leadership

Accomplishment of goals is not the same as leadership. There is a need for leadership in groups and, the larger the group, the more leaders will be necessary. True leaders will do just that: lead. They will not seek to control the group. They will demonstrate by example the better approaches to life and living. Growth and abundance will be their goal, but it will be the goal for the entire group, not only for leadership. Each member of the group will be vital for the accomplishment of the goals. The leadership will be known for its ability to share and distribute resources. This represents strong yin energy.

This is not to take away any individuality or personal rights. The individual contribution is necessary, and each will be as unique as the person themselves. True leadership will not insist on uniformity. True leadership will embrace diversity. True leadership and the community as a whole will carry respect for each individual's right to a peaceful life without fear. True leadership will require a measure of responsibility in each member of the community. A level of self-governance must exist. This means that a mature outlook from each individual will be a prerequisite before this community can fully form.

The acceptance of personal responsibility will allow for the cessation of blaming others for strife and catastrophe. It will lead to people coming together to attain an opportunity for growth to all beings on the planet. This, then, requires a global vision and a strengthening of knowledge regarding those who share the earth with you.

Personal responsibility will be best served if you seek first to understand others rather than attempting to convert them to your way of thinking. Conversion of any kind, but especially forced conversion, is an old form and is outdated. Many have been converted from healthy and natural living to unsuitable lifestyles through fear. Much has been lost through conquest of others and the elimination of their cultures and knowledge. Do away with this thinking now and move towards comprehension of other beings.

Look to ways to improve your daily life through adaptation to and implementation of other ways of being in the world. You need not abandon all your traditions; simply open up to the thoughts of others. Recognize the intrinsic value of the experiences of others. This is the way of Source.

Your Choice Regarding Fear

Fearful things occur. Mighty events happen through natural processes, and the physical realm is not always a safe place. Be realistic in matters, but do not give in to imagined or created fears. You are more powerful than you may realize in the face of reports of doom. Prepare yourselves the best you can for these potentials, but do not live in fear.

It is said that fear is pain borrowed from the future, while anger is pain carried from the past. We pose the question, "What will you fear," but we also ask, "What will cause you anger?" Then we ask, "Which of these will lead you to a peaceful life? Will anger or fear bring joy to your community? How does love grow through the emotions of fear or anger?" In these questions lie the seeds to the future. Seeds need tending if they are to grow to a productive harvest.

Begin now to teach yourself and your children the lesson of decision-making regarding fear and anger. Your children and their children will create answers for problems that you, the generation now living, cannot begin to imagine. Choose to release the energies of fear and anger, transforming them into actions of love or peace. In this way, generations to come will live first in joy and feel the success of a unified community. In this way, generations to come will achieve the peace that you envision now.

Express your love to the future by releasing fear today.

7
Remaining Spiritual During Difficult Times

As above, so below.

Many observe themselves today and ask, "Why is my life not better? Why is life not more perfect for me?" They say, "I am doing many spiritual things and I know many spiritual truths, but yet, I have not ascended above all the difficult times that surround me. Why am I not a spiritual master?"

Spiritual mastery is far more than mere learning of technique or teaching. It is the application of these things in life and existence upon the planet. It is especially important during the most difficult of times. We tell you now that you are living within some of the most difficult times of history. You are doing well, it is true. Some reminders may be in order.

During times of peace, life is like a still pond. Drop a pebble into the pond and the ripples will be orderly and even. During difficult times it is as if many pebbles are dropped continuously into the pond. The surface remains disrupted and there is no evenness to behold. Many ripples diverge and patterns cease to exist. This, then, is like the time you live in today. Many energies are now in conflict.

You will be measurably calmer if you do not engage in these conflicts.

Practice Tolerance of Others

Many now seek to be heard and not to hear. There are many things prevalent in the world today that may creep into your personal attitude. Even in a minor way these may lessen or remove your spiritual clarity. Here are three energies that will create gaps in your peace or joy.

Tolerance is lacking. It is one of the easiest things to practice. Intolerance demonstrates a lack of personal integrity. The need for others to agree with or support you is a demonstration of a lack of personal will or inner strength. It is a sign that the intolerant one carries no true power or energy. They must continually seek approval and support outside of themselves. There is a difference between intolerance and the condoning of behavior that disturbs peace or joy in others.

Greed or self-seeking is a form of intolerance. One who only believes in their personal right and tramples on the lives and happiness of others is in need of adjustment. The dilemma comes for the individual seeking a balance to tolerance and the need to protect oneself and family. There is not a single answer or law to be found that encompasses all situations. While we encourage and advocate peace, there are times that force must be met with force. These times are far fewer than many believe exist. Tolerance of ideas or philosophies is different than tolerance of violent behavior. The latter is a demonstration of passivity, and this is an imbalance. Do not confuse peacefulness with passiveness.

Pursuit of violence or conflict as a way of life is also an imbalance. Many attempt to place a higher purpose to their acts of aggression. Do not be misled by this emotional process. Aggression is yang without yin. It is never a spiritual action. This is not to say a spiritual person will never act with force. Balanced force will stem from true spirituality. Force is different than violence and aggression, however, and a spiritual human will use force as a last result to others' unbalanced behavior.

Seek Your Truth

What is true for you? This will be an answer that changes as your life continues. It will also change as generations pass. Find what is true for you. Speak your truth and stop seeking an ultimate truth outside of you. There may be an ultimate power and truth to all things. It is a far greater thing than you can know. You are small within the universe and your perception of this energy will be different from other beings. Do not insist your vision is better than others or truer. Here is where tolerance truly begins. The acknowledgement that others may see life differently and that theirs is a valid vision will release you from many judgments. The release of judgment will allow you to see the ultimate power more clearly. Ultimate truth is not far off from each one of us.

It is your truth you must speak only and that is a flexible thing. Adapt your beliefs with the addition of new knowledge and emotion. One who holds the same truth all their lives is one who has failed to fully grow. You need not seek to have others agree with your truth. It is not something that needs to be written or spoken. It is a way of living. So we say rather than speak your truth, *live your truth,* and by the demonstration of your personal principles in action, your truth will be tested. If it is found to be wanting in certain times, do not be afraid to adjust or seek new elements to add.

Release the Temptation to Judge

Judgment of others is a pressure that pushes a being far away from peaceful existence. It is not personal judgment that we speak of; it is the judging of other persons. You must make personal decisions or judgments for yourself of what to take in to yourself in thought, emotion and physically. You must judge the best use of time and expenditure of your energies. It is not for others to do this to you, though it is good to seek counsel on matters. Good judgment is a part of wisdom.

Wisdom is a combination of gained knowledge and applied experience. Proper judgment is an aspect of both of these energies.

A life is not right or wrong. In all things, there is the principle of an action producing a reaction. There are few great actions at this time. The lives you lead are more reactive. The choices you make are often based on perceived actions, but these are likely simply reactions to situations in which you are not directly involved. In this, a being does the best they can in seeking a loving resolution, but this is not consistently possible. Remain detached from the outcome and follow the path of love and peace and joy the best you can, doing so for yourself only. By so doing you create the opportunity for better reactions in others. You are not the stone that causes the ripple. You may be the craft the carries others through a storm.

A life, then, is like the weather. Some days there are storms, and these can be fierce and destructive. They are not wrong. There is no cure or solution to a storm, there is only shelter and endurance. Some days are bright and warm. These are not right. It is that we are freer to act to our own purposes in these times, as survival is not an immediate issue.

Affecting the Future

It is an intense period of energies now. There are many reactive situations coming together. A pressure is formed, and it is visible in governmental, religious, and societal trends. It is also visible in the way of Gaia, but we speak now of the direct human experience.

As these pressures continue, entrenched concepts and philosophies will erode and be washed away. In individual lives this will mean adjustments of perception. It will also mean more reactions. Awareness of this probability will increase your ability to gauge the appropriate response. Seek first your own peace and center.

This may sound harsh to some ears. "Is it not in the nature of love to expend one's energies on others?" they may ask. To a certain extent this is true. It is also true that it is not appropriate to waste the energy of love in futile action. Thoughtful loving action is more effective than unfocused love. Neither is wrong, but ask yourself, "Do I wish to be effective? How can I increase and supplement the energy of love in the world at this time?" Understand that in the asking of these questions you now change the nature of life around you. Understand also that you must remain detached from the outcome.

There has never been a truly "Golden Age" on the earth. There have been times of great growth and the increase of knowledge. These times have been turbulent and often destructive of many institutions. In hindsight, it easy to look at the high points of history and assume all was bright. The reality is found deeper. With bright light comes deep shadow.

Yet these times were neither right nor wrong. The time you live in now is most turbulent. What will be the high point when perceived from future generations? Will your personal efforts be known? Likely not. It is many little actions that bring about great changes. Many small things trim the course of a ship. Many waves seek to carry that same ship in directions other than intended. A competent pilot will not judge the waves.

Many waves moving in the same direction are powerful. No wave is the same as another. The greatest of goals is peaceful existence. You are at a distant point now, but the energy expended needs only minor adjustments. Cease looking for ways to disagree. Cease being entertained by conflict and selfishness. Cease seeking only to be heard and begin listening.

Release the need to judge others and feel the return of joy into your life. Seek your own truth and sense the peace that is available to all beings. Accept others' viewpoints and the ensuing love you will feel will grant you access to the Source of all things. In this way, the present times will begin to alter, and a harmonious future will become a vision that all can share.

8
In Dreams

As above, so below.

There are many desires and hopes that we all wish for. It is a shared quality while on the planet to find a state of peaceful existence. Many look outside of themselves for fulfillment, but the real place for such a state to exist is within each entity. It is within each living being to dream. It is also within each one to make the dream active.

Illusions

Some may say that these shared desires are mere dreams or illusions. The belief in a society of equality and co-operative effort, or the desire for peaceful co-existence amongst all beings seems distant and unattainable to many. These ones have lost their ability to hope. They have forgotten how to dream of a better way. It is true that these things appear to be far away. This is an illusion.

There are many illusions available for the family human. An illusion is a perception and has value. The important thing to know about illusions is when to release them and progress your growth. A dream is different than an illusion. A dream comes from within you and can encompass many other beings. An illusion is something you put between you and the rest of the world. A dream has energy that can bring things together. An illusion separates.

There are many opportunities for the family human to practice delineation, that is, the creation of boundaries between one state and another. It is a way of consciously realizing the many levels of existence, but ultimately it is best to return to the realization that all boundaries are artificial. Everything that exists is energy and energy simply transforms from one state to another.

A dream creates power for you, while an illusion draws power from you. A dream can become a reality. If you can create the image, the reality can be beheld. Here lies an important concept: You can create. One of the primary steps to creating is to begin with a dream.

Dreaming is often thought to be something that happens involuntarily while you are asleep. What does that tell you? It tells you that when you are relaxed and at rest, your body, mind, and spirit come together and *naturally* create concepts and solutions to situations that you face while awake and more aware of your lower-vibrational existence. Become practiced at dreaming and you can and will begin to set events in motion that will assist in raising your vibration during the waking state. In a very real way, the better you dream, the better you live.

The Effect of Dreams

Some will ask about nightmares or bad dreams. We tell you now that you must look again at those dreams and seek to see them in a different way. Are they really dreams or are they responses to conscious fear? There is much to fear in the world today but dwelling on these things does not give them an opportunity to fade away. What do you feed your intellect and emotions? The media is full with false fear. Be aware of situations that may cause you harm, but do not invite trouble to you by preparing only for improbable disasters.

A true dream will carry an aspect that a nightmare does not possess. A true dream will carry an energy of wholeness and unity. A nightmare will center around only one being, yourself. Even if it is fear of harm coming to others, likely it is more about how the one having the nightmare feels. It is possible to actively dream in fear and many do just that. It is a reason why the planet is in its current state of existence.

If your dreams are fear-based, your life will increase in the perception of fear. This is why it is important to fill your waking state with concepts of growth and development. The stronger these realities in the state of awakening, the stronger and more natural these things become when you are in the dream state.

This can even affect those who are in close proximity to you. It is often the way of things that others will be affected emotionally first. Usually loved ones can be directly influenced by such action. If you are dreaming of growth, then others will be nourished in their own growth. Here is where responsibility comes in. If you dream of fear or separation, you may create these conditions in your relationships.

As in all things, there is a responsibility to dreaming. There is a possibility of gaining greater ability to respond to dream states. Using dream states to create your life works best when others' best interests are taken into consideration. You can and do affect outcomes in other people's lives.

We do not say that all things in relationships and life are the sole responsibility of one person. All beings act in accordance with their own internal compass. We do say that you can be a powerful force in the energies that move around you and the circle of companions you are engaged with. But powerful creators, those who are strong in the ability to manifest specific outcomes, must learn to influence others with care and respect. It is not healthy to seek control of anyone. This includes, to some extent, your own life. Becoming too specific sets limits on what may be available for your own higher good.

The dream does not require logic. It requires a feeling. The more peaceful the feeling, the more peaceful the reality of existence while incarnate upon this planet. A search for logic in a dream state leads to decreased vibration and the re-instating of limitations on life.

A dream does require the comprehension of limitation. You must understand that the realm of gravity possesses certain boundaries. You cannot be other than what you are. You can *improve* the being you are and dreaming is a strong aspect of this process. Do you desire better health or a stronger body? This will require effort on the physical level, but active dreaming will improve and intensify the results. Things happen much quicker when the higher vibrations are brought into play.

Be prepared to accept the consequences of dreaming. You are the one that sets this energy into motion. Unprincipled imagination can lead you down paths for which you are not fully prepared.

Active Dreaming

Because you are asleep when the dreams most naturally occur, there is little conscious control available. It is often left to what some call their higher self to gain access to the energies available in this state. The term "the higher self" is often misunderstood. It is used in a way that indicates separateness of the entity that is YOU. This higher aspect is the level of increased vibration that is your direct and inseparable connection to the realm of spirit. It is not at any time separate, any more than you are separate from the Source of all things.

Because of your decision to lower your vibration, become incarnate, and experience the realm of gravity, it sometimes requires extra effort to access this connection. The dream state is where this will occur in an involuntary way. It is also the point where, if you are untrained, the visions provided can be most easily misunderstood.

A practiced person, one who is trained in meditation, can and will create a dream effect that presses from the realm of higher vibration, the higher self, into the realm of gravity. The action of meditation is often misunderstood as well. The art of being still is sometimes seen as the goal or purpose of meditation. Simply seeking and finding a place of peace, achieving a centering of oneself, is an excellent skill. Yet there is so much more that can occur once you reach such a state.

This is the point where conscious, active dreaming begins. It is what sets the practice of meditation apart from the desire to pray. A prayer uses a similar energy. The difference is that a prayer is generally a plea requiring an outside response, whereas an active, manifesting meditation is a taking of responsibility. It is the difference between being served a meal and preparing one.

Prayer is effective in times of great need and low personal energy. Meditation and active dream state work is effective always. In each case, the practice will increase in strength if the action is followed by sincere gratitude. Use the power of prayer sparingly. Increase your own ability to respond to all aspects of life.

It is true that physical things can be made manifest. If you have a specific need, begin with an active dream. Be aware that an active dream has greater power when you seek larger goals. It is appropriate to imagine larger concepts than your own individual life and create dreams that encompass family, friends, or even all societies. The fulfillment of a dream can astound the dreamer. It will often take on a shape that they did not or could not have imagined when they began the concept.

Be prepared to accept a new path towards your chosen goal. A true dream will lead into new territories for the dreamer and those they may affect. In the practice of active dreaming, use the primary spiritual principles to guide you. Be peaceful to enter the dream state. Be present in the dream and act in love. Be joyful about the dream no matter what direction the images take. Do not fear to dream of a better future. Dream boldly.

9
A Magical Universe

As above, so below. We speak to you on the matter of physical needs.

We will first offer reminders of how to create. Secondly, we will give insight into the near future and how you can prepare not only yourself, but also affect the entire world in beneficial ways during the coming changes to the planet.

There is a type of magic in this universe. Things that you cannot comprehend by way of physical laws are viewed in this way. Events may seem inexplicably miraculous or magical from a perspective that is based in earthly perception or a trained reality. They are natural occurrences, nonetheless.

To achieve a magical result, it is often a matter of giving space to allow for a specific desire to manifest. If you hold too tightly to the potential reality of a physical happening, there will be a great deal of gravity attached to the outcome. Gravity slows down that which is of a higher vibration.

Powerful Principles Create Better Living

In an effort to assist you to create a better, more spiritual world to exist in while in the physical realm, here are several steps you can take. Many of these will be familiar to you in a personal sense of manifesting. We give the reminder first and ask that you pay attention to what follows.

Create more space in your life. This does not mean that you must eliminate all things. Retain things of value. Move along other items that no longer represent the way you are currently. This often can include people. There are those who may seek to impose limiting beliefs on your reality. Be bold in creating new areas of existence.

Release the need to know how or when something may happen. It is magic. Do not ask how the trick is accomplished. Only enjoy the result.

Let go of limits. Too much definition locks the energy into a course that it may not be able to follow. Be specific, but only up to a point.

Ask for worthy things. A vast sum of money is an unnecessary thing to request. Money is simply a symbol of energy. Why ask for more energy? Why not simply ask for what you want or need? The Universe is filled with the energy you need to create what you desire. Money is an unnecessary step and slows down the achievement of your desire.

Avoid distractions. Make a choice and pursue the goal.

Be in gratitude for what already exists in your life.

Believe. Trust that it will happen. Understand that timelines are not followed in the same way spiritually as physically.

These are powerful principles. Act as if the desire is truth, allow yourself to live in the image of your goal, and speak in terms that indicate you have a vision of the outcome as a solid thing. If you can manage this, you will be well on your way to living an abundant spiritual existence within a physical realm that is experiencing great turbulence.

The State of the World

The practical suggestions we have given are often used for individual satisfaction. It is time to exercise these energies for something bigger than personal gain. There is a global potential available. It begins with an image. It must be inclusive. If you create only for yourself, you may draw resources that others may need.

Witness the current state of society. Why did things turn out this way? An important part of the instability is seated in the desire to acquire vast wealth. Creation of great wealth that was specific for only one or two individuals, or a small group, drew many resources away from those who trusted that their energies would not be re-allocated. This placed a great many people in a situation where they needed to press their manifesting energies into an emergency mode. These types of situations give opportunity for fear and panic to grow and overwhelm others. Events such as the ones you are currently experiencing leave little room for such spiritual motions as joyfulness or feeling peaceful.

We use the example of wealth and currency, but political and ideological realms reflect this same greed for acquisition of all others' resources. It does not have to be this way. It will not continue. This is not a pattern that can be sustained.

The world is at a critical decision point. You have rarely witnessed such a large amount of energy approaching this section of the universe. Already some choices have been created. It is now that society is realizing the consequences of some of these early decisions.

Bring to the forefront of your hearts now what is truly important. Spend conscious moments imaging these outcomes. It is critical for you to do so. It is important to set the example for others by what you do.

Troubling events may continue. Progress toward a more spiritually balanced world will be made, but at a slower pace. There is a certain inevitability to the process. It is a higher vibration.

Regaining a Higher Vision

When you return to the realm of spirit, you are reminded of the purpose of life on the planet. You are given a higher vision and vibration. Upon your next incarnation, you then seek certain styles of life and press for this higher vibration, this world of spirituality and peace. It is something so many dream about. Can it be something unattainable? The blocks to this reality are rooted in lower vibrational desires. The action of conquest or acquisition, the unnecessary belief in ancient theologies, and the denial of new thought and discovery out of fear of change are all elements that prevent spiritual growth in all levels of society throughout the earth.

We tell you now that there are other places, even in the galaxy where you exist, where similar action is going on, that is, the experiencing of Source through a variety of life forms. In the experiencing, there is a continual raising of vibrational awareness that brings these beings closer to a full realization of Source. Few of those beings are resisting the process.

Why does there seem to be a resistance to spiritual growth happening on the planet Earth? It is the way that life developed. It is based on choices made deep in history. This is not to say that the choices were a mistake. The past is not something that needs to be corrected. Rather, we tell you this so you can envision the entire process and gain a full perspective of what you are dealing with. Look how far you have come! Adjustments are available, and the path can become cleaner and clearer for more beings.

It can all happen faster. There has been a movement away from spiritual living. You can observe this easily. Look at the way judgment exists. Look at the way it is broadcast across the world. Listen to the leaders of various countries. Do they speak of progress, or do they create statements of condemnation? This is not an exclusive energy. Both sides of the political spectrum are engaged in this futile waste of time and resources. Yet what do the people in these societies demand from their leaders? Are they themselves thoughtful and considerate of one another? No, rather they reflect the energy expressed by these leaders and thus are led into continued conflict with one another. Is this active spiritual progress?

Understand that spirituality is not a complete separation from the activities of the planet. Complete spirituality is an integration of all activities in society resulting in the promotion of everyone alive, and all future generations, to a higher level of vibration.

Spirituality is also not a solitary energy. You practice your spiritual ways within yourself, that is true. But true spirituality is a connected energy. You feel spiritual when you feel connected to the Universe. Understand that other beings are also aspects of the Universe. You must ultimately connect with them to gain true spiritual existence. Avoiding others will not serve you in a quest for higher vibrational living. We do acknowledge the difficulty in this concept, especially during times such as these.

What Must Be Done

Following the basic concepts we expressed in the beginning will allow you to realize what you personally need. It is the time for all spiritually mature beings to use those same concepts as tools to build a better world. This will help create space for others to actively grow and reach levels of spiritual maturity. Spend specific time in meditation or prayer creating images of peaceful, joyous living for many beings, not just yourself. Have fun with these concepts and allow yourself to feel the love and peace that others may have in the future. Create different ways to imagine the future. Look for opportunities to engage the various senses you possess.

All these imaging sessions that you can conduct are threads to be woven together. Each one is important. None should conflict with the others. It is up to you to seek ways to imagine such an integration of all beings. The magic is in technique. Understand the technique and the technology will follow. Chanting, singing, creating images or meals are a few of the many ways to contribute to a visionary way of life.

Simplification of your existence will go a long way toward the reality of the future beginning within your life. A simpler world is not a primitive world. This is a concept that some will find difficult. The energy to go backwards is currently very strong. A return to agrarian society does not mean that all technology will vanish. The opposite is true. With new techniques and approaches, the world can return to a more pastoral way of life without giving up the advances made in communications and science.

An eventual decline in urban population will cause some difficulties. Empty buildings and sections of large towns will lead some to feel that something is being lost. There will continue to be urban centers. They will exist in smaller ways that are more compatible with the planetary actions and more conducive to peaceful living. Release the current vision of the way things are and you will quickly be able to see the alternatives available to the entire planet.

Base Your Actions on Principled Love

The concepts of love and joy are directly related to the ease of life. If a person is struggling for basic necessities, it is difficult to attain these energies. The images one creates are then for food and shelter in abundance. Here is the seed of greed. There is such an abundance approaching that soon none need feel a lack.

The present day is the time to create channels, physically and emotionally, for this energy to travel through. Those that take the sparse resources from others today are limiting their own future. They may possess many things, but the maxim is true; possessions do not generate peace. We tell you now that possessions also do not hinder peace. Only the striving for more than you need hinders a peaceful existence.

Look for ways to share your existence with others. Look for opportunities to speak words promoting peace.

Act in a joyful manner and be bold when others demand an answer for your action. Why are you joyful? Speak your truth on the matter. Give others reason to follow your example.

Above all, do things out of a principled love. Take action not because you will receive reward, but rather because it is an expression of love. Love is the closest action we can take that emulates Source energy in its purest form. Love without limits and feel your connection to all things increase. As you do, the Universe will channel to you abundant energy to continue to spread a higher vibration.

10
The Wave of Creation

As above, so below.

We bring you information about the approaching changes that you are beginning to experience. Some of you are deep into these changes and find them unsettling. Some of you are feeling at a loss as to what you should be doing on a personal level. Most of you are aware that energy has begun to shift around the planet. Dramatic events, both natural and nationalistic, are shaking society and forcing people to look beyond selfish gain or the worthless actions of public figures.

We do not often offer prophetic information. All too often prophecy can be and is misinterpreted, misunderstood, or held as rigid dogma. Many insist on creating doom-filled scenarios when given real information about future potentials. We tell you this now so that you may read the following words in an appropriate frame of mind.

We say to you that the future is one that will be filled with opportunities for joy and love. We remind you that the future is no different than the present day, in so far as feeling joyful and loving is a choice you can make even in difficult times.

The Return of Creative Power

There is an energy that is returning to this area of the universe. We liken this to an incoming tide, but it is so much more. This powerful aspect of creative source brings refreshing primal strength to reinvigorate a weakened world. The conflicts and strife you experience today will become smoother as this healing power washes away and erodes the broken and rough traditions that mar the paths to peace and happiness.

The approaching wave is a creative thing. It carries with it the essence of the primary nature of the universe. The power inherent in this wave of energy is not destructive. We must say this. For many it may feel like destruction. This is due to the inevitable dismantling of things no longer necessary or pertinent for the planet and surrounding regions of the galaxy. Much that has gone before will be replaced. Systems that once were necessary for stability have become unstable. These systems will be challenged to adapt and grow or be removed and broken down into basic elements.

If this sounds fearful to you, we ask that you examine what you are attached to at this present time. Note we do not say that *all* systems will be challenged. We will say that *most* systems will need to adapt to a new way of existence.

This creative wave corresponds to a higher awareness being felt by many. It is an achievable state in the present day, but few have attained such a higher vibration. The approaching creative wave will create pathways of efficiency that many more will be capable of following to success. There is much that inhibits a higher vibration in the present day.

This adaption will not be instantaneous. Time will continue to pass, and, in the physical realm, all things will change in pace with gravity. There will be three significant indicators that the wave has begun to exert an effect on the planet.

The Arrival of a Generation of Light

The primary visible indicator will be the birth of a new generation of children. We have already seen a new type of child come into existence upon the planet in the recent past. You may personally know some of this generation of young adults. In the last twenty to thirty years, this generation has grown up and taken many societies on a new course. The members of this generation are currently working against deeply entrenched ideologies and so their success is not always apparent. These are the parents of the coming wave of children.

This next generation, the one that is being born onto the planet now and for the past several years, will find that they can accomplish more in a few years than previous generations could achieve in their entire lifetimes. These ones are returning with a strong determination to succeed at raising the vibration of themselves, and thus society. They experienced much horror and tragic death in previous incarnations. They did what they were told was the correct thing, fight and die. Only now are their actions beginning to bear the promised fruit of ending war and violent conflict.

These children will not easily be persuaded to do the will of others. This will make them difficult children to raise using traditional methods. Fortunately, their parents know firsthand of the archaic nature of such child-rearing rules. The partnerships formed between these parents and their children will become a near-perfect example of parent-child relations. The synergy that comes of this will be the largest catalyst for a strong and joyful future.

They may appear self-centered to the eyes of the past. This is true in some ways, but the actual energy they carry is one of self-reliance and self-sufficiency. They will become balanced beings who bring this self-reliant, self-sufficient energy to their societies. Traditions will alter and shift to reflect current needs. These children will bring new energy to human communities. They will streamline progress and education because that is what they want for themselves. Future generations will possess a different set of values based on the changes made.

The Passing Away of the Current Generation

A second indicator will be the passing away of the current generations. This will happen in large numbers. In some cases, this will occur in a very natural way. In other situations, areas of great population for example, the transitioning will occur in a more rapid way.

There is a choice to be made by individuals, but for many this choice will be difficult to achieve. Leaving one's homeland may not be practical. Entering another culture can mean risking unacceptance. It is too late to readjust the population of earth to gain a balance. Too many beings continue to seek to drag old cultural ideas with them and attempt to press them upon existing populations.

The passing of this generation will not be a cause for great sorrow. The changes they wrought are well-documented. These ones have walked a difficult path and deserve a time of spiritual refreshing. Many will be at or near the end of their life span. The attitude of this generation is shifting already, and the prospect of departing one's current incarnation is being more clearly understood as a growth opportunity in a karmic sense.

The karma of the planetary society has recently shifted. You have seen this firsthand. Are you paying attention? Are you fully aware? There is no longer a need to practice a slow method of change. This is unsettling to some. The changes that now approach will occur rapidly, and life can and will be bewildering to many. Do not fear these changes.

The best way to cope with change is to be a part of it. The best way to be a part of change is to instigate it. How can you now begin to initiate changes in planetary society? It is an important question that you must ask yourself. It is primary to your continued spiritual growth. Do not become bogged down in fruitless arguments or ideological wrangling. Pace your energies and direct them towards your immediate community.

A Return to Naturalistic Living

The passing away of a large amount of the human population will cause two things to happen. The first will be the relief of resources. Water and land to live on will become more plentiful. The second will be a necessary return to agrarian living. There will not be massive food production. Economies need large populations to support this type of industry. People will, of necessity, return to a more hands-on lifestyle. Growing their own food, crafting their own houses, or creating their own clothing will once again take on a large part of daily life. This does not mean that technology will vanish. The opposite is true. Much of the personal communication and information technology will continue and undergo further refinement.

You are already aware of the third indicator of the creative wave: a return to a more naturalistic and cooperative vision of partnership with the planet. The movement is termed "green," but could easily be called "blue" as it will eventually be centered around water bodies, especially the oceans.

Technology will drive this indicator. Perhaps the greatest time of innovation in the history of humanity is nearly upon us all. The creative wave of energy will allow for a release of old models based solely on profit margins. The creation of an economy based on the needs of the planet is one that is hard to imagine for many today. It will be a natural way of thinking for the children being born in the next decade.

A Difference like Day and Night

We have termed these new ones the Children of the Sun. They will bring a brighter light to the planet. They will work directly with the energy of the sunlight and also the way plants use sunlight for food. There is more to this phrase than we will address at the present time.

They will also respect the darkness and come to a full and complete comprehension of the human need for nighttime. Nocturnal activity will return to a more natural state as well. Certain harvesting is better achieved in the night and at various phases of the moon. Key health benefits can be derived by certain herbs and plants obtained in such a manner. There is more, and the answer to relieving many diseases awaits discovery in the ocean in the night.

The arrival of this next generation will be a cause for feelings of joy. They possess intelligence above the levels now considered normal. But they are more. Their ability, desire, and capacity for enjoying themselves will be a powerful driving force in their re-creation of human society.

The departure of the older generations will allow for feelings of peace to grow. A contemplative aspect to life will be engendered by the passing away of so many and the realization of all they went through and endured.

As society becomes closer to the earth, beings will spend more time caring for one another. Increased feelings of love will result. A strong, co-operative, and truly connected community will grow naturally and replace the old ways of strife and struggle.

We tell you one more thing: All of these changes will lead to a further period of great growth. As the human race raises its collective vibration to a higher spiritual level, people will find that they can begin to join with higher galactic aspects of life again. To this end, seek love and joy. Practice Peace.

Spiritual Practice

Understand that energy is returning. Understand that options are approaching, and choices are available. Understand your duties, your tasks. Things that are expected of you in the physical realm are not necessarily in harmony with what your spiritual perception of yourself might desire to accomplish.

Stretch your imagery. Create images for yourself but do not put expectations on these images, only create them. Make them variable. Make them changeable and malleable. Allow the images to adapt to new information as it arises. Notice how swiftly new information comes to you.

11
Sense and Spirit

As above, so below.

In this phrase exists a key that all can use. Observation of the world around you can lead to a clearer understanding of the realm of spirit. An aspect of this is to be able to filter away what is untrue. It is vital to observe the things of real value and be aware of what will offer true spiritual growth.

What Makes Sense?

Awareness of the physical world comes to the individual human through what is now known as the five senses. These are listed as sight, sound or hearing, scent, taste, and touch. Each of these is an interaction. The first two are a form of vibrational co-existence. In order to see or hear, first there must be light or movement of atmosphere. Second, there also must exist receptors sensitive enough to accept these vibrations. Thirdly, there must be the ability to interpret the signals.

Can you sense beyond the physical world? The physical human finds limitation in the sensing of spiritual things. The realm of spirit does not rely on the narrow spectrum of light visible to physical beings nor is it limited to existence in an atmosphere. The higher vibrational existence of the realm of spirit means that a keener sense is necessary for those in the lower vibrational levels to receive visions or communications. In a certain way, it is not possible for you to actually see or hear spiritual beings. Yet spiritual visions and messages do exist, largely due to the elegant nature of the human brain. It is a masterful interpreter of communication. It is largely underused, but this is changing.

Other types of humans were skilled in communicating and connecting with each other through a more direct, non-verbal thought process. Aspects of these humans still exist within certain members of the family human to this day, though the branch of humanity that originally carried this trait is essentially vanished. You may view them as primitive but, the truth is, they were very powerfully connected to the rhythms of the planet and each other. They were not so far off from the reality of the spirit realm.

It is almost a disadvantage in the world today to be so directly connected to other humans. You encounter so many beings. So many thoughts can cause discomfort to one who is more clearly attuned to the minds of others.

Those that do not know how to control and filter this continual communication can suffer. They are often thought to be odd. It is better to realize that they are unique amongst you. It is better to release the concept of "normal" and recognize and rejoice at the differences of one another. You are all unique and possess skills that can be honed.

The action of the spiritual realm is not always at a distance from the physical realm. True, some of what occurs is far beyond the comprehension of those in human form, but much is directly relatable to life on the planet. We tell you now, and you have heard this before, that you are spiritual beings in a physical form. You have chosen to exist at this level in order to experience Source from this vantage point. Your humanness is not an accident or a punishment. It is a level of existence that is vital to the workings of the universe. You have chosen this form of expression of energy.

In this you are often given the opportunity of communication with your companions in the spiritual realm. It is you who must filter the rest of the lower vibrations to more clearly comprehend the messages. The brain is a seat of logic and will often translate the vibrations from spirit into images of sight or sound. If you want these messages to be clear and accurate, there must be another component.

The Interpretation of the Heart

The heart also receives vibrations from the realm of spirit. In fact, it is here that spirit speaks first to the individual human. In today's world, the heart is also the most cluttered aspect of individual human beings. This has given rise to the predominance of belief that visions or voices are the only ways to receive a spiritual message. They are useful, but not as efficient as heart communication. Visions and voices can be, and often are, easily misunderstood. Generally, an interpretation of a spiritual message that is filled with fear or sets one group against another is a strong signal that the one who received the message possesses a heavy heart, one that exists without a strong higher vibrational connection.

This is not to say that all communication from spirit is light and happy. There are times that warnings are delivered, or counsel is received that may be direct and admonishing. Always, though, these communications are ultimately for the benefit of all beings, even though they may be directed expressly towards one individual or a small group. We have never sent a message asking one being to destroy another. We have never sent a message speaking of an all-consuming judgment. These are either misinterpretations or direct falsehoods.

A being with a higher vibrational connection within their heart may still see or hear what appears to be a vision or voice. It is the interpretation of the heart that matters.

A strong, higher vibrational connection of the brain with the heart will allow the practical nature of the communication to come through as well. We have never sent a message indicating that if you relax and simply believe, all your troubles will be taken care of. Guidance is given. It is up to each one of you to follow and act. You are spiritual beings in physical forms. Spiritual beings are active beings. Life in the physical form requires work and purpose. This is no different than life in the spiritual form.

Clear Spiritual Messages

We in the spiritual realm have never said, "Kill another human being." This does not mean do not protect yourselves. It does mean that you should seek a way to raise vibrations in others. There are many options open to resolve conflict. The first and foremost is to eliminate the source of the conflict. Cease following ideologies that are archaic or promote the granting of power to a single being or select group. If the majority of the family human were to simply take this single action, the planet would experience almost instant release from the tensions existing today.

We in the spiritual realm have never said, "Worship one aspect of Source." This does not mean to live a life without reverence. Revere *all* aspects of Source, including your fellow beings and also your own self. Act with respect and in a manner that demonstrates how you would like to be treated.

These are not new words. They are also not easily misinterpreted. Then how has the society you exist within come to act in an opposite way? It is based solely on individual response. Do you act in this way? Do you think in this way? Most importantly, do you feel these principles deep within your heart?

There are many messages in vibrational existence. Which do you choose to allow into your center? Which do you radiate from your core?

It is now a time for clear action on the part of each being. The energy that has been low for so long is returning. The change, the shift in natural reality, is approaching. You are creative beings and can assist in the shaping of this energy. Channeling it into paths of creative peace is a choice available to each one of you, but no one does this for you.

It is here that we can observe how many ways there are to access a state of spirituality. It is not simply through music or visualization. These may be the most common of avenues, but they are by no means exclusive channels. There are those who translate spiritual messages into taste, scent, or touch. A true spiritual message will always involve an aspect of creativity.

Sensing the Future

There is one more aspect of the senses we will address. We have stated this before: The division of the senses is in many ways an impediment to spiritual sense. In the realm of spirit, there are few true divisions. You now live in a time of changing perception. Your spiritual growth is made more difficult by the separation of your faculties of observation. This is one of the major changes occurring within all humanity today.

Again, we point you to the new technologies and the dominant motion toward inter-connectedness. The next generations will, as individuals, observe more of the world society than ever before in the history of the existence of the family human. Those alive today can touch upon this, but your role in the shaping of the future is more directly related to the opening of all of the senses to the reality of things beyond the physical realm.

The future generations, the ones being born today and especially their children, are going to envision the world and all societies in a more unified, more synergistic way than many today are willing to imagine. Vague images of a peaceful world will take on sharper clarity when individuals can simply look at hand-held devices and see friends existing in multiple physical locations. The idea of peace will be more of an imperative when members of other language groups find they are able to understand one another in nearly instantaneous dialogue. Peace will not be something to work for. It will be an organic growth across the world.

There are difficulties to overcome. Supply of these technologies needs to be driven by economics in the current climate of society. This will not change measurably.

What will alter are the elements of society themselves. Places that are struggling economically or with basic necessities are being served by many growth-minded institutions that use these technologies. The populations in these areas are being altered and educated in ways that could not be conceived of one hundred years ago. There will be a point of balance where the awareness of different possibilities will spread. The movement of individuals to gain access to their own versions of these technologies will spur the economics to create a supply of product for them.

The increase in the sensing of the rest of the world *by* the rest of the world will have the effect that many spiritual-minded beings have envisioned for many years. The unification of peoples by the sharing of their sensory experiences will accomplish what governments and religions have been unable or unwilling to achieve.

The brilliance of the human family is beginning to shine once again. These technologies will not take you further from the planet, but rather involve you deeper with its rhythms. The sense of peace that exists within Gaia will become linked to the future generations.

In this you can find joy. Clear your senses. Open your heart to a higher possibility of existence on earth. Expressing love for the future will assist in increasing the pace of peace. The benefit is yours to accept. The future is yours to create. Take the actions now and sense the amazing way life will become.

Spiritual Practice

Take some time each day to imagine what you wish, not only for yourself, but also for the entire planet. Do not spend time on explanation or detail. Do not concern yourself with what is the right system of government or societal structure. The future will be far different from what you can imagine anyway.

Imagine peace now. Begin the creation of peace for the world. Imagine peace. Begin the creation of peace within your life this way. Imagine peace. You have heard these words before. Be aware of the power of them now. Image peace.

12
On the Matter and Meaning of Prophecy

As above, so below.

The future holds great interest to many beings. Often it is simply a desire to know that life will be safe and secure for the individual and their family or tribe. This is not a worthless concern. Much information can be gained simply by observing the natural world and the patterns found therein. Time spent in contemplation can allow a person access to wisdom. This is not something limited to only a few beings. It can be experienced by every single conscious being in existence.

Often while spending such contemplative moments, you may find information that seems to have no point of origin, knowledge that previously you did not possess. With practice, this can occur with regularity. It is a tapping into the greater consciousness of Source. There may be within these times a transcendence of gravity, a sort of rescinding of time to a person's vision. It is these moments when other times and potentials can be revealed. The appropriate term for this is "prophecy."

Yet prophecy is not a vision of actual events. Rather, it is a sight of potentials and sometimes probabilities of what may come about, the end result of actions taken. Yet actions can be altered, and results can be changed.

To someone who is experiencing this for the first time, the vision can have an unbalancing effect. This can allow for misleading thoughts and interpretations. The meaning of prophecy is often lost when the vision is misinterpreted. Humans have long lived in a survival mode. The so-called fight or flight syndrome can kick in when new information is presented. Danger has been a normal state and peaceful life has been rare through much of recorded history.

When a vision is publicly presented, the visionary is often greeted with skepticism. What do they see that others cannot? When a vision is proved true, the value of future visions is realized, and the visionary may achieve a ranking that may not be continually deserved. A channel of information, like a river, is not necessarily consistent. Circumstances alter and skills change. The prophet or channel who gains the vision must maintain his or her own internal balance and be cautious as to the nature of the information. The ability to deliver information in a clear and accurate manner is one that can be learned and honed. Some beings are more natural at this than others. In the past, many have failed in their accuracy.

A Difference between Prophecy and Channeling

Often within a channeled message there is a hint of potential futures. The purpose of all truly channeled material is guidance. Sometimes this is spiritual guidance, other times it is more practical. Rarely does the information come through as a specific warning of great disaster. Yet, when seeing a certain potential, some will focus only on this material. They may receive the spiritual images in a complete way, but the glimpse of potential danger will overcome the actual intended meaning for someone who is unskilled in communication. The once necessary desire to be forewarned of danger overcomes the actual intent of seeking guidance and raising of vibration amongst the tribe, family, or gathering.

Communication arrives from many directions. It also radiates outwards in many directions. A channel or visionary must continually direct the information appropriate for each separate audience. Some persons will be unprepared for certain information. They are like infants who are unable to eat solid food. It is the responsibility of the channel to supply only what can be digested or understood by the audience of the moment. Saving certain knowledge for another time when the hearers are more mature in their comprehension is necessary in many cases.

True channels will direct attention away from themselves. True prophets will not become caught up in their own places in the world. The message will take prominence in life, and the repercussions will be accepted. This does not mean that a prophet will bluntly offer the message with little or no regard for the feelings of others. As we have said, the audience must be considered. Traditional beliefs must be taken into account, even if the message is meant to discount those same beliefs. There is a balance that must be achieved and not all have succeeded in this goal.

The realm of prophecy is not exclusive to any one type or class of human. In fact, all humans carry the prophetic potential. What is required is the patience to hone this skill. Most of humanity does not care to practice such patience. In fact, most of humanity would prefer to silence their own prophetic ability or voice. It is not a place where one can be comfortable. Comfort is not the goal of a prophet. Neither is discomfort.

Who is Listening?

Skilled prophets will create a space for belief to grow, where listening can be transformed into understanding. A focus on the positive aspects of the information will be a primary part of the message. In presenting those elements that will provide growth opportunities for the individual, prophets can often overcome initial distrust or resistance to change.

True prophets will be balanced spiritual beings. Their prophetic messages likely will be few in nature. They will not become attached to the outcome of those messages. They will know that the future is malleable and accept that what once was true or probable can easily be altered. They will in fact rejoice in the aversion of destruction or the minimizing of the effects of a natural occurrence such as an earthquake, tsunami, or fierce storm. Heeding the message of a prophecy can save many lives, and much anguish will be avoided.

Often the counsel of a prophet will be extremely practical in nature. Many will ask for detailed information on a vision, especially if disaster or danger is involved. The prophet must exercise caution in dealing with such ones. The prophet must not artificially create answers to satisfy demands by others. It is better to point to the positive steps that can be taken to reduce risk and loss.

Not all prophecy is couched in spiritual terms. Much prophecy exists in this time that is scientific in nature. Visions based on scientific models are as valuable as those based in intuition. Often these prophecies are more detailed. This has the effect of making people accept information and begin to believe that it is a foregone conclusion. In all prophecy, you must allow for new information to arise and alter the vision. In all prophecy, you must remain aware that the probable future envisioned may change, based on actions taken today.

No judgment should be placed on a prophecy. It is neither right nor wrong. Each vision is a perception. Balanced beings will weigh many factors in considering any action they take. The prophecy is simply information interpreted in a specific way. For example, some will hear of the potential of rain. They may choose to leave behind an umbrella. If it rains, they must accept the consequences of their decision. If it remains clear, they must not gloat over a good decision. It is not the fault of the information. It is an exercise of free will, as is acting on the information gained from a prophesy.

The State of the World

Many see the way people are acting in this time in history and believe that certain courses or beings will cause destruction or chaos. In a sense, this is true. But the actions of a few can be eliminated by the determination of many who act in a balanced way.

We tell you now that a choice point has been reached. The course of energies taken by the societies of the planet will not swiftly lead to peace. Division will be inherent for some time longer. This is not meant to create depression. Rather, we say these things now so that you, the individual, the undivided ones, can pause and see clearly what is ahead of you.

A resurgence of unbalanced yang energies is currently in motion across the planet. This does not alter the extended future when yin will rise. It only delays this occurrence. Yang is not the enemy. Yang is merely unbalanced at this time, as it has been for several centuries.

What can you do? This is a difficult time. You may feel a level of depression. Your response to this will be the key to rebalancing the yang energies. Maintain *your* center. We have said these things many times before, and it is practical wisdom for any time in existence. It is more urgent now. Avoid confrontation whenever possible, but do not fear confrontation.

Do not join in when divisive energy seeks to judge others. Focus on what is important. Look for ways to grow and promote growth in others. When you observe people seeking to create limitations on others, imposing their own concepts of morality on individuals who are doing no harm to others, actively move away from them. Do not allow others to create fear within your own being. You need not argue a point. Only remove yourself from the place of contention. By this action, you will give space for these energies to expire.

Remain in love with all persons, even those who cause these divisions. They may be frustrating, but understand that they have succumbed to fear and are seeking to balance themselves in whatever way they can. The sight of many unbalanced peoples clinging to one another gives the illusion of stability, but something inherently unstable eventually breaks apart of its own accord. That is the natural way of the physical realm.

Love is a powerful attraction. Allow the growth of love within yourself. It is the energy of Source. All will eventually be balanced through this power. Darkness does not remain in the presence of light. The greater the light, the swifter the recession of dark.

A Definitive Timeline

We tell you very specifically that right now in your life you must re-examine who you are, what you think and believe, and how you are responding to global events. Shift your energies where necessary and do this boldly. Press the energies of love and peace outwards from your core. This is not a battle. There is nothing to be won or lost. This is a balancing, and it begins with each individual. Fine-tune your thinking. Take note of your reactions and turn them into an action that promotes growth for all beings.

It has long been easy for others to predict war and famine, especially without giving a definitive timeline. We tell you now that we have given a time period of no more than one hundred years for the peaceful resolution that so many can and do envision. The world will become a very different place within this next century. Much of the contentious action you witness today will be unknown. We have said that your actions in the present day promote this result.

We tell you now that you can shorten this timeline of one hundred years. You can see the beginning of a peaceful future within this current generation. There are more things to find joy in than there are to fear. Act now in love and in joy. Seek peace in all that you think and feel. Create the truth of the prophecy of peace.

Spiritual Practice

We invite you now, this very moment, to make a different path for yourself! Choose to re-evaluate your position in this incarnation. Ask yourself large questions and do not be afraid to answer them honestly and aloud.

It all begins with the simple action of you making a choice. What do you want in your life? What do you want to see or do? What do you want to learn or experience? Who do you want to meet? What do you want to achieve while on the planet? What do you want to achieve after you have left the planet? What do you want to achieve when you return to the planet? These are not questions that can be answered with logic. They must be answered from the heart.

13
Becoming Whole

As above, so below.

In a sense, there is very little time to pass in the realm of spirit. Time is a concept based more in gravity, although at lower vibrational levels of spiritual existence we are still very aware of and, in many cases, subject to the energy of passing time. It is the nature of dealing directly with the family human, and it is a joy for those of us in spirit who connect with you on a regular basis. Time is a way of quantifying existence for humanity.

It is an obvious thing to see the great separations that exist in contemporary society. Why, you may ask, is there such great conflict? If this is what occurs upon earth, how can we be a reflection of spirit? How can "below" be "as above?"

Conflict in the Realm of Spirit

In the past, many seers have felt that there are battles and struggles in the realm of spirit, what some would call the heavens. This is a perception based on what they observed in gravity. It is also based on fear and certain ego-based assumptions. It is a vision rooted in the search for power over others and the instillation of a system of judgment to hold that power. Many sought and still seek to make a name for themselves, a legacy that will last through the ages. This is a futile thing to pursue. Time will erase all vestiges of individual existences. It is the energy that is passed on that has true meaning.

The observed struggles, what some seers have considered battles, is the attempt at quantifying the results of effort or energy expended during the course of a human life.

In gravity, you have created certain markers that demonstrate a perception of success. These markers are often external and include the amassing of items and objects. The true mark of spiritual growth is never external and, in the realm of physical existence, is the most difficult thing to gauge, even for the one who is growing.

The disturbance foreseen by ancient seers is simply the effect of many perishing from their physical existences in great fear and confusion, arriving within the realm of spirit in such a state and becoming further confused when things are not as they thought or were taught they would be. The conflict is one where they seek to create a place of judgment for themselves and others. This is action at the lower levels of the spirit realm, those nearest to existence on the planet. The higher realms of spirit are not this way.

These energies, as they return to spirit, are in a powerful state of creation as they pass from one plane to the next. They isolate themselves and others, resisting the wash of love and acceptance that many feel upon their return to the spirit realm.

The Wash of Love

Glimpses of the wash of love can be found in stories of near-death experiences. It is often translated into terms of color. Many people witness a glow of white or beings clothed in white light. This is a poetic way of seeing a truth. The way into the spirit realm is not one of vision alone. To attempt to explain the spirit realm using only the senses of the family human is difficult and cannot truly be accomplished. The physical realm is limited by the gravity that holds and shapes light. In the absence of gravity, we experience a sense of unification with all things. We experience all things through themselves. In gravity, you experience all things as separate and with boundaries.

Begin to understand that the separation of the senses into five is unnecessary and limiting. Realize that all your senses are in fact one and you will instantly feel a lift. It is what happens when a member of the family human is near death. There is no artificial need to separate the observations being experienced. You witness the universe as it truly is and sense, then, the wash of love that encompasses us all.

The Sense of Separation

Is one note better than another? You see how differing vibrations cannot be judged against each other. In this way there is variety in the universe. Source has allowed the components of itself to be witnessed in various ways.
As an aspect of Source, the reason for existence becomes clearer. Witness the universe in every way you can. This benefits you and, through you, all other energies. Resist this knowledge and you put yourself in a separate and

limited place. It is a decision. At the end of physical incarnation, you will be offered the true vision of energetic existence. You cannot fail.

Growth is simply the way of all things. The cycles you observe while in the realm of physical form are just that: cyclical. All energy transforms. A seed that fails to take root still succeeds in becoming one with the sphere of biological growth. Basic components become others and the seed continues in a differing form. You do so also. Yet there is a predetermination to a form of life in place at this time. The human can become something other. In this, the ancients were not mistaken. It is less a process of judgment, however, and more the result of choices. Your karmic path can be chosen and followed by the inherent energy of the vibrational family you exist within.

Like a singer creating a new version of an existing song, life is improvisational. Why limit variety? Clearly Source does not! To sing one or two notes for all existence is possible. Some choose such a way. These energies are vast and provide a constancy of reality. Within this context exists the rest of this universe and all of us.

We are given freedom to create. To let the opportunity lay at rest is also a choice. Do you choose to be the seed that does not take root? You will continue in a different form. This is not a judgment; it is energy in transformation. It Source experiencing itself through itself.

The Continuity of Life

The idea that one human energy continues intact from age to age is ego-based. You do not remain the same person within a single incarnation, or even within a single year of that incarnation. Life is a series of changes, and the changes are continuous. We all exist within a continuum, a mindstream. This continuum is one of constant creation. The less aware of this process beings are, the lower their vibration and the less harmony they feel within an existence. The higher the awareness a being has of this continuum, the less the need for individual self-identification and separation from all things. The more unified people feel within themselves, the more connected they are to the energy of the universe around them; they will be viewed as spiritual beings without the need for self-proclamation.

Each moment is a seed that can potentially ripen at some new moment in the future. The seed is not the tree from whence it came. It is a continuation of the energies of the tree. There is a separation of the elements of the tree: root, trunk, branch, and leaf, but it is the tree in a complete state that produces the seed. To view yourself as a separate entity of the universe and to believe you are complete and fulfilled and need do no more growth is to enter into the state of stagnation.

The Purpose of Guides

The temptation to remain separate is an aspect of the conflict that occurs within the lower levels of the realm of spirit. The action to prevent stagnation of energy is why the arrangement of spiritual guides has been created. The linking of those incarnate upon the planet with those dwelling in the realm of spirit is intended to ensure a continued elevation of all life. Gravity will encourage a level of slowing of energy. It is what creates the concept of time, and in that one thing, we see how the idea of separateness occurs.

There are some that would then seek to stop time or escape gravity. This is to miss the point of existence. You are in the realm of gravity in order to witness it and participate fully in the actions available to you. You have retained consciousness above the rest of the life forms for this reason. The marking of time and the realization of your mortality is a way of encouraging you to attend to these experiences with some urgency. It is to bring to mind the need for living life fully.

You also retain the concept of spirituality far above other life forms. This puts you in the place of stewardship, not ownership, of partnership, not rulership. You do not rule or own the planet or its life forms any more than you own or rule your heart or lungs. These act without thought, yet they are not independent of you. You, though, are dependent upon them. Proper stewardship of your heart and lungs will ensure a continued existence of vitality and allow you to enjoy the planet and witness things in a fully realized way.

Awareness of your mortality and your limited time should heighten the sensory experiences and inform your life. Raising your vibration in this way, you become more fully engaged as an energetic being and sense the great forces in which you exist. The wash of love becomes not only something you receive upon entry to the realm of spirit but something you prepare others for while still incarnate.

Love is a cleansing power. It brings a light into beings and allows them to see what is true. It assists in connecting beings to one another by bringing a heart connection into life. It is only through love that existence is fulfilled. It is only through love that beings can find the truth of peace and experience full joy.

14
A Vision of Current Events

As above, so below.

We speak again of the current times and the path through these moments in history. Much has gone before. Much is ahead. The course will never be completely smooth. There will always be challenges and tests of ability.

We say again, you have chosen to be here now. You are in the midst of one of the greatest shifts in your recorded histories. Vast energies are coalescing throughout the galaxy. It is you who bring them together in harmony around the planet. Those alive today are amongst the spiritually strongest of all humanity. Yet, you can rightfully wonder, "Why all the turmoil? What is the solution? What can I do as an individual?"

Gain Balance and Perception

In these current days, it may seem to a spiritually minded person as if the planet will never experience peace. The events occurring appear frightening, and it is easy to allow a lower-vibrational point of view to creep into our hearts. How will the family human ever gain control over such looming disasters, both ideological and ecological? What can anyone actually do to prevent great destruction from happening on the planet?

We tell you now: Refocus your perception. Viewing such great events will surely make you feel small. Imagine that you are on the edge of a chasm looking down. Such a vision will make most beings feel unbalanced. They might jump back reflexively, seeking safety. They may jump back without looking. Others might be behind them or perhaps there might be another edge that they could fall from. It may be safe, but it may not. The better reaction is to remain still while you find your center of balance and assess the situation in which you find yourself.

The events of the planet today are quite like this illustration. Many individuals, businesses, and governments are acting by reflex. It is a search to maintain what has been gained in the past. We tell you now, the past has passed. There are new ways approaching. Change is a constant thing and often gradual. It is different now. The changes approaching are swifter than you upon the planet are used to. This is not said to cause fear, only to help you have a different perception. It is information that can assist you to see what action to take.

The Energy of Being Human

The human is a creature of action. Like all things, there is a mixture of energies within each human. We often term these *yin* and *yang*. This means *peace* and *action*. Too often, when a human is imbalanced, the energy becomes *passive* and *aggressive*. The balance of energy on the planet today and for several centuries past has been just that. Yang has taken a precedence over yin and life has become aggressive.

In recent decades there has been a movement to raise the energy of peace, or yin. There are moments when it appears that there is success in this, but there also are moments where it appears that yang will always overcome such efforts. Many feel so today. It is an easy conclusion to draw if you are only looking at the chasm as a source of danger and are seeking to escape from the edge.

The chasm may represent difficulties in progress, but this does not negate the value of continued forward motion. There is beauty ahead. Yang will balance with yin. It begins within each human. The responsibility is yours.

Maintain Your Center

Test where you are. Do you use words like power or force as if they are something to gain from others? Do you speak as if you are separate from others or if your particular group or tribe is better or superior? Do you let your focus dwell on inflammatory speech? Do you see things in terms of winning or losing?

Even if you see another side of issues, even if there is ample evidence and there are facts that support your perception, there is never a true gain in an "attack and defeat" mentality. You can gain no true balance if you are pushing or being pushed against. Balance is within you. It is also within others. Those who seek control over others are not seeking balance within themselves. They are, in effect, unbalanced beings.

No true progress can be made if beings committed to imbalance are allowed to control society. The question then arises, "How are they prevented from acting in such a way?" The answer is that they are not prevented. They can only be minimized in their effect.

Allowing others to reap the consequences of their own actions is a real and valid approach to life and living. It is the only one that will instruct the individual human in a deep manner. Accepting responsibility for your own actions will lead to a level of wisdom. Seeking to make others responsible for your life will weaken your spiritual connection. Seeking to place blame is a way of "againstness." This will not bring balance to you or another human.

If you find that you are in disagreement with someone else, seek a way of peace, a common ground. If there is no agreement available, do not continue to waste time or energy. The world is large. If you find that you are in disagreement with many people, take time to examine your own thoughts and feelings.

A Time for Motion

We do not speak of neutrality. We speak of appropriate use of your personal energies. Neutrality is a state of non-movement. It is a stillness, and there is a time for being still. The time for motion is now here. But what motion? We have already commented on reflexive actions. These are unthinking movements that may take you further into unknown areas of imbalance. We say now, exercise movement with caution and awareness.

Above all else, find your own internal balance. This may mean turning off any external devices that input fear-based thoughts. This may mean simply staying silent while others around you argue or fuss. In ceasing to accept any input or give any comment, you will begin the process of filtering out what is trivial and of no lasting consequence. This is vital for gaining further balance. This is vital for your perception of what is *actually* true.

The movement we speak of here is internal movement, the action of progressing your mind, your thoughts, and emotions in an equal way. Your thoughts are yang energy. Your emotions are yin. To attain balance, they must be harmonious.

There is another form that motion takes. It is the movement of your physical self, not simply exercise, but mindful movement. It is not only the basic strengthening of the muscles and bones, but also a search for greater coordination and spatial awareness. Simple walking with purpose is a beginning. More is needed. Basic forms like Tai Chi or Qi Gong will add greatly to your understanding of your physical existence. Practices of yoga are helpful, but understand that there is more to yoga than fashion and weight loss. These are spiritual practices, and simply learning the movement or posture is barely the beginning of the benefit you may gain.

There is an additional gain to maintaining your center. Others around you will begin to feel the stillness and balance that you are experiencing. They will become aware of what is missing from their lives. They too will begin to seek balance from inside of themselves.

The Passing of Time

In this day and age, there are many who have a history of supporting the raising of yin energy. They are aging. The future is uncertain for them. It is this that weakens them and causes imbalance. What they envisioned for themselves may have been taken away by events on the planet. Their lives may have been simplified. Do not despair at this simplification. All life in the near future will become simpler.

In this simplification, there will be more satisfaction in existence. Life will be more centered on things that bring true strength to your physical form. We say that change is here. It does not need to be a fearful thing, yet many desire to see only a return to ways of the past. All humanity is in the process of change. This means that all humanity must experience a re-balancing of energies upon the planet. Equality for all will change the way supplies and goods are distributed. Value must become an equal thing. It is this that is causing the most difficult of changes.

Think of what this will actually mean to beings across the entire globe. Equality of physical necessities will then bring greater opportunities to pursue education and discovery. More knowledge will allow for more balance in personal lives leading to a happier, steadier family base.

It is not a lowering of the yang energy that will allow progress. Yang propels progress. It is the raising of yin that brings purpose to the action of such a strong yang energy. Those that have used yang for purposes of imbalance and personal gain must and will deal with their own personal consequences. They may have gained in artificial ways. The true gain of balance between the spiritual and physical life is what will allow peace to occur.

Understanding of your true desires will assist you to become undivided by the stress of artificial expectations. The energies of love and peace already exist on the planet. It is no secret where they are. Do not allow other energies to press your balance.

As the years pass, those who are older may not see firsthand the effect they create. It will be something that is bequeathed to the next generation and the next after that. It is a worthy thing to leave a legacy of joy. It is far more worthy to do so in the face of adverse times and energies.

Focus your days, not on the acquisition of things, but rather on the creation of the elements of a true spiritual life. Balance is achieved through the cultivation of love and joy. Peace is achieved in the sharing of these elements.

It begins with you. It benefits you in the greatest way possible. You will return. Why would you choose another path?

Spiritual Practice

To act in a balanced way in an unbalanced world is to set the example for others. It is a way to create the future as you want it to exist. It is the only way to promote true peace. It is the thing that will set you apart and on the leading edge of the wave of energy that is approaching.

15
A Time of Light and Unparalleled Growth is Imminent

As above, so below.

You are here to witness and also participate in the continuing shift of energy. It is true that we have entered into these moments in a stronger spiritual position than might have been expected a decade ago. Does this bring excitement to you? Is your heart filled with anticipation? Some are feeling fear. Is this necessary?

Currently, the family human is trained to think in terms of events. This is a different way of thought than that of almost any previous version of human society. The universe is a constant process, a continuum. Many waited with anticipation for the year 2012, believing great changes would occur. They expected an event, something rapturous or catastrophic. This is far from how the universe works.

Sense the Darkness Fading

The sense of great change is not incorrect. The perception of violent or sudden change is, at best, wishful thinking. What is happening can be likened to the winter solstice.

During winter on the planet, days get darker and shorter just prior to the moment of solstice, but as always after that one day, the light begins to lengthen and the days gain warmth. Energy returns, and growth is once again possible and natural.

The winter supplies may likely run low as time moves forward. Those who fail to plan for times of low energy will suffer. Those who are working toward raising their vibration are finding that they need less to sustain themselves in this time. Again, it is not an instant action. We tell you now that this long winter-like decade will come to a conclusion swiftly. Light is not far off.

We do not indicate peril. Dark does not equate with danger. Dark indicates a period of rest and dormancy. What the shifting of energy means is that a period of growth is approaching.

We emphasize again that this will not be realized in an instant. When the energy reappears, it will seem bright in contrast to the previous times we have existed in. We tell you now that the brilliance that will grow over the next century will cast a greater brightness than the planet has ever seen while occupied by the family human.

Over the next decade, however, those alive on the planet will be called to act in certain ways that will benefit all the beings currently awaiting incarnation. These actions will have swift effects on those still alive as well. You are witnessing the edge of an age of growth. It is a time where knowledge will increase, certainly, but more importantly, it is an age of increased emotional and spiritual stability. It will long be remembered as not just a Golden Age, but *The* Golden Age.

Your current work is setting the stage for this era. Your field of endeavor is yourself. In this, we can say that many are doing excellent work. It is true that it is for the future that you work, but you will continue growing in ways that have been unknown to life and the great experiment taking place on this planet. Life, though long separated and segregated, is beginning to unify and blend together. The purification of energy around this amazing planet is reaching new levels.

The Action of the Harmonic Coalescence

Some will feel a sense of regret as they realize they likely will not be on the planet for the finishing of the time of change. Understand that you have helped create the opening harmonies that precede this time of coalescence. Just as your past participation in the Harmonic Convergence and the Harmonic Concordance helped cleanse and purify your personal energies and open the planet to steady and stable change, so too will your presence create the blending of generations necessary to bring the Harmonic Coalescence to its full strength.

Your spiritual behavior now, in essence, acts like the plow to the field. As you transition from your current incarnation, your energy will act in a fertilizing way. Do not resist this change. Understand and continue to understand that all may not physically appear to be a fulfillment of a spiritual wave of change. Know that many things need to be overturned and broken apart before the metaphorical soil is fully prepared to accept the seeds now arriving.

We tell you now that there will likely be a large loss of living beings during this time of change and shifting. Do not fear such a thing. Many of you will find yourselves in positions of assisting others to make a peaceful transition from earth to realms beyond. This is not to say that you will be the cause of anyone's passing. Rather, that you will give comfort and firm assurance to those that have aged or fallen ill.

We in the spirit realm await them with the Wash of Love. They will be welcomed and well cared for, as you will be when your transition occurs. The population of the planet has long been understood to be in a state of imbalance. The coming years will see balance restored to many things.

Beings of Great Light Are Near

Many of you have already begun to sense that we are no longer alone in our sector of the universe. Many realize on an intuitive level that there are higher levels of existence in other portions of the Universe. We tell you now that there is a purer group of physical life forms in the neighborhood of the solar system. They require certain conditions before they are able to join with you. Those conditions are not physical. These beings are highly developed spiritually, and the same way is being prepared for you.

It is not simply that they are waiting to arrive on the planet; it is also the planet itself that draws them near. The vibrational rising of the family human sets the tone for the earth to also move in a higher harmonic way. In order for the beings that now approach earth to coalesce here, they need this vibration to attain and maintain a certain level.

Many of you will be off the planet as this begins. When you return, it will be a very different place. The strife you are currently experiencing will no longer exist. The global society of beings will exist in a deeply harmonious state.

The year 2012 could be said to be the beginning of this time.

As you live through the coming decade, you will find yourself asking if all of this is true. There will be some continued stress. There will not be a swift and sudden enlightenment of all beings. There are too many now who insist on defending old ways. There are too many who are entrenched in believing that acting in warlike ways will bring peaceful conditions. They feel that if they take all they can, somehow others will have what they need. They believe that only they are correct, and all others are in error. They are not open to the changes occurring every day. They misinterpret events to support old systems of belief.

Do not fall prey to this way of thinking. Do not engage in worthless word matches with such people. Do not give your attention, and thus your energy, to the chattering of those who create fear. There are those who see the times shift and alter. They seek to profit from that which should be creating joy by twisting the moments to emphasize the sadness and anger.

The family human is rising upward. There are those who wish that society would return to a lower level. They are emissaries of old energy. This energy will be filtered out and away.

Your spiritual practice is the key to this. Your ability and willingness to find and create peaceful moments for yourself will show others the path to attaining peaceful moments for themselves. These moments then become more common, and the events begin to turn into a process. The returning energies will power this movement and, incrementally, life on the planet will improve.

You will next see this improvement clearly in the shift in consciousness regarding waste disposal and the creation of waste itself. By the conclusion of the next decade, pollution will be well controlled, and the areas of the earth impacted the most by residue and garbage will have made significant recovery. This will not happen automatically. Being aware of your role and participating in this action will bring you a swift rise of personal energy.

Think of yourselves as elements of light. When the darkness the world is experiencing is deep, imagine that *you* are the stars that guide others. The stars themselves do not ask for others to follow them. They do not seek to be worshiped. They do not call attention to themselves. They only shine in the dark in a natural way. You are beings of great light.

Sentient life about the planet consists of both spiritual and physical beings. We are all together in our journey. The journey is reaching a marker, but it is not over. Join with your spiritual companions and those of others as we seek, pursue, and strive for a complete vision of a future of love, joy, and peace.

16
Regard Source

As above, so below.

These opening words indicate a cohesive universe, one where the true nature of life is evident only when you regard all aspects of existence. The scope of such a statement is a profound force for increased awareness.

As a member of the family human, you are gifted with a higher ability to sense the world around you and to manifest the life you desire. As a spiritual being having a physical experience, you are gifted with the innate ability to affect the future of the universe, both in the realm of physical life and also in the higher vibrational realm of spirit, or "below" and "above." Above all other creatures, the individual human, the undivided one, can create a world that nurtures the qualities of spirituality. Where does such an ability come from?

Energy Centers

A central point of creation exists. All things physical and spiritual stem from this one point where Source chose to begin. The location is not necessary to know. It is necessary to know where *you* are located. The original source of all energy has spread out into particles, and you are an aspect of this energy. No matter what form your energy takes, it is always an aspect of Source. From one energy center came countless others. These reconfigure with amazing frequency and delightful variety.

Energy still radiates out from this central point, but the vast amount of Source is in motion throughout the universes. We still refer to this place as the Source Point, but it is more important for beings in this area of the galaxy to focus on themselves as elements of Source. Any central source of energy can be referred to as a chakra, a term of which many are aware. In fact, *you* are a chakra. Few fully comprehend the magnitude of importance of the energy centers they carry within themselves.

The Source of Affection

As a particle or aspect of Source, energy radiates out from you. As the energy moves from a central point, it will affect other waves of energy also moving outward from other similar points, or beings. The more familiar the energy waves that meet are, the more pleasant the experience. In this way, there comes into existence the quality of Source we term affection.

No energy center can exist without being touched by others. It is simply not possible. There can be great distance placed between one energy center and another, but eventually all aspects of Source will again connect. Within the human experience, a similar situation may develop. Some will keep others at a distance, not allowing connections to occur. Such a decision is contrary to the elemental workings of Source. It is a decision caused by fear. There is often a reason for such fear, but the results are never a true feeling of safety. The fear of being close cannot be resolved through distance.

Source is not afraid to be close to itself. Do you fear other beings? This is not a natural way of energy. A drop of rain does not keep separate from the ocean. Rather, they join together without effort or struggle.

Awareness of Change

There is no true safety while incarnate. This may cause some to feel fear. We say this only to indicate that awareness is a vital quality of Source. The more you are personally aware of the physical world around you, the less likely you will find need for the fear of untimely events. This awareness of the lower levels, the lower vibrational aspects of existence, will then ground and assist your awareness of higher vibrations, such as emotion or intentions of others, or even yourself.

Awareness can increase a safe sensation, but it cannot guarantee safety. Change is a constant thing, and this means that each segment of your existence will be different from all others. Adapt and flow to the energy of change and you will find life easier.

A quest for absolute certainty will prove to be futile. Source did not intend for certainty to be a common quality of existence. Source did not fear constant change; Source created constant change.

This is not to say that change simply for change's sake is an ideal to strive towards. Even a swift river follows a course. The banks may alter and change over time. The river may swell or wither depending on other conditions such as rainfall or snow melt. At times, a river may dry up completely and vanish. Shifting of the crust of the planet may divert the course of even mighty rivers. Yet a river remains a river while water flows.

Allowing your life energy to flow within a certain pattern is a natural thing. The difference between the experience of a human and all other forms of life is the amount of awareness available and also the ability to use such a quality to make informed decisions to shift your own flow. You can ask the question, "What if?" You can set mighty forces into motion if the answer becomes, "I will!"

Spiritual Vision

Awareness of the concept that you and all other things, both matter or otherwise, are in fact aspects of Source should humble and empower you. This one thing brings down upon the individual an enormous amount of responsibility. It is here that you respond to the higher call of Source. It is here that you raise your own vibration.

One chakra that exists within the human form is termed the Third Eye. This is the most useful energy center when seeking awareness. It is also the most underused and often misunderstood of all the chakras. It is here that you observe yourself internally. It is, in its way, a diagnostic energy. Too many humans attempt to stare outward, seeking answers from elsewhere. This is a way of denying their own spiritual power. It causes strain to the Third Eye and results in poor spiritual vision. This energy is for the individual alone. It is not to examine others.

Pause now and blink your Third Eye. When your actual optical eyes are weary, you blink and water them. This allows them a rest and to refocus. Proper use of the energy of the Third Eye will serve to refresh your perspective. It will allow for a higher vision of purpose.

Those who are spiritually tired are often staring too long into the subject of spirituality. They look for techniques or rules to raise their vibration, but they have lost the ability to reasonably exist within the physical realm. Their logic will not assist in a spiritual quest. The realm of spirit carries a logic of its own. It is not different from the realm of the physical, but it is only truly understood from "above." You will return to the realm of spirit soon enough and higher logic will be revealed to you at that time. So do not struggle at spiritual growth. It is a natural thing and needs only to be tended and watered. Be fertile, be creative, and spirituality will become a natural way for your energy to travel.

The Source of Love

Did Source exert great effort in the creation of the cosmos? The energy released is great, but it was not considered work. It simply is. The action became the very reason for Source energy to exist. The action taken was not a question. The question was and still is, "What will prove to be?"

When you chose to create, there is often a logical goal available. When creation is at its purest, there is no detailed intention, only the idea of creative energy expressed. Source did not choose a master plan to follow in great detail. Source chose to allow certain energetic principals to come into existence and play with each other.

Beauty exists because Source appreciates such a thing. Do you also feel the element of beauty in your life? Do you find yourself to be beautiful? If not, how then will other aspects of Source be capable of seeing your beauty? Do you comprehend your beauty? You are beautiful.

We have said that Source is love. This is an important thought. If you think in this manner, then all things around you, all other aspects of Source, are potential centers of loving energy. A lack of happiness is a lack of this primary power. It would be correct to say that degrees of love are the measure of an individual's ability to feel joyful and peaceful.

As love is an inherent and basic energy within all things, choose to love more and observe your joy and peace increase. This is not based on how much you are loved, but on how much love you create. Do not be concerned with the returning of energy in this matter. There is no risk in loving, only in the expectation of a return. The return is far reaching. It is an investment in the coming ages.

You shape the future of all humanity in this way. If many begin to act in such a way, the need for conflict will dissipate on all levels. The basic nature of all things will be revealed to be a joyfulness of life and the expression of our individual awareness. When all are able to exist creatively, a level of peace will encompass the planet.

Accept your position as an aspect of the center of all creation. Radiate your purest energy to all beings without exception. As above, where love is the primary power that drives us all, so below, where many seek love and joy and peace, just like you.

17
Do You Love?

As above, so below.

This phrase indicates a level of constancy of energy that exists in both the spiritual realm and also the physical. Not all energies translate in a pure manner from realm to realm. A lowering of vibration can alter the energy of Source. Raising of vibration can transform something mundane into something enlightening. The single energy that does not alter is that of love. Love is also the energy that can most rapidly facilitate transformation.

Many state that they desire increased feelings of love to enter their lives. In truth, all beings need this power to survive and succeed. Love is the central power of the universe, and we are each distinct aspects of the universe. Thus, love does not only begin outside of our selves. When we are strong in this power internally, we draw others to us and the energy then grows exponentially. Love is the most natural of all energies. It is also the most difficult to balance at lower levels of vibration.

The Illusion of Love

Some may resist, or act in ways that seem to counter love. They present a challenge to the society of spiritual beings that is now growing in number upon the planet. They appear to be destructive forces, bent on taking peace away from the planet. They do not appear to accept reason. They seek power and adulation. These things are mere shadows of the true strength of love. Those who lack in personal power often willingly accept and follow such ones blindly. Followers give the illusion that the one followed is loved. In times of turmoil, such an illusion is often quickly dissolved.

For strong spiritual beings, it is difficult to muster even the desire to express love towards such ones. It seems a waste of energy. The temptation may grow to actively oppose those who do damage to others. This is not always an error, but the motivation must always be to restore the strength of love and community, equality, and balance. This requires that spiritually minded beings possess a strong sense of unconditional love.

The importance of the state of unconditional love is relative to a person's desire to be spiritual. It is not a prerequisite to existence. It cannot be generated outside of a being. There must be a selection of action, a conscious decision to act in an unconditionally loving manner.

This is a difficult path when others around you choose another way. The path from the lower vibrations to higher is never an easy one. The desire to gain spiritual abundance is often challenged by the pull of things of physical value. It is a truth that you cannot carry your physical possessions with you into the realm of spirit. Possessions of this nature are transient. Experiences and true knowledge gained add to a being's potential for wisdom, but also are temporary. What is wisdom to a child may seem to be foolishness to an adult. So it is with a spiritual being who observes the one immersed in the pursuit of physical gains.

Here is where love must enter. It is not that the spiritual being is better. Leave out the judgment you may feel over one who appears to be of a lower vibration. The opportunity for sudden enlightenment exists always. Those that may appear as "enemies" may tomorrow be instantly transformed into beings of great light. This can also go the opposite way. The action of unconditional love is not the same as the action of agreement.

Are You Truly a Spiritual Being?

The question, "Do you love?" can be accompanied by the question, "Should you love?" There is a danger in this second query. It sets up the concept of separation and categorization. It begins a path of judgment. Remain aware as you ponder the answer within your core being. One might better ask, "Can the energy of love be wasted?"

The easy answer is no, love is never wasted. But in the answer is another question, "How much time should one spend in loving another when there is no return?" Here, then, is a strong point. There is a difference between active love and the general state of love.

Living in the state of unconditional love still requires discretion of resources. Acting in a loving way is the result of that discretion. Choosing where to send the energy of love is often a case of having a similar vibration with another. This is an easy path.

When you find another who is on a similar plane of existence, you are naturally attracted, and the way seems clear to both of you. Decisions and agreement come with little or no discussion. There is little friction because you both carry similar perspectives. All things look the same to both beings involved. There is no decision to be made about the use of personal resources. You are in a flow together and all is naturally balanced.

The caution is that two or three in agreement can begin to believe they have the "correct" path for many others to follow. Better to accept what is pleasant at present, than to seek to persuade others to your perspective. Your personal approach to spiritual life and living is not a thing that is transferable to another being. Agreement is not always an indication of unconditional love.

A truly spiritual being does not need anyone to be in agreement with their point of view. It is not something that even needs to be communicated verbally. Spiritual action will say more than many words. Truly spiritual beings will be content within themselves. They will also find that other like-minded ones will simply appear in their lives. The action of love will draw such ones together. It will also allow for others to move along their own path.

Love in Return

Those that wish to increase the love in their lives do not have to rely simply upon themselves. Finding others that share similar interests is a beginning to a path. Understanding that you must grow from that point is vital. Within that idea is the possibility that you may move away from those with whom you shared commonality. You will likely grow at different rates. This does not mean that you will cease to express friendship, which is a form of love. If you are growing, this means that you personally have a greater energy of love to express.

This returns us to the question of loving difficult beings. The answer lies in the question, "How do you wish to be treated?" All beings, especially on the physical plane of existence, experience imbalance. Moments of weakness or misdirected energy occur even to strong spiritual beings. At those times we desire others to behave in a certain way, to not further damage our strength or prevent a regaining of balance. We wish for understanding, and also patience.

There is an internal obligation, true. But it is good when we receive loving energy from others at those moments of reduced personal power. The caution is that some will choose to stay in a weak condition and merely accept the love shown. Always seek to raise your strength and continue your growth. Others can assist, but the responsibility is yours alone.

How do we raise our strength? By acting in love. Just as we wish for loving energy in times of low power, the expression of love to others at those times will often draw strength to us. The decision to express love always results in love being returned. It is not always returned from the same direction you send it.

Expression of love in a more general way does not guarantee a return in kind. Expectation of such a return is perilous to the continued state of unconditional love. Loving actions done with a view of recognition for their existence are not as pure as love expressed privately.

Understand that all beings desire and need love. Understand that loving another is a decision you must make. Understand that sending love to another is never a waste of energy.

There may be times when you choose to limit the amount of your strength going outwards to others. This is not a stopping of love. It is a redirecting of love and an exercise of spiritual discretion.

Knowing love is not the same as *being* love. Many know that they are loved and express a level of love in return to those that first love them. The higher action, the one that raises a being's vibration, is to seek ways to *be* the energy of love.

In every moment of a person's life, if they can allow love to be the power behind every action and decision they make, the level of spiritual feeling will increase. In so doing, the level of connectedness will also increase, and the feeling of separation will dissipate. Love allows for transformation.

On the planet there is much that can and will create opportunities for others to lose their balance and their desire to express love. We tell you now that nothing will engender the prospect of peace and the feeling of joy as the expression of the power of love. It is the primary energy of Source and inhabits all things. It is a singular state of existence and the highest indicator of a being's level of spirituality.

We ask you again, "Do you love?" We tell you now, "You are loved."

Spiritual Practice

We want you to feel love now. We want you to go to your heart. Feel that. You see, you cannot *think* love.

Let your heart love right now. Where does it grow from? It does not come from anywhere outside of you, does it? It comes from within you. So, what does the energy of love touch first? It touches you. You are now loving yourself first.

Let the energy radiate out from you. You cannot run out of this. The energy of Source is love. It is the closest thing we can say of this. What started all of this, what you feel when you love, is a particle of Source, right there, pure. Feel love. Be that energy. Be love.

Spiritual Practice

Imagine that you are in a place that touches your heart. Do not be concerned as to where it may be exactly on the planet. Only imagine a place that feels right to you as an individual. Imagine that you are in that place. Next imagine a task or project that brings joy and happiness to you. This does not need to be something altruistic or charitable. We are talking about your fulfillment at this point. The imagining of a project is essential. Creative energies are energies that are in motion. Something must be accomplished, or they will not function well. Imagine that you are accomplishing this project.

There are some who would want to limit what you could expect. We remind you now that the universe is vast and plentiful. Think big. Set big goals. Make plans and set a purpose for your life that exceeds what others expect from theirs. Look to the future by raising your eyes. You will see things in the distance, great things, and you will pattern your feelings and your thoughts in such a way as to expect to always see and experience great things.

18
Essence and Existence

As above, so below.

Many feel that human existence is in a precarious position. It is common for the media to discuss and speculate on the nature of large-scale destruction of life on the planet. This creates an atmosphere of fear. It is true that life is in a reduced state in the current day. It is not true that you need to embrace the weakening force of fear.

Many are concerned about their ability to survive coming changes. Some seek a fantasy where they will not be required to be present while changes on the planet take place. Some simply occupy themselves with distractions that lead nowhere. We have said before and now say again that this is a time for all beings to be aware. This is especially true when we speak to spiritually minded ones.

Balanced Existence

A concern for your continued existence is inherent in your vital force. You cannot deny the drive to live and grow. Much emphasis is put on physical survival. This is not wrong to consider, but to consider only the physical level of existence is to deny the underlying power that causes you to exist in the first place.

The concept of physical existence is one that needs to be brought into balance. The strength of this drive often covers over the deeper aspects of life. This will alter and shift as time continues. Quickly now an emphasis will grow on meaning of life over survival. The difference is between the essence of life and the simple struggle for existence.

Many beings who seek a higher vibration are already aware that there is more to life than a basic day to day routine. Conversely, they also recognize that simplifying their routines can be a portal to understanding their personal essence or, as it is sometimes termed, their higher self. The ability to recognize your personal reality is a key to continued purifying of your essence.

Not all beings grow in a fruitful way. Those that do not comprehend the ability to choose aspects of their reality in the realm of gravity are ones who must contend with a more primal existence. They react to what occurs around them, never taking full responsibility for the outcome of their karmic path.

We all exist. Not everyone senses their essence. Because someone does not sense their essence does not mean they are without a higher purpose. We all possess this higher self or calling. Even those in the spiritual realm have a calling beyond mere spiritual existence. If you do not possess a clear sense of your essence, it is important to increase your awareness in this matter.

The search for your essence can be tricky. It may seem as though the harder you look, the more elusive the truth of your personal reality becomes. This is the way with many things when they are approached from the point of gravity, that is, the physical realm. First, understand that in the seeking, there is no end goal, no final reward or conclusion.

Ultimately, our true essence is far higher in vibration than any merely physical path can illustrate. However, we are currently in the state of gravity and must make do with the information available to us.

Elemental Affinities

A being can have a strong penchant for certain earthly elements. Equally, they may feel a strong empathy for certain life forms. Plants or specific animals can draw us to a very particular path during stages of our existence. These affinities grant us clues as to our true essence.

Your essence may be one of light bringing, which on earth is represented by a kinship with the element of fire. It may be one of support, represented by the element of earth. It may be an essence of thought, which indicates a kinship with things of wind or air or flight. It may be an essence of emotional activity, which corresponds with water. You can see clearly that there are no firm boundaries. Yet each of us carries one of these elemental essences within us. Successfully connecting to other beings will be easier when these essences are taken into consideration.

Essence is the energy that exists within our karmic entity. It is the interior force that takes over when we are not thinking. However, it is more than emotional reaction. It is a viable power that is revealed when we are under great stress. How do we approach things that trouble us? How do we handle disease or problems? Is there a balancing energy that we seek? Is there a search for the comfort of others? Essence comes through when we are in our most natural state. It is the tone of our dreaming and the basis for our imaginings. The images we dwell on indicate the nature of our essence. They indicate the strength or lack of connection to our higher self.

There are those who experience strong karmic echoes. This is not the same as their true essence. A being who believes they should be served, or one who seeks power or domination over others is not fully realizing an essence. They are reacting to karmic echoes of the past. Likely their higher self is seeking a balance from previous incarnations. A belief in one's superiority is not necessarily wrong. It is a perceptive thing and, while in gravity, can be quantified in physical ways. In the higher realms of spiritual existence, superiority and entitlement are not issues that arise. They are not an energy of balance, and thus not an energy of Source's purpose.

It is important to note that our karmic entity is not separate from us at any time. It is what connects us at all times to the Source of the universe. It is the conduit that brings us creative energies. How strong is your connection to your karmic entity? It can be strengthened.

We can alter our existence. We cannot change our essence.

Strengthening Your Essence

Your essence is a combination of vibrations. Clarifying the vibrations that exist around you and within you will strengthen your karmic entity. All other beings, sounds, colors, or scents are vibratory in nature. Not everything works in harmony. This is not a judgment. One color may clash with another. Neither color is wrong or a mistake.

They simply do not go together in an optimal way. Yet, some combinations of color appeal to one being but not another. Thus, it is a perceptual thing.

Finding the optimum combination of vibrations for yourself is the way to strengthen your essence and thus increase the power of your karmic path. Elimination of the need for others to agree with or approve of your choices is a strong step to releasing judgment. Others may still feel a need to bring you to a certain way of thinking, feeling, or belief. This may impede the strengthening of your essence but will not prevent it. Should you find there is too much of a counter-vibration to your quest, a decision must be made as to whether the vibration can be kept or must be released.

Your essence does not rely on things outside of your karmic entity, yet it is interconnected like all things that emanate from Source. If you feel that you are at the mercy of the forces of the universe, as if you have no choice, then you likely are in the mode of basic existence. If you recognize that you personally are an active and creative force of the universe, you are close to expressing your true essence.

The key is increasing your awareness of your own connection to all things. This requires sentience, that is, awareness through the use of your physical senses. But more is necessary. You must go beyond the physical. The path to increasing your awareness is through understanding that the physical senses must first become one sense. Let no separation continue between sight, sound, smell, and touch. When you acknowledge and then fully realize that there is a single physical sense, you will find the path to perception heightened. This is how Source views all aspects of itself. This is how Source views you.

The Search for Your Essence

It is said that time is of the essence. It is truer to say that time is an aspect of your essence. The use of time in unworthy ways is a path to limiting your true essence while on the planet. It is only the human animal that allows itself to be sidetracked and distracted with unworthy thoughts or the pursuit of power over other beings. Many humans allow their personal unique essences to be suppressed.

A search for your essence is a key to spiritual growth. This search is called many things. The avenues that can be pursued include meditation and contemplation. But you are not limited to such things. Any pursuit that allows for the observation of life upon the planet will help you gain access to deeper wisdoms.

Observing others' search for meaning and value can draw clear parallels and pathways for your own search. The study of ways of belief or thinking is an avenue that has served many in the past. This way still holds some value, but it is not necessary to adopt a belief system. In fact, such a thing can cause one to slow down and become more attached to physical existence. Learn the stories and draw from their sources an understanding of the principles of Source.

Essence holds together all the experiences of existence. It is the power that presses energies into the form of a karmic entity, allowing for coherence at a higher level and a continuum of consciousness. Not all beings are experiencing continued consciousness. The energies of those who allow lower vibrations to absorb them will be find redistribution of their essence.

You will know clearly that your essence, and thus your karmic entity, is being strengthened when you experience certain continued feelings of growth and fulfillment. The spiritual concepts of peace and joy are inherent in a purified essence. A clearer signal will be when you find yourself expressing various forms of love to all beings. This is a test, and it is true that you exist within a time of testing and purifying.

Take to heart the clear knowledge that you can strengthen, not just your physical presence, but a larger energy, that of your higher self, your very essence. In this, you produce a stronger karmic path for the future of all beings.

Spiritual Practice

We offer a challenge to you of silence, or quiet. Stay quiet for one day. This does not mean do not talk or respond to others, only wait before you reply. Silently observe what others say and communicate. Is what they say worthwhile? Are the words *you* choose worthy of a spiritual being?

Do not fill silence with noise like communications from certain devices. Do not judge these things. Only, accept a day of quiet.

Notice what forms of communication you regularly accept into yourself. What do you allow to commune with you? If you find that there are many things of little value, ask, "What am I communing to Gaia? Why should she listen to me? What do I unintentionally communicate with my vibrations to both the realm of my physical home and also the realm of my spiritual home?"

19
Time and Change

As above, so below.

How old are you? How old do you feel? How old is humanity? Do you feel like you belong here now? Do other times beckon you? Do you feel that the present day is somehow wrong or extremely imbalanced? Asking these types of questions can lead to an alteration in your perception of the course of history.

In recorded history, we see times of great change. Many study these moments and devote much time seeking an understanding of the changes that occurred. Some explore the idea of, "What if?" They ponder the implications of certain events having different outcomes. What would life be like today if there had been no wars during the 19th and 20th Centuries? What would the world know today if nations choose to integrate with other cultures rather than quell native civilizations in colonial movements?

We tell you now that a time of unprecedented change has already begun. Will the world choose a different way to express energy than in the past? Much depends on you.

Time Compresses

The course of all forms of energy proceeds in waves and currents. The course of life in all forms proceeds in the same way. We see in history the peaks and troughs of these waves of energy. What you do not clearly see is the way the energy is expressed in a higher vibrational existence. As waves of change occur, great pressure is placed in the realm of gravity, affecting time itself.

As great changes approach, time is compressing. Imagine a spiral, like a spring, being placed under pressure. When relaxed, the spring's coils are at a distance. When pressed together, they can be near to touching. The action of time can be compared to that spiraling spring. When great waves of energy approach, the spiral of gravity-based time is brought into a tighter space. Events appear to be closer, sometimes happening simultaneously. Have you recently experienced slight disorientations regarding the timing of events in your life? Have you felt difficulty recalling when or if something has occurred? You are not alone in this! There is nothing wrong with you in this regard.

The strength of the energy that is arriving is greater than at any time in the past two thousand years. There have been powerful waves in the interim, but nothing that will affect the planet and the beings living on and around it quite like this.

Running Out of Time

It may appear that you personally have less time to accomplish daily tasks. It may seem as if time has sped up. This is very true.

Again, imagine time as a spiral. Many believe that we are reaching an "end time," and there is some truth to that idea. What we are reaching is an end to a *cycle of time*. As time winds into the center of the spiral, the space between the minutes, hours, months, and years grows shorter. However, time does not stop, and space does not cease to exist. We will begin to cycle back out of this tightened center of the spiral in the coming years. The perception, then, will be that the pace of time once again lengthens. This will be especially true from the perspective of those in the physical realm.

As we proceed through the approaching shift in and around the planet, we will find that time once again relaxes. We will not feel so rushed or pressed for time. Breath itself will come easier as the coils of time release.

Those who cling to a spot on a coil that is moving apart will find themselves stretched and pulled in a futile attempt to hold on to what is past and vanishing. The end result, however, will be the same as if they willingly went with the flow of time. The difference will be that they are off balance and out of a place of comfort. They also may have prevented others from experiencing a smooth transition from one level to another.

The spiral will continue to decompress and the space and time between the coils will continue to grow. It is a natural law and there is no preventing this action. Those who believe otherwise will create an opportunity for suffering on their own part. There is no need for this. The universe has abundant resources and energies to supply all beings with what they need. Do you feel stretched? Are you holding too tightly to the coils of the past?

A Desire for Change

Many are currently dissatisfied with the course of events of human existence. Life is clearly out of balance on the planet earth. There is much that disrupts the course of happiness, and even for those of you practicing a higher vibrational path, it can often be very difficult to maintain a growth-oriented attitude.

Other beings may press against you in ways that are difficult to comprehend. The temptation to cast judgment is powerful, sometimes overwhelming. Understand that others also feel the same pressure. Be careful not to judge those who have been swept into the strong current of events. Many who seek to better the planet have fallen into swift-moving streams that do not lead to true solutions. The fact is, there is currently no clear channel available for true progress outside of the individual, the undivided one.

Be careful to avoid getting caught up in external causes. There is energy approaching that will alter our approach to the problems the family human is facing. Spending time in these pursuits will be taking time away from the primary purpose of all humankind. Balance yourself. This is the more effective use of your energy at this point of time. This is not to say that you should ignore the challenges being presented in the current times. Do what you can and begin to be aware of your attitudes towards the planet. Remain centered on your personal progress.

One of the greatest changes that will happen is the increase of compassion for those with whom you do not agree. You can start now by reaching out your hands to others more often. It is a difficult thing to do in times of stress. It is also a way of relieving the stressful nature of the times. Agreement is not a requirement to practicing loving and peaceful relations between beings.

The desire for change is powerful. The changes that occur may not happen the way you personally would like them to. They likely will be surprising to a great many beings. If you have too specific a desire, disappointment may follow. Broaden your vision. Encompass principles rather than rules. Create conduits rather than laws. Open channels for energy to course through. This will be more beneficial than supporting dams and locks that attempt to control energy.

Everyone will experience the change. There are no prohibitions that will disqualify anyone. The question is, how easily will people accept the change? A higher level of spirituality will allow for a smoother transition. Those who possess a higher vibration are more apt to be unattached to the outcomes of the changes. There are those who make claims to high levels of spirituality, but they are still in anticipation of a specific series of events. They are attached to a preset vision of what may occur. These times will be most difficult for them. When their preconceived notions do not follow through in reality, fear will begin to take precedence over their claimed faith.

Some wish to be on the side of a single, absolutely correct deity. This is a fundamental misunderstanding of how the universe is structured. In essence, there is no absolute right or wrong when it comes to behaviors in the realm of gravity. There are some choices and outcomes that carry better results than others. There are choices made that may not be beneficial for the continuance of life. These choices and the elements that create them will not necessarily prevent someone from finding a strong connection to Source. Source connection can be found in the deepest moments of emotional stress. Source connection can be an instantaneous thing, but when this occurs, all other connections are shaken or separated. Better to approach Source connection in a steady way, a process rather than an event.

Past Life

This current compression of time has allowed many to access past lives. This can be fun in certain ways and also useful in understanding the continuity of the karmic experience. With knowledge of where you have been, you can better choose where you wish to travel towards. For many, however, they have become stuck in their vision of the past. It is perhaps the main difficulty that needs to be overcome by the family human today. More should be looking forward. Stop thinking about the past and begin looking forward.

The future is creatable. Build it with consciousness and purpose. Believe in the power of the future generations to express their gratitude backwards. Do you express your gratitude to what has gone before? It is a difficult thing, for we often only see the horrors of the wars and economic and natural disasters. These energies are being filtered and purified. You are also in a purification process. Your light will shine brighter as these times conclude.

It is wise to remember that new times begin as others conclude. Allow for a continuum of energy to exist in your imaging of your own future. Allow for a peaceful rendition of the present to encompass your vision of what may happen next. Image the joy that can be felt in the future by those who will be incarnate on the planet. Act in the firm belief that peace is an attainable and sustainable commodity of energy that can be bequeathed and inherited by the children of the future. Love the present moment and the space you are in.

Spiritual Practice

We ask you now: What is within your life that you would change and what is outside of your life that you would choose to add? It is a time of change, and you have the opportunity to direct this energy for your benefit.

20
Return to the Light

As above, so below.

The future arrives with each instant of time. Often the family human looks to the future and seeks to make a controlled plan, to designate a specific outcome. It is good to have a goal, an image of what you desire your personal future to look like. It is also important to remain flexible in those plans. It may be better to create a purpose for yourself and to allow the plans to form in smaller increments of time. We will speak of the coming days, and in so doing, help you to see further and understand the meaning of our words.

There is a steady movement in the universe. It is affecting you directly now and in the very near future. The very concept of light is shifting. When we speak of light, the meaning is twofold. First, literal light, is that which allows vision and sight in the physical realm. It is also what allows for growth. It is one of the necessary things, along with air and water, that assists life to successfully exist on the planet.

Second, we will speak of spiritual light, the higher vibrational state of being. This is the focus of all true spiritual traditions. It gives one the ability to see beyond the basic existence of life on the planet.

A Shift in Light and Life

In the world today, there are many who live in areas where artificial light dominates the region. There are few places of dense population that experience deep nighttime conditions. This is changing human society and has been for some years. It does not alter the core needs of humanity for specific sleep cycles. Some adapt well to such conditions, but most merely endure. Darkness and the night contain an energy that is also necessary for physical growth. Deprivation of this energy can lead to tension within an individual's existence. This will impede a being's spiritual growth, taking away their natural balance.

There are many sources of artificial light. Examine your life and take note of each one of these sources. Ask yourself how often these light sources are actually on during the period of time when your physical form is seeking rest and rejuvenation. Can adjustments be made? This is not a judgment on these things. It is said only to make you aware of an area of life that is changing. The return of a more natural nighttime experience is approaching many on the planet. It may be disconcerting at first, but it will eventually provide a relief to the majority of members of the planet.

This will be the signal for a shift in the population of the planet as well. Those who were born in the middle of the twentieth century are moving to the end of their cycle of incarnation. Their children are thinking differently about life, and they have begun to raise the next generation in a very different way. All around the globe, there is a changing attitude towards how life could be lived. There is a strong energy towards connection and communication. There is a growing desire to have more physical space, but closer contact, between beings. The technology to support such a vision of life is in existence now.

This is the beginning of a movement that will shape the next century. Fewer people will exist in large urban centers. A growth of smaller enclaves of like-minded individuals will appear. The tendency toward centralization will shift.

Although this may seem to indicate a variance rather than coalescence, as we have indicated is in progress in prior communications, it is actually a way to strengthen and balance the future of humankind, bringing many more together in a place of peaceful co-existence. These will not be communities divided from each other; rather, they will be self-contained, supportive places that connect many threads together. Society will become stronger still, and great freedoms will be enjoyed by more individuals.

This requires more responsibility from each member of the family human. Each person in a community will have opportunity to carry their own weight and to work within their skill preference. This is happening now in many of the businesses around the globe.

Oppression will be relieved, and the decision of the group will no longer be dominated by outside or personal interests. In this, nations other than the North American continental governments are beginning to take the lead. A more natural rhythm to life will exist.

This is not to say that urban centers will cease to exist. Their function will simply shift. They will become destinations for culture, education, and learning. They will be places to go to when large decisions need to be debated and decided. They will be places of distribution and also industry, and people will still find homes there. What will cause the change?

A reduction in population is approaching. This need not be viewed as a potential disaster. It is likely a conscious decision that will be made out of the realization that the resources of the planet are being challenged in the way they are currently used. A change in society will relieve this situation and also reveal more efficient and beneficial ways to utilize energy. The base of this change will occur in areas of great population growth.

The spread of ideas and education is speeding up. The humans who have lacked the knowledge to improve their societies soon will have nearly instant access to techniques and technology that will increase their balance. They will use these ideas in surprising ways, and their successes will fuel the changes in other parts of the globe. It will be the connection of youth that powers the core change.

Children of Light

The sons and daughters being born and raised now will carry a new way within their very genetic code. They will no longer tolerate artificial divisions. They will no longer perpetuate ancient, limiting thought. These children will not seek power over others through religion. They will seek shared experience and a desire for harmony. They will carry a new light.

The rebalance of light and dark, day and night, on the physical level of life will give space for many to spend quieter, more contemplative times. It is this that leads to a return and strengthening of spiritual light.

Currently, many find the need to set aside time for meditation or prayer. The members of the upcoming generation will integrate their spiritual practices seamlessly into their daily life. This is a way of existence that has been uncommon on the planet for several thousand years. The return of this spiritual light will provide relief to all aspects of physical existence.

Today, many can imagine such a way of life. It may seem far off, out of reach. This does not mean you should not strive for such an existence. It is more difficult to achieve at present, but there are ways to move towards this life.

What light is important to you, artificial sources, or spiritual enlightenment? With which form of light do you spend the most time? We have counseled everyone to touch the earth more regularly. We add to this, touch the stars. It is the action of looking upward that stimulates the imagination in the family human. It is never truly dark in the night. The light that exists is softer. When the moon is present, it is reflective. Can you arrange for some of your time to be spent in a softer, more reflective way?

The future flows from the actions of the present moments. Do you possess a vision of the future? Do you contemplate your purpose? Do you feel that such a thing comes from outside of you?

The individual points of light in the night sky are, in reality, bright and powerful energies. They are viewed from a distance and so may seem small. They can provide guidance to those who navigate the waters of earth.

You are a being of spiritual light. You are also a bright and powerful energy. When you are viewed from the distance of the future, will you be seen as someone to guide others? The world is now rapidly changing. Make plans in smaller increments of time. Remain flexible in all that you do. Image the planet as a place of love and joy. The potential for this exists right now. Envision the future as a place of peace. In this way, you affect the probability of such a future.

The future approaches. Light will help us all see farther. Act as an agent for love and peace, and your light will help dispel the spiritual darkness.

Spiritual Practice

Do this now. Sit quietly and invite your spiritual companions to join you. Perhaps make a cup of tea and, as you sip the brew, invite your spiritual friends to join in the tasting. Or find a space of warm sunlight and, as you observe the way the colors exist, let your companions see what you see. Then ask, "What else is there? What am I missing?" Then sit in silence and simply observe.

What do you enjoy? What quiet activity or peaceful place do you attend to that you might invite beings of a higher vibration to witness through you? In the exchange, you will be offered the opportunity to see beyond your own level. Would you enjoy this?

Spiritual Practice

It is important now to commune, to communicate with the earth. Gaia is telling you something. This means sitting quietly more often. Do not expect literal voices to arrive in your ears. Simply listen for new thoughts and concepts to grow within you.
    Simply be still.
    Simply be.

It is important now to commune, to communicate with the earth. Gaia is telling you something. This means sitting quietly more often. Do not expect literal voices to arrive in your ears. Simply listen for new thoughts and concepts to grow within you.
    Simply be still.
    Simply be.

About the Author

Jeff Michaels is a well-respected Author, Channel, Spiritual Adviser, and Metaphysical Teacher. He is on a life-long path of service with over forty years' background in ministry, crisis intervention, hypnotherapy, energy work, and creating and leading motivational workshops. His commitment is to guide others to find and follow their own personal spiritual path. His direct style is well-balanced with humor, helping his clients regain or maintain joy in the challenge of living.

Jeff and his partner, Jill Q. Weiss, owned and operated Quintessence, a much-loved *Peaceful Oasis*, offering quality products and services in Crystal Lake, Illinois and Huntington Beach, California. We are now focused on completing Jeff's Mystical Histories.

Please visit www.jeffreyjmichaels.com to discover future offerings. We are grateful for the opportunity to share these writings with you.

More Onereon Writings by Jeff Michaels

How to Become the True You
Who is the True You?

Who are you at your karmic core?
Who would you be without outside influences?
What is your true karmic purpose?

Become Us All
Visions of Death and Life

Is death an ending or is it a transformation
of energy, a continuation of experience?
*"Sentient life around the planet consists of both spiritual
and physical beings. We are together on our journey."*

The Age of Change
A Challenging Path to the Future

Do you sense it?
Are you aware of moments of destiny occurring?
The energy of change is moving rapidly. It cannot
be stopped. It can be useful. It can be channeled.
The higher perspective offered within these pages
can inspire you to form powerful channels of
energy to create the results and future you desire.

www.ingramcontent.com/pod-product-compliance
Lightning Source LLC
Chambersburg PA
CBHW061922220426
43662CB00012B/1770